# Charity accounting and taxation

# Charity accounting and taxation

THIRD EDITION

**Robert Vincent**
**Amanda Francis**
Buzzacott

*Contributors*
Philippa Booth
Jon Clarke
Amanda Francis
Ian Hayes
Ray Mayes
Robert Vincent

**Butterworths Tolley**
London, Edinburgh & Dublin
2001

| | |
|---|---|
| United Kingdom | Butterworths, a Division of Reed Elsevier (UK) Ltd, Halsbury House, 35 Chancery Lane, LONDON WC2A 1EL and 4 Hill Street, EDINBURGH EH2 3JZ |
| Australia | Butterworths, a Division of Reed International Books Australia Pty Ltd, CHATSWOOD, New South Wales. |
| Canada | Butterworths Canada Ltd, MARKHAM, Ontario |
| India | Butterworths India, NEW DELHI |
| Ireland | Butterworth (Ireland) Ltd, DUBLIN |
| Malaysia | Malayan Law Journal Sdn Bhd, KUALA LUMPUR |
| New Zealand | Butterworths of New Zealand Ltd, WELLINGTON |
| Singapore | Butterworths Asia, SINGAPORE |
| South Africa | Butterworths Publishers (Pty) Ltd, DURBAN |
| USA | Lexis Law Publishing, CHARLOTTESVILLE, Virginia |



A CIP Catalogue record for this book is available from the British Library.

ISBN 0 406 90428 6

Typeset by Kerrypress Ltd, Luton, Beds.
Printed and bound in Great Britain by The Cromwell Press, Trowbridge, Wiltshire.

# Preface

This is the third edition of *Charity Accounting and Taxation* and follows the format of previous editions, namely it is a mixture of textbook information and critical comment interspersed with illustrative examples taken from the published accounts of over seventy charities. It incorporates all relevant legislation affecting charity accounting and taxation as at 31 December 2000.

The purpose of the book is to act as a companion to other textbooks, helping the reader to understand some of the more difficult issues that have been posed by recent developments in charity accounting. Liberal use has been made of references to the Charities SORP 2000 and we are grateful to the authors for allowing us to reproduce many sections throughout the text of this book.

We have updated the early chapters of the book to incorporate information concerning changes in the structure of the Charity Commission, changes in the law affecting trustees, particularly the Trustee Act 2000, and changes affecting the preparation of company accounts.

The later chapters dealing with taxation issues have been largely re-written to take account of the major changes introduced in the Finance Act 2000, while the chapter on VAT has been considerably expanded.

We are grateful to the hundreds of charities who have so willingly sent us copies of their reports and accounts. The examples drawn from these are really the backbone of this book.

Our thanks are due to those who have helped to put this edition together, particularly Richard Corden of the Charity Commission and the Buzzacott charity team.

Robert Vincent
Amanda Francis
Buzzacott
March 2001

# About the authors

**Robert Vincent** was a member of the 1995 Charity SORP committee and until recently was the chairman of Buzzacott. He continues to advise charities on strategic and practical issues. He is a trustee of several educational charities and also of two common investment funds.

**Amanda Francis** is the head of Buzzacott's Charity Team. She is a lecturer on Financial Reporting by Charities for the Institute of Chartered Accountants in England and Wales, and also speaks frequently at seminars focusing on particular sections of the voluntary sector. She advises charities on the presentation of their report and accounts, within the context of their overall strategy.

**Ray Mayes** was a member of the Auditing Practices Board working party which was responsible for the production of APB Practice Note 11 'The Audit of Charities'. He is also the author of 'Preparing Company Accounts' published by ABG Professional Information.

**Jon Clarke** is an ex-inspector of Taxes with a wide knowledge of corporate and personal tax. In addition, he has built up a specialism in VAT. These skills, together with those of the Buzzacott tax team, are used to benefit charities by helping them to identify and solve problems and take advantage of the available tax reliefs. He is author of 'Tax Aspects of Charities' published by Accountancy Books.

**Philippa Booth** is a VAT consultant with Buzzacott, specialising in those areas which impinge upon charities and not-for-profit organisations. She works closely with **Ian Hayes**, the partner responsible for the firm's VAT services to charities, who has also contributed to this book.

# Contents

# Table of statutes

References in the right-hand column are to paragraph numbers. Those paragraph numbers in **bold** type indicate where the legislation is set out in full or in part.

# Table of SORP 'Accounting by charities' references

References in the right-hand column are to paragraph numbers. Those paragraph numbers in **bold** type indicate where the SORP reference is set out in full or in part.

CHAPTER 1

# Charity

## 1 DEFINITION

**1.1** Traditionally charity has been synonymous with love. It is an attitude of mind; an emotion; a virtue. It is also an activity; it is not something that can simply be contemplated, it needs to be done.

**1.2** So what activities are loving and charitable? It is often said that charity begins at home. The love and care shown by the members of a family to each other are clear examples of charitable activity. In his first epistle to the Corinthians St Paul said that love suffereth long, and is kind; love envieth not; love vaunteth not itself, is not puffed up, . . . beareth all things, believeth all things, hopeth all things, endureth all things.

**1.3** While it is helpful and important to bear in mind that these are the characteristics of charity we have to be a little more precise in the way in which we use the word for the purposes of this book. While it may be true that charity begins at home it is equally true that it does not stop there but extends into a variety of activities. The most obvious of these are the relief of suffering and poverty, the advancement of humanity and the protection of the environment. These activities demonstrate a care for friends, neighbours and the public generally.

**1.4** It is this concept of benefiting the public which is central to the legal definition of charity.

**1.5** The organisations which have been set up to carry out activities for the benefit of the public are commonly called charities. These are the organisations to which the advantages of charitable status should be accorded. Charitable activity at home is to be thoroughly encouraged but as it is normally for the benefit of the family rather than the public it does not bring any tax relief!

**1.6** Essentially, therefore, we are dealing in this book with those organisations which have been established for charitable purposes and which, in the main, will be registered under the Charities Act 1993 with the Charity Commission.

## 2 CHARITABLE PURPOSES

**1.7** Charitable purposes have been described in many eloquent ways including St Paul's letter to the Corinthians and the preamble to the Statute of Charitable Uses in 1601, to name but two. While St Paul concentrated on the generosity of spirit behind the action, the Statute of Charitable Uses was more concerned with describing the types of activity that were regarded for the public benefit. Apart from curing the sick, giving alms to the poor, providing shelter for the homeless and similar compassionate activities, the Act included the building of sea walls, highways, the building of houses of correction and the provision of soldiers. Doing things, therefore, for the public benefit includes improving communications, defence, maintaining law and order, and caring for the environment. Most of these activities are now undertaken chiefly by the government, but it is important to remember that, if undertaken privately, they may well qualify as charitable activities provided that there is seen to be a measurable benefit to the public.

**1.8** Most readers will be familiar with the classification of charitable activities included in Lord McNaghten's judgment in *Income Tax Special Purposes Comrs v Pemsel* (1891) 3 TC 53, HL. This consisted of the relief of poverty, the advancement of education, the advancement of religion, and other purposes beneficial to the community, not falling under any of the preceding heads. This still remains the leading legal authority on what activities can be said to be carried on for charitable purposes. Marginal cases have been considered by the courts in the intervening years and thousands of cases are considered annually by the Charity Commission from those applying for charitable registration.

**1.9** There are many organisations which may claim that they carry on an activity that is for the public benefit but they will not all achieve charitable status. This is because the objectives of a charity must be solely for charitable purposes. Clubs and trades unions normally exist for the benefit of their members and so, while much of their work may in their view be for the benefit of the public, a large part of it is also for their mutual benefit. Similarly many businesses may argue that they exist to provide a service to members of the public, nevertheless they do so in order to make a profit for themselves. The crucial difference, therefore, between these organisations and charities is that the latter exist solely for the benefit of their beneficiaries.

**1.10** It not infrequently happens that a charity strays into some activity which is not regarded as charitable and the effects of this are considered in Chapter 17. Where it is a relatively minor infringement there may be no serious repercussions. Particular care, however, needs to be taken to avoid crossing the narrow lines of legality affecting:

(a) trading activities; and
(b) political lobbying.

**1.11** These items are considered in Chapter 18.

## 3 ADVANTAGES OF CHARITABLE STATUS

**1.12** The biggest single advantage of charitable status is the exemption from most forms of direct taxation and a certain amount of relief from indirect taxation. This aspect is considered in detail in Chapter 18.

**1.13** Other benefits of charitable status include certain legal advantages. For example, charitable trusts cannot fail for uncertainty, they can be written in perpetuity and, if their original purposes cease to exist, application can be made to the Charity Commissioners for a scheme whereby they can be reconstituted for another similar purpose. For instance, a charity established with an endowment to provide water troughs for horses in Liverpool eventually found itself with little or no demand for its services but with some assets. Under ordinary Trust Law such assets would eventually have passed indirectly to the Treasury via the Duchy of Cornwall as 'bona vacantia'. Under Charity Law, however, the trustees were able to apply for a scheme under what is now s 16 of the Charities Act 1993 to enable the charity to continue with wider charitable objects. This is done by making application to the Charity Commissioners, proposing the additional objects sought. The Charity Commissioners then have the task of considering the application in the light of the 'cy-pres' doctrine, which means they have to decide what is the next best objective to the original. In this case it might have been to help the animal protection societies in Liverpool or perhaps a national society connected with the care of horses. Either way the charity did not die.

**1.14** Although registration with the Charity Commission subjects the trustees of the charity to the supervision of the Charity Commissioners, this can also be an advantage as the Charity Commissioners' job is not simply that of registrar and overseer; they are also there to give assistance to charity trustees in matters relating to the administration of their trust (see **1.28 ff**).

**1.15** A further advantage of charitable status is the additional credibility that it gives to any organisation appealing for donations. Not only is this desirable when appealing for funds from the public, it is essential if seeking support from charitable trusts. They have to ensure that they apply their funds for charitable purposes only and are very reluctant to give money to organisations which are not themselves charities for fear that it can or may be used for a non-charitable purpose. That could endanger their own status.

**1.16** There are no discernible disadvantages attaching to charitable status.

## 4 CONSTITUTION

**1.17** A charity need not have any special constitution provided that there is sufficient evidence of its objects and internal regulations. For most charities it is usual to have some formal constitution usually drawn up with the help of a solicitor. The following are the most normal forms of constitution.

### Trust

**1.18** A simple declaration of trust stating that the trustees hold the property so settled on charitable trusts will normally suffice provided it is quite clear that the funds cannot be used for any other purpose. Some such trusts are drawn up with very wide charitable objects while others are more specific to reflect the wishes of the settlor. In many cases the initial amount settled is a nominal sum to which greater sums are added later by the settlor or others through donations etc.

**1.19** In some cases the initial settlement into the trust is substantial, such as a house left by will to be held as a capital asset for the benefit of the charity and not to be spent. In such cases the initial asset is considered to be a 'permanent endowment' and there are particular accounting requirements concerning permanent endowments, as is explained in Chapter 5 and further referred to in Chapter 6.

*CAFOD: 30 September 1999*

**Aims and Policies**

The Catholic Fund for Overseas Development 'CAFOD', is governed by a Trust Deed dated 29 September 1982 and is registered under the Charities Act 1993, No 285776. Under this Trust Deed the objectives of the Fund are:

(i) the relief of poverty throughout the world;
(ii) the advancement of education throughout the world;
(iii) the advancement of the Christian religion throughout the world;
(iv) the relief and prevention of sickness, disease and physical or mental disability throughout the world; and
(v) such other charitable purposes anywhere in the world as are for the benefit of the United Kingdom community.

## Company limited by guarantee

**1.20** A charity formed as a company limited by guarantee has the advantage that the trustees, or directors to give them their proper title, are afforded the protection of limited liability as regards the debts of the company and their own responsibilities are as defined in the Companies Acts. As the legal responsibilities of trustees can be very considerable and potentially very costly to themselves it is more common to constitute large charities as limited companies. Major charities, such as OXFAM, Barnardos, the Save the Children Fund, Help the Aged and the British Heart Foundation are all constituted in this manner.

**1.21** There is the additional advantage that the company structure is familiar to most people who have dealings with the commercial world. Memorandum and articles of association, the powers and duties of the directors, the holding of annual general meetings and the appointment of auditors are all familiar matters which are included in the constitution. The titles are sometimes changed from director to trustee or member of council. Otherwise the structure is the same as any other company except for the fact that there is no share capital, only the nominal personal guarantees given by subscribers.

*The Samaritans: 31 March 1996*

**Governance**

The Samaritans is both a company limited by guarantee and a registered charity; it was incorporated as a company on 11 April 1963, having been founded by the Reverend Chad Varah on 2 November 1953.

The directors of the company and the trustees of the charity are the members of the Council of Management whose names are given on the page opposite [not reproduced]; the Council meets twice a year to consider statutory and financial business and to determine policy for the Movement.

Much of the work of the Council is delegated to its Executive Committee comprising the Chairman and Vice Chairmen, the Honorary Officers and elected representatives from the 13 regions; the Executive met five times in the year under review and further work was undertaken by the Executive working through its sub-committees.

All of this work is greatly assisted by all the staff at the General Office.

The reporting and accounting requirements are the same as for other companies and these are discussed in Chapter 3.

**Scheme of the Charity Commissioners**

**1.22** Several charities, particularly those whose original trusts have become out of date or unworkable for some reason, are governed by a 'scheme' made by the Charity Commissioners under ss 16 or 17 of the Charities Act 1993.

> *The corporation of Trinity House: 31 March 2000*
>
> **Trusts of the charities**
>
> The Corporate Charity is governed by the Royal Charter of 1685 and supplemental charters of 1870, 1894, 1910, 1939 and 1978.
>
> The Trinity Homes and Mariners' Charity is governed by a scheme of the Charity Commission dated 7 August 1995.

**Unincorporated association**

**1.23** Many local charities such as Women's Institutes or Parent Teacher Associations and similar charities that are dependent on a membership, governed by a management committee, will produce a rule book or constitution which is their governing instrument. For many such organisations model constitutions are available from their national coordinating body. The National Council for Voluntary Organisations also produces model constitutions to suit various charities. Their address is given in Appendix 1.

*Age Concern: 31 March 1996*

**Charitable status**

Age Concern England is an unincorporated association and is registered as the 'National Council on Ageing' with the working names 'Age Concern England' and 'Age Concern'. Its charity number is 261794.

**Associated organisations**

Age Concern England is a central resource to a nationwide movement of Age Concern and Old Peoples Welfare organisations. These financial statements only reflect the affairs of Age Concern England and its trading subsidiaries.

### Industrial and provident or friendly society

**1.24** Some charities, particularly housing associations, are incorporated under the Industrial and Provident Societies Act 1965 and these enjoy substantially the same benefits as those incorporated under the Companies Acts. Friendly societies are perhaps less familiar to people in ordinary commercial life, although there are many non-charitable organisations which are incorporated in this manner such as trades unions. While the accounting requirements for both industrial and provident or friendly societies are very similar to those of limited companies, special care must be taken in the case of registered social landlords to comply with the very detailed and complex accounting requirements issued by the Housing Corporation under the Housing Acts (see **3.12** ff).

### Other constitutions

**1.25** Although the foregoing are the most common constitutions for charities, there are some older and larger charities which have been constituted by Royal Charter. These include the Royal National Lifeboat Institution (RNLI), the Imperial Cancer Research Fund, the Red Cross, the Royal Society for the Protection of Birds (RSPB), and the British and Foreign Bible Society. Some charities are formed under their own special Acts of Parliament such as the National Trust Acts 1907 to 1971 and the RSPCA Act 1932. In all of these cases their constitutions will be governed by their own charter or special Act. In the future there may arise the Charitable Incorporated Institution as an alternative to the Company limited by guarantee (see comment at end of **3.8**).

**Comment**

**1.26** It is surprising how many published accounts of charities used to give no indication of the charity's constitution. In many cases it was only apparent from the terms of the auditors' report, which stated that the accounts complied with this or that Act. Following the publication in 1995 of the Charity SORP (Accounting by Charities, Statement of Recommended Practice) the position has improved immensely.

**1.27** It would be helpful if all charities included in their annual report and accounts brief details of their constitution and their principal objects. Indeed this was one of the recommendations of the 1995 Charity SORP. Most charities now include in their annual report and accounts such details. One of the recommendations in the revised SORP published in October 2000 details in paragraph 30 what further legal and administrative information should be shown in the annual report. In summary these are:

'*(a)* *the name of the charity*
*(b)* *an indication of the nature of the governing document ... how the charity is constituted ... the charity registration number*
*(c)* *the names of trustees ... the method of their appointment*
*(d)* *the address of the charity*
*(e)* *the names and addresses of bankers, solicitors, auditors and investment advisers*
*(f)* *details of specific restrictions imposed by the governing document*
*(g)* *a summary of any specific investment powers and their authority.*'

This is examined in detail in Chapter 4.

## 5 CHARITY COMMISSION

**1.28** The Charity Commission consists of a chief commissioner and four other commissioners, two of the five, at least, being barristers or solicitors, and a staff of around 550. It has three offices, one each in London, Liverpool and Taunton. Its role is to supervise and promote the effectiveness of charities. In general it acts in response to the needs of charity trustees but increasingly it is becoming pro-active in instituting inquiries into possible mismanagement or abuse of charity property.

**1.29** Under the Charities Act 1993 s 1(3) the Charity Commissioners have:

'*the general function of promoting the effective use of charitable resources by encouraging the development of better methods of administration, by giving charity trustees information or advice on any matter affecting the charity and by investigating and checking abuses.'*

**1.30** They have powers to institute inquiries, call for documents, order audits and exchange information with a wide range of public bodies, including the police and the Inland Revenue. In extreme cases, they can suspend or replace trustees or even appoint receivers to protect or salvage charity assets. They are, however, forbidden by law from acting themselves as administrators of any charity. That is the responsibility of the duly appointed charity trustees.

**1.31** The Charity Commission maintains the Central Register of Charities which contains legal, financial and operational details of about 190,000 charities. The Register can be viewed at any of the Commission's offices, which are listed in Appendix 1. Information from the Register can also be requested by telephone, post or e-mail. An abbreviated version of the Register, covering all charities but giving less information, can be accessed through the Commission's website.

Charities are classified by reference to:

- their field of activity (eg medical, environment, welfare);
- the identity of their beneficiaries (eg children, young people, the elderly); or
- their method of operation (eg sponsors or undertakes research).

The Charity Commission also keeps copies of charities' constitutions and latest submitted accounts, all of which are available to the public for a fee to cover copying cost.

**1.32** The Register is open to inspection during normal office hours and at any time via the internet. Section 4 of the Charities Act 1993 says that 'an institution shall for all purposes other than rectification of the register be conclusively presumed to be or have been a charity at any time when it is or was on the register of charities'. It is, therefore, a simple matter to verify whether or not an organisation purporting to be a registered charity is such or not.

**1.33** A significant part of the Charity Commission's time is taken up with registration of new charities, considering schemes for alteration of existing charities and dealing with legal complexities. It is unusual for the Charity Commission to interfere directly in the affairs of any charity unless its suspicions have been aroused by its own monitoring activities or by members of the public, by the media or by the auditors or independent examiner. It will, however, respond to calls for help from charity trustees. It does this through its Charity Support Service which responded to 22,000 requests for advice or assistance in 1999.

**1.34** The monitoring role of the Charity Commission had been rudimentary up to 1990 but has improved enormously since, largely as a result of the computerisation of the Register and additional investment in resources. All charities on the Register now automatically receive Annual Return forms for completion and reminders if they are ignored. Annual accounts are demanded along with the annual returns and these accounts are selectively scrutinised by Charity Commission staff. Whereas in 1988 less than 10% of charities were filing accounts, by 1998 between 80% and 90% were doing so.

**1.35** The Official Custodian for Charities is a 'corporation sole' set up by Parliament to hold property in trust for charities and provide certain services for them free of charge. His office is a division of the Charity Commission. He may hold land or personal property on behalf of charity trustees. Up to 1991 the Official Custodian also held stocks and shares on behalf of charity trustees, collecting dividends and recovering income tax and accounting to each charity free of charge.

**1.36** During 1990 the Official Custodian handled £85m worth of capital transactions and received £94m worth of dividends and interest on behalf of 41,000 charities.

**1.37** Between 1992 and 1995 the investment holding function of the Official Custodian was phased out, largely as a cost saving exercise. This considerable task was accomplished most efficiently and all the stocks, shares and cash were transferred to the trustees of the charities concerned who, thenceforward, have had to make other arrangements for the collection of dividends and recovery of tax.

**1.38** In order to mollify the effects of this divestment by the Official Custodian, the Charity Commission encouraged charities to consider using Common Investment Funds (CIFs), especially charities which are unable to afford the services of professional financial advisers. These funds are created by schemes made by the Charity Commission in accordance with s 24 of the Charities Act 1993. They operate in a similar way to unit trusts and used to be able to invest in a wider manner than individual charities. [But see Trustee Act 2000, **2.4ff**.] Moreover charities can register units in the name of the charity rather than individual trustees thus avoiding the problems associated with changes in the board of trustees. As CIFs are exclusively for charities, the managers ensure that all dividends and interest are remitted gross.

**1.39** The Charity Commission is primarily concerned with providing support to charities on the one hand and acting as the sector regulator on the other. It is split into divisions carrying out these operational functions:

(a) Registration (all offices);
(b) Charity Support (all offices);

(c) Monitoring (Liverpool office);
(d) Investigation (all offices).

These are functions supported by specialised policy, legal, accounting and resource management services.

The Policy Division provides the steering for such matters as the charities SORP, legislative changes, external relations and the promotion of standards. It reports directly to the Chief Commissioner.

**1.40** Communication with charities is achieved through:

- mailings of Charity Commission News twice a year;
- completion every year by trustees of Annual Return and Database Update Forms;
- Commission staff attending and speaking at conferences and other events;
- visits by Commission staff to individual charities; and
- articles contributed by Commission staff to the press and appearances on TV and radio.

In a typical month, 350,000 hits are registered on the Commission's website, and around 44,000 copies of the Commission's leaflets are given out on request.

**1.41** The jurisdiction of the Charity Commission is limited to England and Wales. Schedule 2 of the Charities Act 1993 lists those charities in England and Wales which are exempt from the jurisdiction of the Charity Commission. These consist mainly of universities, museums and other bodies which are subject to other regulatory bodies.

**Comment**

**1.42** Since the publication of Sir Philip Woodfield's *Efficiency Scrutiny of the Supervision of Charities* in 1987, which disclosed many shortcomings and made 46 recommendations for improvement, the Charity Commission has made huge strides forward. It is now an effective regulator, and an accessible source of advice and assistance. Its continuing effectiveness will depend upon matching resources to the needs of charities and liaising with the technical groups and umbrella bodies within the charity sector.

CHAPTER 2

# Trustees' responsibilities

## 1 TRUSTEES' LEGAL RESPONSIBILITIES

**2.1** Charity trustees, by whatever titles they are known, are those persons who are appointed to take responsibility for the general control, management and administration of the charity (Charities Act 1993 s 97(1)). Their appointment is made by the governing instrument. Their responsibilities can be broadly summarised as follows.

**2.2** The Trustee Act 1925 provides that all trustees have an absolute duty to carry out the terms of their trust and not to commit or allow any breach of that trust. They may find themselves personally liable for any loss suffered by the beneficiaries of the trust if they fail in this primary obligation through wilful default or neglect.

**2.3** As custodians of the trust property, the trustees are responsible for the proper maintenance of real property, investment of cash and care of all other assets including prompt collection of debts, tax recoverable and the like. These responsibilities are similar to those of a company director but the standard of care may be more exacting for trustees.

**2.4** The Trustee Act 2000 seeks to replace the Trustee Investments Act 1961 which defined the classes of investment open to trustees. Broadly speaking the 1961 Act required trustees, unless their governing instrument gave them wider powers, to invest at least 25% of their funds in cash deposits or fixed interest Government securities and not more than 75% in equities. In selecting equities trustees could only choose companies which had paid dividends in each of the past five years, thus precluding privatisation issues, new technology stocks and other opportunities.

**2.5** Under the provisions of the Trustee Act 2000 trustees are given the same powers as an absolute owner to invest in any investments subject to an overriding duty of care to:

(a) show such skill and care as is reasonable, making allowance for his or her knowledge, experience or professional status;

(b) consider the need for diversification and the suitability of investments;
(c) obtain and consider proper advice where appropriate;
(d) consider the size and risk of the investment;
(e) consider the need to produce a balance between income and capital growth;
(f) consider ethical implications.

**2.6** The Trustee Act 2000 also empowers trustees to delegate their investment management to professional investment managers, subject to their overriding responsibility to review the management regularly. Included in their delegation is the power to appoint nominees or custodians to hold investments on behalf of the trustees.

**2.7** Pending the enactment of the Trustee Bill 2000, the Trustee Investments Act 1961 remained in force affecting all charity trustees who did not have express wider powers of investment contained in their governing instrument. To overcome these restrictions many trustees took advantage of s 24(7) of the Charities Act 1993 which empowers all charity trustees to invest in Common Investment Funds and Pooling Schemes set up by the Charity Commission. These are considered further in Chapter 15.

## Delegation of powers

**2.8** In practice, trustees often have to operate by delegating their tasks to full-time employees and these in turn may employ professional advisers to assist on such matters as fundraising, money management and investment advice. Care should be taken to ensure that the governing instrument allows trustees to delegate their powers. In many cases, particularly those regarding investment management, the trustees will remain legally responsible for the investment management even though a reputable firm of managers has been appointed to act. In general, trustees will be protected against any claim made against them for breach of trust or other failure caused by an employee or agent if they can show that they exercised due care in appointing that person and continued to exercise reasonable control over him or her through reporting procedures etc.

**2.9** The Charities Acts 1992 and 1993 define further the responsibilities of charity trustees, particularly in connection with their public accountability and compliance with fund raising regulations.

**2.10** The Charity Commissioners (see **1.28 ff**) have responsibility for the general supervision of charities in England and Wales other than those which are specifically exempted by the Charities Act 1993 Sch 2. Their leaflets give detailed guidance to charity trustees on a variety of issues and these are listed in Appendix 2. For exempt charities or those operating from Scotland, Northern Ireland and the Republic of Ireland, an indication of the trustees' legal responsibilities is given in Chapter 15.

## 2 SCOPE OF RESPONSIBILITY

**2.11** The governing instrument must define precisely the limits of the trustees' responsibilities and, in case of doubt, the trustees themselves should record their understanding of their responsibilities in the trustees' minute book.

**2.12** It is of paramount importance that there should be no confusion over what matters are within the responsibilities of the trustees and what matters are outside. The old tradition of 'beating the bounds' of a parish whereby the councillors and parish clerk solemnly walked round the perimeter of the parish once a year is, perhaps, a good image for trustees to bear in mind when considering the content of their annual report and accounts.

**2.13** Paragraph 31(b) of SORP asks trustees to include in their annual report, after the explanation of the charity's objects and mission, '*a description of the organisational structure of the charity and how decisions are made*'. Questions to be considered will include the following:

(a) Is the charity part of a wider network?
(b) If so what is its relationship — a branch, a holding company, an autonomous body under an umbrella organisation? (The Glossary in Appendix 1 of the SORP defines these relationships.)
(c) What is the charity's relationship with other organisations with which it co-operates in pursuit of its charitable objectives — does it have a participating interest eg 20% share in a trading company?
(d) Does the charity share administration with another charity? If so which, if either, controls the other?

**2.14** Having established the way in which the charity is organised, the trustees are in a position to mark out the scope of their legal responsibilities and, therefore, the extent of their accountability.

**2.14** *Trustees' responsibilities*

> *British Red Cross Society: 31 December 1998*
>
> The British Red Cross Society ('British Red Cross') has pleasure in presenting the Trustees' Report and the audited Consolidated Financial Statements of the Society for the year ended 31 December 1998.

**2.15** From the foregoing paragraphs, it is self-evident that the charity accountant must at the outset have a written memorandum setting out all areas of trustee responsibility and all other areas relevant to the accounts which are outside that responsibility. The trustees' report will summarise this in the description of the charity's organisation and the notes to the accounts will include the accounting policies which will explain what is included and how, and what is excluded and why. (See Chapter 5.)

## 3 MANAGEMENT STRUCTURE

**2.16** Consideration of the scope of the responsibilities of the trustees will dictate the type of management structure that will be most suitable to the organisation. It does not matter what the objects of the charity are; it is purely a question of the size and complexity of the organisation and its management requirements. It is dangerous, therefore, to generalise. The charity should examine its own needs for effective management and control, consult its own advisers and look upon itself as unique. That said, there are certain guidelines that are common to all organisations to which trustees should pay heed.

**2.17** Trustees are normally non-executive and unpaid, though possibly very active members of a charity. While being legally responsible for the actions of the charity, they will very often delegate the tasks for the day-to-day running of the charity to full-time executives. Typically, the charity will have a governing board of trustees which will appoint a chief executive who will be responsible for managing the charity's affairs through departments and branches staffed partly by fully paid personnel and partly by volunteers.

**2.18** It is the chief executive's responsibility to install an appropriate internal control system, office procedures, an accounting system and a management reporting system to enable him or her to control the business of the charity, and to report periodically to the board of trustees.

**2.19** In a very small charity, which consists virtually of a single crusader, that person may be both the trustee and the chief executive having to do everything, with the help of a few volunteers. While allowances may be made in such circumstances, if substantial monies are involved that person must have very strong regard for their trustee position and ensure that they can account not only for the money received, but also for their actions in dealing with it. It is no good pleading lack of resources when things go wrong; it is up to the instigator to ensure that there are adequate control procedures to fit the circumstances.

**2.20** For a larger charity, the trustees must ensure that they have a chief executive who is properly qualified for the work that he or she may be asked to do. They must be satisfied that the structure is efficient and properly matched to the tasks of the charity. If there is a divisional or branch structure, there should be proper lines of communication which are well tested and operate effectively. This becomes even more important if the charity is operating internationally.

## 4 CONSTITUTION

**2.21** However the charity is constituted, the trustees should consider, in the light of their responsibilities and management structure, whether the constitution is suitable to the nature and scale of the charity's operations. Circumstances will change as the charity's activities develop and the original constitution may no longer be appropriate. The following checklist may be helpful.

(a) Does the charity enter into significant contracts of employment or for the supply of services, premises, equipment and the like? If so, perhaps a corporate structure with limited liability should be considered.
(b) Is the charity grant making from an invested endowment fund? If so, a simple declaration of trust or trusts should be sufficient.
(c) Is there a membership base to the charity? If so, beware giving each member a vote in the affairs of the charity. It can become politically divisive, cumbersome and expensive to administer. Better to restrict votes to members of an elected council.
(d) Is there a branch structure? Should each branch be a separate autonomous charity or should it be under the control of the 'head office'?
(e) Is the trustee body self-perpetuating? Would it be beneficial to instil some compulsory change?

**2.22** In general, simple charities with few employees, few contractual obligations and one centre of operation should be constituted by a trust deed. This will limit the degree of statutory compliance to the Charities Act 1993 as far as accountability is concerned. More complicated charities may find it preferable to be constituted under the Companies Act 1985 as a company limited by guarantee. This has two major benefits:

(a) In the event of the charity becoming insolvent, the trustees will be protected by the limited liability of the company. Any unpaid creditor wishing to claim against a trustee would have to prove wilful default or negligence on the part of the trustee under the Insolvency Act. In the case of an unincorporated charity becoming insolvent, the boot is on the other foot. If the trustees are unable to meet the liabilities of the charity they must justify the position to the creditors or possibly to the Charity Commission, or to any receiver or administrator or liquidator who may be appointed.

(b) Most people are familiar with the structure and working of a company and therefore if there are a large number of employees of and contractors to the charity, a corporate structure with corporate procedures is likely to be more understandable and acceptable than an unincorporated body.

## 5 TRUSTEES' INSURANCE

**2.23** In view of their responsibilities and potential liabilities it may be prudent to consider insuring against some or all of the inherent risks. The Charity Commission have considered this and concluded that they have no objection to the provision of such insurance by the charity, provided that the policy excludes breaches of trust or duty or reckless disregard of either by the trustee, and the cost is justifiable having regard to the risk.

**2.24** There are basically two classes of risk; those which will affect the assets of the charity and those which will affect the trustees personally. Clearly trustees should ensure that the assets of the charity are safeguarded and, to the extent that their own actions or inactions put them at risk, they may consider taking out insurance, the cost of which can be borne by the charity. Such risks will be losses arising from bona fide decisions taken by the trustees in the ordinary course of carrying out their duties.

**2.25** Cover cannot be obtained to protect trustees personally against claims for wilful default or neglect.

**2.26** The following is an example of a typical note in a set of accounts dealing with this aspect:

> *Bernardo's: 31 March 1999*
>
> The charity purchased insurance for Council members and officers of the company during the year to indemnify them against possible liabilities incurred by them in relation to their duties. The cost of this insurance was £7,800.

## 6 REPORTING DUTIES

**2.27** Charities Act 1993 s 45 requires all charity trustees other than those who are exempt or excepted from such obligation to prepare an annual report and this, together with the accounts, audited or independently examined as appropriate, should be filed with the Charity Commission within 10 months of the accounting year end. This applies to all charities with incomes in excess of £10,000 a year, incorporated and unincorporated alike.

**2.28** The annual report or trustees' report must comply with the requirements of reg 10 of the Charities (Accounts and Reports) Regulations 1995 and paras 26 to 32 of SORP. These are considered in Chapter 4.

**2.29** The accounts of the charity which accompany the annual report will comply with the appropriate governing statute (see Chapter 3). Most will comply either with the requirements of the Charities (Accounts and Reports) Regulations 1995 or those of Sch 4 or Sch 8 of the Companies Act 1985. In either case, they will be expected to comply with the requirements of SORP and consist of:

- Statement of financial activities.
- Balance sheet.
- Cash flow statement (if required by Financial Reporting Standards).
- Summary income and expenditure account (if required by charity with endowment).
- Notes to the accounts.

**2.30** The trustees are responsible for selecting and applying consistently appropriate accounting policies and for the preparation of the accounts. In practice, they may delegate this function to the charity accountant, but just as they must be involved in defining the scope of their responsibilities and, therefore, their accountability, so they must take an active part in approving the accounting policies upon which their accounts are based.

## 7 REMUNERATION OF TRUSTEES

**2.31** The general rule of law is that a trustee must not make a profit out of his position of trust, or put himself in a position where his duties and responsibilities as a trustee might conflict with his own personal interests. This is taken to mean that a trustee cannot be paid for holding the office of trustee per se. It is, however, common practice for trust deeds to contain a 'charging clause', allowing professional trustees, such as solicitors or accountants to be paid for their services. Such payments are legally acceptable insofar as they represent fees for their professional services rendered as distinct from being fees for simply holding the office.

**2.32** There is growing opinion to suggest that this rule is too restrictive. In the case of some larger charities the amount of time demanded of trustees is often so onerous that it is doubtful if suitable candidates for the office can continually be found without some monetary compensation. There is also the anomalous position of the chief executive and senior staff, all of whom may be paid as staff, but many of whom could be regarded as being 'persons having the general control and management of the administration of the charity' (Charity Commission's definition of charity trustees). Those holding such posts need to make it clear that they are not in control and are not trustees. This is the anomaly. Trustees include not only persons with that title, but directors of companies established for charitable purposes, members of the executive committees of unincorporated associations established for charitable purposes and people who hold money raised from an appeal to the public for a charitable cause. None of these must profit from their position of trust. But should they forfeit significant earnings instead?

**2.33** The official view at present, contained in Charity Commission leaflet CC11, is that charity trustees should not receive payment for their services other than reasonable out-of-pocket expenses. Paid executives should expressly be excluded from being members of the board of trustees. Professional advisers charging a charity for their services should normally not be trustees either. Exceptionally, and only with the consent of the Charity Commissioners, professional trustees may make reasonable charges in respect of the professional service that they render if the governing document provides for this.

**2.34** The Charity Commissioners, while sympathising with the problems of overworked, unpaid trustees, believe that the dangers inherent in possibly creating a class of professional, paid, non-executive trustees are too ominous to support. In their recently re-published guidance note CC11 they say:

*'Our starting point, following the lead of the Court, is that the office of trustee is unpaid. It is only if the trustees can show that payment is necessary and*

*reasonable for the proper administration of the charity that we authorise it, ie that it is not simply desirable or convenient for a trustee to be paid, but that there are no other workable options.'*

CC11 goes on to give detailed guidance on the circumstances in which the Charity Commission may allow payment to trustees and the degree of monitoring that may be required by the non-paid trustees.

**2.35** Since publication of the Charities Acts 1992 and 1993 more and more trustees have become aware of their responsibilities and the time that they need to devote to the affairs of their charity if they are to fulfil their duties. Sometimes they find that their employers will not pay them for all or any of the time that they have to take off for their trustee work. In such circumstances the Charity Commissioners will authorise payment of some 'compensation for loss of earnings' to trustees, where the charity can show that it would be adversely affected if that person was unable on financial grounds to accept the office of trustee.

CHAPTER 3

# Accounting requirements

**3.1** All charities are obliged to give an account of their stewardship but to whom and in what form is not always clear. The key lies in the document constituting the charity and this in turn leads to the authorities that regulate its activities. Most, but certainly not all, charities in England and Wales are subject to the supervision of the Charity Commission and the requirements of the Charities Act 1993. Many charities are incorporated as limited liability companies and must, therefore, also comply with the requirements of the Companies Act 1985. There are others carrying on particular activities which are required to be accounted for in particular ways, such as registered social landlords.

**3.2** The purpose of this chapter is to cover the main statutory accounting requirements that are likely to affect most charities and introduce the revised charity SORP Statement of Recommended Practice (Accounting and Reporting by Charities), which seeks to give guidance on the practical application of accounting norms in a way that will satisfy all of those requirements.

## 1 CHARITIES ACT 1993

**3.3** The accounting requirements under the Charities Act 1993 are contained in ss 41–49 of the Act and the Charities (Accounts and Reports) Regulations 2000, which have been made pursuant to ss 42, 43, 44, 45 and 46 of the Act.

### Charity accounts, reports and returns – summary of Charities Act 1993

**3.4** The following is a summary of the main requirements.

**Section 41** Keep accounting records sufficient to:

(a) disclose at any time, with reasonable accuracy, the financial position of the charity at that time, and

(b) enable the trustees to prepare accounts which comply with the requirements of the regulations under s 42.

**Section 42** Prepare annually a statement of accounts complying with regulations.

(a) Charities with incoming resources up to £100,000 pa may produce a receipts and payments account, and a statement showing their assets and liabilities. They may alternatively opt to produce full accrual accounts with a balance sheet.
(b) Charities with incoming resources of over £100,000 pa must provide full accounts on the accruals basis, in accordance with the requirements of reg 3 and Sch 1. These require the trustees to prepare:
    (i) a Statement of Financial Activities (SOFA) analysing the incoming resources and the application of resources in a way most appropriate to the charity's operations,
    (ii) a balance sheet,
    (iii) notes amplifying, explaining and disclosing items included in the accounts.

The principles upon which the accounts should be prepared are contained within the Regulations and are set out in *Charity Accounts and Reports : Core Guide*, which incorporates the relevant sections of both the Act and the Regulations. It is available from HMSO.

**Section 43** Accounts of charities with gross income or total expenditure in the year or in either of the two preceding years exceeding £250,000 to be professionally audited. Accounts of charities with gross income or total expenditure between £10,000 and £250,000 to be either professionally audited or independently examined. The duties of the auditor or independent examiner are set out in the regulations, and are discussed further in Chapter 16.

**Section 44** The Secretary of State to make regulations conferring powers on the auditor or independent examiner to have access to all necessary information. These are contained in reg 8.

**Section 45** Trustees to prepare and file, for charities over the £10,000 threshold, an annual report in accordance with reg 10. This will give legal and administrative details about the charity, explain the objects, policies and organisation, and give a narrative report on its activities, achievements and developments, commenting on the financial position in relation to all of these in the context of the long-term objects of the charity. This is dealt with more fully in Chapter 4.

**Section 46** Special provisions for exempt and excepted charities:

(a) exempt charities to keep 'proper books of account' and, if not otherwise regulated, to prepare annual accounts under this Act consisting of an income and expenditure account and balance sheet;
(b) excepted charities need not submit accounts, unless they have elected to register. They must however prepare accounts and they must also submit an annual report with accounts if requested to do so by the Charity Commissioners.

**Section 47** Annual reports and accounts lodged with the Charity Commission are open to public inspection.

**Section 48** Trustees to lodge an annual return for any charity with a gross income or total expenditure in excess of £10,000.

**Section 49** Criminal liability of persons persistently in default in relation to accounting requirements.

## 2 COMPANIES ACT 1985

**3.5** The Companies Act 1985 as amended by the Companies Act 1989 and statutory regulations sets out the requirements for the preparation of company accounts which will include all charities incorporated or registered under the Companies Acts. The following are the main points covered:

(a) the format of the accounts;
(b) the content of the accounts; and
(c) the rules for determining amounts included in the accounts.

**3.6** There is a fundamental requirement for accounts to show a true and fair view (s 226) and many trustees and charity accountants consider this to be a major point when deciding whether or not to follow precisely the rules laid down in the Act. Bearing in mind that the authors of the Companies Act probably did not have charitable companies in the forefront of their minds when drafting the regulations, it is likely that certain aspects will not suit the reporting requirements of a charity. It should, however, be a rarity that this section has to be invoked by a charity. In general, corporate charities must abide by the accounting provisions of the Companies Act 1985.

**3.7** In the past some charities have considered it necessary to depart from these requirements on the basis that the accounts would not otherwise give a true and fair view. With the advent of SORP which applies equally to incorporated and unincorporated charities, this is likely to become even rarer.

## Preparing company accounts

**3.8** The following is a summary of the accounts provisions contained in the Act which have been extracted from *Preparing Company Accounts*, by Ray Mayes of Buzzacott, published by Accountancy Books 1999. Some items, especially those relating to shares, are not applicable to charitable companies but they are left in for the sake of completeness.

### INTRODUCTION

The Companies Act 1985, as amended, lays down provisions relating to:

- prescriptive formats of accounts;
- the content of accounts;
- principles and rules for determining amounts included in the accounts.

This section summarises accounts provisions of the Companies Act 1985, insofar as they relate to accounts ('individual accounts') that are prepared in accordance with the Companies Act 1985 s 226.

### ACCOUNTS

Full accounts prepared for shareholders must be prepared for all companies, irrespective of size. The full accounts of a 'small' company, however, are less detailed with reduced disclosure requirements. A small company may also take advantage of the FRSSE (Financial Reporting Standard for Smaller Entities). A company qualifying as 'small' or 'medium-sized' may, in addition, prepare 'abbreviated' accounts for filing with the Registrar of Companies.

Depending on certain size criteria, small companies may be exempt from the requirement for audit. Dormant companies may also take advantage of audit exemption.

### COMMENT

A charitable company which is 'small' will still be required to comply with the charity SORP and this may mean disclosing more information than is required under the Companies Act or the FRSSE.

## TRUE AND FAIR VIEW

There is a fundamental requirement for full accounts (individual accounts or group accounts) to show a true and fair view. This applies irrespective of whether or not the accounts are subject to audit or independent reporting accountants' review. Any decision concerning the method of accounting or means of disclosing information must take this basic requirement into account.

## FORMAT OF ACCOUNTS

The form and content of individual accounts is covered by Sch 4 to the Act (companies generally) and Sch 8 (small companies). The Schedules prescribe the required formats from which companies may choose. Schedule 4A deals with the rules for the form and content of group accounts.

Once a format has been adopted, the company must use the same format for subsequent years unless, in the directors' opinion, there are special reasons for changing; these must be disclosed in the year of change.

Every balance sheet and profit and loss account must show the items listed in the adopted format if, of course, they apply either in the financial year or the preceding year.

Adopting a particular format is not as restricting as it may seem, as there are a variety of options, for example:

- departure is allowed if it is made to ensure a true and fair view (see above);
- certain headings may be combined;
- immaterial items may be disregarded;
- more information can be given if directors so wish;
- some information may be given in notes instead of on the face of the accounts.

A company's accounts may include other items not listed in the various formats but there are three specific items which may not be treated as assets in a company's balance sheet:

(a) preliminary expenses;
(b) expenses of and commissions on any issue of shares or debentures; and
(c) costs of research.

ACCOUNTING PRINCIPLES

Company accounts are required to be prepared in accordance with the principles set out in Sch 4 (companies generally) and Sch 8 (small companies). These principles are the fundamental accounting concepts that underlie accounts and are also incorporated within Financial Reporting Standards (FRSs) and Statements of Standard Accounting Practice (SSAPs) generally and (for small comapanies adopting it) the FRSEE.

The basic accounting principles are as follows.

- **Going Concern** The company or reporting entity is to be presumed to be carrying on business as a going concern.
- **Consistency** Accounting policies must be applied consistently within the same accounts from one financial year to the next.
- **Prudence** The amount of any item must be determined on a prudent basis....
- **Accruals** All income and charges relating to the financial year to which the accounts relate must be taken into account, without regard to the date of receipt or payment.
- **Individual determination** In determining the aggregate amount of any item, the amount of each individual asset or liability that falls to be taken into account shall be determined separately.
- **Netting** Amounts in respect of items representing assets or income must not be set off against amounts in respect of items representing liabilities or expenditure (as the case may be), or vice versa.

For fixed assets, stocks, investments and goodwill, rules regarding valuation, accounting and disclosure are laid down.

Historical cost principles are stated as the normal method of accounting but alternative bases (eg revaluation and current cost) are allowed provided that details and related historical cost figures are disclosed.

Only 'realised' profits can be included in the profit and loss account. 'Realised' profits are defined as profits which are treated as realised in accordance with generally accepted accounting principles (basically in accordance with SSAP2).

**Comment**

This causes one of the main difficulties when trying to fit the Companies Act requirements within the Statement of Financial Activities, recommended by the SORP see Chapter 6 which requires the inclusion of 'unrealised' investment gains.

ACCOUNTS DISCLOSURES

Schedule 4 (companies generally) and Sch 8 (small companies) to the Companies Act 1985 set out the information required to be disclosed in a company's accounts, including that relating to the following heads:

| | |
|---|---|
| Disclosure of accounting policies | *Sch 4.35–58* |
| Share capital and debentures | *Sch 8.35–51* |
| Fixed assets | |
| Investments | |
| Reserves and provisions | |
| Provision for taxation (deferred tax) | |
| Details of indebtedness (nature of security | |
| Guarantees and other financial commitments | |
| Interest | |
| Tax | |
| Turnover analysis | |
| Staff details | |

DIRECTORS' REPORT

The directors of a company have to prepare an annual report (directors' report). Small companies are now permitted to omit much of the information otherwise required to be included in the directors' report.

Companies, other than small companies, must provide the following details:

- **Principal activities** 'The principal activities of the company and its subsidiary undertakings in the course of the year,'
- **Names of directors** The names of directors at any time during the year.
- **Review of business** 'A fair review of the development of the business and its subsidiary undertakings during the financial year and of their position at the end of it.'
- **Dividend** Amount of dividend payment, if any, recommended.
- **Post balance sheet events** Particulars of any important post balance sheet events affecting the company and its subsidiary undertakings.
- **Future developments** Indication of likely future developments in the business of the company and its subsidiary undertakings.
- **Research and development** Indication of research and development activities, if any, of the company and its subsidiary undertakings.
- **Land and buildings** Any significant and substantial difference in market value of interests in land at the year end from balance sheet amount.

- **Directors' share interests** Directors' interests in shares or debentures of the company of any other body corporate in the same group (ie its holding company or *corporate* undertaking). (These details may optionally be shown in the notes to the accounts, rather than in the directors' report.)
- **Directors' share options etc.** Options granted or exercised in group companies.
- **Acquisition of the company's own shares** Details of acquisition of own shares.
- **Political and charitable gifts.**
- **Employment of disabled persons, and employee involvement** (companies with 250 or more employees only).
- **Policy on payment of creditors** (public companies; not small or medium sized companies).

AUDIT REPORTS

Full statutory accounts (together with an audit or accountants' report, if appropriate) are required for shareholders for all companies. The availability or otherwise of audit exemption will determine whether the accounts should be accompanied by an auditors' report, an accountants' report or neither type of report.

The auditors of a small company which has taken advantage of the special provisions in its full statutory accounts are no longer required to state specifically whether in their opinion the annual accounts have been properly prepared in accordance with the provisions 'applicable to small companies'.

The auditors must consider whether the information given in the directors' report is consistent with the accounts and, if not, must state that fact in their report. There is no requirement to state in what respect it is inconsistent.

Where abbreviated accounts are prepared (under the 'small' and 'medium-sized' company filing exemptions), a special auditors' report is required stating that in the auditors' opinion:

- the company is entitled to deliver abbreviated accounts; and
- the abbreviated accounts have been properly prepared.

When the full statutory accounts are unaudited the abbreviated accounts should be accompanied by an accountant's report on the full accounts, only if it is required.

DORMANT COMPANIES

Provided they comply with certain conditions, the Companies Act 1985 permits dormant companies not to appoint auditors.

The Act permits a company which:

(a) has been dormant since the end of the previous financial period;
(b) is entitled to the benefit of the accounting exemptions applicable to 'small' companies, or would have been so entitled but for the fact that it was a member of an 'ineligible group'; and
(c) is not obliged to prepare group accounts;

to agree by special resolution not to appoint auditors (providing there is no specific requirement in the company's articles to appoint auditors).

Companies which take advantage of this provision may file 'small company' abbreviated accounts (an abbreviated balance sheet and notes), without an auditors' report provided the balance sheet contains a statement by the directors that the company was dormant throughout the financial year to which the accounts relate.

### PUBLICATION OF NON-STATUTORY ACCOUNTS

Where a company publishes non-statutory accounts (that is, abridged accounts giving less than full statutory accounts disclosure or other than as part of the company's statutory accounts), those accounts must state:

(a) that they are not the company's statutory accounts;
(b) whether statutory accounts (ie either full annual or abbreviated accounts) have been filed;
(c) whether the auditors have reported on the statutory accounts (under s 235 CA 1985) or, if appropriate, whether the company's reporting accountant has made a report for the purposes of s 249A(2) on those accounts;
(d) whether the audit report or accountant's report (for the purposes of s 249A(2)) was qualified, or modified, as the case may be.

The full audit report or accountants' report (as the case may be), however, is *not* to be published with non-statutory accounts.

Simplified accounting information, abridged accounts, announcements of company results to employees or the press, might be classified non-statutory accounts.

### GROUP ACCOUNTS

A parent company which has 'subsidiary undertakings' is required (with certain exceptions) to prepare group accounts in the form of consolidated accounts of the company and its subsidiary undertakings. Consolidation is not restricted to subsidiaries which are companies.

Group accounts are required to comply with the provisions of Sch 4A to the Companies Act 1985 as to the form and content of consolidated accounts and additional information to be given. Schedule 4A provides, *inter alia*, for the following:

(a) elimination of group transactions;
(b) provisions for acquisition and merger accounting;
(c) treatment and disclosure of 'minority interests';
(d) non-consolidated subsidiary undertakings;
(e) joint ventures and associated undertakings;
(f) preparation 'as if' the group were a single company.

A subsidiary may be excluded from consolidation on the grounds of:

(a) immateriality;

and *must* be excluded in the following circumstances:

(b) severe long-term restrictions;
(c) temporary control – holding with a view to subsequent resale;
(d) activities are 'so different' from those of other undertakings as to be incompatible with the obligation to give a true and fair view.

APPROVAL AND SIGNATURE OF ACCOUNTS

The requirements for the approval and signature of the directors' report, the accounts and the auditors' report were amended by the Companies Act 1989 and SI 1992/2452 and have been further amended by SI 1994/1935.

A company's annual accounts must be approved by the board of directors and signed on behalf of the board by a director of the company. The signature must be on the company's individual balance sheet and the name of the signatory must be stated. Previously, the signature of *two* directors was normally required and, although this is still permissible, it is no longer a requirement under the Companies Act 1989.

The directors' report must also be approved by the board of directors and signed on their behalf by a director or the secretary of the company; the name of the signatory must be similarly stated.

The auditors' or accountants' report must state the names of the auditors or reporting accountants (as the case may be) and be signed by them.

The above requirements also apply to the approval and directors' signature of abbreviated accounts.

The balance sheet and directors' report of a small company which have been prepared in accordance with the special provisions for small companies must each contain a statement by the directors to that effect.

This completes the extract from *Preparing Company Accounts*, by Ray Mayes of Buzzacott, published by Accountancy Books 1999.

**Comment**

During the debate on the Charities Bill in 1992 an undertaking was given by the Government to review the accounting requirements under company legislation as they affect charitable companies with a view to bringing these into line with the accounting requirements under the Charities Act. This undertaking is hopefully being fulfilled. A member of the DTI Companies Directorate has been working with the Charity Commission Policy Group and a consultation paper was promised. In March 1998 the DTI launched their review of company law and from this has sprung the concept of the Charitable Incorporated Institution (CII). It remains to be seen whether this will eventually remove charitable companies from the jurisdiction of the DTI and the Companies Acts and place them under that of the Charity Commission and The Charities Acts.

## 3 INDUSTRIAL AND PROVIDENT SOCIETIES

**3.9** The charities constituted under the Industrial and Provident Societies Acts must comply with the accounting provisions contained in the Industrial and Provident Societies Act 1968. The relevant provisions for industrial and provident societies are as follows:

**(a) Books of account** *References*

Every society is required at all times (a) to keep proper books of account which will give a true and fair view of its transactions, assets and liabilities; and (b) to maintain a satisfactory system of control over its books of account, its cash holdings and its receipts and remittances. *s 1*

Books of account need not be in the form of bound books, but if they are kept in some other form the society must take adequate precautions to guard against falsification and facilitate its discovery. *s 2*

**(b) Revenue accounts and balance sheets**

Every revenue account prepared by a society must give a true and fair view of the income and expenditure to which it relates, whether this is the income and expenditure of the society as a whole or the income and expenditure in respect of a particular business. For each year of account the society must prepare one or more revenue accounts which between them will give a true and fair view of the society's income and expenditure as a whole for that year of account (to be included in the society's annual return for that year). *s 3(1)–(3)*

Every balance sheet of a society must give a true and fair view of the state of the society's affairs as at the date of the balance sheet. *s 3(4)*

The committee of management are under a duty to take all reasonable steps to secure compliance with these requirements. A member of the committee who fails in his duty commits an offence, unless he can prove that he reasonably believed that a competent and reliable person had been charged with the duty of securing compliance and was in a position to discharge the duty.

A society may not publish any revenue account or balance sheet unless it: *s 3(5)*

(i) has been audited by the society's last-appointed auditor(s) and incorporates a report by the auditor on its compliance with the relevant requirements relating to the revenue accounts, balance sheet and books of account;

(ii) has been signed by the secretary and two committee members on behalf of the committee.

A society is not obliged to prepare or publish any account or balance sheet beyond those needed for the completion of its annual return. If, however, a society does prepare or publish any additional revenue account or balance sheet (eg half-yearly accounts, or yearly accounts in a form differing from those in the annual return), every such revenue account or balance sheet must comply with the relevant requirements.

**(c) Annual returns**

The form of the annual return will continue to be prescribed by the Chief Registrar. But in every annual return for a year of account beginning on or after 1 January 1969 there must be included the annual revenue account or accounts required under [the preceding paragraph] and a balance sheet as at the end of the year. These and any other accounts contained in the return must have been examined by the society's auditors and the return must be accompanied by a copy of the auditors' report on the accounts for the period included in the return. *s 11(2)(3)*

A copy of the auditors' report must accompany every copy of an annual return for a year of account beginning on or after the 1 January 1969 which is supplied to any member or person interested in the society's funds under s 39(5) of the 1965 Act. *s 11(5)*

## 4 FRIENDLY SOCIETIES

**3.10** Charities constituted under the Friendly Societies Act 1992 must comply with the requirements of that act and The Friendly Societies (Accounts and Related Provisions) Regulations 1994. In particular the following is of relevance:

*References*

(a) **True and fair requirement**
The annual financial statements of all Friendly Societies are required to show a true and fair view. Friendly Societies are required to follow the accounts regulations and applicable accounting standards and related pronouncements issued by the Accounting Standards Board. *s 70*

(b) **Audit requirements**
Auditors are required to report on the truth and fairness of the financial statements and to perform their work in accordance with Auditing Standards. An additional opinion that is required to be published concerns the consistency of the financial statements with the report of the committee of management and its compliance with the 1992 Act and the regulations made under it. *s 73*

**3.11** The Friendly Societies (Accounts and Related Provisions) Regulations 1994 prescribe the format and content of the annual accounts and committee of management report to be prepared in respect of friendly societies. The provisions include the following:

*References*

(a) **Income and expenditure account and balance sheet**
The income and expenditure account should be prepared in accordance with prescribed format and headings. The balance sheet must similarly be produced in accordance with prescribed headings. The regulations detail the order and headings under which the income and expenditure account and balance sheet should be prepared. *s 1* *s 2*

The regulations further state that amounts in respect of items representing assets or income may not be set off against amounts in respect of items representing liabilities or expenditure or vice versa.

**(b) Accounting principles and rules**

A Friendly Society is presumed to be carrying on a business as a going concern. Accounting policies must be consistently applied. The amount of any item must be determined on a prudent basis. In particular, only income arising by the balance sheet date must be included in the income and expenditure account. All liabilities or losses that have arisen or are likely to arise in respect of the financial year to which the accounts relate or a previous financial year must be taken into account, including those which only become apparent between the balance sheet date and the date on which the accounts are signed. Income and charges relating to the financial year to which they relate must be taken into account, without regard for the date of receipt or payment. Each asset or liability must be determined separately in determining the aggregate amount of the item. *s 6*

## 5 REGISTERED SOCIAL LANDLORDS

**3.12** Brought into existence mainly by incorporation under the Industrial and Provident Societies Act 1965, housing associations became known as Registered Social Landlords (RSLs) under the Housing Act 1996. Their objective is to provide affordable housing to those on low incomes; and many charities, particularly those providing residential care, have established themselves as RSLs or have linked themselves with existing RSLs.

**3.13** As RSLs are to some extent dependent upon statutory funding through the Housing Corporation which was established in 1964, those charities which operate through RSLs must comply with the appropriate accounting requirements. Formerly contained in the Housing Associations Act 1985 and the Registered Housing Associations (Accounting Requirements) Order 1988, these are now to be found in 'The Accounting Requirements for Registered Social Landlords – General Determinations 1997 and 1998'.

**3.14** This general determination only applies to RSLs in England. There are, however, similar orders which apply to Northern Ireland, Scotland and Wales.

**3.15** Basically the balance sheet and income and expenditure account should follow the formats of the Companies Act 1985. Paragraph 29 of the 1997 Determination requires there to be a distinction between housing activities and other activities. Further updates of the Determination can be expected in the future.

**3.16** In addition to the General Determination, there is the Statement of Recommended Practice (SORP) 'Accounting by Registered Housing

Associations' issued in February 1994 by the National Housing Federation. A revised SORP was issued in March 1999 and applies to accounting periods ending on or after 23 March 2000.

**3.17** Like the SORP 'Accounting and Reporting by Charities' this SORP has a wider application and is to be adopted by registered social landlords throughout the UK. It gives guidance on accounting practice, formats and accounting policies. Where applicable, it takes precedence over SORP 'Accounting and Reporting by Charities', para 14 of which states:

*'Where necessary these recommendations should be adapted to meet:*

*(a)* *any statutory requirements relating to the form and content of accounts, such as are contained in companies legislation, the Industrial and Provident Societies Acts 1965 to 1978 in determinations made by the Housing Corporation under the provisions of the Housing Act 1996 or regulations made under the Law Reform (Miscellaneous Provisions) (Scotland) Act 1990.*
*(b)* *any requirements imposed by the charity's own governing document to the extent that these exceed statutory requirements.'*

**3.18** As explained in more detail in **3.9** Industrial and Provident Societies are required to:

- keep proper books of account and give a true and fair view of their affairs and explain their transactions;
- maintain satisfactory systems of control;
- lodge an annual return with accounts with the Registrar of Friendly Societies.

**3.19** Under the Housing Act 1996 Sch 1 para 18 similar provisions apply.

**3.20** The conduct of charities operating as registered social landlords is set down in the Housing Act 1996 and the National Housing Federation Code of Governance which was published in September 1995. In addition, finance officers should have regard to the Housing Corporation's determinations and circulars regarding financial controls and financial reporting.

**3.21** In addition to the accounts, the board of an RSL is expected to produce an annual report covering the operation of the association, its performance and its prospects.

## 6 OTHER SOURCES OF ACCOUNTING REQUIREMENTS

**3.22** The activities in which the charity is engaged may require it to register with local authorities, regulatory bodies or other organisations which may have their own particular accounting requirements. These will generally be in addition to and not in place of any other statutory accounting requirements listed in this chapter. If the charity has been constituted by a simple trust deed, regard should be had to the terms of the trust deed which may also contain specific requirements relating to the accounts.

## 7 STATEMENT OF RECOMMENDED PRACTICE – SORP

**3.23** Whilst the Accounting Standards Board takes responsibility for setting accounting standards which have general application such as Financial Reporting Standards (FRSs) and Statements of Standard Accounting Practice (SSAPs), they have delegated responsibility for Statements of Recommended Practice (SORPs) to the regulatory authority responsible for the industry or sector concerned.

**3.24** Thus the SORP 'Accounting and Reporting by Charities' has been issued in its revised form in November 2000 by the Charity Commission and applies to all accounting periods beginning on or after 1 January 2001. Other more specialist SORPs have been issued, including one on higher education, the HEI SORP, and another on registered housing associations (now registered social landlords) – see **3.12** above.

**3.25** The status of the SORP is that of recommendation rather than requirement. However to conclude that this leaves it as optional whether to follow the recommendations or not is a dangerous presumption. In the preamble to the SORP there is a statement by the Accounting Standards Board which includes the following:

*'On the basis of its review, the ASB has concluded that the SORP has been developed in accordance with the ASB's code of practice and does not appear to contain any fundamental points of principle that are unacceptable in the context of present accounting practice or to conflict with an accounting standard or the ASB's plans for future standards.'*

**3.26** This is colloquially referred to as 'negative franking' and effectively elevates the SORP to the status of current best practice. Therefore any charity which chooses not to follow or to ignore a recommendation must be able to justify its decision.

**3.27** Paragraph 9 of SORP contains the following statement in this respect:

*'Trustees may occassionally find that following a recommendation is incompatible with the obligation to give a true and fair view. They should then use the alternative accounting treatment which gives a true and fair view and provide*

*particulars (in accordance with paragraph 280) of any material departure from the recommendations in this SORP, in the Annual Report and the notes to the accounts.* ***A departure is not justified simply because it gives the reader a more appealing picture of the financial position or results of the charity.'***

**3.28** The Charities (Accounts and Reports) Regulations 1995 and 2000, issued under the Charities Act 1993 lend further weight to the SORP. Paragraph 3 of Part III of Sch 1 specifically requires that the values of assets and liabilities in a charity's accounts should be determined in accordance with the principles set out in the SORP.

**3.29** The recommendations in the SORP as best practice should therefore always be followed by charities producing accounts which are required to show a true and fair view, except in two cases:

(a) if the recommendation is incompatible with the obligation to give a true and fair view;
(b) if the recommendation is incompatible with statutory accounting requirements imposed on the charity. In this case the recommendation should be adapted to meet the special circumstances as nearly as possible.

## Summary of the SORP

### 3.30 Purpose of charity's annual report and accounts

*'The purpose of preparing a charity's annual report and accounts is to discharge the charity trustees' duty of public accountability and stewardship.'* *(para 3)*

*'The report and accounts should:*

*(a) provide timely and regular information on the charity and its funds;*
*(b) enable the reader to gain an understanding of the charity's activities and achievements;*
*(c) enable the reader to gain a full and proper appreciation of the charity's financial transactions during the year and of the position of its funds at the end of the year.* *(para 4)*

### 3.31 Scope

*'This SORP is intended to apply to all charities in the United Kingdom and the Republic of Ireland regardless of their size, constitution or complexity.*

*However, where a separate SORP exists for a particular class of charities, the trustees of charities in that class should adhere to that Statement of Recommended Practice.'* *(para 12)*

## 3.32 Content

| | | |
|---|---|---|
| (a) Trustees' annual report | – | This should include:<br>(i) legal and administrative information about the charity<br>(ii) narrative information on:<br>– the objects<br>– organisational structure<br>– relationship with other organisations<br>– how trustees decide: strategy, policies on reserves, investment, grant making, funding deficits, internal controls, risk assessment.<br>– activities and achievements<br>– financial position<br>– future plans. (paras 26–32) |
| (b) Accounts structure | – | This defines what should be included in the accounts and how:<br>(i) accounting concepts and standards<br>(ii) accounting for separate funds:<br>Unrestricted – general and designated<br>Restricted – income and capital (endowments)<br>Endowments – permanent and expendable<br>(iii) accounting for gains and losses<br>(iv) accounting for the movement of funds<br>(v) reconciling funds<br>(vi) accounting for branches. (paras 33–55) |
| (c) Statement of financial activities | – | This shows the total incoming and total outgoing resources of the charity including capital gains and losses |
| | – | It gives an analysis of both incoming and outgoing resources |
| | – | It separates restriced funds from unrestricted funds |
| | – | It shows for each class of fund whether there is a net inflow or outflow of funds |
| | – | It provides a reconciliation of all movements in the charity's funds |

| | | |
|---|---|---|
| | | – Detailed guidance is given on all relevant issues. (paras 56–180) |
| (d) | Balance sheet | – This shows all the assets and liabilities of the charity<br>– It represents the resources available to the charity and how they are deployed<br>– Details of inalienable or historic assets and contingent liabilities may be contained in notes rather than on the face of the balance sheet. (paras 181–271) |
| (e) | Cash flow statement | – Application (paras 272–276) |
| (f) | Accounting policies | – This includes recognition of incoming resources such as legacies and grants<br>– It deals with deferred income, life memberships etc<br>– Expenditure policies include costs of generating funds, management and administration, as well as direct charitable expenditure<br>– Recognition of liabilities especially in relation to grants payable is considered (paras 277–291) |
| (g) | Summary financial information | – General principles (paras 292–297) |
| (h) | Special sections | – Consolidaton of Subsidiary Undertakings (paras 298–319)<br>– Associates, Joint Ventures and Joint Arrangements (paras 320–330)<br>– Charitable Companies (paras 331–343) |
| (i) | Accounting for smaller charities | – This explains the application of FRSEE to charities<br>– The position for charities with income below £250,000 (paras 344–358) |

**Comment**

**3.33** The SORP applies to all charities (both incorporated and unincorporated) except registered housing associations (now registered social landlords), universities and common investment funds, all of which have their own SORP.

**3.34** While it is important to comply with the statutory requirements governing the accounts of the charity, which are set out in this chapter, it is equally important to do so in accordance with the recommendations of the SORP, which are considered in detail in the following chapters.

CHAPTER 4

# Trustees' report

## 1 DUTY TO PREPARE ANNUAL REPORT AND ACCOUNTS

**4.1** Paragraph 26 of SORP makes it clear that the trustees are responsible for the whole of the annual report of a charity, including the accounts, and accordingly they should take care to ensure the accuracy of:

(a) the trustees' narrative report, *'describing what the charity is trying to do and how it is going about it...'*
(b) the disclosure of the legal and administrative details of the charity;
(c) the accounts of the charity and notes thereto.

**4.2** Paragraphs 27–29 of SORP impose the following further duties upon trustees in relation to the Annual Report and Accounts:

(a) include any other information required by law;
(b) confirm that the accounts comply with current statutory requirements and those of the charity's governing instrument;
(c) approve the report and accounts as a body, authorising one of their number to sign on their behalf with the date of approval;
(d) if any trustee considers that the report and accounts should not have been approved, he or she should report their concerns to the Charity Commission or other regulator;
(e) the trustees annual report should be attached to the annual accounts together with the auditors' or independant examiner's report as required.

## 2 LEGAL AND ADMINISTRATIVE DETAILS

**4.3** Paragraph 30 of SORP sets out the requirements regarding the disclosure of the legal and administrative details of a charity.

**4.3** *Trustees' report*

*'The legal and administrative information provided in the trustees' annual report should include:*

*(a)* *the name of the charity. . .*
*(b)* *an indication of the nature of the governing document (eg trust deed; memorandum and articles of association; Charity Commission Scheme; Royal Charter etc) and how the charity is (or its trustees are) constituted (eg limited company; unincorporated association; trustees incorporated as a body etc). The charity registration number (in Scotland the charity recognition number) and the company registration number should also be provided;*
*(c)* *(i)* *the names of the current charity trustees — (up to 50);*
  *(ii)* *the names of any other persons who have served as trustees in the financial year;*
  *(iii)* *the method of appointment or election of trustees;*
  *(iv)* *the name of any other person or body entitled to appoint one or more of the charity trustees;*
  *(v)* *where the charity trustee is a company, the names of its current directors or other persons managing it;*
*(d)* *the address of the principal or registered office of the charity. . .;*
*(e)* *the names and addresses of any other relevant organisations or persons. This should include the names and addresses of those acting as bankers, solicitors, auditor (or independent examiner or reporting accountant), and investment or other principal advisers;*
*(f)* *details of any specific restrictions imposed by the governing instrument concerning the way in which the charity can operate;*
*(g)* *a summary of any specific investment powers and their authority (eg the governing document; Charity Commission Order etc).'*

For an example of such information, see the extract from the annual report and accounts of Help the Aged on page 45.

**Comment**

**4.4** While it would seem to be a matter of common sense that these details should be given in every annual report, it is surprising how many charities take it for granted that the reader will instinctively know all about them. It is, therefore, helpful to have this checklist when starting to prepare the annual report.

**4.5** Apart from the details listed in para 30 of SORP it is also helpful to give a prominent indication of the main objects of the charity so that the reader is immediately aware of the field in which it operates. It is astonishing how often this is omitted, probably because the writers assume that the readers already know. The objects of the charity, if not obvious from its title, should be clearly stated at the very outset, preferably on the front cover.

## *Help the Aged: 30 April 2000*



As required by the Articles of Association, Priscilla Campbell Allen, Peter Bowring, Jo Connell and Anne Harris, retire by rotation and, being eligible, offer themselves for re-election.

In accordance with the Memorandum and Articles, Dr Chai Patel was appointed during the year, retires and being eligible, offers himself for re-election.

The Charity regrets to announce the death of George Davis and recognises and acknowledges his contribution as a Trustee for many years, including five years as Chairman of the Board of Trustees and three years as a Vice President.

The Charity thanks and recognises the contribution of Lady Macpherson who served as a Trustee for more than six years and resigned on 19 August 1999.

The Board is grateful for the additional advice and expertise of the following people who have served on advisory committees:

Joan Bartlett (Servite Housing)

Tony Carter (Greater London Forum for the Elderly and National Pensioners' Convention)

Daphne Clark (Sutton Housing Trust)

Peter Fletcher (Peter Fletcher Associates)

Christopher Flind (Chairman, Richmond, Twickenham and Roehampton District Health Authority)

Judith Hunt

Vera Ivers (Older Womens Network UK)

Susan Kingsley (Church Commissioners Association)

Nina Patel (Institute on Ageing and Ethnicity)

[*continued on following page*]

*Help the Aged, continued*

Sir Harry Roche (retired)
Lucianne Sawyer (UK Home Care Association)
Paul Seymour (Watson Wyatt Partners)
Peter Townsend (The Townsend Centre for International Poverty)

**Auditors**

Hays Allen
Southampton House
317 High Hoborn
London WC1V 7NL

**Solicitors**

Wedlake Bell
16 Beford Street
Covent Garden
London WC2E 9HF

**Bankers**

Barclays Bank Plc
Pall Mall Corporate Banking Group
50 Pall Mall
PO Box 15162
London SW1A 1QB

**Stockbrokers**

Charles Stanley and Company Limited
25 Luke Street
London EC2A 4AR

## Trustees' Responsibilities

Help the Aged is constituted as a Company Limited by Guarantee and as such is subject to Company Law. Its Trustees are required to prepare financial statements for each financial year which give a true and fair view of the state of affairs of the Charity and of the surplus or deficit for that period. In preparing those financial statements, the Trustees are required to:

- Select suitable accounting policies and apply them consistently
- Make judgements and estimates that are reasonable and prudent
- State whether applicable accounting standards have been followed, subject to any material departures disclosed and explained in the financial statements
- Prepare the financial statements on the going concern basis unless it is inappropriate to presume that the company will continue its operations

The Trustees are responsible for keeping proper accounting records which disclose with reasonable accuracy at any time the financial position of the company and to enable them to ensure that the financial statements comply with the Companies Act 1985. They are also responsible for taking reasonable steps for the prevention and detection of fraud and other irregularities.

### Specific Restrictions imposed by the Memorandum and Articles of Association

The Memorandum of Association provides that the Company shall not dispose of the whole of its freehold or leasehold properties or any part thereof exceeding 25% except with the sanction of the Company in General meeting by Special Resolution first obtained.

## 3 NARRATIVE INFORMATION

**4.6** The trustees' narrative report is perhaps the most important part of the annual report as it links the financial facts shown by the accounts to the objects of the charity and the policies being pursued to achieve those objects. It enables the trustees to explain both successes and disappointments; it also enables them to explain any unusual items in the accounts which they fear may give a misleading impression to their supporters, for example, a sudden influx of cash at the year end.

**4.7** Paragraph 31 of SORP provides a full checklist of the narrative information that should, if relevant, be included in the trustees' report.

Whilst every charity '*should adapt the narrative according to its own particular circumstances*', para 31 of SORP expects all reports to include the following:

- an explanation of the objects of the charity;
- a description of the organisational structure of the charity;
- a statement regarding relationships between the charity and connected organisations;
- a review of the activities, developments and achievements of the charity during the year and plans for the future;
- a statement of the charity's policies, in particular:
  the charity's policy on reserves stating the level of reserves held and why they are held;
  the investment policy and performance against policy;
  grant making policies...
- where funds are in deficit an explanation of why they are in deficit and what action is to be taken on them;
- a statement confirming that the major risks to which the charity is exposed as identified by the trustees have been reviewed and systems have been established to mitigate those risks.

**4.8** Regulation 7 of the Charities (Accounts and Reports) Regulations 2000 gives further reinforcement to the recommendations of paras 30 and 31 of SORP.

For all charities Reg 7 requires trustees to include in their annual report:

- the financial year to which the report relates
- a brief summary of the main activities and achievements of the charity during the year
- the name of the charity
- the number assigned to it in the register and, in the case of a charitable company, the number with which it is registered as a company

- the principal address of the charity and, in the case of a charitable company, the address of its registered office
- particulars of documents regulating the purposes and administration of the charity
- the names of the charity trustees and any person or body entitled to appoint a charity trustee
- a description of the policies regarding income reserves, investment selection and making grants.

**4.9** For charities with gross income in excess of £250,000 Regulation 7 lists the following further requirements:

- instead of a brief summary of activities and achievements there should be a review of all activities, including
  - — material transactions, significant developments and achievements of the charity during the year in relation to its objects;
  - — any significant changes in those activities during the year;
  - — any important events affecting those activities which have occured since the year end and any likely future developments in these activities; and
  - — where any fund was in deficit at the beginning of the year, the steps taken by the trustees to eliminate that deficit;
- a statement as to whether the charity trustees have given consideration to
  - — the major risks to which the charity is exposed; and
  - — systems designed to mitigate those risks;
- a statement regarding the performance during the financial year of the investments belonging to the charity (if any);
- a description of the organisational structure of the charity;
- a description of any assets held by the charity or by any trustee on behalf of another charity, and particulars of any special arrangements regarding safe custody and their segregation from the assets of the charity, together with a description of the objects of the charity on behalf of which the assets are held.

**Comment**

**4.10** At first sight Reg 7 and paras 30–31 of SORP look dauntingly bureaucratic and repetitive. Some trustees may think that their report will simply consist of a list of disclosure points for compliance purposes. This, however, is not doing either the regulations or the SORP justice. Broken down to their essentials they are asking trustees:

(a) to give details about the charity's structure and administration;
(b) to explain its objects and policies;
(c) to review its activities and achievements;
(d) to comment on the fund balances at the year end in the context of

the objects of each. Are they adequate? Are they excessive? What are they proposing to do about it?

(e) to show an awareness of the main risks faced by the charity and the need to implement systems to mitigate them.

**4.11** The report may be a lengthy document or simply a few paragraphs. The main point is that it should help to explain and interpret the figures shown in the accounts, to make the 'Report and Accounts' a cohesive integral document. The sub-headings of para 31 of SORP are intended to act as a prompt to help trustees to identify relevant matters for inclusion.

**4.12** Although it is succinctly worded, para 31 of SORP demands considerable thought on the part of the trustees, who may find it necessary to lengthen their report significantly to cover fully the subjects on which they are asked to comment. We welcome this as a further move in the direction of greater accountability but the burden should not be underestimated. Following the publication of the previous SORP, the need for trustees to consider the optimum level of reserves was topical; the new SORP adds the need for trustees to make a statement confirming that they have considered the risks to which the charity is exposed.

**4.13** A well-prepared trustee's report will have identified its target audience and communicated the main messages concerning the charity's progress by linking them to the salient features in the accounts. Thus supporters of the charity will, by reading the report, be able to judge whether their support has been worth while and whether they feel inclined to continue to support it in the future.

**4.14** In order to ensure that clear and accurate messages come through, trustees should consider the structure of their report and the structure of their accounts. For example, the main expenditure headings in the Statement of Financial Activities should represent the main charitable activities of the charity on which the trustees are reporting. If they do not then the structure of the report or the accounts or both should be revised. Similarly, if significant resources are earmarked for one particular purpose, it will make the trustees' report clearer if the balance sheet can show these as a designated fund, separate from the other unrestricted funds. This aspect is considered further in Chapter 5.

**4.15** While the trustees' report may sometimes be drafted by the charity accountant or even the auditors, it must be made abundantly clear to the trustees that it is *their* report and that they must take responsibility for it. This is now dealt with in a 'statement of responsibilities' which may form part of the trustees' report or be shown as a separate statement accompanying the accounts. The auditors have a duty under Statement of Auditing Standards No 600

(SAS600) to distinguish their responsibilities from those of the trustees. This is discussed further in Chapter 16.

**4.16** Apart from the overall financial picture, the trustees are reminded of the need to consider the finances on a fund-by-fund basis to ensure that each is being used for its own purposes and is capable of meeting its commitments. If one becomes overextended the trustees should say what they are doing about it.

**4.17** Although the trustees' report is fundamentally a narrative explanation it can be illustrated with pictures, graphs, pie charts etc to help emphasise particular points. Indeed such diagramatic portrayal of figures extracted from the accompanying accounts helps the ordinary reader to understand the main features of the accounts themselves.

The example from ChildLine on the following page shows how such an illustration breaks up the narrative and emphasises the point.

## 4 FUNDS HELD AS CUSTODIAN TRUSTEE

**4.18** Paragraph 32 of SORP makes clear that it is for the managing or executive trustees to prepare the annual report and accounts — not custodian trustees. Custodian trustees are those whose sole role is to hold assets on behalf of a charity. They should therefore make their records available to the trustees of the charities for whom they hold the assets so that they can be included in the latters' accounts.

*Childline: 31 March 1999*

**Review of the year**

During the year to 31 March 1999, ChildLine was able to increase the number of trained volunteer counsellors to over 930. This means we can now answer more than 3,500 of the calls children make to the charity each day. In the course of the year, ChildLine gave substantial counselling to over 130,000 children who were contacting us for the first time, a 14% increase on 1998. We continued to provide special project lines, such as our bullying and children-in-care numbers, in addition to the mainstream service.

ChildLine's 24-hour service to the children of the United Kingdom is provided from our London-based headquarters. BT continues to provide these premises and we are most grateful for their ongoing support. The service is also provided at times of peak demand from our national offices in Scotland (Glasgow) and Wales (Swansea and Rhyl), and from the Midlands (Nottingham), North West (Manchester) and Yorkshire and the North East (Leeds) regions of England. We are indebted to McDonald's Restaurants Limited for their ongoing support in Manchester and to our landlord in Swansea who has provided us with a major concession on the rental costs. A full analysis of donations in kind is included in Note 6. The total value of these is now £262,954.

Special Northern Ireland lines are currently operated from our Manchester base, but we have started the process of staff recruitment and continue to search for premises within the province to provide a local service.

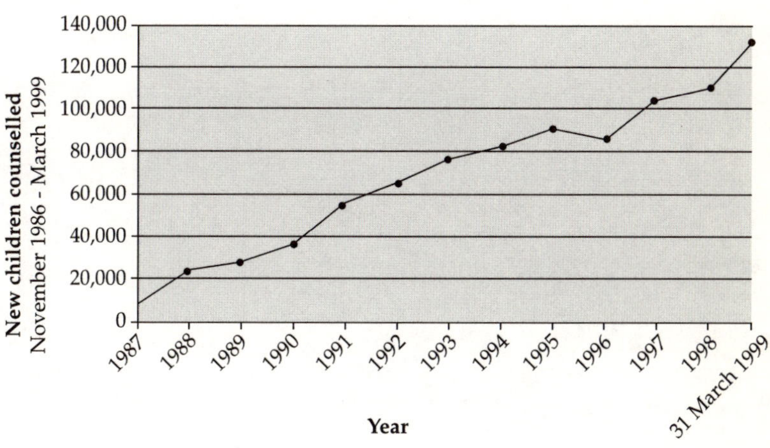

CHAPTER 5

# Accounting policies and accounts structure

## 1 GUIDELINES

**5.1** Paragraph 277 of SORP emphasises the need to explain the basis of the preparation of the accounts of a charity.

*'Charity accounts should include notes on the accounting policies chosen which should be the most appropriate in the particular circumstances of each charity for the purpose of giving a true and fair view. . .'*

**5.2** In paras 33–35 the SORP goes on to say that: *'Accounts intending to show a true and fair view must be prepared on the going concern assumption and the accruals concept and provide information that is relevant, reliable, comparable and understandable. . .'* – and that they must also comply with recognised accounting standards. These consist of Statements of Standard Accounting Practice (SSAPs), Financial Reporting Standards (FRSs) and Urgent Issues Task Force (UITF) abstracts, all of which fall within the authority of the Accounting Standards Board. The SORP gives helpful guidance on the application of these standards in an appendix.

**5.3** The first thing upon which the trustees need to decide in relation to their accounts is the scope of their accountability. What needs to be included: volunteers' activities; branches; overseas activities; connected charities; subsidiary or associated companies? For many charities such as churches, missionary societies and international relief agencies, these are the most difficult questions to resolve as quite often there is a lacuna between the strict legal responsibility and the practical ability to exercise control. To a large extent the trustees may have to rely upon the reports and returns made to them by those working for the charity in the field.

**5.4** Nevertheless the first imperative as regards the accounts is to decide and define their scope (see Chapter 2). On occasions this may result in the accounts being limited.

**5.5** In their annual review for 1996/97 the trustees of UNICEF UK Committee make it clear that the total support for UNICEF from the

UK was £36.2 million, of which the government gave £25.5 million direct and the UK committee was responsible for and accounted for the rest.

*UK Committee for UNICEF: 31 March 1996*

**1 Accounting policies**

(e) Direct contributions to UNICEF from Her Majesty's Government totalling £25,464,900 (*1995: £21,363,553*) are not included in these financial statements.

**5.6** Having established the boundaries of the accounts the next step is to decide upon the accounts structure that is needed to control and communicate the financial transactions of the charity. The main considerations are as follows.

(a) **Funds structure** Are the trusts upon which funds are given to the trustees clearly known? Do they restrict the trustees further than the general trusts under which they receive other monies for the charity? If they do, then they must be kept separate from the general unrestricted funds.
(b) **Branches** Are the branches an integral part of the charity, or have they such autonomy and independence as to make them totally separate from the charity?
(c) **Connected charities** Are there parallel charities working in concert with the charity? Are they under common control or administration? Should their activities be aggregated with those of the charity? If not, what if anything needs to be said about them?
(d) **Consolidation** Have all subsidiary undertakings corporate or otherwise been consolidated with the parent charity's accounts? Does this distort the overall picture of the charity's activities?
(e) **Associated undertakings** Does the charity have a material interest, say 20%, in a company owned by a consortium?

**5.7** The answers to all these questions will have a significant bearing upon the accounts structure of the charity. It is worth spending considerable time examining each of these aspects which are dealt with later in this chapter.

## 2 ACCOUNTING POLICIES

**5.8** Once the trustees have agreed the scope of their accountability and have broadly established the accounts structure that is needed to comply with this, their next step is to define the accounting policies which form the basis for their accounts.

**5.9** These are covered in paras 277–291 of SORP. The following is a summary of the matters to be considered:

- *accounts are prepared in accordance with the SORP and accounting standards;*
- *compliance with the Charities Act or Companies Act or other legislative requirement;*
- *based on historic cost, except for investments (and possibly fixed assets if revalued);*
- *any material departure from the SORP or accounting standards with explanation and justification;*
- *details of any branches or other entities not included and why;*
- *specific policies regarding material incoming resources eg legacies, gifts, intangible income, grants receivable, deferred income, subscriptions, endowment income, resources received net of expenditure;*
- *specific policies for the recognition of liabilities including constructive obligations;*
- *policy for including items within categories of resources expended;*
- *methods and principles for the allocation and apportionment of costs between different categories of expenditure;*
- *bases of capitalisation of fixed assets for the charity's use;*
- *bases of valuation of investments;*
- *basis of inclusion of unrealised and realised gains and losses on investments;*
- *basis for inclusion of stocks and work in progress;*
- *description of the different types of fund held by the charity and the policy for transfer between funds and allocations to and from designated funds;*
- *other relevant polices eg pension contributions, foreign exchange gains and losses, exceptional items, finance and operating leases, treatment of irrecoverable VAT.*

### Comment

**5.10** The detailed requirement for the disclosure of accounting policies is given in Chapter 13 (**13.4 ff**). Suffice it to say at this stage that, in line with the exhortation given in Chapter 2 regarding the trustees' responsibilities in relation to the accounts, it is their responsibility to select 'suitable policies'. These policies should reflect the main accounting aspects affecting the charity — its sources of income, its application of those resources and the way in which it accounts for its major assets, land, buildings and other fixed assets. They will also introduce the main funds structure of the accounts which will indicate the purposes for which the balances on the funds are held (see the example taken from the Multiple Sclerosis Society).

*Multiple Sclerosis Society: 31 December 1999*

**Notes to Consolidated Accounts**

**1. Accounting policies**

a) The accounts are prepared under the historical cost convention with the exception of investments which are stated at market value. They comply with the requirements of Statement of Recommended Practice 'Accounting By Charities' ('SORP') and are in accordance with applicable accounting standards.

b) These are consolidated accounts representing the accounts of the Society and its three subsidiary companies (see pages 16 and 17 for company details).

The Society accounts include the assets, liabilities and funds, and the income and expenditure of the Society's branches including regions, respite care centres and holiday homes and are compiled from the audited accounts and returns supplied by branch treasurers and the trading company. Details of the number of branches consolidated in these accounts appear in note 2.

c) General accumulated funds are unrestricted funds available to the Society for its general purposes and include funds designated by the Society for a particular purpose; the use of such designated funds remains at the discretion of the Society's officers and trustees.

d) Restricted funds are funds subject to restrictions imposed by the donor or by the specific terms of appeal under which the funds are raised. The restrictions are binding upon the Trustees of the Society.

e) All income is accounted for when the Society has entitlement, there is certainty of receipt and the amount is measurable. For legacies entitlement is taken as the earlier of the estate being settled or payment being received. Previously probate date was taken as the date of entitlement and the Trustees have elected to adopt a more prudent basis. The impact of this change in accounting policy is shown as a prior year adjustment and explained in note 20.

f) All expenditure is accounted for on an accruals basis. The Society makes research grants on the recommendation of its Medical Research Advisory Committee. Grants are charged to the Statement of Financial Activities in the year which they are awarded.

g) The governance, management and administration expenses reported in note 4 relate to the whole of the Society's activities

[*continued on following page*]

*Multiple Sclerosis Society, continued*

and a proportion of these charges are allocated to expenditure headings on a basis consistent with the use of the resources.

h) Investments are stated at market value. It is the Society's policy to keep valuations up to date such that when investments are sold there is no gain or loss arising to previous years. As a result the Statement of Financial Activities includes those unrealised gains and losses arising from the revaluation on the investment portfolio throughout the year. Disclosure is made in note 7 to the financial statements of the difference between historic cost and the sales proceeds of investments sold during the year.

i) Tangible assets are included at cost and depreciation is provided on a straight line basis, in order to write off the assets over their useful lives.

The depreciation rates are as follows:

| | |
|---|---|
| Freehold land | Nil |
| Freehold buildings | 2% |
| Leasehold buildings | Remaining term of lease |
| Termination payment on Lease (Effie Road) | Remaining term of lease |
| Computer equipment | 33⅓% |
| Motor Vehicles | 25% |
| Fixtures | 20% |

k) Stocks are valued at the lower of cost and net realisable value.

## 3 ACCOUNTING FOR SEPARATE FUNDS

**5.11** Whilst the main purpose of the accounts is to give an overall view of the incoming and outgoing resources and the resultant financial position at the year end, there are additional requirements for charities that have to account for more than one fund under their control:

*'The accounts should provide a summary of the main funds, differentiating in particular between the unrestricted income funds, restricted income funds and endowment funds. . .'* *(para 37)*

**5.12** This can present complications, particularly where the charity earmarks projects and enters into funding agreements with various trusts or government authorities. The accounts must be capable of producing the overall picture, while at the same time providing an account of the movement on each of the main funds.

**5.13** To ensure that both aims are achieved it is necessary to classify the funds of the charity. Appendix 3 of SORP explains the legal position regarding the funds of a charity. The major distinction is between *unrestricted funds*, ie those that are expendable at the discretion of the trustees in furtherance of the objects of the charity, and *restricted funds* which are subject to specific trusts declared by the donor within the objects of the charity.

**5.14** Further distinctions must be made within the categories of restricted and unrestricted funds. Restricted funds may be restricted income funds or they may be restricted as to the use of capital which must be retained while the income may be used for unrestricted purposes. Such capital funds, if restricted in perpetuity, are called 'permanent endowments'; if the trustees have power to convert them into income funds, they are called 'expendable endowments' until such time as the trustees exercise the power.

**5.15** To complicate matters further, the trustees may place their own restrictions on the use of part of the unrestricted funds. They may do this by *designating* amounts to be set aside, for instance for 'replacement of buildings'. Such designated funds have many of the characteristics of restricted funds but, except where donors give specifically to these funds, they remain unrestricted and the trustees can use their discretion to change their earlier decision if they so wish. Once, however, new money is raised specifically for the designated fund its character then changes from unrestricted to restricted.

The following chart on 'The Funds of a Charity' may help readers to classify their receipts among their funds.

| **The Funds of a Charity** | | |
|---|---|---|
| *Nature of Fund* | *Restricted* | *Unrestricted* |
| 1. Capital funds<br>Property or cash given to the charity to be held in perpetuity as capital, the income from or use of the asset being for either restricted or unrestricted purposes. | Permanent endowment | |
| Property or cash given to the charity to be held as capital but giving the trustees power to use the capital for income purposes. The end uses may be either restricted or unrestricted, but until the power is exercised the capital will remain restricted. | Expendable endowment | |
| 2. Fixed asset funds<br>Reserves set aside by trustees to represent investment out of income in fixed assets either for the use of the charity or as income producing investments.<br>(Technically this is an income fund but as it has been applied to achieve the long-term purposes of the charity it may be helpful to show this designated fund separately from the other income funds.) | | Designated fixed asset fund |
| 3. Income funds<br>Property or cash which has been given to fund a particular project, or to be used for a particular purpose, or in a particular region or manner. | Restricted income fund | |
| Property or cash which has been set aside by the trustees for a particular purpose, eg cyclical maintenance, roof replacement, research or staff pensions. | | Designated income fund |

**5.16** In order to cope with the separate accounting that is necessary to distinguish individual funds a suitable coding structure is essential in order to allocate all incoming and outgoing resources correctly.

**5.17** Guidance is given in SORP in paras 36–50 and also in SORP Appendix 3.

**Funds structure**

Paragraphs 36 and 37 of SORP give a diagram showing the main classifications of separate funds and require accounts to provide a summary of the main funds differentiating in particular between the unrestricted income funds, restricted income funds and endowment funds.

*'The notes to the accounts should provide information on the structure of the charity's funds so as to disclose the fund balances and the reasons for them. . .'*
*(para 49)*

In particular the assets and liabilities representing each type of fund should be summarised and analysed (eg investments, fixed assets and net current assets) between the funds and any which appear in deficit should be explained in the trustees report.

Save the Children Fund describe the composition of their funds in their accounting policies.

*Save the Children Fund: 31 March 2000*

**Fund accounting**

General unrestricted funds are the accumulated annual surpluses and deficits on general funds and the unrealised gains of the investment portfolio. They are available for use at the discretion of the trustees in furtherance of the general charitable objectives.
Designated funds are amounts which have been put aside at the discretion of the Board of Trustees and comprise:

(i) A base reserve: the level of which is £10m. This is to allow sufficient resources for Save the Children to fundamentally reshape in the event of major downward revisions to long-range financial forecasts.

(ii) A tangible fixed assets reserve: which represents the extent to which funds are invested in tangible fixed assets for use by the charity, and are therefore not available for other purposes.

(iii) An emergency response reserve: this designation enables the organisation to draw funds to become operational in emergency situations in advance of money being made available through special appeals or from grant-awarding bodies. The reserve is replenished as expenditure take place.

Restricted funds are funds subject to specific conditions imposed by the donors.

Endowment funds represent assets received which may not be exhausted: only the income may be used.

## Reconciliation of funds

However the funds struture is presented, and liberal use of the notes is recommended for the detail, there must be a reconciliation of the opening and closing balances of each fund. This not only enables the donors to track their restricted fund but to see how it fits in to the general finances of the charity as a whole.

Thus, para 48 of SORP emphasises the following:

*'Reconciliation of funds*

*The Statement of Financial Activities should reflect the principal movements between the opening and closing balances on all the funds of the charity. It should be analysed between unrestricted income funds, restricted income funds and endowment funds (permanent and expendable combined'.*

This is illustrated in the accounts of CAFOD for 1999 (see next page).

Chapter 6, which deals with the Statement of Financial Activities, gives further guidance on the separation of funds.

## Comment

**5.18** The separation of funds is one of the more difficult aspects of charity accounting. It demands first definition and then consitency of treatment. Definition can be achieved by a written memorandum setting out the purposes of each fund, its sources of income and the allocation of expenditure to it.

**5.19** Consistency refers to the basis of allocation. For example, a charity may agree to apportion the cost of salaries of a department over the projects administered by that department acording to the time spent on each project by each member of staff. Another charity may find such a basis of apportionment of cost too complicated and adopt instead a fixed percentage of the total cost to be allocated to each project. Either method may be acceptable but what is not acceptable is to chop and change from one to the other.

**5.20** If it is thought necessary to change the basis of allocation then, depending upon its materiality, it may be necessary to explain it in the accounting policies, showing the effect of the change on the respective funds.

## CAFOD 30.9.99
## (Catholic Fund for Overseas Development)

| Statement of Movement of Funds | Year to 30 September 1999 | | | | | Year to 30 September 1998 | | | | |
|---|---|---|---|---|---|---|---|---|---|---|
| | Development | | | Emergency | Total | Development | | | Emergency | Total |
| | Unrestricted £000 | Restricted* £'000 | Total £'000 | Restricted £'000 | Total £'000 | Unrestricted £000 | Restricted* £'000 | Total £'000 | Restricted £'000 | Total £'000 |
| Fund balances at start of year | 6,967 | 968 | 7,935 | 3,344 | 11,279 | 7,522 | 475 | 7,997 | 2,483 | 10,480 |
| Net inflow/(outflow) of funds after transfers | 719 | (502) | 217 | 2,791 | 3,008 | (555) | 493 | (62) | 861 | 799 |
| **Fund balances at close of year** | **7,686** | **466** | **8,152** | **6,135** | **14,287** | **6,967** | **968** | **7,935** | **3,344** | **11,279** |
| **REPRESENTED BY:** | | | | | | | | | | |
| Fixed assets | 3,451 | 262 | 3,713 | — | 3,713 | 3,596 | 218 | 3,814 | — | 3,814 |
| Net current assets | 4,239 | 204 | 4,443 | 6,135 | 10,578 | 3,609 | 750 | 4,359 | 3,344 | 7,703 |
| Amounts due after one year | (4) | — | (4) | — | (4) | (238) | — | (238) | — | (238) |
| **TOTAL NET ASSETS** | **7,686** | **466** | **8,152** | **6,135** | **14,287** | **6,967** | **968** | **7,935** | **3,344** | **11,279** |

**Notes to pages 5 and 6**
CAFOD did not change any of its principal activities during the above financial years.

There were no gains and losses other than those included above.

*Restricted includes permanent endowment funds; see note 13

Transfers between funds represent unrestricted funds being used for emergency purposes and emergency funds being used for post-emergency rehabilitation projects.

## 4 BRANCHES

**5.21** Appendix 1 of SORP is a glossary of terms and defines branches as *'entities or administrative bodies set up, for example, to conduct a particular aspect of the business of the reporting charity, or to conduct the business of the reporting charity in a particular geographical area. They may or may not be legal entities which are separate from the reporting charity'*. The definition recognises its own limitation by going on to explain different types of branch, including charities which may have nothing to do with the activities of the reporting charity, but which are under the control of the reporting charity (see para **5.27**). It helpfully lists some of the characteristics, any one or more of which may indicate that the entity is a branch:

*'(i) it uses the name of the reporting charity within its title;*
*(ii) it exclusively raises funds for the reporting charity and/or for its own local activities;*
*(iii) it uses the reporting charity's registration number to receive tax relief on its activities;*
*(iv) it is perceived by the public to be the reporting charity's local representative;*
*(v) it receives support from the reporting charity through advice, publicity materials, etc.'*

**5.22** Paragraph 53 of SORP says that *'all branch transactions should be accounted for gross in the reporting charity's own accounts...'*. This is normally done in one of two ways, either by aggregating the activities of all branches under generic headings or by identifying the contributions made by each branch.

**5.23** If the branch and the reporting charity are both incorporated as companies then the method of accounting for the branch within the accounts of the main charity is by means of consolidation (see **5.30 ff**).

**5.24** Paragraph 52 of SORP draws attention to the distinction between a branch and a connected charity:

*'Separate legal entities which may be known as branches but do not fall within the definition of a branch in the Glossary should prepare their own Annual Report and Accounts and, if they are connected charities the relationship should be explained in the trustees report...'*

(See para **5.26**.) An example of such a situation is a local charity which raises funds for more than one national charity. It may be regarded as the local branch of each national charity but clearly is not exclusively under the control of any of them.

### Comment

**5.25** The biggest practical problems concerning branches are first to identify them, secondly to decide whether they are under the control of the reporting charity or not, and thirdly to set in place a uniform and

*Westminster Roman Catholic Diocesan Trust: 31 December 1999*

**Scope of the accounts**

The accounts include the assets, liabilities and transactions of the following:

Curial funds

The Curial funds are used to support the Archbishop and Bishops in providing Diocesewide services and pastoral care and to meet the cost of central administration. The Curial funds are administered by staff within the Curial (or Central) Offices in the Westminster Cathedral complex.

Parochial funds

The Parochial funds are administered, with guidance from the Central Finance Office, by the parish priests and are used to carry out the work of the Church within local areas and to help fund the Curia.

Westminster Cathedral Limited

A wholly owned subsidiary trading company carrying out general trading activities which relate to Westminster Cathedral and whose object is to generate profit for the benefit of the Cathedral.

**Fund accounting**

The Curical Funds

The Curial Funds can be used across the whole of the Diocese and are subdivided between:

- The general fund comprising those monies which may be used towards meeting the charitable objectives of the Charity and used across the whole of the Diocese at the discretion of the Directors of the Corporate Trustee.
- The designated funds being monies set aside out of general funds and designated for specific purposes by the Directors of the Corporate Trustee.
- The restricted funds being monies raised for, and their use restricted to, a specific purpose, or donations subject to donor imposed conditions.

The Parochial funds

These comprise legacies, donations, trust income and interest and relate to specific parishes. As the monies must be utilised by individual parishes and cannot be used across the whole of the Diocese, the funds are all regarded as restricted for the purpose of these accounts.

controllable system of reporting by branches to the main charity. Control is the key word. If the trustees are legally responsible for the activities of the branch, they must ensure that they can account for them and, to do so, they will have to have in place effective accounting controls and procedures. Having said that, regard should also be given to the circumstances. Some branches operate in remote parts of the world with limited resources. A pragmatic view needs to be taken on the level and quality of reporting expected; but, nevertheless, if material, the activities of the branch should still be included in the accounts with appropriate notes if necessary to explain the basis on which they are included.

## 5 CONNECTED CHARITIES

**5.26** Connected charities are defined in Appendix 1 of the SORP as '*those which have common, parallel or related objects and activities and either common control or unity of administration. Within this category may be charities which come together under one umbrella organisation*'. Usually they are separate charities run by the same people. All that is normally required in the accounts of each is a note to indicate the relationship between each charity and details of any transactions between them, as explained in para 157 of SORP.

**5.27** Charities which are members of an '*umbrella organisation*' should give an indication of how many members there are, their areas of activity and how the reader can contact them. If there have been material transactions between the connected charities and the reporting charity these should be disclosed.

**5.28** Sometimes, however, the relationship amounts to one being subordinate to the other and in this case the controlling charity should account for the activities of the other as though it were a trust established for special purposes of the controlling charity. It will be treated as a branch and be included, probably as a restricted fund, in

*Barnardo's: 31 March 1999*

| | |
|---|---|
| Subordinate Charities | Included in Restricted and Endowment Funds are assets held on behalf of 10 trusts which are constituted as separately registered charities. These have purposes which are consistent with the objects of Barnardo's and are under common control. As such, their results have been included in the consolidated statements presented. |

the accounts of the controlling charity. This situation is referred to in paras 302 and 51–55 of SORP (see **5.21**).

**Comment**

**5.29** One might ask why there is a need to disclose dealings with connected charities. Are they more important than dealings with unconnected charities? Clearly it is a regulatory matter to ensure that charities which are effectively run from the same office or by the same people are not using one of the charities to hide the reality of the overall situation. For example two charities with differing year ends could hide accumulated reserves by making donations to each other just before their year end. This regulatory aspect is reinforced by the fact that connected charities are now included in the SORP under '*related parties*'.

**5.30** Apart from the regulatory aspect, it is important for trustees to determine precisely the relationship between their charity and any other – is it a branch, is it a 'special trust' (ie subsidiary charity), is it connected or is it independent?

## 6 CONSOLIDATION

**5.31** Consolidation of accounts is required where there is a corporate hierarchy of parent and self accounting subsidiary undertakings. The only exception is the 'special trust' subsidiary of an unincorporated charity, as described in **5.21** and **5.28** above and referred to in para 302 of SORP.

**5.32** In all other cases the parent charity and its charitable and non charitable subsidiary undertakings will form a group. The parent charity '*should prepare consolidated accounts including all its subsidary undertakings except where:*

(a) *the gross income of the group in the accounting period is no more than the audit threshold (currently £250,000)*
(b) *the subsidary undertaking's results are not material to the group*
(c) *the accounts have to be aggregated under charity legislation in England and Wales*'. *(para 300)*

**5.33** '*The normal rules will apply regarding the method of consolidation, which should be carried out on a line by line basis as set out in FRS2.*' *(para 309)*

**Comment**

**5.34** There was a concession in the previous SORP whereby a charity could in certain circumstances bring in the results of a trading subsidiary as a single line to represent its net contribution or cost to the charity's resources. This is no longer available and the normal rules for consolidation on a line by line basis must be followed. It was feared that this might result in a distortion of the overall picture conveyed by group accounts by including gross figures of trading income and expenditure when the charity's main interest was only in the net contribution made by such activities.

**5.35** This argument however is countered first by the need to show the major activities of the group on the face of the accounts gross and second by the recommmendation to treat similar items in the same way, eg '*operating activities for generating funds in the charity should be combined with similar activities in the subsidiary, and charitable activities within the charity should be combined with charitable activities in the subsidiary. . .*'.
*(para 310)*

**5.36** One of the more helpful results of this approach is that it resolves the problem previously posed by the apparent anomaly of a charity shop carrying on a charitable activity on the one hand of selling donated goods, ie converting gifts in kind into cash, and selling bought in goods on the other, ie trading. Now both activities can be combined.

*'Activities for generating funds can include selling donated goods and bought in goods. . .'* *(para 106)*

Consolidated accounts will combine these activities whether carried on by the charity or its trading subsidiary under the heading of '*activities for generating funds*'.

**5.37** Practical guidance is summarised in para 311 of SORP which recommends charities to: '*choose appropriate line headings within the permissible format of the Statement of Financial Activities and suitable amalgamations of activities. The headings should be expanded and changed to reflect the underlying activities of the group*'.

**5.38** Additional segmental information may sometimes be needed in the notes in order to distinguish the key results of the charity from those of its subsidiary undertakings.

*'Examples of those items which should be separately disclosed include the costs of generating funds management and administration and the costs of charitable activities.'* *(para 318)*

## 7 ASSOCIATES, JOINT VENTURES AND JOINT ARRANGEMENTS

**5.39** Paragraphs 320–330 of SORP give guidance on how to identify associates and joint ventures and distinguish them from parents or subsidiaries. Reference is made to FRS 9 which determines the relationship between the entities involved.

**5.40** *'Where a charity has a long term participating interest in another undertaking and exercises significant influence over its operating and financial policy then this is likely to be an associate undertaking. Where a charity benefically holds 20% or more of the voting rights in any undertaking it will be presumed to have a participating interest and significant influence...'*

*(para 322)*

**5.41** Associates should be included in the accounts based on the net equity method, ie the net interest in the results to be shown in one line after the *'net incoming/(resources expended)'* line in the SOFA and the net interest in associates to be shown in a separate line within fixed asset investments.

**5.42** A joint venture arises where there is a separate entity controlled by two or more undertakings. The accounting for a charity's share in a joint venture seems rather clumsy but it is explained in para 326 of SORP as: *'the gross equity method'*. It involves including gross incoming resources from the joint venture on a line by line basis, then deducting the total from the total incoming resources and then adding back the net interest in the results as a separate line in the same way as for associates.

**5.43** Where a charity carries out activities in partnership with other bodies but without creating a separate legal entity, it should account for its gross share in the incoming resources from the joint arrangement and for its gross share in the resources expended in the same way as for a branch (see **5.21ff**). In this case there may be a contingent liability in respect of joint and several liability to be considered.

*Oxfam: 30 April 2000*

At 30 April 2000, Oxfam had an interest in the following subsidiary and associate undertakings, all of which are registered in Great Britain.

| Organisation Name | Class of share capital held | Portion held by parent company | Portion held by other group companies | Nature of business |
|---|---|---|---|---|
| Oxfam Activities Limited | Ordinary | 100% | — | Promotes fair trade and raises funds through trading activities |
| cafédirect Limited | Ordinary | — | 25% | Promotes fair trade |
| cafédirect Limited | Preference | — | 25% | Promotes fair trade |
| Living on the line Limited | Ordinary | 100% | — | Promotes education |

In addition, Oxfam India Trust is included within the accounts of Oxfam.

The share capital of Oxfam Activities Limited, 2,000 ordinary shares of £1 each, is wholly owned by Oxfam and its nominee.

The share capital of Living on the Line Limited, 2 ordinary shares of £1 each, is wholly owned by Oxfam and its nominee.

CHAPTER 6

# Statement of Financial Activities

## 1 PURPOSE

**6.1** The Statement of Financial Activities is a single accounting statement which analyses all capital and income resources and resources expended by a charity in the year on all its funds, and contains a reconciliation of those funds.

**6.2** Paragraph 56 of SORP summarises the overall objectives of the statement:

*'The Statement of Financial Activities is a single accounting statement with the overall objective of showing all the incoming resources and resources expended by the charity in the year on all its funds. It is designed to show how the charity has used its resources in furtherance of its objects for the provision of benefit to its beneficiaries. It shows whether there has been a net inflow or outflow of resources, including capital gains and losses on assets, and provides a reconciliation of all movements in the charity's funds.'(para 56)*

### Comment

**6.3** One of the most fundamental changes to come out of the Charities (Accounts and Reports) Regulations 1995 and SORP was the abandonment of the traditional income and expenditure account in favour of the Statement of Financial Activities. The income and expenditure account was seen to have a number of disadvantages when applied to a charitable organisation. For example, it:

- concentrated on the 'bottom line' or the surplus or deficit for the year;
- did not explain fully the charity's activities nor the fact that the primary concern of a charity is to provide benefits to its beneficiaries rather than a corporate pursuit of gain for the benefit of shareholders;
- failed to recognise the different types of fund, particularly restricted funds.

**6.4** The Statement of Financial Activities addresses all of these problems and provides the essential link with the second primary statement, the balance sheet, via the reconciliation of funds. It concentrates attention on the resources available to the charity and how the trustees have applied them.

**6.5** The Statement of Financial Activities is a columnar statement analysed in appropriate detail to show all incoming resources, both capital and revenue, in the financial year, and how and to what extent the charity's funds have been spent. Part I of Sch I of the Charities (Accounts and Reports) Regulations 1995 sets out how the statement should be constructed. This is reinforced and expanded upon by paras 57 to 73 of SORP. The following examples taken from CC66—SORP 2000: Example reports and accounts (published by the Charity Commission) show the basic construction of a Statement of Financial Activities under the revised SORP.

*CC66 – SORP 2000: Example reports and accounts*
*(Dorsetshire Drugs Advice Centre: 31 March 2002)*

**Statement of Financial Activities (including Income and Expenditure Account) for the year ended 31 March 2002**

| | Notes | Unrestricted Funds £'000 | Restricted Funds £'000 | Total Funds 2002 £'000 | Total Funds 2001 £'000 |
|---|---|---|---|---|---|
| **Incoming resources** | | | | | |
| Donations | 2 | — | 5,000 | **5,000** | 6,796 |
| Activities to further the charity's objects: | | | | | |
| Grants and contracts for advice and information, outreach work and training project | 3 | 95,535 | 150,000 | **245,535** | 207,304 |
| Activities to generate funds: | | | | | |
| Charity shop | | 19,465 | — | **19,465** | 17,242 |
| Investment income and interest | | 900 | 765 | **1,665** | 1,324 |
| **Total incoming resources** | | 115,900 | 155,765 | **271,665** | 232,666 |
| **Resources expended** | | | | | |
| *Costs of generating funds* | | | | | |
| Charity shop | | 11,773 | — | **11,773** | 11,225 |
| Fund-raising and publicity | | 5,798 | — | **5,798** | 1,893 |
| *Charitable expenditure* | | | | | |
| Advice and information | | — | 67,008 | **67,008** | 59,876 |
| Outreach work | | — | 68,391 | **68,391** | 53,316 |
| Training project | | 80,836 | — | **80,836** | 63,606 |
| Management and administration | | 10,108 | 1,250 | **11,358** | 7,372 |
| **Total resources expended** | 4 | 108,515 | 136,649 | **245,164** | 197,288 |
| **Net incoming resources – Net income for year** | 5 | 7,385 | 19,116 | **26,501** | 35,378 |
| Gain on revaluation of investments | 9 | 762 | — | **762** | 202 |
| **Net movement in funds** | | 8,147 | 19,116 | **27,263** | 35,580 |
| **Total funds at 1 April 2001** | | 20,249 | 1,316 | **21,565** | (14,015) |
| **Total funds at 31 March 2002** | 13 | 28,396 | 20,432 | **48,828** | 21,565 |

Movements in funds are disclosed in Note 13 to the financial statements.

*CC66 – SORP 2000: Example reports and accounts (The ABC Charity: 31 March 2001)*

**Consolidated Statement of Financial Activities (incorporating an Income and Expenditure Account) for the year ended 31 March 2001**

| | Notes | Unrestricted Funds £'000 | Restricted Funds £'000 | Totals 2001 £'000 | Totals 2000 £'000 |
|---|---|---|---|---|---|
| **Incoming resources** | | | | | |
| Donations and gifts | 2 | 4,130 | 3,200 | **7,330** | 6,000 |
| Legacies | 3 | 2,150 | – | **2,150** | 1,330 |
| Building appeal | 17 | – | 400 | **400** | 900 |
| Activities in furtherance of the charity's objects: | | | | | |
| Government grants for residential care | 17 | – | 700 | **700** | 400 |
| Fees for residential care | | 1,200 | – | **1,200** | 1,000 |
| Activities for generating funds: | | | | | |
| Merchandising income | 4 | 1,140 | – | **1,140** | 900 |
| Investment income | 5 | 350 | 50 | **400** | 475 |
| Net gain on disposal of fixed assets | | 20 | – | **20** | 30 |
| Total incoming resources | | 8,990 | 4,350 | **13,340** | 11,035 |
| **Resources expended** | | | | | |
| *Cost of generating funds:* | | | | | |
| Fund-raising costs | | 480 | 210 | **690** | 550 |
| Building appeal costs | 17 | – | 15 | **45** | 110 |
| Merchandising costs | 4 | 870 | – | **870** | 710 |
| Investment management fees | | 80 | 10 | **90** | 110 |
| | | 1,430 | 265 | **1,695** | 1,480 |
| *Charitable expenditure:* | | | | | |
| Costs of activities in furtherance of the charity's objects: | | | | | |
| Residential care costs | | 1,400 | 1,030 | **2,430** | 2,545 |
| Childcare | | 1,000 | 2,400 | **3,400** | 3,150 |
| Emergency services | | 1,800 | 1,300 | **3,100** | 2,800 |
| Information and Education | | 90 | 10 | **100** | 300 |
| Support costs | | 110 | 80 | **190** | 180 |
| Management and administration | | 210 | 60 | **270** | 230 |
| | | 4,610 | 4,880 | **9,490** | 9,405 |
| **Total resources expended** | 6 | 6,040 | 5,145 | **11,185** | 10,885 |
| Net incoming resources/ (resources expended) before transfers | | 2,950 | (795) | **2,155** | 150 |
| Transfers between funds | 17 | 15 | (15) | **–** | – |
| **Net incoming resources/ (resources expended)** | | 2,965 | (810) | **2,155** | 150 |
| Net gains on investment assets | 11 | 100 | – | **100** | 250 |
| **Net movement in funds** | | 3,065 | (810) | **2,255** | 400 |
| Fund balances brought forward at 1 April | 17 | 6,300 | 3,900 | **10,200** | 9,800 |
| Fund balances carried forward at 31 March | 17 | 9,365 | 3,090 | **12,455** | 10,200 |

All of the above results are derived from continuing activities. All gains and losses recognised in the year are included above. The surplus for the year for Companies Act purposes comprises the net incoming resources for the year plus realised gains on investments and was £2,225,000 (2000: £230,000). Page 10 gives details of changes in resources applied for fixed assets for charity use.

## 2 THE BASIC CONSTRUCTION

**6.6** The basic concept behind the Statement of Financial Activities is to analyse all the charity's incoming resources and resources expended such that the reader of the charity's accounts can gain an immediate understanding of where its resources came from and what it has spent its resources on during the year. As a minimum it should also distinguish between unrestricted income funds, restricted income funds and the endowment funds of the charity. All the charity's incoming resources and resources expended should be categorised between these funds, although, of course, a charity may not have all three types of fund.

**6.7** Where a charity does have more than one type of fund then the Statement of Financial Activities should show, in columns, the movements on each type of fund as well as the total movement on all funds. Comparative figures are required but normally these will be for the total movements only rather than for each type of fund.

**6.8** Paragraph 69 of SORP provides the following table setting out the basic outline of the Statement of Financial Activities.

| Description | Unre-stricted Funds | Re-stricted Funds | Endow-ment Funds | Total Funds | Prior Year Total Funds |
|---|---|---|---|---|---|
| Incoming resources | | | | | |
| Total incoming resources | A | A | A | A | A |
| Resources expended | | | | | |
| Total resources expended | B | B | B | B | B |
| Net incoming resources before transfers = A–B | C | C | C | C | C |
| Gross transfers between funds | D | D | D | D | D |
| Net incoming resources before revaluations and investment asset disposals = C + D | E | E | E | E | E |
| Gains and losses on revaluations of fixed assets for the charity's own use | F | F | F | F | F |
| Gains and losses on revaluations and disposals of investment assets | G | G | G | G | G |
| Net movement in funds = E + F + G | H | H | H | H | H |
| Total funds brought forward | I | I | I | I | I |
| Total funds carried forward = H + I | J | J | J | J | J |

**Comment**

**6.9** The above table sets out the minimum information that needs to be incorporated into a Statement of Financial Activities. If deemed appropriate there is nothing to prevent a charity disclosing additional information. For example, in some instances it may be preferable to split out the unrestricted fund column into two columns – one for the general fund and one for designated funds. This will be particularly

**Imperial Cancer Research Fund: 30 September 1999**

Consolidated statement of financial activities for the year ended 30 September 1999

| | Note | Unrestricted funds £'000 | Designated funds £000 | Restricted funds £'000 | **Total 1999 £'000** | Total 1998 £'000 |
|---|---|---|---|---|---|---|
| **Incoming resources** | | | | | | |
| Fundraising: | | | | | | |
| Legacies | | **47,558** | – | – | **47,558** | 46,038 |
| Donations | | **15,296** | – | **1,335** | **16,631** | 12,890 |
| Regional activities | | **6,511** | – | **4,022** | **10,533** | 10,546 |
| Corporate fundraising | | **1,862** | – | **1,013** | **2,875** | 1,680 |
| Miscellaneous | | **128** | – | – | **128** | 662 |
| | | **71,355** | – | **6,370** | **77,725** | 71,816 |
| Other sources: | | | | | | |
| Grants | | – | – | **4,052** | **4,052** | 4,900 |
| Investment income | | **5,091** | – | **28** | **5,119** | 4,841 |
| | | **5,091** | – | **4,080** | **9,171** | 9,741 |
| Retail and trading operations: | | | | | | |
| Sales of donated goods in shops, including donations | | **25,795** | – | – | **25,795** | 24,602 |
| Trading subsidiaries' income | 2 | **10,226** | – | **23** | **10,249** | 11,616 |
| **Total incoming resources** | | **112,467** | – | **10,473** | **122,940** | 117,775 |
| Less: shops' expenses | 7 | **(20,796)** | – | – | **(20,796)** | (22,248) |
| trading subsidiaries' expenses | 2 | **(8,533)** | – | – | **(8,533)** | (9,274) |
| **Incoming resources available** | | **83,138** | – | **10,473** | **93,611** | 86,253 |
| **Resources expended** | 7 | | | | | |
| Direct charitable expenditure: | | | | | | |
| research expenditure | | **53,478** | – | **10,715** | **64,193** | 55,331 |
| Other expenditure: | | | | | | |
| Fundraising costs | | **19,842** | – | – | **19,842** | 14,482 |
| Management and administration costs | | **737** | – | – | **737** | 841 |
| **Total expenditure** | | **74,057** | – | **10,715** | **84,772** | 70,654 |
| **Surplus/(deficit) for the year** | | **9,081** | – | **(242)** | **8,839** | 15,599 |
| **Associates** | | | | | | |
| Net profit/(loss) on associates | 10 | **21** | – | – | **21** | (21) |
| **Other** | | | | | | |
| Net investment gains/(losses) | 9 | **5,372** | – | **87** | **5,459** | (245) |
| Transfer between funds | 14 | **(21,929)** | **21,929** | – | – | – |
| **Change in net assets** | | **(7,455)** | **21,929** | **(155)** | **14,319** | 15,333 |
| **Funds at 30 September 1998** | | **71,651** | **46,409** | **6,399** | **124,459** | 109,126 |
| **Funds at 30 September 1999** | | **64,196** | **68,338** | **6,244** | **138,778** | 124,459 |

The notes to these accounts form an integral part of the consolidated financial statements.

relevant where significant amounts of money have been designated for a particular purpose and the charity wishes to emphasise that these are not regarded as 'free' or general reserves. A good example of this is the 1999 accounts of the Imperial Cancer Research Fund.

**Incoming resources – A**

**6.10** The first section of the Statement of Financial Activities lists out the various categories of incoming resources per type of fund. It is important to emphasise that transfers between funds, which are internal to the charity, are not regarded as an incoming resource, and nor are the gains and losses on revaluations of assets or the gains and losses on the disposal of investment assets which are shown separately further down the Statement of Financial Activities (see **6.19** below). Gains on the disposal of tangible fixed assets used by the charity are, however, regarded as incoming resources.

**6.11** The details regarding the analysis of incoming resources are detailed in Chapter 7. However, para 59 of SORP makes it clear that the analysis of the incoming resources should be that which is appropriate to the charity.

*'The various categories of incoming resources should be analysed as appropriate to the charity and should be shown separately where material as recommended below:*

*Incoming Resources*

*(i) donations, legacies and similar incoming resources (paragraphs 87–94):*
*(ii) incoming resources from operating activities of the charity distinguishing between (paragraphs 101, 108)*
  *(a) activities in furtherance of the charity's objects; and*
  *(b) activities for generating funds;*
*(iii) investment income (paragraphs 112–113);*
*(iv) other incoming resources (eg net gains on dispoals of fixed assets for use by the charity) (paragraph 118).*
*(v) the total by column of the above resources arising in the year.' (para 59)*

**Resources expended – B**

**6.12** In the next section of the Statement of Financial Activities resources expended should be summarised between the cost of generating funds and charitable expenditure, and totalled, distinguishing between fund types. The detailed requirements regarding the classification and analysis of resources expended are detailed in Chapter 8. Suffice it here sufficient to say that charitable expenditure should be analysed to show separately:

(a) grants payable in furtherance of the charity's objects;
(b) costs of activities in furtherance of the charity's objects;
(c) support costs for (a) and (b) where material;
(d) resources expended on managing and administering the charity.

These classifications do permit some flexibility in the detailed headings for resources expended. This allows them to be adapted to best portray the activities of the charity. Such flexibility is not permitted for other sections of the Statement of Financial Activities.

**Comment**

**6.13** The SORP recognises the fact that in practice a few individual charities may need to expand on the structure set out in the table given at 6.8 above in order for the accounts to show a true and fair view and convey a proper understanding of the nature of the charity's activities. In all cases, however, it is recommended that there be a clear link between the incoming and outgoing resources and, in particular, the functional split of activities.

**6.14** The link referred to above by the SORP is of fundamental importance to the reader of the accounts. For example, a charity which runs a residential and nursing care home may include within its incoming resources section 'Residential and care fees'. It would therefore be sensible for the charitable expenditure section of the statement of financial activities to include a heading such as 'Residential and care costs'.

**Transfers – D**

**6.15** The next section of the Statement of Financial Activities should record, gross, all transfers between the various categories of funds. Detailed explanations of the movements should be given in the notes to the accounts.

**Comment**

**6.16** Generally such transfers will be in respect of designations made during the year, where general and designated funds are shown separately; augmentation of restricted funds out of general funds, either to meet expenditure not covered by restricted income or to boost an appeal, for example; or the transfer of restricted funds to general or other funds provided the restriction has been removed by the donor or the Charity Commission.

**6.17** The total of transfers between funds should always be zero as the transfers should cancel one another out.

**6.18** Immediately following the transfers section should be a sub-total (E) giving the net incoming or outgoing resources for the year before revaluations and investment asset disposals as required by para 3(d) Part I Sch I of the Charities (Accounts and Reports) Regulations 1995.

## Gains and losses – F and G

**6.19** The next section of the Statement of Financial Activities comprises the gains or losses on revaluations of all assets and, stated separately, gains or losses on the disposal of investment assets. Where an asset is revalued the Statement of Financial Activities should distinguish between revaluations relating to assets held for use by the charity itself and those relating to investment assets (para 3(e) Part I Sch I of the Charities (Accounts and Reports) Regulations 1995).

**6.20** Paragraph 64 of SORP states:

*'The next section records separately (see also paragraphs 155–156):*

*(i) gains and losses on revaluation of fixed assets for the charity's own use; and*
*(ii) gains and losses on the revaluation and disposal of investment assets.'* *(para 64)*

## Comment

**6.21** The requirement set out in the 1995 SORP to show realised and unrealised gains on investment assets separately has been abandoned reflecting the stance taken already by many charities in practice. This is discussed further in Chapters 7 and 10.

## Net movement of funds – H

**6.22** By adding the net gains to, or deducting the net losses from, the net incoming resources we arrive at the figure for the net movement in the charity's funds for the year.

**6.23** Paragraph 67 of the SORP addresses the issue of discontinued activities or the acquisition of new ones:

*'In order to comply with Financial Reporting Standard 3 (FRS 3) where a charity has discontinued any of its operations or acquired new ones, the Statement of Financial Activities should distinguish between continuing, discontinued and acquired operations. This will normally apply to the whole of a distinctive type of activity of a charity but not to the development or cessation of new projects within that activity.'* *(para 67)*

In practice this is unlikely to impact on many charities.

## 3 RECONCILIATION OF FUNDS

**6.24** Paragraph 48 of SORP states:

*'The Statement of Financial Activities should reflect the principal movements between the opening and closing balances on all the funds of the charity. It should be analysed between unrestricted income funds, restricted income funds and endowment funds (permanent and expendable combined).'* *(para 48)*

### Comment

**6.25** The reconciliation of funds statement is an integral part of the Statement of Financial Activities, and provides the link between the Statement of Financial Activities and the balance sheet, ie the final total of each column of the Statement of Financial Activities should be the balance on each of the fund categories shown on the bottom half of the balance sheet.

**6.26** The following is an example of a Statement of Financial Activities for a non-incorporated charity which illustrates each of the above points.

*Church of England Children's Society: 31 March 2000*

**Consolidated Statement of Financial Activities for the year ended 31 March 2000**

| | Note | General Funds | Restricted Funds | Endowment Funds | Total Funds 2000 | Total Funds 1999 |
|---|---|---|---|---|---|---|
| | | £000 | £000 | £000 | £000 | £000 |
| **Incoming resources** | | | | | | |
| Legacies | | 5,874 | 0 | 0 | 5,874 | 7,520 |
| Donations | | 3,655 | 7 | 0 | 3,662 | 2,010 |
| Collecting boxes | | 1,860 | 17 | 0 | 1,877 | 2,005 |
| Parish giving | | 1,746 | 33 | 0 | 1,779 | 1,820 |
| Events and other activities | | 3,838 | 7 | 0 | 3,845 | 3,626 |
| Shops | | 3,516 | 0 | 0 | 3,516 | 3,385 |
| **Total fundraising income** | | **20,489** | **64** | **0** | **20,553** | **20,366** |
| Fees and grants | 2 | | | | | |
| – from local authorities | | 5,172 | 0 | 0 | 5,172 | 5,402 |
| – from central government and others | | 2,437 | 116 | 0 | 2,553 | 1,553 |
| Miscellaneous income | 3 | 718 | 0 | 0 | 718 | 447 |
| Investment income | 4 | 1,317 | 0 | 207 | 1,524 | 1,843 |
| **Total incoming resources** | | **30,133** | **180** | **207** | **30,520** | **29,611** |
| Less shops operating costs | 5 | (2,929) | 0 | 0 | (2,929) | (3,079) |
| **Incoming resources available** | | **27,204** | **180** | **207** | **27,591** | **28,532** |
| **Resources expended** | 5,6,7 | | | | | |
| Direct charitable expenditure | | 27,534 | 182 | 207 | 27,923 | 26,089 |
| Other expenditure | | | | | | |
| – Management and administration | | 1,276 | 0 | 0 | 1,276 | 1,520 |
| – Fundraising | | 9,201 | 0 | 0 | 9,201 | 5,092 |
| **Total resources expended** | | **38,011** | **182** | **207** | **38,400** | **32,701** |
| Transfers between funds | | (2) | 2 | 0 | 0 | 0 |
| **Net outgoing resources for the year** | | **(10,809)** | **0** | **0** | **(10,809)** | **(6,169)** |
| Net realised gains on investment assets | 9 | 8,118 | 0 | 0 | 8,118 | 1,976 |
| **Net (expenditure)/income for the year** | | **(2,691)** | **0** | **0** | **(2,691)** | **(4,193)** |
| Net unrealised (losses)/gains on investment assets | 9 | (6,667) | 0 | 591 | (6,076) | (1,196) |
| Net gain on revaluation of properties | | 0 | 0 | 0 | 0 | 0 |
| **Net movement in funds** | | **(9,358)** | **0** | **591** | **(8,767)** | **(5,389)** |
| **Fund balances at 1 April** | | **44,726** | **0** | **6,671** | **51,397** | **56,786** |
| **Fund balances at 31 March** | | **35,368** | **0** | **7,262** | **42,630** | **51,397** |

All the activities of the group and the Society are continuing.
There are no other recognised gains or losses.
The notes on pages 18 to 28 form part of these financial statements.

## 4 ADAPTATION OF FORMATS

**6.27** Pararaph 70 of the SORP acknowledges that there may be instances when, in order to give a true and fair view of the charity's activities the format of the Statement of Financial Activities may need to be amended or expanded. In particular, para 71 suggests that some charities may wish to insert an additional subtotal after the 'Cost of generating funds' heading to give a figure for '*net incoming resources available for charitable application*'. A further subtotal may also be inserted to show the total for charitable expenditure.

### Comment

**6.28** It is important that the Statement of Financial Activities portrays very clearly the manner in which the charity has applied its resources. Many charities will find that the adaptation referred to in para 71 of the SORP is very useful. It enables the reader to determine very quickly the amount expended on charitable activities and to compare this with the amount available. It might also emphasise the efficiency (or not) with which the charity has generated funds by comparing clearly the total incoming resources with the net incoming resources available for charitable application.

**6.29** The Statement of Financial Activities is a complex statement and for this reason it is important that where there is nothing to report in either the current or the preceding period the heading should be omitted.

## 5 SUMMARY INCOME AND EXPENDITURE ACCOUNT

**6.30** In addition to producing a Statement of Financial Activities a number of charities will need to produce a summary income and expenditure account also. This requirement will affect those charities which are governed by the Companies Act 1985, or similar legislation, or have endowment funds.

**6.31** A separate summary income and expenditure account will also be needed if required by the charity's governing instrument.

**6.32** This summary statement and all relevant notes will need to be appropriately cross-referenced to the Statement of Financial Activities from which the summary amounts will be derived.

### The problem

**6.33** The Statement of Financial Activities includes, in incoming resources, endowment capital receipts and excludes realised gains and losses on the disposal of investments, which are dealt with 'below the line' along with unrealised gains and losses on investments and revaluations of other fixed assets. As a result the Statement of Financial Activities cannot always double as an income and expenditure account because FRS3 will not allow the inclusion of capital receipts, nor the exclusion of profits or losses on the realisation of fixed assets.

**Solution 1 – adapt the Statement of Financial Activities**

**6.34** Where the Statement of Financial Activities of a charity constituted under the Companies Act 1985 does not include movements on endowment funds during the year, and where it is possible to separate out realised and unrealised gains and losses on investment assets, the charity may be able to adapt its Statement of Financial Activities. The changes required are as follows:

(a) immediately above the heading 'Incoming resources' insert another heading 'Income and Expenditure';
(b) add to the heading 'Net incoming/outgoing resources for the year' the total for realised gains on investments and annotate the resultant subtotal with the heading 'Net income/expenditure for the year';
(c) immediately above the heading 'Net income/expenditure for the year' place another heading 'Statement of Total Recognised Gains and Losses';
(d) add to the 'Net income/expenditure for the year' unrealised gains or losses on investments and gains or losses on the revaluation of fixed assets for the charity's own use to arrive at the 'Net movement in funds'.

**6.35** Thus the Statement of Financial Activities would comprise two distinct sections – an income and expenditure account and a statement of total recognised gains and losses. The format of the latter statement will be:

Net income/expenditure for the year
Net unrealised gains (losses) on revaluation

Net movement in funds
Balances brought forward

Balances carried forward

**6.36** The following examples taken from the accounts of Catholic Marriage Care Limited and the Church Housing Trust illustrate the adaptation of the Statement of Financial Activities in order to satisfy the requirements of the Companies Act 1985 and FRS3.

*Catholic Marriage Care Limited: 31 March 2000*

**Statement of financial activities**
Year to 31 March 2000

| | Notes | Unrestricted funds General fund £ | Unrestricted funds Designated funds £ | Restricted funds £ | **Total 2000 funds £** | Total 1999 funds £ |
|---|---|---|---|---|---|---|
| **Income and expenditure** | | | | | | |
| **Incoming resources** | | | | | | |
| Grants receivable | 1 | 294,376 | – | 45,000 | **339,376** | 312,956 |
| Contributions from autonomous centres | 2 | 23,531 | – | – | **23,531** | 15,970 |
| Investment income and interest receivable | 3 | 29,656 | – | – | **29,656** | 42,449 |
| Donations and voluntary income | 4 | 15,192 | – | – | **15,192** | 45,143 |
| Independent services | | 9,411 | – | – | **9,411** | 25,488 |
| Natural family planning | | 10,761 | – | – | **10,761** | 10,734 |
| Annual conference | | 18,537 | – | – | **18,537** | 28,607 |
| Counselling and training | | 17,082 | – | – | **17,082** | 33,057 |
| Miscellaneous income | 5 | 9,133 | – | – | **9,133** | 9,084 |
| **Total incoming resources** | | 427,679 | – | 45,000 | **472,679** | 523,488 |
| **Resources expended** | | | | | | |
| Direct charitable expenditure | | | | | | |
| Services | 6 | | | | | |
| Counselling and training | | 180,295 | – | 150 | **180,445** | 171,696 |
| Natural family planning | | 21,704 | – | 23,514 | **45,218** | 55,947 |
| Support costs | | 215,605 | – | 7,448 | **223,053** | 238,087 |
| Projects | 7 | 221,260 | – | – | **221,260** | 217,047 |
| | | 638,864 | – | 31,112 | **669,976** | 682,777 |
| Other expenditure | | | | | | |
| Fundraising and publicity | 8 | 9,757 | – | – | **9,757** | 44,101 |
| Management and administration of the charity | 9 | 49,418 | – | – | **49,418** | 66,996 |
| **Total resources expended** | | 698,039 | – | 31,112 | **729,151** | 793,874 |
| **Net (outgoing) incoming resources before transfers** | 10 | (270,360) | – | 13,888 | **(256,472)** | (270,386) |
| **Transfers between funds** | | 306,300 | (306,300) | – | **–** | – |
| **Net incoming (outgoing) resources for the year** | | 35,940 | (306,300) | 13,888 | **(256,472)** | (270,386) |
| **Realised gains on investments** | | – | – | – | **–** | 402 |
| **Statement of total recognised gains and losses** | | | | | | |
| **Net income (expenditure)** | | 35,940 | (306,300) | 13,888 | **(256,472)** | (269,984) |
| **Unrealised (losses) gains on investments** | | (1,517) | – | – | **(1,517)** | 13,890 |
| **Net movement in funds** | | 34,423 | (306,300) | 13,888 | **(257,989)** | (256,094) |
| **Balances brought forward at 1 April 1999** | | 213,727 | 1,045,449 | – | **1,259,176** | 1,515,270 |
| **Balances carried forward at 31 March 2000** | | 248,150 | 739,149 | 13,888 | **1,001,187** | 1,259,176 |

*Church Housing Trust: 31 March 2000*

**Statement of financial activities**
Year to 31 March 2000

| | Notes | Unrestricted funds £ | Restricted funds £ | **Total 2000 £** | Total 1999 £ |
|---|---|---|---|---|---|
| **Income and expenditure** | | | | | |
| **Incoming resources** | | | | | |
| Donations | | 213,119 | 244,208 | **475,327** | 403,258 |
| Legacies | | 151,507 | – | **151,507** | 97,296 |
| Grants receivable | | | | | |
| National Lottery Charities Board | | – | 25,904 | **25,904** | 43,058 |
| Investment income and interest receivable | 1 | 49,647 | – | **49,647** | 45,147 |
| Rents receivable | | 12,898 | – | **12,898** | 14,505 |
| **Total incoming resources** | | 445,171 | 270,112 | **715,283** | 603,264 |
| **Resources expended** | | | | | |
| Direct charitable expenditure | | | | | |
| Grants payable | 2 | | | | |
| Grant of properties to English Churches Housing Group | | 199,600 | – | **199,600** | – |
| Other | | 187,789 | 220,008 | **407,797** | 406,393 |
| | | 387,389 | 220,008 | **607,397** | 406,393 |
| Research and support costs | 3 | 91,596 | – | **91,596** | 83,854 |
| | | 478,985 | 220,008 | **698,993** | 490,247 |
| Other expenditure | | | | | |
| Fundraising and publicity | 4 | 115,900 | – | **115,900** | 76,618 |
| Management and administration of the charity | 5 | 81,421 | – | **81,421** | 78,148 |
| **Total resources expended** | | 676,306 | 220,008 | **896,314** | 645,013 |
| **Net (outgoing) incoming resources for the year** | | (231,135) | 50,104 | **(181,031)** | (41,749) |
| Realised gains on investments | | 6,254 | – | **6,254** | – |
| **Statement of total recognised gains and losses** | | | | | |
| Net (expenditure) income for the year | | (224,881) | 50,104 | **(174,777)** | (41,749) |
| Unrealised (losses) gains on investments | | (22,512) | – | **(22,512)** | 12,114 |
| **Net movement in funds** | 7 | (247,393) | 50,104 | **(197,289)** | (29,635) |
| **Balances brought forward at 1 April 1999** | | 653,754 | 368,396 | **1,022,150** | 1,051,785 |
| **Balances carried forward at 31 March 2000** | | 406,3361 | 418,500 | **824,861** | 1,022,150 |

### Comment

**6.37** It is hoped that in the course of time the need to continue to produce a summary income and expenditure account will wither away. Already the Department of Trade and Industry are working with the Charity Commission to propose amendments to the Companies Act accounting regulations to bring them more in line with Charities Act regulations as far as charitable companies are concerned. Perhaps it is not stretching optimism too far to look forward to a suitably amended FRS3 to accommodate the Statement of Financial Activities.

### Solution 2 – a summary income and expenditure account

**6.38** The purpose of the summary income and expenditure account is solely to provide a reconciliation between the information given in the Statement of Financial Activities and that required by the Companies Act and FRS3. It is for disclosure purposes only in order to comply with those requirements.

**6.39** Paragraph 337 of the SORP sets out the requirements.

*'Where a summary income and expenditure account is required, it should be derived from and cross referenced to the corresponding figures in the Statement of Financial Activities. It need not distinguish between unrestricted and restricted income funds but the accounting basis on which items are included must be the same as in the Statement of Financial Activities. It should show separately in respect of continuing operations, acquisitions and discontinued operations:*

*(a) gross income from all sources;*
*(b) net gains/losses from disposals of all fixed assets belonging to the charity's income funds;*
*(c) transfers from endowment funds of amounts previously received as capital resources and now converted into income funds for expending;*
*(d) total income (this will be the total of all incoming resources - other than revaluation gains - of all the income funds but not for any endowment funds);*
*(e) total expenditure out of the charity's income funds;*
*(f) net income or expenditure for the year.*

*In practice, the format may need to be modified to comply with specific statutory requirements or those of the charity's own governing document.'*
*(para 337)*

**6.40** To prepare the summary income and expenditure account it will be necessary to prepare as a working document a schedule reconciling the net movement of funds as shown in the Statement of Financial Activities to the gross income of continuing operations required by FRS3. Taking the Church of England Children's Society example given earlier in this chapter this reconciliation schedule would have been as follows.

| | | 2000 £000 | 1999 £000 |
|---|---|---|---|
| **Net movement in funds per SOFA** | | (8,767) | (5,389) |
| Add: | total resources expended | 41,122 | 35,780 |
| | realised losses on investments | – | – |
| | unrealised losses on investments | 6,076 | 1,196 |
| | revaluation losses of tangible fixed assets | – | – |
| | | 38,431 | 31,587 |
| Less: | non-charitable trading income (net) | (1,071) | (277) |
| | endowment fund receipts | – | – |
| | realised gains on investments | (8,118) | (1,976) |
| | unrealised gains on investments | – | – |
| | revaluation gains on tangible fixed assets | – | – |
| **Gross income of continuing activities** | | 29,242 | 29,334 |

**6.41** The example, below illustrates the resulting summary income and expenditure account.

*Church of England Children's Society: 31 March 2000*

**Consolidated Summary Income and Expenditure Account for the Year Ended 31 March 2000**

| | Note | Total 2000 £000 | Total 1999 £000 |
|---|---|---|---|
| Gross income of continuing operations | | 29,242 | 29,334 |
| Non-charitable trading activities: net income | 1 | 1,071 | 277 |
| Total income of continuing operations | | 30,313 | 29,611 |
| Total expenditure of continuing operations | 5,6,7 | 41,122 | 35,780 |
| Net expenditure for the year before transfers and investment asset disposals | | (10,809) | (6,169) |
| Transfer to restricted funds | | 0 | 0 |
| Net income/(expenditure) before investment asset disposals | | (10,809) | (6,169) |
| Gain on disposal of fixed asset investments | | 8,118 | 1,976 |
| **Net Income/(Expenditure) for the year** | | **(2,691)** | **(4,193)** |

Total income comprises £30,133,000 for unrestricted funds and £180,000 for restricted funds. A detailed analysis of income is provided in the Statement of Financial Activities.

Detailed analyses of the expenditure are provided in the Statement of Financial Activities and Notes 5, 6 and 7.

Net income/(expenditure) before investment asset disposals for the year of (£10,809,000) comprises (£10,809,000) net income of unrestricted funds less £0 net expenditure of restricted funds, as shown in the Statement of Fiancial Activities.

The Summary Income and Expenditure Account is derived from the Statement of Financial Activities on page 14, which, together with the notes to the accounts on pages 18 to 28 provides full information on the movements during the year on all the funds of the group.

Such a statement is further illustrated by an example from The British Butterfly Conservation Society's 2000 accounts.

*The British Butterfly Conservation Society Limited: 30 June 2000*

**Consolidated summary income and expenditure account**
**Year to 30 June 2000**

| | Notes | **2000** **£** | 1999 £ |
|---|---|---|---|
| Gross income on continuing operations | | **1,061,577** | 1,107,153 |
| Non-charitable trading activities: net (expenditure) income | 4 | **(300)** | 14,649 |
| Total income of continuing operations | | **1,061,277** | 1,121,802 |
| Total expenditure of continuing operations | | **884,558** | 701,171 |
| **Net income for the year** | | **176,719** | 420,631 |

Total income comprises £703,008 (1999—£442,943) for unrestricted funds and, £358,269 (1999—£678,859) for restricted funds. A detailed analysis of income by source is provided in the statement of financial activities.

Turnover of non-charitable trading activities amounted to £nil (1999–£6,404). A detailed analysis of the trading results is shown in note 4.

Detailed analyses of the expenditure are provided in the statement of financial activities and notes 5 to 7.

The summary income and expenditure account is derived from the statement of financial activities on page 17 which, together with the notes to the accounts on pages 24 to 35, provides full information on the movements during the year on all the funds of the group.

## 6 DISCONTINUED AND ACQUIRED OPERATIONS

**6.42** Very occasionally a charity will discontinue a particular class of its operations or acquire new ones. When this happens para 67 of SORP states that the Statement of Financial Activities should distinguish between continuing, discontinued and acquired operations as required by Financial Reporting Standard No 3 (FRS3).

*Women's Royal Voluntary Service: 31 March 1996*

**Continuing Activities**

On 1 April 1995, in accordance with a legal transfer of undertakings, the activities, assets and liabilities of WRVS head office, the hospitals department and other administrative offices of WRVS, all of which formed part of a registered charity (Charity Registration No 254891), were transferred to Women's Royal Voluntary Service.

A detailed analysis of incoming and outgoing resources relating to the activities introduced in the year is given in note 20 to the accounts.

An analysis of incoming resources and resources expended between activities previously included and those introduced during the year is as follows:

| | **Unrestricted funds** | | | | |
|---|---|---|---|---|---|
| | **General and non-charitable trading funds** | **Designated funds** | **Restricted funds** | **Total 1996** | **Total 1995** |
| | **£** | **£** | **£** | **£** | **£** |
| **Incoming resources** | | | | | |
| Activities | | | | | |
| Previously included | 280,725 | – | – | 280,725 | – |
| Introduced in the year | 6,472,119 | – | 22,334,049 | 28,806,168 | 839,337 |
| **Total incoming resources** | 6,752,844 | – | 22,334,049 | 29,086,893 | 839,337 |
| **Resources expended** | | | | | |
| Activities: | | | | | |
| Previously included | 1,119,182 | – | – | 1,119,182 | 69,619 |
| Introduced in the year | 6,003,087 | – | 21,599,483 | 27,602,570 | 1,360,422 |
| **Total resources expended** | 7,122,269 | – | 21,599,483 | 28,721,752 | 1,430,041 |
| **Net (outgoing) incoming resources before transfers** | | | | | |
| Activities: | | | | | |
| Previously included | (838,457) | – | – | (838,457) | (69,619) |
| Introduced in the year | 469,032 | – | 734,566 | 1,203,598 | (521,085) |
| **Net (outgoing) incoming resources before transfers** | (369,425) | – | 734,566 | 365,141 | (590,704) |

CHAPTER 7

# Incoming resources

## 1 GUIDELINES

**7.1** Paragraph 22 of SORP describes the recommended content of a charity's accounts as a report in financial terms on the activities and resources of the charity. In particular, it states that the accounts should include a Statement of Financial Activities which should show *'all incoming resources and all resources expended by it and reconciles all changes in its funds.'*

**7.2** In this chapter, therefore, we examine how charities account for the 'incoming resources' received by them.

**7.3** Paragraph 59 of SORP states that the incoming resources should be summarised in the statement in a manner appropriate to the charity. Equally, it is important that all incoming resources are analysed in a manner sufficient to enable the reader of the accounts to gain an accurate appreciation of their principal elements, but, on the other hand, should not be excessively detailed. If necessary, additional supporting analyses can be given in the notes to the accounts.

**7.4** Paragraph 59 of SORP requires:

*'The various categories of incoming resources should be analysed as appropriate to the charity and should be shown separatley where material as recommended below:*

*Incoming Resources*

*(i)* *donations, legacies and similar incoming resources (paragraphs 87–94);*
*(ii)* *Incoming resources from operating activities of the charity distinguishing between (paragraphs 101–108);*
   *(a)* *activities in futherance of the charity's objects; and*
   *(b)* *activities for generating funds;*
*(iii)* *investment income (paragraphs 112–113);*

*(iv)* *other incoming resources (eg net gains on disposals of fixed assets for use by the charity) (paragraph 118);*
*(v)* *the total by column of the above resources arising in the year.'(para 59)*

*CC66 — SORP 2000: Example reports and accounts (Example D — Overseas Aid)*
**Consolidated Statement of Financial Activities for the year ended 30 September 2001**

| | Notes | Unrestricted funds £'000 | Restricted funds £'000 | 2001 Total £'000 | 2000 Total £'000 |
|---|---|---|---|---|---|
| **Incoming resources** | | | | | |
| Donations, legacies and similar incoming resources | 2 | **6,897** | 3,797 | **10,694** | 10,991 |
| Activities in furtherance of the charity's objects: | | | | | |
| Contracts for operational programmes | 3 | – | 4,746 | **4,746** | 4,567 |
| Activities for generating funds: | | | | | |
| Shop income | 4 | **8,573** | – | **8,573** | 6,596 |
| Investment income and interest | 5 | **190** | 39 | **229** | 202 |
| **Total incoming resources** | | **15,660** | **8,582** | **24,242** | **22,356** |

## Comment

7.5 The above example shows how any of the headings set out in para 59 of SORP may need to be expanded or emphasised as appropriate to describe the main sources of funding the activities of the charity.

7.6 This chapter will consider the resources made available to charities under each of the following heads:

- donations, legacies and similar incoming resources
- legacies
- gifts in kind
- intangible income
- fundraising proceeds
- cash collections
- life subscriptions
- grants receivable
- trading activities
- investment income
- gains and losses on fixed assets for charity use
- gains and losses on investment assets
- tax recoverable.

7.7 First, however, we need to examine the general principles which should be followed in recognising incoming resources.

## 2 RECOGNITION – BASIC PRINCIPLES

**7.8** Paragraphs 75 to 84 of SORP set out the principles to be followed with regard to the recognition and disclosure of incoming resources. In particular, paragraphs 75 and 76 define the basic principles regarding recognition as follows:

*'The value of all resources – both for income and endowment funds – accruing to the charity should be recorded in the Statement of Financial Activities as soon as it is prudent and practicable to do so. In all cases incoming resources should not be recognised until the conditions for receipt have been met and there is reasonable assurance of receipt. This will be dependent on the following three factors being met:*

*(a) entitlement – normally arises when a particular resource is receivable or the charity's right to it becomes legally enforceable;*
*(b) certainty – when there is reasonable certainty that the incoming resource will be received;*
*(c) measurement – when the monetary value of the incoming resource can be measured with sufficient reliability.'* *(para 75)*

*'All incoming resources should be reported gross whether raised by the charity or its agents. Netting off expenditure against income is only allowable for small fundraising events where it will not materially understate the gross incoming resources and gross resources expended for the event. However, in no case should the charity's own staff costs be netted off against the proceeds of any such events when reported in the accounts.'* *(para 76)*

**Comment**

**7.9** The revised SORP has re-emphasised the concept that income should be recognised as soon as it is prudent and practicable to do so. In addition the SORP sets out the three factors which will determine whether or not income should be recognised. Greater emphasis has been placed on these factors than was the case in the 1995 SORP. This will normally be when the charity becomes legally entitled to the income. This increased emphasis clarifies a number of issues, particularly in relation to legacies and cash collections, but the over-riding principles will continue to create both accounting and audit problems (see below).

## 3 RECOGNITION OF INCOMING RESOURCES SUBJECT TO RESTRICTIONS

**General**

**7.10** Paragraph 85 of SORP emphasises that:

*'The fact that an incoming resource is for a restricted purpose does not affect whether or not it is recognised in the Statement of Financial Activities.'*
*(para 85)*

**7.11** Incoming resources of a restricted fund which have been recognised in the Statement of Financial Activities and have not been spent by the end of the financial year will be carried forward in that fund.

## Comment

**7.12** The following example shows a charity which, having received restricted income during the financial year and not spent it all, has carried forward the balance at the end of the year.

*Help the Aged: 30 April 2000*

**Consolidated Statement of Financial Activities**

For the year ended 30 April 2000

| | Notes | Unrestricted funds £'000 | Restricted funds £'000 | Endowment funds £'000 | Total 2000 £'000 | Restated Total 1999 £'000 |
|---|---|---|---|---|---|---|
| **Incoming Resources** | | | | | | |
| Donations and gifts | | 5,630 | 12,158 | – | **17,788** | 15,889 |
| Legacies receivable | | 8,094 | 456 | – | **8,550** | 9,998 |
| Grants receivable | | 214 | 1,992 | – | **2,206** | 1,149 |
| Sales of donated goods | | 24,897 | – | – | **24,897** | 26,693 |
| Income from housing | | 3,743 | – | – | **3,743** | 3,498 |
| Gifted Housing properties | | 626 | – | – | **626** | 1,048 |
| Investment income | 2 | 172 | 341 | – | **513** | 549 |
| Net gain on disposal of tangible fixed assets | | 848 | – | – | **848** | 472 |
| Net profit from trading activities | 3 | 1,179 | – | – | **1,179** | 610 |
| **Total incoming resources** | | **45,403** | **14,947** | **–** | **60,350** | **59,906** |
| Less: Costs of selling donated goods | | 21,315 | – | – | **21,315** | 22,209 |
| **Incoming resources available** | | **24,088** | **14,947** | **–** | **39,035** | **37,697** |
| **Resources expended** | | | | | | |
| Direct charitable expenditure: | | | | | | |
| UK and overseas aid programmes | 4 | 1,475 | 12,867 | – | **14,342** | 12,185 |
| Housing | | 6,584 | – | – | **6,584** | 5,121 |
| Information, campaigning and education | | 4,357 | 291 | – | **4,648** | 4,025 |
| Support costs | | 2,011 | – | – | **2,011** | 1,900 |
| | | 14,427 | 13,158 | – | **27,585** | 23,231 |
| Other expenditure: | | | | | | |
| Fundraising and publicity | | 8,400 | 1,116 | – | **9,516** | 9,836 |
| Management and administration of the charity | | 482 | – | – | **482** | 467 |
| | | 8,882 | 1,116 | – | **9,998** | 10,303 |
| **Total resources expended** | 5 | **23,309** | **14,274** | **–** | **37,583** | **33,534** |
| **Net incoming resources** | | **779** | **673** | **–** | **1,452** | **4,163** |

[*continued on following page*]

| | | | | | | |
|---|---|---|---|---|---|---|
| *Help the Aged, continued* | | | | | | |
| **Net movement in funds** | | **779** | **673** | **–** | **1,452** | **4,163** |
| **Fund balances brought forward at 1 May 1999** | | **25,862** | **5,956** | **517** | **32,335** | **28,172** |
| **Fund balances carried forward at 30 April 2000** | | **26,641** | **6,629** | **517** | **33,787** | **32,335** |
| Designated funds | | 17,158 | | | | |
| Other unrestricted funds | 20 | 9,483 | | | | |
| | | 26,641 | | | | |

All transactions are derived from continuing activities.
All recognised gains and losses are included in the Statement of Financial Activities.

### Pre-conditions on use

**7.13** Paragraph 85 of SORP goes on, however, to stress the importance of distinguishing between incoming resources that are subject to restrictions on the use to which they can be put and those which will only be received once certain conditions have been fulfilled. The SORP states:

*'There is an important difference for accounting purposes between restrictions on the purposes for which a particular resource may be used and conditions which must be fulfilled prior to its receipt or use by the charity. If receipt is dependent upon pre-conditions which cannot be or have not been met, then the incoming resource should not be recognised in the Statement of Financial Activities or the balance sheet. A similar treatment should continue to be applied where the charity is unable to meet, even at a later stage, any pre-conditions for its use.'* *(para 85)*

### Comment

**7.14** A good example of income subject to pre-conditions arises from the current trend for grant making institutions to award grants subject to the charity obtaining matching funding from elsewhere. Until the matched funding has actually been secured, and the charity is certain of its receipt, the original grant should not be recognised in the charity's accounts either, but merely disclosed by way of note.

### Pre-conditions as to timing of use

**7.15** Donor imposed conditions as to the timing of related expenditure could also affect the timing of the recognition of the incoming resource if the restrictions amount to a pre-condition. Paragraph 79 gives an example of such a case and expands on the situation:

*'In addition charities often receive incoming resources by way of grant or donation to fund general or specific activities. Charities are normally entitled*

*to these incoming resources when they are receivable. This is the case even if the resources are received in advance of the performance of the activity and they should not be deferred. Incoming resources may be deferred only when the donor has imposed restrictions on the expenditure of resources which amount to pre-conditions for use (eg the receipt in advance of a grant for expenditure in a future accounting period). However, when the conditions for receipt have been met then the charity is entitled to the incoming resources and must recognise them in the Statement of Financial Activities. Incoming resources cannot be deferred simply because the related expenditure has not been incurred.'* *(para 79)*

## Comment

**7.16** Paragraph 79 is essential to prevent any form of departure from the accruals concept of accounting in charity accounts. Care is needed, however. If taken literally, and to its extreme, the requirement to defer income that will be used for expenditure in a future accounting period could result in incoming resources being equated exactly to expenditure each year with any excess incoming resources being deferred simply because they have not been spent. Income should only be deferred where the person or institution providing it has specifically stated that it is to offset expenditure in a given period.

The following example illustrates the treatment of deferred income in the notes to the Statement of Financial Activities.

*Royal College of Psychiatrists: 31 December 1999*

**10 Grants receivable**

| | Unrestricted funds £ | Restricted funds £ | **Total 1999 £** | Total 1998 £ |
|---|---|---|---|---|
| Member and trainee service | | | | |
| Department of Health (DoH) | | | | |
| Basic Specialist Training | – | 46,046 | **46,046** | 51,328 |
| Contribution to Higher Specialist Training | – | 45,375 | **45,375** | 50,391 |
| Contribution to Overseas Doctors Training Scheme | – | 47,892 | **47,892** | 44,158 |
| Miscellaneous | – | 5,314 | **5,314** | – |
| | – | 144,627 | **144,627** | 145,877 |
| Research unit | | | | |
| Department of Health (DoH) | – | 776,634 | **776,634** | 548,710 |
| Gatsby Charitable Foundation | – | 100,000 | **100,000** | 100,000 |
| BUPA | – | 39,003 | **39,003** | 12,000 |
| | – | 915,637 | **915,637** | 660,710 |
| | – | 1,060,264 | **1,060,264** | 806,587 |
| Total incoming resources | – | 1,238,383 | **1,238,383** | 1,019,601 |
| Less: Deferred income—grants received in advance | – | (178,119) | **(178,119)** | (213,014) |
| | – | 1,060,264 | **1,060,264** | 806,587 |

## 4 DONATIONS, LEGACIES AND SIMILAR INCOMING RESOURCES

**7.17** This section of the Statement of Financial Activities is intended to show incoming resources of a voluntary nature, usually given by the founders, patrons, supporters and the general public, government and non-statutory bodies such as businesses and charitable foundations and trusts. It will include grants which provide core funding or of a general nature but will not include those which are specifically for the performance of a service or production of charitable goods (for example, a service agreement with health authorities for the provision of hospice care in a hospice). In addition, this section of the statement of financial activities may include incoming resources from membership subscriptions, gifts in kind, intangible income and sponsorships where these are regarded as donations rather than payment for goods and services.

**7.18** Paragraph 88 of SORP requires:

*'The material components of donations legacies and similar incoming resources should be shown separately on the face of the Statement of Financial Activities or in the notes to the accounts.'* *(para 88)*

### Legacies

**7.19** Paragraphs 89 to 93 of SORP state:

*'It is good practice to monitor a legacy from the time when notification is received to its final receipt. A charity should not, however, regard a legacy as receivable simply because it has been told about it. It should only do so when the legacy has been received or if, before receipt, it becomes reasonably certain that the legacy will be received and the value of the incoming resources can be measured with sufficient reliability.'* *(para 89)*

*'There will normally be reasonable certainty of receipt for example, as soon as a charity receives a letter from the personal representatives of the estate advising that payment of the legacy will be made or that the property bequeathed will be transferred. It is likely that the value of the resource will also be measurable from this time. However, legacies which are not immediately payable should not be treated as receivable until the conditions associated with payment have been fulfilled (eg the death of a life tenant).'* *(para 90)*

*'It is unlikely in practice that the entitlement, certainty of receipt and measurability conditions will be satisfied before the receipt of a letter from the personal representatives advising of an intended payment or transfer. The amount which is available in the estate for distribution to the beneficiaries may not have been finalised and, even if it has, there may still be outstanding*

*matters relating to the precise division of the amount. In these circumstances entitlement may be in doubt or it may not be possible to provide a reasonable estimate of the legacy receivable, in which case it should not be included in the Statement of Financial Activities.'* *(para 91)*

*'Where a charity receives a payment on account of its interest in an estate or a letter advising that such a payment will be made, the payment, or intended payment, on account should be treated as receivable.'* *(para 92)*

*'Similarly, where a payment is received or notified as receivable (by the personal representatives) after the accounting year end, but it is clear that it had been agreed by the personal representatives prior to the year end (hence providing evidence of a condition that existed at the balance sheet date), then it should be accrued in the Statement of Financial Activities and the balance sheet.'* *(para 93)*

***'Disclosure***

*Where the charity has been notified of material legacies which have not been included in the Statement of Financial Activities (because the conditions for recognition have not been met), this fact and an estimate, where possible, of the amounts receivable should be disclosed in the notes to the accounts.'* *(para 94)*

**Comment**

**7.20** Until the publication of the 1995 SORP the generally accepted basis for accounting for legacies was to bring them into the accounts on a cash basis at the date of receipt by the charity. This, however, was open to abuse, for example, enabling trustees to defer a legacy receipt until after the year end even though the executors were ready to hand over the money beforehand.

**7.21** To redress this the 1995 SORP and the revised version thereof required legacies to be accounted for on an 'accruals' basis. While solving one problem it presented others, which have been addressed in the new version.

- The incoming resources section of the Statement of Financial Activities may include legacies that had not been received at the balance sheet date. The lack of clarity in the 1995 SORP meant also that some legacies recognised as income, were probably not actually received for some considerable time thereafter. This gave a false picture of the liquidity of the charity at the end of the financial year. The revised SORP has clarified the position by stating clearly that it is considered unlikely that the three factors governing recognition of legacy income, ie entitlement, certainty and measurability, are likely to be achieved until the charity has received a letter from the executor or administrator advising of an intended payment of money or assets. It is still felt advisable, however, to highlight material outstanding legacies as a separate debtor figure and explain the position with regard to the legacies in the notes to the accounts.

- Trustees will need to assess the likely amount of any legacies which have been notified to them. This may not always be easy, particularly with regard to residuary legacies, and in cases where the amount cannot be estimated or measured it may be more appropriate to exclude the legacy from the statement of financial activities but to include a note to the accounts disclosing details of the legacy and why it has not been accrued for.
- Charities may not be aware of all legacies to which they have become entitled at the end of a financial year.
- It will be virtually impossible for an auditor or independent examiner of a charity's accounts to test the completeness of legacy income. He or she will be reliant on assurances obtained from the trustees that they have informed the auditor of all legacies of which they have been notified. Additional evidence can be obtained from the charity's solicitors, from published death notices, from specialist agencies such as Smee and Ford and from a review of post year end receipts.

**7.22** In view of the huge impact a legacy can have on the accounts of a charity, and its unpredictability both as to amount and timing of receipt, many charities may seek to modify the application of paras 89 to 94 of SORP, for example by including only such legacies as they know they will receive within the early months of the following accounting year. In the past the argument for doing this might be either that the doubt over the timing of the receipt makes the legacy 'incapable of measurement' or that to include such an amount as an incoming resource in the current period would not show a true and fair view of the position because of the uncertainty as to actual receipt and amount. The additional clarity provided by the revised SORP means that the credibility of this argument is now almost non-existent. In very basic terms if a charity now has a letter informing it of an intended payment or transfer, that amount should be accrued for in the Statement of Financial Activities. Details of all material legacies notified to the trustees at the year end, but not included in the accounts because the recognition factors have not been satisfied, should be given in the notes. In certain cases it might even warrant special mention in the trustees' report.

**7.23** This is an area of continuing difficulty and debate, but the thrust of SORP is to seek recognition in the accounts of all incoming resources as and when they are known to be due to the charity, when it has a legally enforceable entitlement to them and when they can be quantified. In the case of legacies this must be when the charity is notified that it is legally entitled to the legacy so that there is reasonable certainty of its eventual receipt and when it is told of an impending payment or transfer of monies, ie it can be quantified for accounting purposes.

**7.24** What is beyond argument is that charities should no longer adopt the approach of crediting legacies to an equalisation reserve and taking the income into the Statement of Financial Activities over a number of years nor of delaying their receipt and recognition until convenient for accounting purposes. Legacies should be regarded as part of the ordinary incoming resources of the charity.

**7.25** We are aware that the practice of treating legacies as an incoming resource in full in the year they are received still causes anguish for a number of charities, simply because the size and the frequency of receipt of such sums is unpredictable and, therefore, uncontrollable. Trustees naturally wish to retain control and like to compare figures to budget estimates and the previous year. The inclusion of legacies often makes such comparison difficult and, some might argue, misleading. However, it shows the truth. It is not, in our view, helpful to try and hide the event, rather it is better to explain it, if significant, in the trustees' annual report.

*Save the Children: 1999/2000*

**Legacy pledgers**

This year nearly 300 supporters pledged gifts to Save the Children in their wills, worth an estimated £3.6 million. So far, more than 2,700 people have chosen to support Save the Children in this way.

We recieved two particularly large bequests from supporters who wished to benefit future generations of children. Alan Spennock left us all of his estate, worth more than £550,000. James McNulty also bequeathed his entire estate, worth over £305,000. The combined total of these bequests would be enough to support a three-year programme to protect working children in the Sahel region of West Africa from hazardous and exploitative labour.

*Barnado's: 31 March 1999*

**Income**

i) Donations except in relation to legacies are accounted for at the time of receipt at head office. Legacies have been included in the statement of financial activities where probate was granted prior to the balance sheet date and where receipt took place shortly after the year end. Other legacies notified are not accrued due to uncertainties of value and timing of receipt. The amount notified in relation to such legacies is disclosed in Note 12.

## Gifts in kind

**7.26** Paragraphs 95 to 98 of SORP describe the basis of recognising gifts in kind and the related disclosures. The paragraphs state:

*'Incoming resources in the form of gifts in kind should be included in the Statement of Financial Activities in the following ways:*

*(a) Assets given for distribution by the charity should be recognised as incoming resources for the year within donations, legacies and similar incoming resources only when distributed.*

*(b) Assets given for use by the charity (eg property for its own occupation) should be recognised as incoming resources when receivable. Where the donor intended the assets to be used on a continuing basis then they should be accounted for in accordance with para 80 [see 7.28 below.]*

*(c) Where a gift has been made in kind but on trust for conversion into cash and subsequent application by the charity, the incoming resource should normally be recognised in the accounting period when receivable. However, in certain cases this will not be practicable and the incoming resource should be included in the accounting period in which the gift is sold. The most common example is that of second-hand goods donated for resale, which, whilst regarded as a donation in legal terms is in economic terms similar to trading and should be included within "activities for generating funds"'.* *(para 95)*

*'In all cases the amount at which gifts in kind are brought into account should either be a reasonable estimate of their gross value to the charity or the amount actually realised.'* *(para 96)*

***'Disclosure***

*The basis of any valuation should be disclosed. Where material, an adjustment should be made to the original valuation upon subsequent realisation of the gift.'* *(para 97)*

*'Referring to 95(a) above, where there are undistributed assets at the year end, a general description of the items involved and an estimate of their value should be given by way of a note to the accounts provided such value is material.'* *(para 98)*

### Comment

**7.27** The requirements with regard to gifts in kind should not present any significant problems and most charities are adhering to the principles laid down in paras 95 to 98.

**7.28** However, care does need to be taken to ensure that the circumstances surrounding the gift are examined, particularly if the gift is of an asset which is of substantial value. For example, was the gift subject to any conditions? If so, did these conditions impel the trustees to treat the gift as either an addition to the permanent endowment or as a new permanent endowment? If so, the gift should be valued and treated as incoming endowment fund resources, with any income therefrom treated as either unrestricted or restricted income according to the conditions of the gift. Similarly, the gift itself may be subject to conditions on its use. If this is the case the asset should be treated as incoming resources of restricted funds. Where the asset is to be retained for continuing use by the charity itself, the restricted fund will be reduced by transfers of amounts equivalent to any depreciation or amortisation charges over the expected useful life of the asset concerned in accordance with para 80 of SORP.

*Oxfam: 30 April 2000*

**c. Gifts in Kind**

**Blankets and clothing**, etc. received and given to overseas projects are included in the accounts at market value at the time of export. Goods held pending despatch are not included in the accounts. Goods which have been dispatched overseas but are not yet distributed from Oxfam-controlled stores are included in the value of aid provided and are not included on the Balance Sheet. This is taken to be the point at which the goods have a value to the beneficiary.

**Food aid from the World Food Programme and the European Union** for which Oxfam accepts full responsibility for distribution is included in income at its market value, and under 'Resources Expended' at the same value.

**Properties, investments, and other fixed assets** donated to the charity are included as donation income at market value at the time of receipt.

*Save the Children: 31 March 2000*

**Gifts in kind**

Gifts in kind include food, clothing and medical supplies. The Consolidated Statement of Financial Activities classifies gifts in kind as resources arising and expended when they are received in the field. No value has been placed on stocks of goods as yet undistributed.

Except for gifts from the European Union, the gifts in kind are valued by officers of Save the Children with regard to market prices when distributed in the field. Those gifts received from the European Union are required to be valued at their insurance value.

Gifts in kind also include campaigning and fundraising goods and services which have been valued by officers of Save the Children either at market value or, where a market value is not available appropriate estimates are made.

## Intangible income

**7.29** Paragraphs 99 and 100 of SORP state:

*'A charity may receive assistance in the form of donated facilities, beneficial loan arrangements, donated services or services from volunteers. Such assistance is generally referred to as "intangible income". Such intangible incoming resources should be included in the Statement of Financial Activities where another party is bearing the financial cost of the resources supplied and the benefit is quantifiable and measurable. (This will not normally apply to commercial discounts except where they are clearly intended as a donation.) Where there is no financial cost borne by another party for the provision of the assistance (eg in the case of volunteers), the intangible income should not be included in the Statement of Financial Activities. The value placed on resources included in the Statement of Financial Activities should be the financial cost to the third party of providing them. However, where this information is not available or if the charity considers the value to be less than the costs borne by the third party, a reasonable estimate of their gross value to the charity should be given. An equivalent amount should be included as expenditure under the appropriate heading in the Statement of Financial Activities.'* *(para 99)*

***'Disclosure***

*The notes to the accounts should give an analysis of intangible incoming resources included in the Statement of Financial Activities distinguishing appropriately between the different major items eg seconded staff, loaned assets etc. Material intangible incoming resources which are not included in the Statement of Financial Activities (eg volunteers) should be commented on in the Trustees Annual Report (see paragraph 31(d)).'* *(para 100)*

## Comment

**7.30** The amount of any intangible income to be included in the Statement of Financial Activities should be assessed by reference to its value to the charity. This is not necessarily the market value or rate of the facilities or services. For example, suppose a charity were looking to rent some office space in London. The charity would almost certainly have some idea of the market rent it was willing to pay for the facilities it acquired – say £15,000 per quarter. If the charity was fortunate enough, instead, to be offered, rent-free, suitable premises in Park Lane, London, W1, then the value of those premises for the purposes of the charity's accounts would not be the rental value of the Park Lane accommodation but the £15,000 per quarter that the charity would otherwise have had to incur, ie the value of the facilities to the charity itself.

**7.31** Whereas it is generally accepted that it is impracticable to value the voluntary services provided by supporters, it is necessary to estimate the value of any secondments of paid staff to the charity, where the person seconded is carrying out a task that the charity would otherwise have had to employ someone to do. In this case, the value of the secondment is the salary paid by the employer or the salary the charity would have been willing to pay an employee to carry out the task(s) if less. This may, of course, be dictated by the funding body; for example where local authority staff are seconded to a charity in which the authority is interested.

> *Macmillan Cancer Relief: 31 December 1998*
>
> **Gifts in kind**
> The Charity benefits from the many thousands of voluntary hours and unclaimed out-of-pocket expenses contributed by a very large number of supporters. In addition, companies, organisations and individuals have, in many cases, provided the use of facilities, equipment and premises for various activities and meetings without charge. It would be impossible to place a value on all these gifts in kind for which the Charity is extremely grateful and without which much of the work undertaken could not be achieved.
> In addition, where Macmillan Cancer Relief receives the benefit of the services of secondees, these are included in the Statement of Financial Activities at values appropriate to the Charity. The proceeds of other items such as pictures, property or shares are taken to income upon sale or, if retained for investment purposes, are recorded at a reasonable valuation.

## Cash collections

**7.32** Funds collected for a charity and to which it is legally entitled, but which it has not received by the year-end, should normally be included in its Statement of Financial Activities as incoming resources and in its balance sheet as 'collections in progress' as a current asset.

**7.33** Funds in the form of cash collections in the hands of, or otherwise under the control of, persons other than the charity trustees as at the year-end should, where material, be brought into account as incoming resources of the year in accordance with the returns received from the collectors. Where it is not practicable to ascertain the actual amount it should, if considered material, be estimated (eg by apportioning the amount subsequently ascertained or received between the relevant accounting years) on a reasonable and consistent basis according to the known circumstances and the results of control checks made from time to time.

## Comment

**7.34** A sensible approach should be adopted when accounting for cash collections. Inevitably there is the difficulty of ascertaining the actual amount collected at the end of each financial year, but as the accounts are not published until some months after the accounting date it should be a relatively straightforward exercise to estimate the amount collected by reference to the total amount subsequently received and apportioning on a time basis.

## Life subscriptions

**7.35** Paragraph 283 of SORP merely states that the basis for including subscriptions for life membership should be disclosed. It is generally accepted that life subscriptions should be included as income in the Statement of Financial Activities on a consistent basis (eg if the life subscription is twenty times the annual subscription, one twentieth of it might be recognised as income each year). At the end of each year, the balance carried forward to future years should be included in the Balance Sheet as deferred income under 'liabilities'.

## Comment

**7.36** The requirements set out above are adopted by most charities with life subscriptions, although the period over which the income is amortised varies widely. Some charities whose life subscriptions merely entitle the member to receive the charity's newsletters and attend meetings continue to credit life subscriptions, in full, to the Statement of Financial Activities in the year in which they are received.

> *The Wildlife and Wetlands Trust (WWT): 31 December 1999*
>
> **Membership Subscriptions and Adoption Schemes**
> Annual and Life Fellow subscriptions are credited to income in the year in which they are receivable. In prior years Life Fellows subscriptions were treated as a receipt in advance and are reduced by the value of annual benefits each year.

> *The National Trust: 28 February 1999*
>
> **Accounting for income**
> Membership income, admission fees, gifts, legacies and appeal income are accounted for as and when the income is received. Annual subscriptions from members are included in full in the year they are received. Life membership subscriptions are credited to the life membership equalisation account and from there to income in ten equal annual instalments.

## Incoming resources from operating activities

**7.37** Paragraph 101 of SORP requires:

*'For the purpose of analysing incoming resources from operating activities, such activities fall into two principal categories.*

*(a) activities in furtherance of the charity's objects.*
*(b) activities for generating funds.'* *(para 101)*

**7.38** These broad headings need to be expanded as appropriate to reflect the activities being carried out by an individual charity. To avoid disclosing immaterial categories, activities may be aggregated at a suitable level with the possibility of further subdivisions being given in the notes to the accounts.

## Comment

**7.39** The aim of the SORP in subdividing incoming resources in this way is to link incoming resources and resources expended more clearly. Thus by grouping together all incoming resources which are in the nature of a payment for the provision of the charity's services (or goods), whether they be trading income, grants with conditions which make them similar to receipts from trading such as receipts under service agreements with local authorities, etc, the total can be compared directly with the cost of providing the services (or goods). Similarly, income arising out of activities specifically for generating funds can be compared directly with the cost of generating them.

**7.40** This classification will lead to greater use of ratio analysis in interpreting charity accounts and inevitably to assessing performance and comparing charities. Whilst some may welcome this, such analysis must be carried out with care. Charities which seem to carry out similar activities are often subtly different and these differences can have a marked impact on financial results. (For example, one charity may employ a fundraiser whereas another may be fortunate enough to have volunteers to assist with the raising of funds). Additional disclosure in the notes to the accounts and in the trustees' report explaining ratios that, at face value, may appear far from satisfactory will therefore become essential.

## Activities in furtherance of the charity's objects

**7.41** Paragraph 104 of SORP states that this category of incoming resources may include:

*'(a) the sale of goods or services as part of the directly charitable activities of*

*the charity (known as primary purpose trading) or the letting of non-investment property in furtherance of the objects.*

*(b)* *the sale of goods or services made or provided by the beneficiaries of the charity;*

*(c)* *incoming resources from government or public authorities where these are received in the normal course of trading under (a) or (b) eg fees for respite care;*

*(d)* *grants in specifically for the provision of goods and services as part of the directly charitable activities or provided by the beneficiaries;*

*(e)* *ancillary trades connected to a primary purpose in (a) and (b) where the principal aim is to provide a service to the charity's beneficiaries.'*

*(para 104)*

**Activities for generating funds**

**7.42** Activities for generating funds are described by the SORP as those activities which

*'are not part of the directly charitable activities but are carried out in order to generate incoming resources to support those activities. This will include fundraising events such as jumble sales, firework displays and concerts (which are legally considered to be trading activities) and those sponsorships and social lotteries which cannot be considered as pure donations'.* *(para 105)*

**7.43** Paragraph 106 of SORP provides some examples of activities for generating funds:

*'Activities for generating funds can nclude selling donated goods and bought in goods, providing services to other than the charity's beneficiaries, licensing arrangements, the letting of non investment property and many others. Whilst selling donated goods is legally considered to be the realisation of a donation in kind (see paragraph 95(c)), in economic terms it is similar to a trading activity and should be included in this section. Ancillary trades where the principal aim (whilst still providing a service to the beneficiaries) is to generate incoming resources to support or contribute to the other charitable activities, should also be included in this section. Sometimes all these activities are carried on separately and other times mixed together in a single enterprise.'*

**7.44** The accounting for grants receivable will depend on whether the grant is for the purchase of a fixed asset or towards revenue expenditure. The treatment of 'capital' grants or grants for the purchase of tangible fixed assets is dealt with in para 80 of SORP:

*'Where either incoming resources are given specifically to provide a fixed asset or a fixed asset is donated (a gift in kind), the charity will normally have entitlement to the incoming resources when they are receivable. At this point, all of the incoming resources should be recognised in the Statement of Financial Activities and not deferred over the life of the asset. As explained in*

*paragraph 79 the possibility of having to repay the incoming resources does not affect their recognition in the first instance. Once acquired, the use of the asset will either be restricted or unrestricted (see paragraph 86). If its use is unrestricted the trustees should consider creating a designated fund reflecting the book value of the asset. The relevant fund will then be reduced over the useful economic life of the asset in line with its depreciation. This treatment accords with the requirements under accounting standards for the recognition of assets and liabilities and provides the most appropriate interpretation of SSAP 4 for charities.'* *(para 80)*

**7.45** Grants received towards the cost of revenue expenditure must be divided between those for core funding and those that resemble trading income receivable under service contracts with government and local authorities.

**7.46** Core grants should be recognised as part of 'Donations, legacies and similar income' once any conditions for receipt have been complied with. If there is any likelihood of a grant having to be repaid then this fact should be explained in the notes to the accounts.

**7.47** Core grants restricted to future accounting periods should be deferred and recognised in those future accounting periods, with the basis of any apportionment explained in the notes to the accounts. Grants for immediate financial support and assistance, or to reimburse costs previously incurred, should be recognised immediately in the Statement of Financial Activities. A description of the sources of any material core grants should be disclosed in the notes to the accounts.

**7.48** Grants from government and other public authorities are specifically referred to in para 114 to 117 of SORP:

*'Incoming resources from the government and other public authorities arise in many and varied ways such as grants, contracts and service agreements. They include resources from the European Union and other EU bodies and incoming resources from the National Lottery.'* *(para 114)*

*'These resources should be treated in a similar manner to other incoming resources and included under the relevant headings of the Statement of Financial Activities which will normally be "donations legacies and similar incoming resources" or "activities in furtherance of the charity's objects" (see paragraphs 87 and 101–104).'* *(para 115)*

*'These resources should also be dealt with in accordance with any conditional terms which create a special trust and therefore a restricted fund, though this can be difficult to determine in practice. Sometimes the conditions may represent the authority's expectations of service provision without imposing a restriction but each case must be judged on its own merits. However, where the incoming resources are for a service (or goods) and, upon full performance of the service, any*

*surplus funds can be retained and used for general purposes, this most likely indicates that the incoming sources and related expenditure will be unrestricted. Whereas, if upon full performance any surplus is retrievable by the authority then the resources are most likely to be restricted.'* *(para 116)*

***'Disclosure***

*The notes to the accounts should give a description of the sources of any material incoming resources, by category. For example this could distinguish between type of authority and resources such as fees, grants and service agreements.'* *(para 117)*

## Grants receivable

**7.49** The following examples illustrate the accounting for both income and capital grants.

*WRVS: 31 March 1996*

**WOMEN'S ROYAL VOLUNTARY SERVICE NOTES TO THE ACCOUNTS FOR THE YEAR ENDED 31 MARCH 1996**

**1 Principal accounting policies**

(d) Grants receivable
- (i) Home Office grant-in-aid
  Grant-in-aid allocated to revenue is credited to the statement of financial activities on an accruals basis.
- (ii) Grant from the Ministry of Defence
  Funding from the Ministry of Defence is accounted for on an accruals basis. Any funding unappropriated at the end of each accounting period is deemed to be repayable to the Ministry of Defence.
- (iii) Food project grants
  Grants received from local authorities for the purchase of kitchen equipment and motor vehicles used by food projects, and towards the initial setting up costs and running expenses of each individual project, are credited to the statement of financial activities in full in the year in which they are received and treated as restricted funds. The restricted funds are reduced each year by an amount equal to any expenditure on such assets and the initial setting up costs incurred.
  This represents a change in accounting policy. In previous years any unspent grants have been treated as deferred income in the accounts of the group. A prior year adjustment has been made to reflect this change of policy (note 19).

[*continued on following page*]

*WRVS continued*

(iv) Other capital grants

Other capital grants received towards the cost of tangible fixed assets are credited to the statement of financial activities in full in the year in which they are received and treated as restricted funds. The restricted funds are reduced by annual transfers of amounts equivalent to any depreciation charges over the expected useful life of the asset concerned.

*WRVS: 31 March 1996*

**WOMEN'S ROYAL VOLUNTARY SERVICE NOTES TO THE ACCOUNTS FOR THE YEAR ENDED 31 MARCH 1996**

**2 Grants receivable**

| | **Unrestricted funds** | | | | |
|---|---|---|---|---|---|
| | **General fund** | **Designated funds** | **Restricted funds** | **Total 1996** | **Total 1995** |
| | **£** | **£** | **£** | **£** | **£** |
| GROUP | | | | | |
| Home Office grant-in-aid (see (a) below) | 6,200,097 | – | – | 6,200,097 | 1,327,906 |
| Ministry of Defence grant (see (b) below) | – | – | 1,633,113 | 1,633,113 | 1,545,437 |
| Food projects' grants (see (c) below) | – | – | 122,432 | 122,432 | 500,486 |
| Other grants | 140,937 | – | 107,432 | 248,369 | – |
| | 6,341,034 | – | 1,862,977 | 8,204,011 | 3,373,829 |
| CHARITY | | | | | |
| Home Office grant-in-aid (see (a) below) | 6,200,097 | – | – | 6,200,097 | – |
| Less: grant-in-aid attributed to WRVS Office Premises Limited | (1,107,697) | – | – | (1,107,697) | – |
| | 5,092,400 | – | – | 5,092,400 | – |
| Other grants | 140,698 | – | 107,432 | 248,130 | – |
| | 5,233,098 | – | 107,432 | 5,340,530 | – |

(a) An annual grant from the Voluntary Services Unit of the Home Office to assist with core expenditure and the administration of premises used by the charity and the group.

(b) An annual grant allocated to WRVS Services Welfare Limited and used to provide welfare and support to army service men and women serving on army bases throughout the world.

(c) Grants recieved from local authorities for the purchase of kitchen equipment and motor vehicles used by food projects, and towards the intial setting up and running costs of each project.

## Trading activities

**7.50** As described more fully in Chapter 18, trading activities are not charitable activities and should not, therefore, be carried on by charities. There are, however, two major exceptions to this rule:

- if the trade is exercised in the actual carrying on of a primary purpose of the charity, eg independent schools; or
- if the work in connection with the trade is mainly carried on by the beneficiaries of the charity, eg disabled workshops.

**7.51** Thus a charity established to care for the sick can run a hospital, nursing home, day centre, hospice etc. If fees are charged for the services provided, the activity is broadly defined as trading, but provided any surplus that is earned is applied towards the charitable objectives, it falls within the first exception. Similarly, any sale by the charity of work made by the patients while in the charity's care will fall within the second exception.

**7.52** Other permissible operational income will include regular forms of trading income appropriate to the charity which relate directly to its activities. An operatic society will have receipts from sales of theatre tickets, programmes, advertising, recording royalties etc; a museum will have receipts from entry fees, private functions, book and poster sales etc.

**7.53** The profits of some forms of occasional trading are also relieved from tax by extra-statutory concession of the Inland Revenue, and are normally allowed as ancillary to the objects of a charity. Typical examples of such trading, which is generally for the purposes of raising funds, include jumble sales, firework displays, carnivals etc. Unless the amounts involved are significant, the amounts are probably best dealt with in the Statement of Financial Activities as a net figure. The activities described in paragraphs **7.51** and **7.52** above will fall within the category 'activities in furtherance of the charity's objects' whereas those described in this paragraph will fall within the heading 'activities for generating funds'. An analysis of incoming resources from both categories should be given in the notes to the accounts to supplement the analysis on the face of the Statement of Financial Activities. It should be sufficiently detailed to enable the reader to understand the main activities carried out by the charity and the main components of the gross incoming resources receivable for each activity.

**7.53** *Incoming resources*

*South Bank Centre: 31 March 2000*

**Statement Of Financial Activities**

*for the year ended 31 March 2000*

| | Notes | Restricted Funds £000 | Unrestricted Funds £000 | Total Funds 2000 £000 | Total Funds 1999 £000 |
|---|---|---|---|---|---|
| **Incoming resources** | | | | | |
| Income from trading activities | 4 | – | 9,077 | 9,077 | 8,580 |
| Sponsorship and donations | | – | 162 | 162 | 285 |
| Grants for lottery projects | 13 | 689 | – | 689 | 15 |
| Funding for other site development projects | 13 | 819 | – | 819 | – |
| Operating grant | | – | 13,879 | 13,879 | 13,218 |
| Interest receivable | | – | 197 | 197 | 295 |
| Total incoming resources | 13 | 1,508 | 23,315 | 24,823 | 22,393 |

*South Bank Centre: 31 March 2000*

**4 INCOME FROM TRADING ACTIVITIES**

| | 2000 £000 | 1999 £000 |
|---|---|---|
| Own promotions | 2,401 | 1,976 |
| Hall & space rentals | 2,601 | 2,625 |
| Retail & catalogue sales | 941 | 911 |
| Concessions & car parking | 2,357 | 2,216 |
| Other income | 776 | 842 |
| Profit on sale of tangible fixed assets | 1 | 10 |
| | 9,077 | 8,580 |

The total value of box office ticket sales for the three concert halls was £10.882m including VAT (1999 — £12.178m). This includes takings for SBC's own promotions and those collected on behalf of external promoters: takings for the external promoters are then paid over net of any letting charges.

**7.54** Most charities with substantial trading activities will channel these through a trading subsidiary either to minimise risk or avoid ultra vires activity. The trading results of the subsidiary undertakings themselves should be accounted for in accordance with the rules for consolidation. These are detailed and discussed in Chapter 5.

### Comment

**7.55** Most charities have little difficulty in complying with these requirements although there are often concerns about the 'application' of charity funds invested in non-profitable, non-charitable trading companies and the financing of such companies.

**7.56** One area of particular difficulty, however, arises in connection with charity shops which sell mainly donated goods, a charitable activity, but which may also sell bought in goods, a trading activity. This problem, and those of a similar nature, is dealt with in para 107 of SORP:

*'It may be possible to segregate the incoming resources and resources expended for each different type of activity (this may have to be done for tax purposes) but an enterprise carrying on a mix of activities will often be viewed as a single economic unit. Charity trustees should consider the balance of the activities being undertaken to determine the most appropriate place to include the incoming resources from such enterprises but having done this the mix of incoming resources need not be segregated further. For example a shop may mainly sell donated and bought in goods, but it may also sell a small amount of goods made by its beneficiaries and incidentally provide information about the charity. It would be acceptable to class all the incoming resources from the shop as "shop income" under "activities for general funds".'* *(para 107)*

## Investment income

**7.57** Paragraph 113 of SORP states:

*'The notes to the accounts should show the gross investment income arising from each category of investment in accordance with para 238.'* *(para 113)*

Note: para 238 referred to here requires that investments should be analysed between the following categories:

- investment properties
- investments listed on a recognised stock exchange or ones valued by reference to such investments, such as unit trusts and common investment funds
- investments in subsidiary or associated undertakings or in companies which are connected persons
- other unlisted securities
- cash and settlements pending held as part of the investment portfolio
- any other investments.

## Comment

**7.58** In most cases this should not present charities with any problems but it will enable the reader of a charity's accounts to carry out a crude but nevertheless relatively meaningful analysis of investment yields. The inclusion of investment income gross is a good discipline for charities to ensure that tax is reclaimed regularly, provided that is, that the debtor for tax recoverable is visible among the debtors.

*Barnardo's: 31 March 1999*

| | 1999 £000 | 1998 £000 |
|---|---|---|
| **6 Investment income and interest** | | |
| Listed investments United Kingdom | 4,328 | 4,063 |
| Listed investments Overseas | 701 | 296 |
| Short term deposits | 156 | 552 |
| Rents and ground rents | 235 | 98 |
| Loan and other interest | 558 | 720 |
| | 5,978 | 5,729 |

## Gains and losses on fixed assets for charity use

**7.59** Two types of gain or loss can arise with regard to fixed assets. The first is where an asset is revalued, either upwards or downwards, thereby resulting in an unrealised revaluation gain or loss. The accounting of such gains or losses is detailed and discussed in Chapter 10.

**7.60** The other type of gain or loss in relation to fixed assets for charity use is a realised gain or loss, arising when an asset is sold, scrapped or otherwise disposed of.

**7.61** Paragraph 156(b) of SORP states:

*'Gains on the disposal of fixed assets for the charity's own use should be included under the heading "other incoming resources". Losses on disposal should be treated as additional depreciation and included appropriatley in the resources expended section of the Statement of Financial Activities.'* *(para 156(b))*

**Comment**

**7.62** Most charities should have little difficulty in complying with the SORP requirements.

**7.63** In the past some charities have tended to deal with significant gains or losses within the funds on the balance sheet rather than disclosing them on the face of the income and expenditure account. This has often had a misleading result where, for example, there has been a deficit on the income and expenditure account but a substantial gain on the sale of, say, a freehold property. On the face of it the charity has lost money while the balance sheet shows an increase in net assets. The SORP requirements should prevent this situation arising in the future.

**7.64** As discussed in Chapter 10, difficulties arise concerning assets used by a charity which have hitherto not been valued or which have been written off. Paragraph 195 of SORP recommends that a 'reasonable estimate of the value to the charity should be used'. Trustees often argue that not only will the resultant value be meaningless as they have no intention of selling the property, but the unrealised gain to be shown in the

Statement of Financial Activities will be positively misleading as it will imply that the charity has increased its available resources.

**7.65** We sympathise with this concern. Our suggestion is that, in cases where a valuation is to be included where none existed before, the adjustment should be made at the beginning of the year as a prior year adjustment so that the comparative figures are restated to reflect the uplift in value. While complying with the recommendation of para 195 of SORP, this will avoid the distortion of showing an apparent increase in resources in one year. Consideration should also be given to 'designating' the revaluation gain if it belongs to general fund assets.

## Gains and losses on investment assets

**7.66** Paragraph 156(d) of SORP states:

*'Any gains and losses on investment assets (including property investments) should be included under the gains and losses on the revaluation and disposal of investment assets. Realised and unrealised gains and losses may be included in a single line.'* *(para 156(d))*

*The Baring Foundation: 31 December 1999*

**Statement of Financial Activities for the year ended 31 December 1999**

| | Unrestricted Funds Total 1999 £ | Unrestricted Funds Total 1998 £ |
|---|---|---|
| **Income and Expenditure relating to Continuing Activities** | | |
| **Incoming Resources** | | |
| Donations | 714,553 | 676,849 |
| Investment income | 2,608,434 | 2,400,059 |
| Other income | 2,344 | 27,846 |
| Total Incoming Resources | 3,325,331 | 3,104,754 |
| **Resources Expended** | | |
| Direct charitable expenditure: | | |
| Grants | (3,408,646) | (3,459,846) |
| Other direct charitable expenditure | (170,110) | (188,122) |
| Other expenditure: | | |
| Managment and administration of the charity | (159,675) | (167,702) |
| Total Resources Expended | (3,738,431) | (3,815,670) |
| **Net (Outgoing)/Incoming Resources** | (413,100) | (710,916) |
| **Statement of Total Recognised Gains and Losses** | | |
| Net gain on investments | 13,311,018 | 7,133,047 |
| **Net movement in Funds** | 12,897,918 | 6,422,131 |
| Funds balances brought forward at 1 January 1999 | 72,888,359 | 66,466,228 |
| **Funds balances carried forward at 31 December 1999** | £85,786,277 | £72,888,359 |

**Comment**

**7.67** The calculation and treatment of gains is discussed in more detail in Chapter 10. In many cases, charities should have little problem complying with SORP, but others may find that their investment managers insist on additional charges for supplying the necessary information.

**7.68** Again, in the past some charities have credited or debited investment gains or losses directly to the funds on the balance sheet. As with tangible fixed assets this creates a misleading picture of a charity's activities and should be prevented under SORP.

**7.69** Some charities argue that gains on investments should not be included within the Statement of Financial Activities. The 'growth' of an investment is often largely inflationary and merely represents the amount required to maintain the real value of the investment. SORP has recognised this particular point by excluding all investment gains from the 'incoming resources' section of the Statement of Financial Activities. However, it is important to show that there has been a movement in the net worth of the charity, be it an increase or a decrease, and this is done by means of the 'gains and losses on revaluations and investment asset disposals' section.

**7.70** The need to no longer show separately realised and unrealised gains and losses is welcome and reflects the fact that the only figures that matter to the charity are the closing values of the investment pool compared to the opening values. It makes no difference whether or not investments were changed in between.

**Tax recoverable**

**7.71** Income received in circumstances where a claim for repayment of tax has been or will be made to the Inland Revenue (this includes income received under a deed of covenant and by Gift Aid) should be grossed up for tax recoverable and the gross figure included as income. The tax recoverable should be accounted for as a debtor until the charity recovers the amount involved.

**Comment**

**7.72** The grossing up of income received net of income tax is a good discipline to ensure that tax is reclaimed regularly from the Inland Revenue.

*Marie Curie Cancer Care: 31 March 2000*

**(f) Donations, legacies and other forms of voluntary income**

All income is accounted for when receivable and includes associated tax reclaims. Bequeathed properties awaiting disposal are valued on behalf of the Council and are included within legacy income. Entitlement to legacy income is taken to be probate date.

*The Trust of St Benedict's Abbey, Ealing: 31 August 2000*

**Dividends and interest**

Dividends and interest, together with any associated tax credit, are credited to the statement of financial activities in the period in which they are receivable

CHAPTER 8

# Resources expended

## 1 INTRODUCTION

**8.1** Appendix 1 of SORP defines resources expended as follows:

*'Resources expended means all costs incurred in the course of expending or utilising the charity's funds. This includes all claims against the charity upon being recognised as liabilities by the trustees, as well as all accruals and payments made by the trustees of a charity, and all losses on the disposal of fixed assets (other than investments), together with all provisions for impairment of fixed assets.*

*This is to be distinguished from total expenditure which does not include losses on the disposal of fixed assets nor amounts paid for the acquisition of fixed assets nor any amounts paid out of endowment funds. Total expenditure is required to be calculated in the determination of whether a charity has crossed the thresholds for independent examination or audit set by regulations made under the Charities Act 1993 or The Charities Accounts (Scotland) Regulations 1992.'*

**8.2** Paragraph 131 of SORP states that resources expended should be split into two main categories, being the costs of generating funds and the actual cost of charitable activities.

**8.3** In this chapter we look at how expenditure should be analysed and look at each of the recommended headings in some detail. We also consider how to allocate expenditure over each of the expense headings and deal with capital expenditure, aspects of the Companies Acts and accounting for irrecoverable VAT.

## 2 ANALYSIS OF EXPENDITURE

**8.4** Given the requirement set out in para 131 of SORP that resources expended should be analysed between the cost of generating funds and the cost of charitable activities, paras 132 to 138 of SORP expand on this and identify sub-headings that should be used to categorise expenses. In particular, paras 132 to 134 define what is meant by the cost of generating funds whilst paras 136 and 137 define charitable expenditure.

***'Costs of Generating Funds***

*These are the costs which are associated with raising funds from all the possible sources of incoming resources. This will mainly be fundraising costs (Appendix 1: Glossary) in attracting donations, legacies and similar incoming resources and the costs of activities for income generation. In addition it may include costs associated with raising funds for the provision of goods and services in the furtherance of the charity's objects, but it should not include any of the costs of performing or supporting those activities. For instance the costs of negotiating a contract or applying for a grant for a charitable activity could be regarded as a cost of generating funds. The costs of carrying out the activity will be costs in furtherance of the charity's objects and the costs of monitoring performance in line with the contract or grant could be support costs.'* *(para 132)*

*'Expenditure on fundraising should be all the costs incurred in raising the fundraising proceeds (see paragraph 60(i) shown in the accounts, including agents' costs where used. This should include publicity costs associated with fundraising or raising the profile of the charity but not those which are used in an educational manner in furtherance of the charity's objects. Such distinctions should be drawn in line with the particular nature and circumstance of each charity and its publicity material. Policies for drawing these distinctions should be disclosed to meet the requirements of paragraph 284.'* *(para 133)*

*'The costs of generating funds should also include investment management costs for both income generation and captial maintenance (also see paragraph 42).'* *(para 134)*

***'Charitable Expenditure***

*Charitable expenditure comprises all the expenditure incurred by the charity in meeting its charitable objectives as opposed to the cost of raising the funds to finance these activities and should be analysed between the following sub-headings.*

*(a)* *grants payable in furtherance of the charity's objects (paragraphs 138–146).*
*(b)* *costs of activities in furtherance of the charity's objects (paragraphs 147–150).*
*(c)* *support costs of (a) and (b) where material (paragraphs 147–150).*
*(d)* *costs of management and administration of the charity (paragraphs 151–152).'* *(para 136)*

*'Costs such as depreciation, amortisation or losses on disposal of fixed assets used wholly or mainly for charitable activites, including where the assets are written off as project expenditure, should be allocated within this section in accordance with the principles in paragraph 153.'* *(para 137)*

**Comment**

**8.5** It will be seen from above that the SORP has continued to require a distinction to be made between charitable expenditure and the cost of generating funds. This latter category has been given greater prominence in the new SORP and should be the first category of expenditure. The thinking behind this is that by being forced to give information regarding the cost of generating funds in this manner, trustees will have to disclose the efficiency of their fundraising activities. It also concentrates attention on the need to maximise the proportion of resources expended which is devoted to the charitable objectives of the charity. However, the change in the classification of management and administration of the charity to charitable expenditure (compared to 'other expenditure' previously) also illustrates the recognition that all charities must incur expenditure on administration and management if they are to carry out their activities effeciently and professionally. It is also hoped that by redefining administration and management as charitable expenditure it will encourage charities to include costs other than the audit fee within this heading.

## 3 ALLOCATION OF EXPENDITURE

**8.6** Paragraphs 132 and 138 of SORP do not give precise definitions or detailed guidance on how expenditure should be allocated to each of the recommended heads. This means that each charity needs to develop its own principles for cost allocation suitable to its own circumstances. These principles should be applied consistently from one accounting period to another.

**8.7** Paragraph 153 of SORP states the following with regard to allocation of expenses:

*'It is not practicable to define precisely what should be included under each expenditure heading as each charity's circumstances will be different. Furthermore, charities will often group expenditure under different headings for internal reporting purposes from those which should be disclosed in the annual accounts. In attributing costs the following principles should be applied:*

*(a) No part of expenditure incurred on activities falling directly within one cost category should be attributed to any other cost category.*
*(b) Items of expenditure which involve more than one cost category, for*

*example the cost of running an office which houses both fundraising and charitable project support functions, should be apportioned on a reasonable, justifiable and consistent basis to the cost categories involved.*

(c) *Where costs should not be allocated to the categories in paragraph 60(i) (costs of generating funds) and 60(ii)(a–c) (grants payable, costs of operating activities, and support costs) they should be included within 60(ii)(d) management and administration of the charity.'* *(para 153)*

**8.8** Paragraph 154 of SORP emphasises the need to explain the basis and principles used for the allocation of all costs in the accounting policies.

**8.9** Further, para 119 of SORP states:

*'All expenditure should be included in the Statement of Financial Activities in accordance with the accruals concept, (Appendix 2: SSAP 2). A liability arises as soon as there is a legal or constructive obligation committing the charity to the expenditure as described in Financial Reporting Standards (FRS's) 5 and 12.'* *(para 119)*

**Comment**

**8.10** The problems associated with deciding on an appropriate basis of allocating expenditure highlights the need for a comprehensive chart of accounts with appropriate sub-divisions so that all expenditure is classified in sufficient detail to enable an objective view to be taken on cost allocation. Take for example the case of printing costs where the same supplier may provide material for the direct mail fundraising, advertising the charity's activities, educating the public, informing volunteer workers and producing the annual report, not to mention the stationery for use in all departments. The most reliable way of allocating the cost is to analyse and code each invoice as it is received and have sufficient printing cost codes in the chart of accounts to accommodate the analysis. In this way each department will bear its appropriate share of such costs. Now that computer accounting systems are widely used, this degree of analysis is within the reach of most charities that are likely to require it.

**8.11** The question of appropriate allocation of costs will recur later in this chapter and is also discussed in further detail in Chapter 5. It should, however, always be remembered that one charity's management and administrative expenses may be another's costs in furtherance of the charity's objects. For example, a charity established to provide recruitment consultancy services to other charities at reduced cost would regard the salary costs of the consultants as expenditure on furthering the objects of the charity. The recipient charity would probably regard the bill from the supplier as a management and administration expense. It is, therefore, always necessary to consider the use to which the goods or services purchased have been put.

**8.12** Once the question of the basis to be used in allocating costs between the various headings has been resolved, it is essential that the accounting policies contained within the notes to the accounts clearly identify the principles that have been applied.

*CC66 — SORP 2000: Example reports and accounts (Dorsetshire Drugs Advice Centre)*

(f) Resources expended are allocated to the particular activity where the cost relates directly to that activity. However, the cost of overall direction and administration on each activity, comprising the salary and overhead costs of the central function, is apportioned on the following bases which are an estimate, based on staff time, of the amount attributable to each activity:

| | |
|---|---|
| Charity shop | 0% |
| Fund-raising and publicity | 15% |
| Advice and information | 20% |
| Outreach work | 20% |
| Training project | 30% |
| Management and administration of the charity | 15% |

*Barnardo's: 31 March 1999*

**Expenditure**

i) All expenditure is accounted for on an accruals basis. Expenditure categories include salaries, depreciation and other costs as analysed in Note 8. Some costs incurred centrally are allocated to categories on the basis of their use of central support services. Such allocations are made on the basis of staff numbers, head count or asset value as appropriate.
ii) Costs of selling donated goods represents expenditure incurred in the operation and management of the Barnardo's chain of shops.
iii) Child care and community work in the UK represents the costs of running projects and providing services. Included in this total are support costs, incurred in providing regional and departmental management.
iv) Informing the public about our work. This includes costs incurred in raising awareness of child care issues and Barnardo's activities in relation to them.
v) Fundraising and publicity costs. These costs are incurred in relation to staff members who are engaged directly in fundraising, and also include the costs of specific publicity campaigns for the raising of donations.
vi) Central management costs relate to the management of Barnardo's assets, organisational administration and compliance with constitutional and statutory requirements.

*Macmillan Cancer Relief: 31 December 1999*

**Resources expended**
Grants are generally made to employing institutions to meet employment, travelling and training costs in the initial years of new appointments. Expenditure on grants is recognised in accordance with the commitments policy set out below. The related costs claimed by the employing institution are set against the commitment on an accruals basis. Any accruals or commitments for unclaimed grants are reversed at the end of the year following that in which the grant expired.

Specific overheads are attributed directly to service support and fundraising functions. Overheads relating to the management of the Charity's assets, its organisational administration and compliance with constitutional and statutory requirements, are reported as management and administration costs. Other non-specific overheads are allocated to service support and fundraising functions based on headcount or level of fundraising activity as appropriate.

## 4 COSTS OF GENERATING FUNDS

**8.13** As explained in **8.4** above this category of expenditure will mainly be fundraising costs. Appendix 1 of SORP defines fundraising costs as follows:

*' "Fundraising and Publicity Costs" comprise the costs actually incurred by a charity, or by an agent, in inducing others to make voluntary contributions to it. Such costs will include the costs of producing fundraising advertising, marketing and direct mail materials, as well as any remuneration payable to an agent. It will normally include publicity costs but not those used in an educational manner in furtherance of the charity's objects.'*

**8.14** Paragraph 135 of SORP requires that where material, the different categories of the costs of generating funds should be shown on the face of the Statement of Financial Activities. It might, therefore, be necessary to have headings such as 'fundraising event costs', 'appeal expenses' and 'investment management fees' on the statement of financial activities itself. Where, however, individual categories are not material the analysis can be relegated to the notes. Such an analysis should, wherever possible, be linked to the incoming resource categories reflecting the funds raised and to enable a true income/cost comparison to be made.

*CC66 — SORP 2000: Example reports and accounts (Aid Overseas)*

**Consolidated Statement of Financial Activities for the year ended 30 September 2001**

| | Notes | Unrestricted funds £'000 | Restricted funds £'000 | 2001 Total £'000 | 2000 Total £'000 |
|---|---|---|---|---|---|
| **Incoming resources** | | | | | |
| Donations, legacies and similar incoming resources | 2 | **6,897** | 3,797 | **10,694** | 10,991 |
| Activities in furtherance of the charity's objects: | | | | | |
| Contracts for operational programmes | 3 | – | 4,746 | **4,746** | 4,567 |
| Activities for generating funds: | | | | | |
| Shop income | 4 | **8,573** | – | **8,573** | 6,596 |
| Investment income and interest | 5 | **190** | 39 | **229** | 202 |
| **Total incoming resources** | | **15,660** | **8,582** | **24,242** | **22,356** |
| **Less: Cost of generating funds** | | | | | |
| Shop expenditure | 4 | **6,494** | – | **6,494** | 6,029 |
| Fund-raising costs | 6 | **1,646** | 113 | **1,759** | 1,584 |
| | | **8,140** | **113** | **8,253** | **7,613** |
| **Net incoming resources available for charitable application** | | **7,520** | **8,469** | **15,989** | **14,743** |

[*continued on following page*]

*CC66 — SORP 2000: Example, continued*

| | | | | | |
|---|---|---|---|---|---|
| **Charitable expenditure** | | | | | |
| Costs of activities in furtherance of the objects of the charity: | 7 | | | | |
| Grants payable to partner organisations | 7,8 | **1,286** | 2,239 | **3,525** | 3,829 |
| Operational programmes | 7 | **1,032** | 4,578 | **5,610** | 5,892 |
| Gifts in kind | 7 | **239** | 1,092 | **1,331** | 1,296 |
| Information, campaigning & education | 7 | **984** | 9 | **993** | 917 |
| Support costs | 9 | **1,502** | 404 | **1,906** | 1,845 |
| Managing and administering the charity | 10 | **470** | 2 | **472** | 466 |
| **Total charitable expenditure** | | **5,513** | **8,324** | **13,837** | **14,245** |
| **Total resources expended** | | **13,653** | **8,437** | **22,090** | **21,858** |
| **Net incoming resources** | 11 | **2,007** | **145** | **2,152** | **498** |
| Total funds brought forward | | **4,006** | 2,695 | **6,701** | 6,203 |
| **Total funds carried forward** | 21, 22 | **6,013** | **2,840** | **8,853** | **6,701** |

*CC66 — SORP 2000: Example reports and accounts (Aid Overseas)*

**4. Shop income and expenditure**

| | **Aid Overseas Trading Ltd £'000** | **Charitable Trading £'000** | **2001 Total Shop Activities £'000** | **2000 Total Shop Activities £'000** |
|---|---|---|---|---|
| Turnover from donated goods | – | 6,985 | **6,985** | 5,366 |
| Turnover from purchased goods | 1,588 | – | **1,588** | 1,230 |
| **Total shop income** | **1,588** | **6,985** | **8,573** | **6,596** |
| Operating expenses | (1,012) | (4,626) | **(5,638)** | (5,187) |
| Management expenses | (452) | (404) | **(856)** | (842) |
| **Shop expenditure** | **(1,464)** | **(5,030)** | **(6,494)** | **(6,029)** |
| **Net income from trading** | **124** | **1,955** | **2,079** | **567** |

This represents income from the sale of donated and bought-in goods through the charity's shops.

The profit of Aid Overseas Trading Limited is gifted to the charity so that there is no liability to Corporation Tax for that entity. Further details are set out in note 15 to the accounts.

*CC66 — SORP 2000: Example reports and accounts (Aid Overseas)*

**6. Fund-raising costs**

| | Unrestricted £'000 | Restricted £'000 | 2001 Total £'000 | 2000 Total £'000 |
|---|---|---|---|---|
| | 640 | 100 | **740** | 721 |
| Staff costs | | | | |
| Consultancy costs | 501 | 6 | **507** | 427 |
| Brochures and material | 264 | 2 | **266** | 249 |
| **Office costs and other** | | | | |
| overheads | 241 | 5 | **246** | 187 |
| | 1,646 | 113 | **1,759** | 1,584 |

## Current practice

**8.15** Most charities currently show their fundraising costs, usually with the appropriate accounting policy note stating the basis of allocation. The main change required by the new SORP is the need to include with fundraising costs the cost of investment management, etc to arrive at a figure for the cost of generating funds.

*The British Butterfly Conservation Society: 30 June 2000*

**1. Principal Accounting Policies**

**Fundraising and publicity**

Fundraising and publicity costs comprise expenditure incurred by the charity in inducing others to make contributions to it and in enhancing its public image.

**6 Fundraising and publicity**

| | Unrestricted funds | Restricted funds | Total 2000 | Total 1999 |
|---|---|---|---|---|
| Group and charity | £ | £ | **£** | £ |
| Staff costs | 5,168 | 1,793 | **6,961** | 247 |
| Advertising and promotion | 9,264 | 7,459 | **16,723** | 3,037 |
| General publicity and publications | 2,761 | – | **2,761** | 9,715 |
| Posters, leaflets and exhibitions | 14,328 | – | **14,328** | 8,275 |
| Office costs | 1,241 | 15 | **1,256** | – |
| | 32,762 | 9,267 | **42,029** | 21,274 |

**8.16** Despite the fact that the practice of netting off is discouraged strongly (see Chapter 13), some charities continue to show only the net proceeds from their fundraising so that either expenditure is not shown on the face of the Statement of Financial Activities and is lost in a note to the accounts, or in a few cases, such expenditure is not identified at all in the accounts. This practice should be avoided and does not comply with SORP.

**8.17** Few charities should have difficulty in grouping their expenditure on fundraising and other means of generating funds together, considering investment management fees, for example, to be part of this category of expenditure. This new emphasis, however, will enable readers of a charity's accounts to gain an appreciation of investment management costs and compare them to the size and nature of the investment portfolio and its performance.

**8.18** The need to distinguish between publicising to simply raise the profile of the charity and that publicity which serves to educate in furtherance of a charity's objects is to be welcomed.

*CC66 — SORP 2000: Example reports and accounts (The ABC Charity)*

| | | Unrestricted funds £'000 | Restricted funds £'000 | **Totals 2001 £'000** | Totals 2000 £'000 |
|---|---|---|---|---|---|
| **Resources expended** | | | | | |
| ***Cost of generating funds:*** | | | | | |
| Fund-raising costs | | 480 | 210 | **690** | 550 |
| Building appeal costs | 17 | – | 45 | **45** | 110 |
| Merchandising costs | 4 | 870 | – | **870** | 710 |
| Investment management fees | | 80 | 10 | **90** | 110 |
| | | 1,430 | 265 | **1,695** | 1,480 |
| ***Charitable expenditure:*** | | | | | |
| Costs of activities in furtherance of the charity's objects: | | | | | |
| Residential care costs | | 1,400 | 1,030 | **2,430** | 2,545 |
| Childcare | | 1,000 | 2,400 | **3,400** | 3,150 |
| Emergency services | | 1,800 | 1,300 | **3,100** | 2,800 |
| Information and Education | | 90 | 10 | **100** | 300 |
| Support costs | | 110 | 80 | **190** | 180 |
| Management and administration | | 210 | 60 | **270** | 230 |
| | | 4,610 | 4,880 | **9,490** | 9,405 |
| **Total resources expended** | 6 | 6,040 | 5,145 | **11,185** | 10,885 |

## Comment

**8.19** A great deal of attention continues to be paid to the ratio of the cost of generating funds to income and the revised disclosure requirements will only increase it. Most charities have a wide range of types of income which have different cost ratios. Legacy income will have a very low cost while a postal appeal could be expensive. Charities are aware of the importance of the fundraising cost ratio, particularly for donors and potential donors who often expect 100% of their donation to be used on charitable activities, and are always looking for more efficient ways of raising money so that the least efficient methods can be dropped. However, this is a difficult problem for trustees since income is money, regardless of whether the fundraising costs associated with obtaining it are 1% or 90%. When cash is needed to carry out the charity's main objects, the trustees face a dilemma when deciding whether to refuse income because its fundraising costs are too high. This is a dilemma facing more and more charities given the continued pressures on charitable giving.

**8.20** As a side issue, it is essential to stress that, when considering expending money on any form of charitable fundraising, the trustees should have given careful and full consideration to the likely response. This is in order both to ensure that the costs of fundraising are justified and to ensure that the charity receives all funds raised (ie response rates, if monitored, are a useful tool for detecting fraud).

**8.21** A few charities have as their sole purpose the raising of money for other charities, and the expenditure on direct charitable objectives therefore consists only of grants to other organisations. If donations from the public are passed a number of times from one charity to another, it would be possible, hypothetically, to extract the grants received and grants made from the accounts of a number of charities, and expose a chain of movements and perhaps even complete a circle. This situation is disturbing, since, of course, each item of income is incurring fundraising and/or administrative costs every time that it passes from one organisation to another and by the time that the donation reaches the ultimate beneficiary the amount has been considerably reduced. Again, it can be argued that this is better than not receiving it at all.

**8.22** SORP, in requiring disclosure relating to fundraising and grants payable to institutions such as other registered charities, is hopefully helping to control such situations and ensure that the Charity Commission requirement that charitable funds are properly applied is met.

## 5 CHARITABLE EXPENDITURE

**8.23** As stated above, paras 136 and 137 of SORP define direct charitable expenditure as follows:

*'Charitable expenditure comprises all the expenditure incurred by the charity in meeting its charitable objectives as opposed to the cost of raising funds to finance these activities…'*

**8.24** Paragraph 92 also requires such expenditure to be analysed between at least four sub-headings:

(i) grants payable;
(ii) activities in furtherance of the charity's objects;
(iii) support; and
(iv) management and administration of the charity.

**8.25** The analysis of charitable expenditure is one of the most important aspects of the accounts as it is the explanation of what has been spent on the objects of the charity. Considerable thought should, therefore, be given to the way in which this is done. In some cases two lines are enough as will often be the case with a grant making charity (ie grants payable and management and administation). In other cases, where the object, for example, is to provide care for the elderly, details relating to the costs of activities in furtherance of the charity's objects and support costs may require several lines. For example, more information may be expected to describe the various ways in which such care has been delivered and the amount spent on each.

## 6 GRANTS PAYABLE

**8.26** Appendix 1 of SORP defines a grant as follows:

*'A grant is any voluntary payment (or other transfer of property) in favour of a person or institution, in furtherance of the objects of the grant maker. The payment or transfer may be for the general purposes of the receipient, or for some specific purpose such as the supply of a particular service. It may be unconditional, or be subject to conditions which, if not satisfied by the recipient, may lead to the grant, or property acquired with the aid of the grant, or part of it, being reclaimed.'*

It should be noted that any payment which a charity makes in return for the supply of goods or services cannot be a grant.

**8.27** The SORP requires detailed analysis and explanation of grants payable where grant-making is material to the charity. For this purpose 'material' is defined as being equal to 5% or more of the total resources expended by a charity in any accounting period.

**8.28** The detailed analysis and explanation required will depend on whether grants are made to institutions or to individuals. SORP is very clear that a grant to an individual is one where it is made for the direct benefit of the individual who receives it, for example to relieve financial hardship. All other grants should be defined as institutional. Thus, for example, a grant that is made to an individual to carry out some research project should be regarded as a grant to the institution with which the individual is connected rather than be shown as a grant to an individual.

**8.29** Regardless of whether grants are given to individuals or to institutions, SORP requires an analysis of grant making activities to be given in the accounts which discloses the total number and the total value of the grants given for different charitable purposes. The actual classifications used will be left to the individual grant-making charity to decide but could, for example, include welfare grants, education grants, medical research grants, grants for the arts, etc. Where grant making is significant a charity might also decide to provide further analysis, for example, showing a geographical analysis of grants payable.

**Comment**

**8.30** This expanded definition of what constitutes an institutional grant (compared to the 1995 version of SORP) should encourage greater consistency in disclosure between grant-making charities. However, it will be interesting to see how grants (or bursaries) towards education costs are classified by different grant-making charities. There are clear arguments for defining such payments as both individual grants and as institutional grants. It will be necessary to look into the specific circumstances in which such grants are made before making a final decision on classification.

**Grants to institutions**

**8.31** Paragraphs 143 and 144 of SORP require the following to be disclosed with regard to grants made by a charity to institutions:

*'In addition,* **in the case of institutional grants,** *and subject to paragraph 146, the trustees should disclose details, as specified in paragraph 144, of a sufficient number of institutional grants to convey a proper understanding of the charity's grant making activities. The number of grants which is sufficient will vary with circumstances. Where a charity has made fewer than 50 material institutional grants in a year all the grants should be disclosed. Otherwise, the disclosure should cover at least the 50 largest institutional grants or any larger number which is necessary for the proper understanding of the charity's grant-making activity. There is no requirement to disclose any grants which are below £1,000 in total.'* *(para 143)*

*'The disclosure for institutional grants should include the name of the recipient institution and the number and total value of grants made to that institution in the accounting year. Where grants have been made to a particular institution for different charitable purposes, the number and total value of the grants made for each purpose should be disclosed. For example, a charity may have made grants to different officers of a particular university for different projects. As has already been explained (paragraph 141), the grants should all be treated as having been made to the institution but an analysis should be given of the number and total of grants made for each purpose.'* *(para 144)*

**Grants to individuals**

**8.32** The disclosure requirements with regard to grants made to individuals are less onerous with only the aggregate value and the number of grants needing to be disclosed.

**8.33** A detailed discussion of the specific disclosure requirements relating to grants payable is contained within Chapter 13 which deals with the notes to the accounts.

**Current practice**

**8.34** Following the publication of the 1995 version of SORP, many grant making charities now provide details of their grant making activities in much more detail than in the past. Much of the information is contained within the notes to the accounts or, where voluminous, in a separate publication as permitted by para 140 of SORP. Few charities provide details on the face of the Statement of Financial Activities itself.

*The Lord Ashdown Charitable Settlement: 5 April 2000*

**Achieving the aims and objectives i.e. Policies**

Applicants to The Lord Ashdown Charitable Settlement must reside within the UK and must provide proof of need. Organisations must provide their most recent audited accounts, a registered charity number, and most important, a cash flow for the next twelve months. Applications should have a stamped addressed envelope attached. It is also important that the actual requests for funds must be concise and preferably *summarised on one side of A4 paper.*

Due to the commitment of nearly all of the funds available, the Trustees are no longer likely to respond to unsolicited applications. In the year to 5 April 2000 The Lord Ashdown Charitable Settlement received in the region of 7,000 applications, out of which there were 361 grants (5% of 7,000) over £250. There was also a further 109 grants (1.5% of 7,000) of £250 and under; the majority of these came from the pool of unsolicited applications. Regrettably, a disappointingly large number of applications will inevitably be unsuccessful. Around 95% of the applications for grants over £250 are rejected.

*The Lord Ashdown Charitable Settlement: 5 April 2000*

**Grants payable (extract)**

During the year ended 5 April 2000 the Trust made grants, and at 5 April 2000 had commitments in respect of grants, in the following categories:

| | **Payable** | For future years | | Payable |
|---|---|---|---|---|
| | **2000** | 2002 | 2001 | 1999 |
| | **£** | £ | £ | £ |
| Arts | **160,350** | – | 40,000 | 132,200 |
| Children/youth | **85,700** | – | 7,200 | 46,700 |
| Community | **1,443,922** | 450,000 | 612,862 | 1,771,902 |
| Disability | **–** | – | 15,500 | – |
| Education | **764,130** | 775,000 | 940,000 | 1,281,801 |
| Hospice and aged | **13,000** | – | – | 15,000 |
| Interfaith/race | **413,650** | 40,000 | 126,800 | 168,850 |
| Medical | **5,000** | – | 5,500 | 53,300 |
| Mental health | **4,500** | – | – | – |
| Preventative medicine | **38,000** | – | 4,000 | 52,500 |
| Students | **50,463** | – | 2,450 | 66,906 |
| Grants of £250 or under | **23,109** | – | – | 22,252 |
| | **3,001,824** | 1,265,000 | 1,754,312 | 3,611,411 |

In addition to the commitments existing at 5 April 2000, the charity has entered into a guarantee agreement whereby it guarantees the salary and pension contributions of the director of the London College of Jewish Studies (formerly Jews' College) for a period of three years commencing 1 May 2000. [*continued on following page*]

*The Lord Ashdown Charitable Settlement, continued*

The largest 50 grants made to Institutions during the year were as follows:

| Recipient | Charity registration number | Purpose of Grant | £ |
|---|---|---|---|
| **Arts** | | | |
| Ebony Steel Band Trust | 308026 | African Caribbean Youth | **72,000** |
| Lyndons Arts Trust | 1060068 | Community arts | **15,000** |
| Stephen Spender Memorial Trust | 1069077 | Artistic development | **20,000** |
| Yaa Asantewaa Arts Centre | 271449 | Black community arts | **55,000** |
| **Children/Youth** | | | |
| Jewish Child's Day | 209266 | Children of Chernobyl | **15,000** |

*Edith Cavell and Nation's Fund for Nurses: 31 December 1999*

**1 Grants paid**

During the year 467 (1998 — 423) grants were paid to individuals with an aggregate value of £113,809 (1998 — £109,735).

## Comment

**8.35** As discussed in Chapter 13 the requirements with regard to grant disclosure continue to cause some disquiet in the charity world. However, as explained in **8.21** above, the added disclosure will provide a means of controlling the situation where donations from the public are passed from one grant making body to another, gradually being eroded before being passed over to the ultimate beneficiary.

## 7 COSTS OF ACTIVITIES IN FURTHERANCE OF THE CHARITY'S OBJECTS AND SUPPORT COSTS

**8.36** Paragraph 147 of SORP requires costs incurred in furtherance of a charity's objects to be analysed on the face of the Statement of Financial Activities using a functional classification:

*'Expenditure on activities in furtherance of the charity's objects (ie on the provision of services or of goods) should be appropriately analysed by the activities of the charity (functional classification) to assist the reader of the accounts in understanding how the charity spends its resources. This should mirror the operational activities in furtherance of the charity's objects in the incoming resources section but may have additional activities which do not generate incoming resources.'* *(para 147)*

**8.37** Costs which cannot be classified as being directly related to the furtherance of a charity's objects may be deemed support costs and should be shown separately on the face of the Statement of Financial Activities. Appendix 1 of SORP defines support costs as follows:

*'"Support costs" of charitable activities comprise costs incurred directly in support of expenditure on the objects of the charity, and can therefore be considered as part of total expenditure directly relating to the objects of the charity. Such costs will include all services (either at headquarters or through a regional network) which are identifiable as wholly or mainly in support of the charity's project work or other charitable expenditure (excluding management and administration costs) if — but only if — they are an integral part of the cost of carrying out the direct charitable objectives of the charity.'*

## Current practice

**8.38** Most charities show the costs of furthering their objects to maximum advantage.

**8.39** Some charities have a tendency to show too much detail on the face of the Statement of Financial Activities so that one loses sight of the essential features of the expenditure. The functional classification of direct charitable expenditure on the face of the Statement of Financial Activities should be sufficiently simple to allow the reader an understanding of the main areas of activity of the charity. If deemed necessary additional detail can be given within the notes to the accounts both as regards the functional classification and the natural classification of the expenditure (see Chapter 13). The extract from the accounts of the Alzheimer's Disease Society on the following page is a good example of the functional classification of expenditure, as is the Aid Overseas example within CC66 — SORP 2000: Example reports and accounts.

## Comment

**8.40** Paragraph 149 of SORP recommends analysis of expenditure in a manner appropriate to the charity but consistent with the classifications used for incoming resources from operating activities. The analysis should enable the reader to gain an understanding of how the charity spends its resources without being excessively detailed. In an effort simply to comply with the legal accounting requirements of the Companies Act or other statutory requirements, or to satisfy the requirements of one particular user of the charity's accounts, the charity accountant or treasurer has, in the past, often overlooked this simple and fundamental responsibility. It is therefore recommended that the analysis of the costs of activities in furtherance of the charity's activities is regularly reviewed, and that occasionally this is done by someone not closely involved with the charity, to ensure that the main elements are being properly communicated.

*Alzheimer's Disease Society: 31 March 1999*

| **Resources expended** | Notes | Restricted funds £ | Unrestricted funds £ | 1999 Group Total £ | 1998 Group Total £ |
|---|---|---|---|---|---|
| Direct charitable expenditure: | | | | | |
| Care services | | 2,995,153 | 3,615,415 | **6,610,568** | 5,861,798 |
| Information and education | | 294,769 | 1,092,914 | **1,387,683** | 1,477,084 |
| Research, caring and other grants | 7 | 890,693 | 160,446 | **1,051,139** | 510,881 |
| Regional development and branch activities | | 3,190,565 | 1,337,484 | **4,528,049** | 4,164,348 |
| | | 7,371,180 | 6,206,259 | **13,577,439** | 12,014,111 |
| Other expenditure: | | | | | |
| Fundraising | | 100,730 | 1,011,444 | **1,112,174** | 1,009,242 |
| Management and administration | 5 and 8 | 121,434 | 220,663 | **342,097** | 240,501 |
| | | 222,164 | 1,232,107 | **1,454,271** | 1,249,743 |
| Total resources expended | 5 | 7,593,344 | 7,438,366 | **15,031,710** | 13,263,854 |

*CC66 — SORP 2000: Example reports and accounts (Aid Overseas)*

| | | Unrestricted funds £,000 | Restricted funds £,000 | **2000 Total £,000** | 2000 Total £,000 |
|---|---|---|---|---|---|
| **Charitable expendiure** | | | | | |
| Costs of activities in furtherance of the objects of the charity: | 7 | | | | |
| Grants payable to partner organisations | 7, 8 | 1,286 | 2,239 | **3,525** | 3,829 |
| Operational programmes | 7 | 1,032 | 4,578 | **5,610** | 5,892 |
| Gifts in kind | 7 | 239 | 1,092 | **1,331** | 1,296 |
| Information, campaigning & education | 7 | 984 | 9 | **993** | 917 |
| Support costs | 9 | 1,502 | 404 | **1,906** | 1,845 |
| Managing and administering the charity | 10 | 470 | 2 | **472** | 466 |
| **Total charitable expenditure** | | 5,513 | 8,324 | **13,837** | 14,245 |

## 8 MANAGEMENT AND ADMINISTRATION OF THE CHARITY

**8.41** Paragraph 151 of SORP defines costs relating to the management and administration of the charity as follows:

*'Expenditure on the management and administration of the charity will normally include both direct and indirect costs under this heading. Direct costs will include such items as internal and external audit, legal advice for trustees and costs associated with constitutional and statutory requirements eg the cost of trustee meetings and preparing statutory accounts. There should also be an apportionment of indirect costs involved in managing and administrating the charity, (as distinct from directly pursuing its charitable activities). This will include a proportion of management (and other staff) time and the overhead costs connected with it, eg office and communications costs.'*

*(para 151)*

**8.42** Paragraph 152 of SORP requires:

*'There should be a clear analysis of all the major items of expenditure on management and administration shown in the notes to the accounts.'*

*(para 152)*

## Current practice

**8.43** Most charities separate their administrative expenses from other categories of expenditure. We have found no examples where administrative expenditure has been shown other than gross on the face of the Statement of Financial Activities.

**8.44** In addition most charities are providing some details of the expenditure analysed to this heading in the notes to their accounts.

## Comment

**8.45** It would be misleading to deduct a grant from management and administration expenses, thereby hiding the true amount of the expenditure on the face of the accounts.

**8.46** Even though grants or donations may be received specifically to defray certain management and administration expenses they should still be included as an incoming resource and not deducted from expenditure.

*Church Housing Trust: 31 March 2000*

**5 Management and administration of the charity**

| | Unrestricted funds £ | Restricted funds £ | **Total 2000 £** | Total 1999 £ |
|---|---|---|---|---|
| Staff costs | 36,308 | – | **36,308** | 38,735 |
| Office costs | 34,995 | – | **34,995** | 30,575 |
| Legal and professional fees | 3,308 | – | **3,308** | (325) |
| Audit and accountancy fees | 4,406 | – | **4,406** | 4,539 |
| Interest payable and similar charges | 2,404 | – | **2,404** | 4,624 |
| | 81,421 | – | **81,421** | 78,148 |

*The Trust of St Benedict's Abbey, Ealing: 31 December 1999*

**7 Management and administration of the charity**

| | Unrestricted funds £ | Restricted funds £ | **Total 1999 £** | Total 1998 £ |
|---|---|---|---|---|
| Professional fees and charges | 32,542 | – | **32,542** | 28,342 |
| Bank charges | 5,693 | 20 | **5,713** | 5,161 |
| Other costs | 4,520 | – | **4,520** | 2,592 |
| | 42,755 | 20 | **42,775** | 36,095 |

**8.47** Management and administration can mean very different things to different people and within different organisations, and because of the flexibility which is possible concerning the definition, it is important that the basis which is used to determine management and administration expenses should be shown among the accounting policies in the notes to the accounts.

**8.48** Many charities remain concerned at the ratio of their management and administration costs to other costs, particularly those expended on direct charitable objectives, and this ratio continues to be a measure by which charities are judged and assessed. Unfortunately, such assessments are often misleading, particularly if comparing incompatible charity structures. Nevertheless, the pressure on charity trustees to reduce management and administration expenses remains, and the temptation to analyse expenses to other headings still exists. We see many examples where management and administration comprises of little more than the annual audit fee! It is important for the charity sector, and the wider public, to realise that a significant amount of such expenditure is essential if the charity is to carry out its objectives efficiently, effectively and professionally. Charities which include only their audit fee as a management and administration expense are failing to present an accurate picture of their affairs and are not complying with SORP.

**8.49** The definition of management and administration expenses will vary depending on the type and size of the charity, and careful thought will be needed in deciding on the principles to be applied in allocating expenditure to this head.

## 9 CAPITAL EXPENDITURE

### Current practice

**8.50** Most charities now capitalise expenditure on tangible fixed assets for use by the charity as required by Financial Reporting Standard 15 (FRS 15) 'Tangible Fixed Assets' and para 190 of SORP. However, there are some charities which, even though the expenditure has been incurred for the purpose of acquiring assets of a long-term nature which will be used to carry on the activities of the charity, write off the expenditure in the year in which it is incurred (eg many schools write off capital expenditure on buildings, equipment and furniture).

### Comment

**8.51** Those charities which treat capital expenditure as revenue thereby reduce their net movement on funds and reduce the assets shown on their balance sheet. While this might be deemed useful for fundraising purposes, it is incorrect and misleading and should be changed to conform with FRS 15 and the SORP.

**8.52** The treatment of tangible fixed assets is dealt with more fully in Chapter 10. Paragraph 192 of SORP states as a general principle:

*'. . . tangible fixed assets should initially be included at their cost of acquisition including costs that are directly attributable to bringing the assets into working condition for their intended use. This can include costs of interest on loans to finance the construction of such assets but only where the charity has adopted this as a policy for all tangible fixed assets and capitalisation should cease when the asset is ready for use. This applies whether assets are bought outright or through hire purchase or finance leasing.'* *(para 192)*

**8.53** The definition contained within SORP should be sufficient to enable charities to decide what expenditure is of a capital nature.

**8.54** Where, therefore, expenditure is incurred by a charity to acquire assets of a permanent nature which will be used to carry out its objectives on an on-going basis, then that expenditure should be treated as capital expenditure and shown on the balance sheet. If the expenditure is incurred to acquire assets which will be consumed within 12 months, then it would be incorrect to capitalise such expenditure, and it should be written off to the Statement of Financial Activities in the year in which it is incurred.

## 10 COMPANIES ACT 1985 FORMATS: APPLICATION TO CHARITIES

### Current practice

**8.55** The Companies Act 1985 Sch 4 requires that all companies prepare their profit and loss accounts in one of two standard formats, either vertical or horizontal, and then in accordance with one of two expense classifications, analysed by either the:

(i) type of operation or purpose, for example cost of sales, distribution costs, administrative expenses etc; or
(ii) type of expenditure, for example purchase of raw materials, staff costs, depreciation etc.

### Comment

**8.56** Most incorporated charities appear to have little difficulty in analysing expenditure so as to comply with SORP and the Companies Act. The first type of expenditure analysis permitted by the Companies

Act corresponds to the functional analysis of expenditure required by SORP to be shown on the face of the Statement of Financial Activities. The second type of expenditure corresponds to the natural classification that should be used in the notes to the charity's accounts under SORP. Hence very few charities should experience problems in complying with both SORP and the Companies Act 1985.

**8.57** Some charities continue to claim that they should be exempted from the SORP and charity accounting requirements. They argue that SORP is only recommended practice and that there is no legal requirement under the Charities Act 1993 for companies to comply with the Charities (Reports and Accounts) Regulations 1995 (other than r 10 regarding annual reports) or SORP. However, this issue has been addressed by the Auditing Practices Board in their guidance to auditors of charities. This guidance states that if the accounts of an incorporated charity are to show a true and fair view then they must comply with SORP. The actual guidance is as follows:

*'Charities which are incorporated under the Companies Act 1985 are required to meet that Act's requirements for the preparation of annual accounts which give a true and fair view of the charitable company's state of affairs at the end of the year and income and expenditure for that year.*

*There is no reference in the Companies Act 1985 to the provisions of the Charities SORP, and trustees of charitable companies are not required to state whether the financial statements have been prepared in accordance with the SORP or to give particulars of any material departure and the reasons for it. Nevertheless, the development and issue of a SORP following the ASB code of practice provides guidance on the application of accounting standards in a manner which takes account of the particular circumstances of a particular type of entity. Consequently, compliance with the requirements of the charities SORP will normally be necessary in order to give the true and fair view required by company law.*

*The form of the auditors' opinion on financial statements of a charitable company includes the expression of opinion on the incoming resources and application of resources, reflecting the SORP's specific primary statement dealing with financial activities of the charities. The wording used in the illustrative examples however recognises that the statement of financial activity is integral to the financial statements as a whole and is considered necessary to give a true and fair view for statutory purposes.'*

**8.58** Thus the overriding factor in deciding whether to depart from the SORP, and to what extent, must be whether such changes are necessary in order to give a true and fair view.

## 11 VAT

### Current practice

**8.59** SSAP 5 requires irrecoverable VAT to be included with the expenditure to which it relates.

**8.60** The majority of charities follow the standard, not necessarily as a positive accounting policy, but probably because it simplifies the bookkeeping entries.

*NCH Action For Children: 31 March 2000*

**Value Added Tax**

As part of NCH's activities are classified as exempt or non-business activities for the purposes of VAT, NCH is unable to reclaim all the VAT which it suffers on its operating costs. Expenditure in these financial statements is therefore shown inclusive of VAT paid.

**8.61** Some charities, however, particularly those in the anomalous position of having to pay VAT while similar state-run operations are able to reclaim it, extract VAT, show the expenditure net and group all the VAT borne as a separate charge disclosed under both 'the cost of generating funds' and 'the cost of activities in furtherance of the charity's objects' as appropriate.

**8.62** Other charities calculate the total sum of irrecoverable VAT paid by them and show this as a separate note in their accounts.

*Macmillan Cancer Relief: 31 December 1998*

**Note 6 Total resources expended**

| | Staff Costs £'000 | Depreciation £'000 | Grant Payments £'000 | Other Costs £ | **1998 Total £'000** | Restated 1997 Total £'000 |
|---|---|---|---|---|---|---|
| Direct charitable expenditure | | | | | | |
| Grants for provision of services and welfare | – | – | 34,275 | – | **34,275** | 27,735 |
| Direct provision of services | – | – | – | 745 | **745** | 594 |
| Support costs | 2,133 | 48 | – | 1,530 | **3,711** | 3,185 |
| | 2,133 | 48 | 34,275 | 2,275 | **38,731** | 31,514 |
| Other expenditure | | | | | | |
| Fundraising and publicity: staff | 6,437 | – | – | – | **6,437** | 6,035 |
| Fundraising and publicity: other expenditure | – | 330 | – | 9,690 | **10,020** | 9,884 |
| Management and administration | 287 | – | – | 287 | **574** | 582 |
| Millennium compliance costs | – | – | – | 557 | **557** | – |
| | 8,857 | 378 | 34,275 | 12,809 | **56,319** | 48,015 |
| Other costs include: | | | | | | |
| Audit fees | | | | | **36** | 34 |
| Irrecoverable VAT | | | | | **1,158** | 1,134 |
| VAT recovered in respect of previous years | | | | | **(101)** | (12) |

## Comment

**8.63** The trustees of a charity have a responsibility to the public to inform them of wasteful government burdens such as VAT suffered by their charity and we applaud those who disclose this amount in their accounts.

**8.64** There are two preferred methods of disclosing the amounts involved:

(i) to calculate the total VAT that is irrecoverable and to disclose this in a separate note to the accounts;
(ii) to calculate the total VAT irrecoverable on each of the classifications of expenditure to disclose these amounts, either on the face of the Statement of Financial Activities itself, or in the appropriate notes to the accounts supporting each class of expenditure.

CHAPTER 9

# Balance sheet presentation

## 1 GUIDELINES

**9.1** Paragraphs 181–188 of SORP give details of what is to be included in the balance sheet and how. In essence these guidelines need to be followed:

- group together the funds of the charity according to their kind, eg permanent endowment, restricted, designated and other unrestricted funds;
- analyse the assets between fixed and current distinguishing fixed assets between intangible fixed assets, tangible fixed assets and investments;
- analyse liabilities between current and long-term liabilities.

**9.2** Paragraph 182 of SORP says that: *'the objective of the balance sheet is to show the resources available to the charity and whether these are freely available or have to be used for specific purposes because of legal restrictions on their use. . .'*

**9.3** Paragraph 186 emphasises that the assets and liabilities should be analysed in a way that enables the reader to gain a proper appreciation of their spread and character.

### Comment

**9.4** The format of the balance sheet of a charity is both familiar and conventional. The important addition is the need to provide a statement showing the division of the assets and liabilities between the main funds of the charity. This can be done either as a separate statement following the Statement of Financial Activities, or as a note.

*Corporation of Trinity House of Deptford Strond: 31 March 2000*

## COMBINED BALANCE SHEET OF THE CORPORATE CHARITY AND TRINITY HOMES AND MARINERS' CHARITY

## at 31 March 2000

| | | ***2000*** | | ***1999*** | |
|---|---|---|---|---|---|
| | **Notes** | **£** | **£** | **£** | **£** |
| **FIXED ASSETS** | | | | | |
| Tangible fixed assets | 12 | | **7,833,710** | | 7,549,395 |
| Investments | 13 | | **41,539,977** | | 38,813,100 |
| | | | **49,373,687** | | 46,362,495 |
| **CURRENT ASSETS** | | | | | |
| Debtors | 14 | **538,273** | | 263,225 | |
| Cash at bank and on deposit | | **294,637** | | 397,368 | |
| | | **832,910** | | 660,593 | |
| **CURRENT LIABILITIES:** amounts falling due within one year | 15 | **601,934** | | 518,061 | |
| **NET CURRENT ASSETS** | | | **230,976** | | 142,532 |
| **NET ASSETS** | | | **49,604,663** | | 46,505,027 |
| **FUNDS** | | | | | |
| *Corporate Charity:* | | | | | |
| Designated funds | 16 | **1,903,221** | | 1,550,594 | |
| Other unrestricted funds | 17 | **6,611,060** | | 6,314,147 | |
| Restricted funds | 18 | **38,907** | | 30,668 | |
| | | | **8,553,188** | | 7,895,409 |
| *Trinity Homes and Mariners' Charity:* | | | | | |
| Designated funds | 19 | **1,039,797** | | 802,186 | |
| Other unrestricted funds | 20 | **2,177,214** | | 2,181,464 | |
| | | **3,217,011** | | 2,983,650 | |
| Permanent endowment funds | 22 | **37,834,464** | | 35,625,968 | |
| | | | **41,051,475** | | 38,609,618 |
| **TOTAL FUNDS** | | | **49,604,663** | | 46,505,027 |

Approved on half the Corporate Board:

PB Rowe

Rear Admiral P B Rowe CBE LVO
Deputy Master, Trinity House

26 September ....2000

*Trinity House: 31 March 2000*

**23 ANALYSIS OF NET ASSETS BETWEEN FUNDS**

| | Corporate Charity | | Trinity Homes and Mariners' Charity | | | |
|---|---|---|---|---|---|---|
| | **Unrestricted funds** | **Restricted funds** | **Unrestricted funds** | **Restricted funds** | **Endowment funds** | **Total 2000** |
| | **£** | **£** | **£** | **£** | **£** | **£** |
| **Fund balances at 31 March 2000 are represented by:** | | | | | | |
| Tangible fixed assets | 6,551,939 | – | 32,271 | – | 1,249,500 | **7,833,710** |
| Investments | 1,892,947 | – | 3,327,106 | – | 36,319,924 | **41,539,977** |
| Current assets | 267,079 | 38,907 | 261,884 | – | 265,040 | **832,910** |
| Current liabilities | (197,684) | – | (404,250) | – | – | **(601,934)** |
| **Total net assets** | 8,514,281 | 38,907 | 3,217,011 | – | 37,834,464 | **49,604,663** |
| **Unrealised gains included above:** | | | | | | |
| On tangible fixed assets | 6,539,158 | – | – | – | 1,249,500 | **7,788,658** |
| On investment assets (see below) | 296,149 | – | 942,793 | – | 26,470,523 | **27,709,465** |
| | 6,835,307 | – | 942,793 | – | 27,720,023 | **35,498,123** |
| **Reconciliation of movements in unrealised gains on investment assets:** | | | | | | |
| Unrealised gains at 31 March 1999 | 123,031 | – | 705,679 | – | 24,481,484 | **25,310,194** |
| Unrealised gains on investment properties in the year | – | – | – | – | 1,008,836 | **1,008,836** |
| Net investment gains on listed investments in the year | 177,714 | – | 280,815 | – | 988,733 | **1,447,262** |
| Realised gains on listed investments calculated on historical costs | (4,596) | – | (43,701) | – | (8,530) | **(56,827)** |
| **Unrealised gains at 31 March 2000** | 296,149 | – | 942,793 | – | 26,470,523 | **27,709,465** |

## 2 GROUPING OF FUNDS

**9.5** Paragraph 183 of SORP recommends that:

*'the funds of a charity should be grouped together in the balance sheet according to their kind. It should distinguish, as a minimum, between, unrestricted income funds, restricted income funds and endowments. Distinctions between permanent and expendable endowment and designated funds can also be made.'*

**9.6** Paragraph 49 of SORP goes on to say that:

*'the notes to the accounts should provide information on the structure of the charity's funds so as to disclose the fund balances and the reasons for them,. . . in particular*

*(a)* *the assets and liabilities representing each type of fund of the charity should be clearly analysed . . .*
*(b)* *disclosure of how each of the funds has arisen, the restrictions imposed and the purpose of each fund . . .*
*(c)* *any funds in deficit should always be separately disclosed . . .*
*(d)* *explanations should be provided for material movements in funds . . .'*

## Comment

**9.7** Although the fund structure of the charity may be complex, the balance sheet should be simple showing only the year end balances of the main funds or groups of funds. These should be set out in a logical sequence, for example beginning with the restricted funds, then the designated funds and finally the balance on the unallocated unrestricted funds, often referred to as the 'general' fund. Alternatively it may be more appropriate to begin with 'Capital Funds', both restricted and unrestricted to show the amount tied up in property and endowment and move down to 'Income Funds' set aside for short-term and general purposes.

**9.8** With the help of the notes explaining the purpose of each fund within each group and the movement of each since the previous year end, the reader is in a position to appreciate the overall deployment of the assets and liabilities of the charity. A more informed judgement can also be made concerning the adequacy or otherwise of the 'free reserves' of the charity, ie those that are not already earmarked for some special purpose. The following example taken from the accounts of the British Museum shows how even a large, complex organisation can summarise this information on two pages.

*British Museum: 31 March 2000 (page one)*

**15.—Statement of funds**

| | At 1 April 1999 £000s | Income £000s | Expenditure £000s | Revaluation/ Investment gains/losses £000s | Movement during year £000s | Transfers between funds £000s | At 31 March 2000 £000s |
|---|---|---|---|---|---|---|---|
| **Funds** | | | | | | | |
| ***Capital Funds*** | | | | | | | |
| *Permanent Endowment Funds* | 9,900 | 0 | 0 | 685 | 685 | 0 | 10,585 |
| *Restricted Capital Funds* | | | | | | | |
| Collection Purchase Fund | 914 | 1,841 | 2,007 | 0 | (166) | 64 | 812 |
| Building Revaluation Fund | 226.961 | 0 | 0 | 8,041 | 8,041 | (8,036) | 226,966 |
| Estates Proceeds | 3,640 | 0 | 0 | 0 | 0 | 11,322 | 14,962 |
| Construction Projects Fund | 29,267 | 22,112 | 0 | 0 | 22,112 | (35,724) | 15,655 |
| Fixed Asset Fund | 36,720 | 0 | 540 | 0 | (540) | 36,598 | 72,778 |
| | 297,502 | 23,953 | 2,547 | 8,041 | 29,447 | 4,224 | 331.173 |

| | | | | | | | |
|---|---|---|---|---|---|---|---|
| *Unrestricted Capital Funds* | | | | | | | |
| Collection Purchase Fund | 0 | 447 | 447 | 0 | 0 | 0 | 0 |
| Building Revaluation Fund | 4,889 | 0 | 0 | 27 | 27 | 0 | 4,926 |
| Fire Safety Security Fund | 2,476 | 0 | 0 | 0 | 0 | (1,000) | 1,476 |
| Great Court Fund | 7,400 | 0 | 0 | 0 | 0 | 0 | 7,400 |
| Gallery Refurbishment Provision | 0 | 0 | 0 | 0 | 0 | 62 | 62 |
| Maintenance Reserve | 824 | 0 | 0 | 0 | 0 | (324) | 500 |
| Construction Projects Fund | 4,234 | 325 | 0 | 0 | 325 | 0 | 4,559 |
| Fixed Asset Fund | 13,637 | 4,337 | 2,422 | 0 | 1,915 | 1,000 | 16,552 |
| | 33,470 | 5,109 | 2,869 | 27 | 2,267 | (262) | 35,475 |
| **Total Museum Capital Funds** | 340,872 | 29,062 | 5,416 | 8,753 | 32,399 | 3,962 | 377,233 |
| British Museum Co Ltd Fixed Assets | 315 | 0 | 262 | (7) | (269) | 1,005 | 1,051 |
| ***Total Consolidated Capital Funds*** | 341,187 | 29,062 | 5,678 | 8,746 | 32,130 | 4,967 | 378,284 |
| ***Revenue Funds*** | | | | | | | |
| *Restricted Revenue Funds* | | | | | | | |
| Restricted Income Trust Funds | 3,366 | 0 | 50 | 195 | 145 | (448) | 3,063 |
| Deferred Income Fund | 2,646 | 2,521 | 1,821 | | 700 | (288) | 3,058 |
| | 6.012 | 2,521 | 1,871 | 195 | 845 | (736) | 6,121 |
| *Unrestricted Revenue Funds* | | | | | | | |
| Unrestricted Trust Funds | 7,616 | 211 | 76 | 118 | 253 | 448 | 8,317 |
| Oriental Research Fund | 128 | 6 | 22 | 0 | (16) | 0 | 112 |
| Reorganisation Reserve | 621 | 0 | 0 | 0 | 0 | (500) | 121 |
| General Funds | 507 | 35,597 | 35,965 | 3,635 | 3,267 | (3,174) | 600 |
| | 8,872 | 35,814 | 36,063 | 3,753 | 3,504 | (3,226) | 9,150 |
| **Total Museum Revenue Funds** | 14,884 | 38,335 | 37,934 | 3,948 | 4,349 | (3,962) | 15,271 |
| British Museum Co Ltd | 5,073 | 9,512 | 9,326 | (65) | 121 | (1,005) | 4,189 |
| ***Total Consoldiated Revenue Funds*** | 19,957 | 47,847 | 47,260 | 3,883 | 4,470 | (4,967) | 19,460 |
| **Total Funds** | 361,144 | 76,909 | 52,938 | 12,629 | 36,600 | 0 | 397,744 |

## *British Museum: 31 March 2000 (page two)*

**Analysis of group net assets between funds**

| | Permanent Endowments £000s | Unrestricted Funds £000s | Restricted Funds £000s | Total 2000 £000s |
|---|---|---|---|---|
| Fund balances at 31 March 2000 are represented by: | | | | |
| Tangible Fixed Assets | | 22,528 | 299,744 | 322,272 |
| Fixed Asset Investments | 10,511 | 8,067 | 2,678 | 21,256 |
| Current Assets | 153 | 35,338 | 34,872 | 70,363 |
| Current Liabilities | (79) | (15,125) | | (15,204) |
| Early retirement provision | | (943) | | (943) |
| Total Net Assets | 10,585 | 49,865 | 337,294 | 397,744 |
| **Unrealised gains included above** | | | | |
| On investments | 868 | 158 | 196 | 1,222 |
| Total unrealised gains at 31 March 2000 | 868 | 158 | 196 | 1,222 |

The Trustees consider that sufficient resources are held in an appropriate form to enable each fund to be applied in accordance with any restriction imposed.

**Capital: Permanent Endowment Funds**

These consist of funds for which only the income can be used. The major part consists of the Brooke-Sewell Permanent Fund. This was established by Mr Percy Thomas Brooke-Sewell with a series of benefactions made during his lifetime specifically for the purchase of Oriental antiquities and works of art.

The Bell Fund is a permanent endowment for which the Trustees of the British Museum act as custodians. The beneficiary of this is the British School of Archaeology in Iraq.

**Capital Funds: Restricted**

These consist of a number of funds for major Museum refurbishment schemes, including monies given towards the Great Court Scheme, which is the Museum's Millennium Project, and for redevelopment of the site now the British Library has vacated the premises.

**Capital Funds: Unrestricted**

These consist of funds designated by the Trustee for various purposes and include:

(a) *Fire Safety and Security*

Monies designated for use in carrying out necessary works to ensure that the Museum complies with the statutory requirements needed to make the Museum a safe and secure environment for public and staff, and to renew the electrical infrastructure.

(b) *Great Court*

The Trustees have set aside £7,400,000 to underwrite the capital costs of the Great Court Scheme.

**Restricted Trust Funds**

These consist of a number of funds where the donor has specified the use to which they may be put. The major funds are as follows:

(a) *Ready Bequest*

A bequest from Miss M Ready to be used for the purchase of Greek and Roman antiquities.

(b) *Sharpe Bequest*

A bequest from Dr D Sharpe to be used for the purchase of books concerned with Ancient Greece or Rome.

(c) *Brooke-Sewell Bequest*

A bequest from Mr P Brooke-Sewell to be used for the purchase of Oriental and Japanese antiquities.

**Unrestricted Trust Funds**

(a) *Shaw Fund*

Agreement is currently being sought from the Charity Commission to share this fund equally with the British Library. However this is subject to any prior call the Museum may have to meet any funding shortfall for the Great Court construction costs. The split referred to above will not be effected until the Great Court project has been completed and all costs settled.

**Revenue: Designate Funds**

*Oriental Reasearch Fund*

A fund established mainly for travel to China in connection with research and fieldwork and for the funding of Chinese academics and students whilst working or studying at the British Museum.

## 3 FIXED ASSETS

**9.9** The principles for the inclusion of intangible and tangible fixed assets are set out in paras 189–241 of SORP. The fact that over 50 paragraphs are devoted to the subject explains why there are two chapters in this book to examine the issues.

**9.10** Fixed assets will include:

- intangible assets held for the charity's use, such as intellectual property;
- tangible assets held for the charity's use, such as freehold land and buildings, leaseholds, plant machinery and motor vehicles, fixtures, fittings and equipment and payments on account of assets in course of construction;
- investments, including investment properties.

**9.11** The values at which fixed assets should be included in the balance sheet are discussed in Chapter 10.

**9.12** It will be seen that a separation must be made between fixed assets held for the charity's use and those held for investment purposes. Where part of a building occupied by the charity is sub-let to provide rental income, an apportionment may be made, if material. Otherwise the primary use of the asset should be the deciding factor — see para 197 of SORP.

**9.13** It is no longer necessary to distinguish between tangible fixed assets used for direct charitable objects and those used for fundraising or administration.

## Comment

**9.14** Under the old SORP it was necessary to spend time apportioning floor space to different activities. Now this only applies to assets used partly for functional use and partly for investment. Even then para 197 of SORP encourages 100% allocation to the principal use rather than apportionment. The following example taken from the 1996 accounts of the National Trust shows the degree of apportionment that was previously required and now will no longer be necessary.

*The National Trust: 29 February 1996*

**Note 15 – Fixed Assets**

| | | Administrative | Properties | Plant Equipment | Motor |
|---|---|---|---|---|---|
| | **Total** | **Freehold** | **Leashold** | **Computers** | **Vehicles** |
| | **£000** | **£000** | **£000** | **£000** | **£000** |
| Cost as at 1 March 1995 | **36,670** | **3,221** | **490** | **24,417** | **8,542** |
| Additions | **5,828** | – | – | **4,929** | **899** |
| Disposals | **(3,075)** | – | – | **(562)** | **(2,513)** |
| Cost as at 29 February 1996 | **39,423** | **3,221** | **490** | **28,784** | **6,928** |

[*continued on following page*]

*The National Trust, continued*

| | | | | | |
|---|---|---|---|---|---|
| Accumulated depreciation as at 1 March 1995 | **20,311** | **–** | **452** | **13,973** | **5,886** |
| Charge for the year | **4,665** | **–** | **3** | **3,373** | **1,289** |
| Disposals | **(2,564)** | **–** | **–** | **(491)** | **(2,073)** |
| Accumulated depreciation as at 29 February 1996 | **22,412** | **–** | **455** | **16,855** | **5,102** |
| Net book amount as at 29 February 1996 | **17,011** | **3,221** | **35** | **11,929** | **1,826** |
| Net book amount as at 28 February 1995 | 16,359 | 3,221 | 38 | 10,444 | 2,656 |

The net book amount at 29 February 1996 represents Fixed Assets used for:

| | **Total £000** | **Direct Charitable Purposes £000** | **Fund-raising £000** | **Membership and publicity £000** | **Administration £000** | **Enterprises £000** |
|---|---|---|---|---|---|---|
| Administrative properties – freehold | **3,221** | **1,761** | **–** | **–** | **1,460** | **–** |
| – leasehold | **35** | **–** | **–** | **–** | **–** | **35** |
| Plant, equipment and computers | **11,929** | **1,976** | **20** | **2,258** | **3,100** | **4,575** |
| Motor vehicles | **1,826** | **1,681** | **–** | **30** | **24** | **91** |
| Total 1996 | **17,011** | **5,418** | **20** | **2,288** | **4,584** | **4,701** |
| Total 1995 | 16,359 | 6,256 | 25 | 2,324 | 3,510 | 4,244 |

A charge for the use of assets is made by the National Trust to The National Trust (Enterprises) Limited

## 4 CURRENT ASSETS

**9.15** Current assets will include:

- stock and work in progress;
- debtors, analysed in the notes between trade debtors, amounts due from subsidiary or associated undertakings, other debtors, prepayments and accrued income;
- investments which are to be realised without reinvestment of the sale proceeds (see para 231 of SORP);
- cash at bank and in hand.

### Comment

**9.16** Paragraph 186 of SORP draws attention to the need to analyse assets and liabilities in a way that enables '*the reader to gain a proper appreciation of their spread and character*'. It may therefore be appropriate to show separately on the face of the balance sheet a significant debtor, for example, which might otherwise be hidden in the notes distorting comparison with the previous year.

**9.17** Similarly, where debts or amounts due from subsidiary or associated undertakings remain outstanding for more than 12 months, consideration should be given as to whether they are current assets at all. Perhaps they should be reclassified as loans and included in investments. If so, the terms of interest, repayment and security may also require consideration. Indeed this may raise the question whether the loan is either a qualifying investment for tax purposes or a justifiable use of charity funds from the point of view of the Charity Commission.

## 5 LIABILITIES

**9.18** Liabilities should be analysed between their current and long term elements. Paragraph 247 of SORP recommends that:

*'The totals for both short-term and long-term creditors should each be separately analysed in the notes giving amounts for the following:*

- *loans and overdrafts*
- *trade creditors*
- *amounts due to subsidiary and associated undertakings*
- *other creditors*
- *accruals*
- *deferred income.'*

**Comment**

**9.19** The presentation of liabilities in the manner recommended is simple enough to follow. The main area of difficulty is in deciding what is a liability. For example, when does a contingent liability warrant inclusion as a provision; or when does a decision by the trustees amount to a legal commitment? These aspects are considered in Chapter 11.

CHAPTER 10

# Fixed assets, valuations and depreciation

## 1 GUIDELINES

**10.1** Paragraph 190 of SORP reminds us that *'Financial Reporting Standard 15 (FRS15) "Tangible Fixed Assets" requires that all fixed assets should be capitalised on initial acquisition and included in the balance sheet at cost or valuation. . .'*

**10.2** The value at which such fixed assets should be included in the balance sheet depends upon the nature of the assets. These are considered under the following heads:

- intangible fixed assets should be included in accordance with Financial Reporting Standard 10 (FRS 10) 'Goodwill and Intangible Assets' —*para 189;*
- tangible fixed assets held for charity use—at cost or valuation, less depreciation—*para 190;*
- tangible fixed assets which are classed as inalienable and historic assets—may be excluded from the balance sheet in certain limited circumstances—*para 211;*
- fixed assets held as investments—at market value—*para 232.*

**10.3** Current assets will normally be included at the lower of cost and net realisable value. An exception will occur where investments are transferred from fixed assets to current assets with a view to their disposal and non-reinvestment as described in para 231 of SORP. In that case they should be included at market value even if that is in excess of cost.

Liabilities should be included in the balance sheet at their settlement value—para 243 of SORP.

## 2 RELEVANT ACCOUNTING STANDARDS

**10.4** Generally accepted accounting practice (GAAP) is to write off the amount spent on an asset over its estimated useful life. This is enshrined in FRS 15. If the asset has no cost because it was a gift or because it was written off in the past, an estimate of its present value and its life expectancy should be made and the asset should be capitalised at that value with an appropriate charge for depreciation in future years to reduce the value to nil at the end of its useful life. Regard should also be had to FRS 11 regarding the impairment of assets. Thus, if the carrying book value of the asset is in excess of the market value an additional charge for depreciation may be required—para 229 of SORP.

### Comment

**10.5** The Accounting Standards Board allows very little latitude for variance from the principles set out in Financial Reporting Standards. This is understandable as otherwise the standards would be steadily eroded. One fundamental principle is that expenditure on an asset should be matched against the period over which the asset is used. This is not a new principle but it is new to many charity trustees, particularly school governors, who may have been used to writing off capital expenditure on buildings, furniture, motor vehicles etc in the year in which it was incurred.

**10.6** By capitalising such expenditure and depreciating if over the life of the asset, not only does the balance sheet reflect more accurately the investment made, but the Statement of Financial Activities will show the annual cost of using the asset. The resulting net book value shown in the balance sheet represents the resource available for use in future years. With this information, trustees are in a much better position to judge the age and condition of the fixed assets used by the charity and to assess the needs for their replacement.

## 3 VALUATION OF FIXED ASSETS FOR THE CHARITY'S OWN USE

**10.7** The value at which a fixed asset, used by the charity, should be included in the balance sheet is set out in paras 190–196 of SORP. Normally this will be its original cost less depreciation. Recommendations concerning the depreciation of such assets are contained in paras 198–202 of SORP, and are considered in the next section.

**10.8** Fixed assets which have been donated should be included at the value at which the gift was included in incoming resources, which should be its estimated market value at the time of the gift. For those assets which have not been capitalised for some years, it may be difficult to ascertain the original cost or even the value at the date of gift. It should however be possible to make *'a reasonable estimate of the asset's cost or current value to the charity. Such a valuation will be regarded as the asset's initial carrying amount and will not be regarded as a revaluation'—(para 195).*

**10.9** Fixed assets which are inalienable or historic, such as ancient monuments, historic buildings or a collection of artistic or scientific works should be included in a separate line in the balance sheet to distinguish them from the other fixed assets used by the charity or held as investments—para 208 of SORP. The value at which such assets are included can be problematical and is considered below in **10.13ff**. There is however a let out contained in para 211 of SORP:

*'It may be difficult or costly to attribute a cost or value to inalienable and historic assets. In such cases these assets may be excluded from the balance sheet if:*

*(a)* *reliable cost information is not available and conventional valuation approaches lack sufficient reliability; or*
*(b)* *significant costs are involved which may be onerous compared with the additional benefit derived by users of the accounts in assessing the trustees' stewardship of the assets.'*

**Comment**

**10.10** Inalienable assets are those which the trustees are not permitted to sell. Historic assets might fall into either the priceless category as being rare treasures or the worthless category of white elephants. It is important for the trustees to give careful consideration to both categories if only to ensure that the treasures are identified and secure, and the white elephants are not an excessive drain on the charity's resources. Even though these may be excluded from the balance sheet under para 211 of SORP, if they are material in relation to the charity, information should be given in the notes to the accounts to explain them more fully giving, for example, details of insurance values unless such disclosure is likely to put the assets at risk of theft or vandalism (see para 215 of SORP).

**10.11** Before adopting the let out of para 215 of SORP trustees are expected to try to estimate a value of their inalienable or historic assets. This can be difficult. How, for example, do you value an asset which is adapted for a unique purpose? There is no *'market'* for it. The answer is to enquire what it, or another asset that could fulfil the same function, would cost to replace or what it might cost to rent. In many cases these questions will enable the trustees to make some reasonable estimate of the value of the asset to the charity.

**10.12** A good example of an asset which is adopted for a unique purpose is a church or temple, or even a school. It may be old or new and it may have a high replacement cost for which it is insured. But what is its current user value? If it did burn down, would the trustees replace it as it was? Or would they pocket the insurance money and merge with a neighbouring congregation or school?

**10.13** In estimating the value of such a building for inclusion in the balance sheet for the first time at anything more than a nominal figure, the trustees should concentrate on two things.

(a) If the building is likely to become redundant and is to be disposed of, consider its net realisable value. This will probably involve the services of a qualified surveyor but the cost should be met out of the eventual sale proceeds.
(b) If the building is to continue in the charity's use, compare its insured value with the amount it might cost to rent alternative space in the vicinity for the same purpose and then multiply that figure by 20. This will give the capital value of the whole property, ie land and buildings, on a yield of 5% which in 2000 terms may be regarded as reasonable.

An alternative approach is to calculate the depreciated replacement cost set out in the Royal Institution of Chartered Surveyors' Statement of Asset Valuation Practice No 3. This suggests that the gross replacement cost of a building is discounted by three factors: economic obsolescence reflecting the age and condition of the building and its cost of maintenance; functional obsolescence reflecting any change of use or need for the building in its present form; and environmental factors reflecting how the building fits in with local planning and environmental policies.

**10.14** By applying the procedures outlined above the trustees may conclude that buildings used in their charity have three different values: 'replacement as new' value based on insurance cover of £1 million; an alternative rental of £10,000 pa × 20 = £200,000; and a depreciated replacement cost of £150,000. It is suggested, in such circumstances, that the trustees adopt a figure of between £150,000 and £200,000 as the opening figure of valuation for such assets because they are clearly in a less than 'as new' condition. Subsequent additions will be included at cost and depreciation will be charged over the estimated future life of the building, say 50 years (see **10.23 ff**).

## 4 REVALUATIONS OF FIXED ASSETS, INCLUDING INVESTMENTS

**10.15** Paragraphs 218–223 of SORP deal with the procedures for revaluing fixed assets, including investments. Apart from investments, revaluation of fixed assets is optional. If a policy of revaluation is applied to one asset it must also be applied to other assets of the same class—para 218 of S0RP. The fact that they have been revalued together with the date and basis of valuation should be disclosed in the notes. Market value is defined in SORP as:

*'the price at which an asset could be, or could be expected to be, sold or acquired in a public market between a willing buyer and willing seller. For traded securities in which there is an established market, the market value basis that is to be used in the valuation for the Balance Sheet is defined as the mid-point of the quotation in the Stock Exchange Daily Official List or at a similar recognised market value. For other assets it is the trustees or valuer's best estimate of such a value.'*

**10.16** Where there is no recognised market to which to refer, the name and qualification of the person making the valuation should be disclosed. If that person is also a trustee or employee of the charity that fact should also be disclosed.

**10.17** Trustees are advised by SORP to *'use any reasonable approach to valuation at least every five years subject only to obtaining advice as to the possibility of any material movements between individual valuations'* (*para 221*). This applies particularly to unquoted shares, and land and buildings. In the former case they should consider the net assets, earnings and dividend record of the company in relation to the charity's shareholding. In the latter case they might consider having a professional valuation every five years—see paras 233 and 234 of SORP.

*British Museum: 31 March 2000*

**Notes to the accounts**

**Museum Tangible Fixed Assets**

| | | Freehold Land and Buildings £000s | Assets in the course c'struction £000s | Investment Properties £000s | Permanent Exhibitions £000s | Plant Equipment Fixtures Fittings £000s | Total £000s |
|---|---|---|---|---|---|---|---|
| Cost or valuation: | | | | | | | |
| At 1 April 1999: | Cost | 0 | 50,088 | 0 | 0 | 0 | 50,088 |
| | Valuation | 210,283 | 0 | 9,597 | 10,536 | 1,712 | 232,128 |
| Additions during the year | | 0 | 41,161 | 0 | 0 | 775 | 41,936 |
| Disposals during the year | | (755) | 0 | (7,281) | 0 | 0 | (8,036) |
| Transfers | | 779 | (3,819) | 1 | 2,992 | 47 | 0 |
| Fixed Assets Valuation Adjustment | | 8,106 | 0 | 63 | (65) | (36) | 8,068 |
| At 31 March 2000: | | 218,413 | 87,430 | 2,380 | 13,463 | 2,498 | 324,184 |
| | Cost | | 87,430 | 0 | 0 | 0 | 87,430 |
| | Valuation | 218,413 | 0 | 2,380 | 13,463 | 2,498 | 236,754 |
| | | 218,413 | 87,430 | 2,380 | 13,463 | 2,498 | 324,184 |
| Depreciation: | | | | | | | |
| At 1 April 1999: | | 0 | 0 | 0 | 0 | 0 | 0 |
| Provided during the year | | 1,795 | 0 | 0 | 540 | 627 | 2,962 |
| Fixed Asset Valuation Adjustment | | 0 | 0 | 0 | 0 | 0 | 0 |
| At 31 March 2000 | | 1,795 | 0 | 0 | 540 | 627 | 2,962 |
| Net Book Value: | | | | | | | |
| At 31 March 2000 | | 216,618 | 87,430 | 2,380 | 12,923 | 1,871 | 321,222 |
| At 31 March 1999 | | 210,283 | 50,088 | 9,597 | 10,536 | 1,712 | 282,216 |
| Net book value at 31 March 2000 represents fixed assets for: | | | | | | | |
| Directly charitable activities | | 213,057 | 85,993 | 2,341 | 12,711 | 1,840 | 315,942 |
| Other activities | | 3,561 | 1,437 | 39 | 212 | 31 | 5,280 |
| | | 216,618 | 87,430 | 2,380 | 12,923 | 1,871 | 321,222 |

The historic cost of the land and buildings is not known; cumulative additions shown above represent purchases since 1 April 1999. The main Museum site at Great Russell Street was valued at 31 March 1999 on the basis of depreciated replacement cost for existing use. The other freehold buildings were valued at total worth in existing use based on open market value. Investment properties were valued at open market value. The Trustees do not consider that there is any material difference between the market value and carrying values in the accounts of any interest in land and buildings held as Fixed Assets.

All valuations were carried out for accounting purposes at 31 March 1999 by Gerald Eve, Chartered Surveyors for the main Museum building at Great Russell Street and by Kinney and Green, Chartered Surveyors for the other freehold land and buildings in accordance with the Guidance Notes issued by the Royal Institution of Chartered Surveyors.

Permanent Exhibitions and Plant, Equipment, Fixtures and Fittings have been adjusted by the application of relevant Office for National Statistics indicies to the net book value at 31 March 1999.

The valuation adjustment of £8,061,000 arises from the application of relevant indicies to the carrying values at 31 March 2000 and has not had a material impact on the depreciation charge for the year. This has been treated in the Statement of Financial Activities as an exceptional item and has not been included in the Income and Expenditure Account as it has no impact on the operating costs of the Museum.

For the present both the Study Centre and Great Court costs are included at cost under the heading Capital Assets in the course of Construction at £14.9 million and £68.1 million respectively.

The freehold of Blythe House was valued at £4,400,000 at 1 April 1989 and has not been revalued since that date. It is jointly occupied with the Science Museum and the Victoria & Albert Museum, is in the process of being transferred to the Trustees of three occupying museums from the Secretary of State for the Environment and is not included above.

**10.18** If trustees carry out a revaluation of fixed assets they should substitute the revalued amount for the book value in the balance sheet and show the resulting gain or loss in the Statement of Financial Activities—para 156 of SORP.

*The Guide Dogs for the Blind Association: 31 December 1999*

**4. Investments**

**a. Movement in Investments During the Year**

| | *1999* | *1998* |
|---|---|---|
| | *£000* | *£000* |
| Market Value at Beginning of Year | **166,919** | 154,569 |
| Acquisitions | **75,304** | 45,183 |
| (Decrease)/Increase in Cash Deposits | **(11,448)** | 6,760 |
| Disposals at Opening Market Value | **(68,332)** | (50,544) |
| Net Uplift on Revaluation | **24,550** | 10,951 |
| **Market Value at end of the Year** | **186,993** | 166,919 |

**b. Analysis of Investments**

| | *1999* | | *1998* | |
|---|---|---|---|---|
| | ***Market Value £000*** | ***Cost £000*** | *Market Value £000* | *Cost £000* |
| Listed Investments | | | | |
| United Kingdom | **120,417** | **89,927** | 107,861 | 77,514 |
| Overseas | **2,047** | **2,223** | 1,460 | 1,336 |
| | **122,464** | **92,150** | 109,321 | 78,850 |
| Unit Trusts | **60,314** | **40,914** | 41,955 | 34,203 |
| Unlisted Investments | **4** | **19** | 4 | 19 |
| Cash Deposits | **3,717** | **3,717** | 15,165 | 15,165 |
| Investment in Subsidiaries | **494** | **504** | 474 | 504 |
| | **186,993** | **137,304** | 166,919 | 128,741 |

The market value of listed investments is the mid-market price quoted on a recognised stock exchange, the value of unit trusts is the mid-bid and offer price of the units and the value of unlisted investments is as determined by Council, all as at close of business at the year end.

Included in unit trusts are two holdings representing more than 5% of the total value of investments, one a holding of £16.5m in the Mercury Asset Management Ltd 33KWS — Overseas Fund, and the other amounting to £9.8m in the 33KWS — Growth and Recovery Fund.

**10.19** In the case of fixed assets used by the charity, if the trustees do not have a policy of revaluation, they should have regard to para 207 of SORP which requires them to disclose significant differences between the carrying value and the market value of interests in land and buildings not held as investments.

**Comment**

**10.20** It is worth emphasing that, although trustees are required by FRS 15 to ascertain a cost or valuation for fixed assets used by the charity, they are under no obligation to revalue them thereafter. They must however consider their value from year to year in order to decide whether or not there is any significant difference between the book value and the market value which should be disclosed.

**10.21** If trustees decide to revalue fixed assets used by the charity they must be prepared to continue to do so every five years or on a rolling basis. This need not be an expensive process. Trustees can adopt any reasonable approach according to the circumstances.

## 5 DEPRECIATION OF FIXED ASSETS (OTHER THAN INVESTMENTS)

**Guidelines**

**10.22** Paragraph 198 of SORP reminds us that:

*'most tangible fixed assets depreciate; that is they wear out, are consumed or otherwise suffer a reduction in their useful life through use, the passing of time or obsolescence. Their value is thus gradually expended over their useful economic life. This expenditure should be recognised by means of annual depreciation charged in the Statement of Financial Activities and shown in the Balance Sheet as accumulated depreciation deducted from the value of the relevant fixed assets.'*

**Comment**

**10.23** The first point to consider is the first phrase – 'most tangible fixed assets depreciate'. Which ones do not? Obviously one hopes that investments do not, but these are considered at **10.33 ff**. Here we are concerned only with assets used by the charity. Many charities would argue that their land and buildings had appreciated in value over the years. But in reality it is only the land value that would have risen. The buildings themselves are likely to have depreciated physically and become expensive to maintain. Perhaps, however, some of the contents or fixtures are of antique and artistic interest. These may well have increased in value rather than depreciated.

**10.24** So it is important at the outset to analyse the fixed assets into categories such as land, buildings, fixtures and fittings, furniture and equipment etc. The cost or book value should be apportioned over each heading and consideration should be given to the length of life of the asset. If it is finite a depreciation policy is needed; if not it is not.

**10.25** This degree of analysis will only be necessary where the fixed assets consist of many items. In such cases it is recommended that a fixed asset register is maintained.

## 6 CALCULATION OF DEPRECIATION CHARGE AND IMPAIRMENT OF FIXED ASSETS

**10.26** Having established the estimated life of a fixed asset the annual rate of depreciation can be determined. Normally this will be established for groups of fixed assets and be disclosed in the accounting policies—para 199 of SORP.

**10.27** *'Exceptions to charging depreciation may only arise if any of the following conditions apply:*

*(a)* *the asset is freehold land. . .*
*(b)* *the depreciation charge and accumulated depreciation are not material because*
  *(i)* *the asset has a very long useful life; or*
  *(ii)* *the residual value (based on current prices) of the asset is not materially different from the carrying amount of the asset;*
  *provided the stringent conditions of Paragraphs 89–91 of FRS 15 are met and the asset is subject to an annual impairment review (except for charities under the threshold for following the FRSEE);*
*(c)* *the assets are inalienable or historic and have not been included in the balance sheet. . .'*

(*para 200*)

**Comment**

**10.28** Exception (b) above introduces the apparently contradictory notions of an asset which has not reduced in value and therefore need not be depreciated, but only provided that a review has been made to ensure that its value has not been impaired.

**10.29** Impairment of fixed assets for use by a charity is considered in paras 224–229 of SORP. Impairment occurs if a functional fixed asset's net book value is higher than its recoverable amount. *'Recoverable amount is the higher of the net realisable value and the value in use. Value in use is normally the present value of the future cash flows obtainable as a result of an asset's continued use. . .'*(*para* 225). Thus a piece of medical equipment may, as a result of technological change, have a negligible realisable value, but still be capable of generating significant income giving it a higher value in use. In such a case there may be no impairment of value.

*British Library: 31 March 2000*

**Notes to the accounts**

**Fixed assets**

**11 (a) Movements**

| | Land & Buildings £000 | Plant & Machinery £000 | Office Equipment £000 | Motor Vehicles £000 | Computer Equipment £000 | Total £000 |
|---|---|---|---|---|---|---|
| **Cost of Valuation** | | | | | | |
| At 1 April 1999 | 440,134 | 24,575 | 20,488 | 120 | 10,412 | 495,729 |
| Prior year adj | (34,201) | — | (9,524) | — | — | (43,725) |
| Recast opening balance | 405,933 | 24,575 | 10,964 | 120 | 10,412 | 452,004 |
| Additions | 191 | 720 | 13 | 24 | 741 | 1,689 |
| MHCA adjustment | 962 | — | — | — | — | 962 |
| Revaluation | 18,127 | — | — | — | — | 18,127 |
| Disposals | (3) | (163) | (172) | (34) | (1,540) | (1,912) |
| **At 31 March 2000** | 425,210 | 25,132 | 10,805 | 110 | 9,613 | 470,870 |
| **Depreciation** | | | | | | |
| At 1 April 1999 | — | 7,299 | 6,720 | 101 | 7,238 | 21,358 |
| Prior year adj | — | — | (2,540) | — | — | (2,540) |
| Recast opening balance | — | 7,299 | 4,180 | 101 | 7,238 | 18,818 |
| Charge for year | | | | | | |
| — St Pancras assets | 7,027 | 4,451 | 1,570 | — | — | 13,048 |
| — Other assets | 569 | 214 | 303 | 1 | 1,579 | 2,666 |
| Revaluation | (7,027) | — | — | — | — | (7,027) |
| MHCA Adjustment | 16 | — | — | — | — | 16 |
| Impairment | 1,470 | — | — | — | — | 1,470 |
| Elimination on Disposal | — | (152) | (160) | (34) | (1,512) | (1,858) |
| **At 31 March 2000** | 2,055 | 11,812 | 5,893 | 68 | 7,305 | 27,133 |
| **Net Book Value** | | | | | | |
| **At 31 March 2000** | 423,155 | 13,320 | 4,912 | 42 | 2,308 | 443,737 |
| At 31 March 1999 | 405,933 | 17,276 | 6,784 | 19 | 3,174 | 433,186 |

**(b) Valuations**

The land and buildings as at 31 March 2000 include seven properties valued at £33,595,000 n 31 March 1999, and one building, St Pancras, revalued at £390,652,000 on 31 March 2000, for which title or lease has been vested in the British Library Board.

| **Site** | | **Land £000** | **Buildings £000** | **Totals £000** |
|---|---|---|---|---|
| St Pancras | Freehold | 27,500 | 363,152 | 390,652 |
| Boston Spa | Freehold | 2,000 | 24,500 | 26,500 |
| Colindale Avenue | Freehold | 2,825 | 2,750 | 5,575 |
| Southampton Buildings | Freehold | 500 | 1,000 | 1,500 |
| Unit 3, Colindale Avenue | Leasehold | 5 | 15 | 20 |
| 22 Micawber Street | Leasehold | — | — | — |
| Building 25, Woolwich | Leasehold | — | — | — |
| Bindery, British Musuem | Leasehold | — | — | — |
| | | 32,830 | 391,417 | 424,247 |

[*continued on following page*]

*British Library, continued*

The St Pancras site was valued as at 31 March 2000, by CB Hillier Parker, Surveyors and Valuers, using the 'Depreciated Replacement Cost' basis of valuation. All remaining land and buildings in use by the British Library were revalued as at 31 March 1999 by Rogers Chapman, Chartered Surveyors, using the 'Worth for Existing Use' basis of valuation.

**(c) Impairment**

Subsequent to the balance sheet date (April 2000). Southampton Buildings has been sold, and the proceeds passed to the Department for Culture , Media and Sport. This has had effect of cancelling the profit rent deemed to exist at the date of the 31 March 1999 valuation, and therefore that valuation is now considered to be fully impaired at the date of this balance sheet.

| **Southampton Buildings** | **£000** |
|---|---|
| Valuation 1999 | 1,500 |
| Accumulated Depreciation | 30 |
| Net Book Value | 1,470 |
| Impairment | (1,470) |

**10.30** Where there is impairment of value, ie the recoverable amount, as defined above, is less than the net book value of the asset, *'the loss should be treated as additional depreciation'(para 229)*.

**Comment**

**10.31** Whilst one wishes to avoid tinkering with depreciation rates, once they have have been established, it is useful to consider whether the resulting net book value of the asset is materially different from its value in use. This will only apply to significant fixed assets used by the charity and the application of the impairment review procedure is likely to be rare for most charities.

## 7 FIXED ASSETS – INVESTMENTS

**Guidelines**

**10.32** Paragraph 231 of SORP recommends that investments, including investment properties and cash held for investment purposes be classified as a separate category within fixed assets. The only exception is where the investment is only being held temporarily and there is an intention to realise it without reinvestment of the proceeds. In such a case it should be reclassified as a current asset.

## Valuation

**10.33** Paragraph 232 of SORP recommends that:

*'all investment assets should be shown at market value on the Balance Sheet or at the trustees' best estimate of market value as described below. Market value best represents a true and fair view of the value of these assets to the charity, given the duty of the trustees to administer the portfolio of investment assets so as to obtain the best investment performance without undue risk. Investment assets should not be depreciated. All changes in value in the year, whether or not realised, should be reported in the gains and losses on revaluations and disposals of investment assets section of the Statement of Financial Activities.'*

**10.34** The question of ascertaining market value for each investment has already been discussed in **10.15 to 10.17 ff**.

## Analysis of investment assets

**10.35** Paragraphs 238–241 of SORP explain the degree of analysis of investments which should be given in the notes to the accounts.

**10.36** First there should be an analysis showing the general spread of investments. Typically this might include:

- investment properties;
- listed investments;
- unit trust and common investment funds;
- shares in subsidiary or associated undertakings;
- other unlisted investments;
- uninvested cash held as part of the portfolio.

**10.37** Secondly, the investments should be analysed beween those in the UK and those outside the UK. For this purpose a company which is listed in the UK is regarded as being a UK investment.

**10.38** Any investments representing over 5% by value of the portfolio should be identified separately. Also, any restrictions which might apply on the realisation of any investments should be noted—para 240 of SORP.

**10.39** Thirdly, *'the notes to the accounts should indicate the value of investments held in each type of fund. This may be included in the overall analysis of assets held in the different type of funds'—(para 241).*

*Church of England Children's Society: 31 March 2000*

**Notes to the Financial Statements for the Year Ended 31 March 2000 (continued)**

| **9 Investments** | **2000** £000 | **1999** £000 |
|---|---|---|
| Group and Society | | |
| **Classified as fixed assets:** | | |
| Being at market value | | |
| Listed investments | | |
| United Kingdom equity | 11,866 | 21,305 |
| United Kingdom fixed interest | 2,263 | 6,201 |
| United Kingdom unit trusts | 8,138 | 7,798 |
| United Kingdom other | 0 | 64 |
| Overseas fixed interest | 358 | 301 |
| Overseas unit trusts | 4,349 | 4,330 |
| Index-linked gilts | 202 | 196 |
| | 27,176 | 40,195 |
| Unlisted investments | 37 | 37 |
| Less provisions | (37) | (37) |
| | 27,176 | 40,195 |
| Being at cost | | |
| Listed investments | 17,589 | 24,532 |
| Unlisted investments | 37 | 37 |
| Less provisions | (37) | (37) |
| | 17,589 | 24,532 |
| **Movements during the year** | | |
| At 1 April | 40,195 | 42,477 |
| Purchases, legacies, donations | 6,493 | 3,186 |
| Proceeds of sales | (21,554) | (6,248) |
| Net profit on sales | 8,118 | 1,976 |
| Decrease in unrealised gains | (6,076) | (1,196) |
| At 31 March | 27,176 | 40,195 |
| **Classified as current assets** | | |
| Short term deposits | 5,564 | 1,779 |
| Staff loans | 60 | 111 |
| | 5,624 | 1,890 |

Investments exceeding 5% of the portfolio are the holding in Shroder Institutional European Fund Income Units representing 9.2% by Value (1999: 6.5%) and Vodaphone Airtouch PLC Ordinary Shares repesenting 7.25% by Value (1999: 2.53%).

CHAPTER 11

# Current assets, liabilities and reserves

## 1 CURRENT ASSETS

**11.1** *'Current assets, other than investments, should normally be recognised at the lower of cost and net realisable value.'* *(para 242)*

**11.2** An asset is current if it is available to be spent in the near future. If is is likely to take longer than 12 months to be converted into cash it is strictly not available and ought not to be included as a current asset. However see **11.4** ff for the method of inclusion of long term debtors.

**11.3** *'Where investments are held as current assets the same disclosure is required as for fixed asset investments.'* *(para 246)*

## 2 DEBTORS AND ACCRUED INCOME

**11.4** *'Debtors should be analysed in the notes to the accounts between short term and long term (above one year) giving amounts for the following:*

*(a) trade debtors;*
*(b) amounts due from subsidiary and associated undertakings;*
*(c) other debtors;*
*(d) prepayments; and*
*(e) accrued income.'* *(para 245)*

**11.5** In the case of grants it is necessary to look at the terms of the grant. Paragraphs 79 and 114–116 of SORP demonstrate the complexity of grants which may be paid in advance or in arrears or subject to conditions which make them repayable in certain circumstances. The grants should, however, be matched as far as possible against the expenditure to which they relate. If, therefore, a grant is known to be forthcoming in respect of expenditure incurred during the year it is proper to accrue the income and include the grant in the debtors.

*The Carr-Gomm Society Limited: 31 March 2000*

**Notes to the accounts**

**12 Debtors**

| | 2000 | 1999 |
|---|---|---|
| | £000 | £000 |
| Net arrears of rent and service charges | 562 | 511 |
| Revenue grants and allowances receivable | 135 | 203 |
| Social Housing Grant receivable | 405 | 59 |
| Other debtors and prepayments | 597 | 350 |
| | 1,699 | 1,123 |

Included in 'other debtors and prepayments' are staff loans of £14,916 (1999—£14,850), repayable within one year.

**11.6** Legacies should be brought into account when they are known to be receivable. If a legacy is known to be due to the charity at the balance sheet date and the amount is reasonably quantifiable and there is reasonable certainty of that amount being received in due course, then it should be included as a debtor. (See para 75 of SORP re entitlement, certainty and measurement.)

## 3 LIABILITIES

**11.7** *'The totals for both short term and long term creditors should each be separately analysed in the notes giving amounts of the following:*

*(i) loans and overdrafts;*
*(ii) trade creditors*
*(iii) amounts due to subsidiary and associated undertakings;*
*(iv) other creditors;*
*(v) accruals; and*
*(vi) deferred income.'* *(para 247)*

**11.8** A liability is current if it is due for payment within 12 months of the balance sheet date. If all or part of a liability is not due for payment until after 12 months, that part of the liability is not current and should be shown with the long-term liabilities. Care needs to be taken over the way in which liabilities are shown which are partly current and partly long term, such as amounts due on a bank loan repayable over five years.

*The Carr-Gomm Society Limited: 31 March 2000*

**Notes to the accounts**

**13 Creditors: amounts falling due within one year**

| | **2000** | **1999** |
|---|---|---|
| | **£000** | **£000** |
| Bank overdraft | 228 | – |
| Social Housing Grant recieved in Advance of scheme costs | 440 | 237 |
| Trade creditors | 384 | 620 |
| Other creditors including taxation and Social Security | 823 | 806 |
| Accruals and deffered income | 1,156 | 1,153 |
| | 3,031 | 2,816 |

**14 Creditors: amounts falling due after more than one year**

| | **2000** | **1999** |
|---|---|---|
| | **£000** | **£000** |
| **Housing property loans:** | | |
| Private Finance | 786 | 800 |
| Greenwich Natwest — residual loans | 88 | 89 |
| Local Authority loan | 38 | 38 |
| | 912 | 927 |

All of the loans are mortgages secured by charges on the Society's housing properties.

The residual loans and local Authority loan are repayable by instalments, the last instalments of which fall due on 31 July 2052

In the year ended 31 March 2000, the interest rates in force were 16.875% for the Local Authority loan (1999—16.875%) and 8.375% to 11.625% for the Greenwich NatWest fixed rate residual loans. No loans remain on the floating rate scheme. Private Finance 6% fixed over 25 years.

| | **2000** | **1999** |
|---|---|---|
| | **£000** | **£000** |
| Loans repayable in five plus years | 874 | 889 |
| Loans repayable between two and five years | 38 | 38 |
| | 912 | 927 |

**11.9** The value at which liabilities, whatever their nature, should be shown in the balance sheet is their settlement value.

## 4 COMMITMENTS

**11.10** A particular problem for charities is to decide whether commitments made before the balance sheet date should be included as liabilities or whether they should be shown as designated funds. The question is: are the trustees obliged to pay the money over, or have they simply decided to do so and are setting it aside in anticipation?

**11.11** Paragraph 119 of SORP says that *'a liability arises as soon as there is a legal or constructive obligation committing the charity to the expenditure as described in FRS 5 and 12'.*

**11.12** Paragraph 123 of SORP deals with charitable commitments where trusts have promised finanical report to a recipient as a constructive obligation. A typical example would be a promise to fund the costs of a researcher for three years without conditions such as performance targets to be met. In this case the charity, having created a valid expectation in the mind of the recipient, should include two thirds of the cost in long-term creditors and one third in short-term creditors.

**11.13** Paragraph 124 of SORP deals with the position where the commitment is dependant upon explicit conditions being met before payment is made. It goes on: *'Such conditions may prevent a grant from being a liability until they are met. However where it is reasonably certain that payment will be made, a liability should be accrued. Where a liability is not accrued such a commitment should normally be treated as a contingent liability . . .'.*

**11.14** The balance sheet treatment of those different grades of obligation is set out in paras 250–271 of SORP. Broadly speaking legal or constructive obligations should be included in full and split between liabilities due within one year and those falling due after one year. Commitments which do not amount to obligations should not be included as liabilities but particulars of any material commitments should be disclosed in the notes to the accounts.

*'The notes should distinguish between those commitments included on the balance sheet as liabilities and those that are intentions to spend and are not included but in both cases should detail:*

*(a) the reason for the commitments . . .*
*(b) the total amount of the commitments . . .*
*(c) the amount of commitments outstanding at the start of the year.*
*(d) any amounts charged in the Statement of Financial Activities for the year.*
*(e) any amounts released during the year . . .*
*(f) the amount of commitments at the end of the year . . .'* *(para 258)*

**11.15** Where commitments do not amount to obligations and are therefore not included as liabilities, it is recommended, if they are material, that they are shown separately within unrestricted funds as designated funds. This 'earmarks' part of these unrestricted funds to meet these commitments and thereby shows what is left available for future commitments. It should be noted however that: *'activities that are to be wholly financed from future income would not form part of such designation'.* *(para 259)*

*CC66—SORP 2000 Example —Aid Overseas: 30 September 2001*

**24.—Commitments**

| | **2001 Group £'000** | **2000 Group £'000** | **2001 Charity £'000** | **2000 Charity £'000** |
|---|---|---|---|---|
| At 30 September 2001, the charity had commitments as follows: | | | | |
| Capital expenditure authorised but not contracted for: | **79** | **200** | **79** | **200** |
| Commitments in respect of grants approved for projects which have not been accrued in the financial statements but will form part of grants: | | | | |
| Within one year | 472 | 319 | 472 | 319 |
| Between one and two years | 180 | 165 | 180 | 165 |
| Between two and three years | 42 | 38 | 42 | 38 |
| | **694** | **522** | **694** | **522** |
| Annual commitments under non-cancellable operating leases for land and buildings which expire: | | | | |
| Within 1 year | 185 | 138 | 137 | 101 |
| In two to five years | 416 | 281 | 416 | 281 |
| Over five years | 393 | 574 | 372 | 553 |
| | **994** | **993** | **925** | **935** |
| Annual commitments under non-cancellable operating leases for motor vehicles which expire: | | | | |
| Within one year | 1 | – | – | – |
| In two to five years | 45 | 46 | 28 | 28 |
| | **46** | **46** | **28** | **28** |

## 5 CONTINGENT ASSETS AND LIABILITIES

**11.16** *'A charity should not recognise incoming or outgoing resources or gains and losses arriving respectively from contingent assets or contingent liabilities in the Statement of Financial Activities or the balance sheet.'*

*(para 262)*

Only when it is virtually certain that a contingent asset will be received or probable that a contingent liability will be incurred should they be included in the accounts. At that point they cease to be contingent.

*'The probability of a contingent asset or liability resulting in a future transfer*

*of resources (to or from the charity) should be continually assessed and the recognition of the asset or liability should be reviewed as appropriate.'* *(para 265)*

**11.17** Material contingent assets and liabilities should be disclosed in the notes to the accounts. These will show the nature of each contingency and uncertainties that are expected to affect the outcome. A prudent estimate of the financial effect, if not included in the accounts, should be given or an explanation as to why it is not practicable to do so — paras 266 and 267 of SORP.

*National Institute for Social Work: 30 June 2000*

**Notes to the accounts**

**16 Contingent liability**

NISW's freehold properties at 5–7 and 9 Tavistock Place were purchased from grants received from the Department of Health and various other supporters. In the event of a disposal of the properties 58.82% of the sale proceeds, being a pro rata contribution, will be refundable to the Department of Health.

## 6 LOAN LIABILITIES/GUARANTEES

**11.18** Paragraphs 270–271 of SORP give details of the disclosure requirements where a charity has pledged assets as security for a loan or other liability. They also require similar disclosure in respect of inter-fund loans and loans to subsidiary companies. Apart from details of the assets charged and the amount of the loan and its proportion to the value of the assets charged, the repayment details and interest should also be given.

**11.19** *'All material guarantees given by the charity, and the conditions under which liabilities might arise as a result of such guarantees, should be disclosed in a note to the accounts.'* *(para 260)*

**Comment**

**11.20** The revised SORP has considerably simplified the thought process that is needed to classify assets and liabilities and how to deal with contingencies. Inevitably there are many borderline cases when one cannot be sure whether or not to include an item in the accounts, but by giving detailed disclosure in the notes and, if sufficiently material, referring to the matter in the trustees' report, the treatment adopted will be well flagged and explained.

CHAPTER 12

# Cash flow statements

## 1 THE REQUIREMENT FOR A CASH FLOW STATEMENT

**12.1** The preparation of a cash flow statement is a requirement of Financial Reporting Standard 1 (Revised 1996) 'Cash Flow Statements' (FRS1) for all charities which exceed certain thresholds. This chapter explains the requirements of FRS1.

**12.2** FRS1 makes a cash flow statement, with comparative figures, a requirement in the accounts of all 'large' charities. To be deemed to be large for these purposes, a charity must meet two or more size qualifications in either its present or previous financial year. The current qualifications as set out in Appendix 2 of FRS1 are as follows:

'*(a)* *gross income in the year in excess of £2.8 million;*
*(b)* *a Balance Sheet total in excess of £1.4 million;*
*(c)* *more than 50 employees.'*

**12.3** The definition in SORP points out that these limits, which are determined from ss 246–249 Companies Act 1985, may change from time to time.

**12.4** The FRS exempts from the obligation to produce a cash flow statement 'subsidiary undertakings where 90% or more of the voting rights are controlled within the group, provided consolidated financial statements in which those subsidiary undertakings are included are publicly available'. This may be applicable where a parent/subsidiary undertaking relationship is considered to exist within a charitable group.

**12.5** As a 'primary statement' the cash flow statement should be given the same prominence in the accounts as the Statement of Financial Activities and the balance sheet.

**12.6** It is not intended to repeat in this chapter all of the requirements and definitions given by FRS1 with which the SORP states the charity's cash flow statement must comply.

## Comment

DEFINITION OF 'LARGE' CHARITY

**12.7** Slightly confusingly, the limits set out above for determining whether a charity is 'large' are the same as for determining whether a company is 'medium-sized' and are not the same as those for determining whether a company is 'large'. This must therefore be remembered when these limits are changed in future.

DEFINITION OF 'GROSS INCOME'

**12.8** The limits stated above refer not to 'turnover' as in FRS1, but to 'gross income'. 'Gross income' is defined in the Charity Commission's guidance notes for the completion of the Annual Return, a copy of which is reproduced in Appendix 3. In summary, it should represent the total incoming recources of all income funds plus gains or profits on the disposal of fixed assets or investments belonging to those funds. Any amounts receivable which are endowments should be excluded. For these purposes, the gain or profit on disposal of fixed assets or investments represents the amount by which the sale proceeds exceed the original cost, not the carrying value. In the case of accounts consolidating the results of a charity and its trading subsidiary, the 'gross income' should be the total of the charity's gross income as defined above (adjusted to remove the profit convenanted by the subsidiary) plus the turnover of the trading subsidiary. For the purposes of determining whether a cash flow statement is required, 'gross income' is not therefore the same as the total incoming resources shown on the Statement of Financial Activities. This in our view, is needlessly confusing.

DEFINITION OF 'BALANCE SHEET TOTAL'

**12.9** The 'balance sheet total' limit is not the total net assets of the charity shown as the total of its balance sheet, but is the total of all of its assets and excludes any liabilities.

## 2 THE OBJECT AND NATURE OF THE CASH FLOW STATEMENT AND THE DISCLOSURE REQUIREMENTS

**12.10** The object of the cash flow statement is to show all of the inflows and outflows of cash of the entity which have occurred in the accounting period in such a way as facilitates comparison of the cash flow performance of different entities and provides information that assists in the assessment of their liquidity, solvency and financial adaptability.

The revised FRS1 requires all cash inflows and outflows to be analysed under one of the following eight standard headings:

(a) operating activities;
(b) returns on investments and servicing of finance;
(c) taxation;
(d) capital expenditure and financial investment;
(e) acquisitions and disposals;
(f) equity dividends paid;
(g) management of liquid resources; and
(h) financing.

**12.11** Where applicable, three supporting reconciliations are required by the FRS.

**12.12** The FRS requires a reconciliation between the 'operating profit' reported in the 'profit and loss account' and the net cash flow from operating activities. This reconciliation should show the effect of the increase or decrease in stocks, debtors and creditors on cash movements resulting from operating activities. Clearly the FRS was written with commercial entities in mind. How charities can deal with this requirement is discussed below.

**12.13** A reconciliation of the movements in 'net debt' is also required in respect of the amounts shown in the financing section of the cash flow statement reconciling from their balance sheet value at the start of the year to their balance sheet value at the end of the year. This reconciliation should disclose separately movements between the two years resulting from cash flow movements (which will appear on the cash flow statement) and other movements with no cash flow effect (eg exchange differences) which should be reported in the notes to the cash flow statement only.

**12.14** Finally, a reconciliation is also required between the amounts on the balance sheet at the start and the end of the year of those items treated as 'cash'. Movements of a non-cash nature should be shown separately and the net cash inflow or outflow from this reconciliation must agree with the total cash movements given by the cash flow statement.

**12.15** Material transactions not resulting in cash movements must be disclosed in the notes to the cash flow statement if the disclosure is necessary for an understanding of the underlying transactions. The commonest disclosure as a result of this is that of material acquisitions of fixed assets which have not resulted in cash movements as they have been given to the charity or have been financed using hire purchase or similar arrangements.

## Comment

CATEGORIES OF INFLOWS AND OUTFLOWS OF CASH

**12.16** The statement should, if applicable, show a net amount for each of the eight categories listed above; any sub-division of these categories can either be shown on the face of the statement or should be disclosed in the notes. The FRS allows the cash flows relating to the management of liquid resources and financing to be combined under a single heading, provided the cash flows relating to each are shown separately and separate sub-totals are given.

**12.17** Clearly, for charities, the categories for taxation and equity dividends paid are unlikely to apply.

THE RECONCILIATION BETWEEN 'OPERATING PROFIT' AND CASH FLOWS FROM OPERATING ACTIVITIES

**12.18** The FRS requires a reconciliation of the operating results shown on the profit and loss account with the cash flows arrived at from the operating activities shown as the opening category on the cash flow statement.

**12.19** In the absence of an 'operating profit' for charities complying with SORP, it is considered that this reconciliation should be from the 'net incoming/outgoing resources before revaluations and investment asset disposals' of the charity, shown on its Statement of Financial Activities, to the 'cash inflow (or outflow) from operating activities'. The treatment of investment income in this reconciliation is dealt with below.

## 3 DEFINITION OF CASH

**12.20** FRS1 gives a detailed and restrictive definition of what should be considered to be 'cash' for the purposes of the cash flow statement.

*'Cash*
*Cash in hand and deposits repayable on demand with any qualifying financial institution, less overdrafts from any qualifying institution repayable on demand. Deposits are repayable on demand if they can be withdrawn at any time without notice and without penalty or if a maturity or period of notice of not more than 24 hours or one working day has been agreed. Cash includes cash in hand and deposits denominated in foreign currencies.'* (para 2)

A 'qualifying financial institution' is defined as:

*'An entity that as part of its business receives deposits and other repayable funds and grants credits for its own account.'*

**12.21** FRS1 requires the total of the inflows and outflows to agree to the total of the increase or decrease in the charity's 'cash' (as defined above) between the start and end of the reporting period.

## 4 PROBLEM AREAS SPECIFIC TO CHARITIES

### Investment income

**12.22** Cash movements resulting from the purchase and sale of investments are required by FRS1 to be disclosed as cash outflows or inflows from 'capital expenditure and financial investment' activities and any cash inflows coming from investment income are treated as part of the cash flows resulting from 'returns on investments and servicing of finance'.

**12.23** FRS1 assumes that the opening movement in the cash flow is the 'net cash inflow or outflow from operating activities', which, as the FRS has been written mainly with commercial companies in mind, excludes any cash inflows from investing activities. (Most trading companies would exclude investment income from their operating profit or loss.) However, SORP includes investment income as an incoming resource and investment income is therefore included in the Statement of Financial Activities' equivalent of operating profit, 'net incoming/outgoing resources before revaluations and investment asset disposals', with which a charity's equivalent reconciliation should begin.

**12.24** A strict interpretation of FRS1 suggests that, in order that charities can comply with the FRS1 requirement to show cash inflows from investment income as part of their cash flows from 'returns on investments and servicing of finance', the reconciliation referred to above from 'net incoming resources' to net cash inflow or outflow from operating activities must treat the amount shown on the Statement of Financial Activities as investment income receivable as a deduction. The net cash inflow or outflow from operating activities will therefore exclude any cash inflow from investment income.

**12.25** However, many charities consider investment income to be an integral part of their 'operations' and do not deduct the investment income from the operating activities. Whichever policy a charity adopts should be applied consistently and, if material, should be disclosed in the accounting policies.

### Treatment of cash held as part of investment portfolio

**12.26** Paragraph 195 of SORP provides for the inclusion of cash as a fixed asset investment if it is held as part of the investment portfolio.

This may include uninvested monies held by investment managers or investments in financial instruments made as part of the charity's investment strategy. To the extent that they meet the definition of cash given above, movements in these amounts must be included in the cash flow statement.

12.27 Below is an example of a charity's cash flow statement.

*Charity Cash Flow Statement: Year to 31 March 2000*

| | Notes | 2000 £ |
|---|---|---|
| Cash inflow from operating activities | A | 133,000 |
| Returns on investments and servicing of finance | B | 13,000 |
| Capital expenditure | B | (33,000) |
| | | 113,000 |
| Management of liquid resources | B | (2,000) |
| Financing | B | (4,000) |
| Increase in cash | C | 107,000 |

Notes to the cash flow statement for the year to 31 March 2000

**A Adjustment of net incoming resources before transfers to net cash inflow from operating activities**

| | **2000 £** |
|---|---|
| Net incoming resources before transfers | **100,000** |
| Depreciation charge | **50,000** |
| Net gain on disposal of tangible fixed assets | **(1,000)** |
| Interest receivable | **(10,000)** |
| Investment income receivable | **(5,000)** |
| Interest payable | **1,000** |
| Decrease in stocks | **3,000** |
| Decrease in debtors | **5,000** |
| (Decrease) in creditors | **(10,000)** |
| **Net cash inflow from operating activities** | **133,000** |

**B Gross cash flows**

| | **2000 £** |
|---|---|
| **Returns on investments and servicing of finance** | |
| Interest received | **8,000** |
| Investment income received | **6,000** |
| Interest paid | **(1,000)** |
| | **13,000** |

[*continued on following page*]

*Charity Cash Flow Statement, continued*

| | |
|---|---|
| **Capital expenditure** | |
| Payments to acquire tangible fixed assets | **(29,000)** |
| Receipts from disposals of tangible fixed assets | **2,000** |
| Payments to acquire investments | **(30,000)** |
| Receipts from the disposal of investments | **24,000** |
| | **(33,000)** |
| **Management of liquid resources** | |
| Purchase of treasury bills | **(10,000)** |
| Disposal of treasury bills | **8,000** |
| | **(2,000)** |
| **Financing** | |
| Repayment of bank loan (note C) | **(4,000)** |
| | **(4,000)** |

**C Analysis of changes in net debt**

| | At 1 April 1999 £ | Cash flows £ | Other changes £ | At 31 March 2000 £ |
|---|---|---|---|---|
| Cash in hand, at bank | 100,000 | 97,000 | – | 197,000 |
| Cash held by investment managers | 30,000 | 20,000 | – | 50,000 |
| Overdrafts | (40,000) | (10,000) | – | (50,000) |
| | 90,000 | 107,000 | – | 197,000 |
| Debt due within one year | (4,000) | 4,000 | (4,000) | (4,000) |
| Debt due after one year | (12,000) | – | 4,000 | (8,000) |
| Current asset investments | 5,000 | 2,000 | – | 7,000 |
| **Total** | 79,000 | 113,000 | – | 192,000 |

**D Reconciliation of net cashflow to movement in net debt**

| £ | £ | |
|---|---|---|
| Increase in cash in the period | 107,000 | |
| Cash repayment of bank loan | 4,000 | |
| Cash used to increase liquid resources | 2,000 | |
| Change in net debt | | 113,000 |
| Net debt at 1 April 1999 | | 79,000 |
| Net debt at 31 March 2000 | | 192,000 |

## Endowment fund movements

**12.28** Endowment fund movements are very specific to charities and consequently FRS1 does not address how they should be dealt with within a cash flow statement.

**12.29** In practice, charities should not include movements in endowments as cash flows from 'operating activities' but should, instead, treat them as increases or decreases in the financing section of the statement. In particular:

(a) endowment monies received in any year, ie donations, etc, should be treated as 'additions to endowments' in the 'financing' section of the cash flow statement;

(b) the receipts and payments arising from the disposal and acquisition of investments representing endowment funds should be shown gross in the 'capital expenditure and financial investment' section of the cash flow statement. These receipts and payments should be shown separately from those relating to investment assets representing other types of fund. The receipts and payments should be sub-totalled to give the 'net movement in cash flows attributable to endowment investments'. A corresponding line should be shown in the financing section for the same amount. The line in the 'financing' section will reflect the increase (cash into) or decrease (cash out of) the endowment fund whereas it will be the opposite direction in the 'capital expenditure and financial investment' section;

(c) on rare occasions where payments are made out of an endowment fund, for example in the case of expendable endowment, this should be shown as a decrease in the 'financing' section;

(d) transactions on endowment funds which do not result in cash flows should not be reported in the cash flow statement (eg depreciation) but major transactions should be disclosed in the notes if necessary for an understanding of the transactions.

**12.30** These somewhat complex disclosures are best illustrated in the following extract of the 'gross cash flows' note to a cash flow statement.

*Extract from a charity cash flow statement illustrating endowment fund movements*

| **Gross cash flows** | **2000** £ | **2000** £ |
|---|---|---|
| **Returns on investments and servicing of finance** | | |
| Interest received | | 10,000 |
| Investment income received | | 7,000 |
| Interest paid | | (2,000) |
| | | 15,000 |
| **Capital expenditure** | | |
| Payments to acquire tangible fixed assets | | (45,000) |
| Receipts from the disposal of tangible fixed assets | | 14,000 |
| Payments to acquire endowment investments | (63,000) | |
| Receipts from the disposal of endowment investments | 71,000 | |
| Net movement in cash flows attributable to endowment investments | | 8,000 |
| Payments to acquire other investments | | (30,000) |
| Receipts from the disposal of other investments | | 26,000 |
| | | (27,000) |

[*continued on following page*]

*Charity Cash Flow Statement, continued*

| | |
|---|---|
| **Management of liquid resources** | |
| Purchase of treasury bills | (20,000) |
| Disposal of treasury bills | 16,000 |
| | (4,000) |
| **Financing** | |
| Repayment of bank loan | (6,000) |
| Net movement in cash flows attributable to endowment investments | (8,000) |
| | (14,000) |

CHAPTER 13

# Notes and disclosures

## 1 INTRODUCTION

**13.1** The main thrust of SORP is to concentrate the report and accounts into three principal statements:

- the trustees' annual report;
- the Statement of Financial Activities (SOFA);
- the balance sheet.

**13.2** If these three statements are to be readily understood they must be succinct and uncluttered. SORP, in relation to the classification of incoming resources and expenditure, suggests that these should be summarised in a manner appropriate to the charity. The accounts should not be excessively detailed. Supporting analyses should be provided in the notes to the accounts.

**13.3** This chapter is therefore concerned with those matters which will be dealt with in the notes to the accounts and can be used as a checklist to ensure that all relevant matters have been considered. It covers the following:

accounting policies
funds structure and movements
connected charities
subsidiary undertakings
associated undertakings
netting off
income from charity shops
detail of income and expenditure
grants payable
concessionary loans
overheads costs
transactions with trustees and related parties
indemnity insurance
emoluments of employees
auditors' and independent examiner's remuneration
ex gratia payments
tangible fixed assets
investments
guarantees
contingent assets and liabilities
secured loans.

## 2 ACCOUNTING POLICIES

**13.4** *'Charity accounts should include notes on the accounting policies chosen which should be the most appropriate in the particular circumstances of each charity for the purpose of giving a true and fair view. The policies should be consistent with this SORP, Accounting Standards and relevant legislation. FRED 21 explains how accounting policies should be determined.' (para 277)*

**13.5** Para 279 of SORP goes on to say that the accounting policies note should state that the accounts have been prepared in accordance with the SORP and accounting standards (or with the FRSSE if applicable), that they comply with the Charities Act or the Companies Act or other relevant statute and that they are based on historic cost except for investments (and perhaps certain fixed assets) which have been included at revalued amounts.

If any part of the accounts does not accord with the SORP the accounting policies note must give the reasons why the trustees judge that the treatment adopted is more appropriate in the circumstances, describe how it departs from the SORP and give an estimate of the financial effect on the accounts. It is stressed that a departure from SORP *'is not justified simply because it gives the reader a more appealing picture of the financial position or results of the charity' (para 280).*

Para 282 of SORP encourages trustees to give brief explanations of specific accounting policies which they have adopted to deal with material items. Examples of such items are contained in paragraphs 283–291 of SORP and cover policy notes on:

- Incoming resources: legacies, grants receivable, gifts in kind etc.
- Resources expended: recognition of liabilities, grants payable, allocation of costs.
- Assets: capitalisation, valuation, depreciation, inalienable property, investments, stocks and work in progress.
- Funds structure: types of fund and policy for transfers and allocations.
- Other items: pension fund, foreign exchange, finance and operating leases, irrecoverable VAT.

**Comment**

**13.6** The first point to make is that the SORP is a guide; it is not to be slavishly followed. It is a question of identifying the material items contained in the accounts and then explaining the accounting policy adopted for each.

**13.7** Before the earlier SORP came into force in October 1995, charities had a wider choice of accounting policies, it being left to the trustees to decide for example whether to bring in certain classes of income on an accruals or cash basis, or to include investments at cost or market value. The biggest impact of the 1995 SORP was that it closed off most of those options, effectively forcing charities to conform on accounting polices. This has been further reinforced by the new SORP 2000. So why do we still have to disclose accounting policies?

**13.8** There are three answers to this question:

- not all readers of charity accounts are necessarily well versed in SORP and they have a right to know the main accounting policies on which the accounts are based;
- despite SORP's tightening grip, there are still areas of choice of accounting policy which need to be explained, eg the basis of allocation or apportionment of costs between direct charitable expenditure, support costs, fundraising, and publicity and management and administration;
- in certain cases trustees may feel justified in adopting an accounting policy which is at variance to that contained in SORP. If so, and if it is material, this must be both explained and justified on the grounds of showing a true and fair view.

**13.9** Many charities may, on practical grounds, find it difficult to comply with every aspect of SORP and will have to compromise. For example they may not be able to account for all their branch activities and find it necessary to exclude some from the accounts. While this is not to be encouraged and may invite an audit qualification, it will considerably alleviate the situation if the matter is disclosed in the accounting polices, together with an indication as to what steps are being taken to correct the omission in future.

The accounts of Imperial Cancer Research for 1999 contain a very full and clear explanation of their accounting policies.

*Imperial Cancer Research Fund: 30 September 1999*

**Notes to the consolidated financial statements**

**1 Accounting policies**
The principal accounting policies, all of which have been applied consistently throughout the year, are set out below:

**Basis of preparation**
These financial statements have been prepared under the historical cost convention, as modified by the revaluation of investments to market value, and are in accordance with Statement of Recommended Practice ('SORP'). The cash flow statement does not fully comply with Financial Reporting Standard 1 (Revised) but provides a clearer understanding of the movement from the statement of financial activities to the change in cash balances.

**Income**
Sales of donated goods in shops, donations and income from regional activities are accounted for when received as the value of such donations cannot be determined prior to receipt. All other income is accounted for on a receivable basis. Legacies and donations received other than in cash are included in income at valuation.

Voluntary income from regional activities includes the net proceeds of events organised by the Groups of Friends. Due to their voluntary nature, collecting full information on every event is impractical.

**Shops' expenses**
Shops' expenses include the direct costs of the charity's shops, office and regional costs relating to retail operations and a proportion of central overheads.

**Fundraising costs**
Fundraising costs consist of the salaries and all directly attributable overheads of the fundraising departments other than those incurred in retail activites plus a proportion of central overheads.

**Management and administration costs**
Management and administration costs consist of expenditure incurred due to charitable status. These include the costs of audit and investment management expenses, salaries and directly attributable overheads of the Council office, and a proportion of central overheads.

[*Continued on following page*]

*Imperial Cancer Research Fund, continued*

**Central overheads**
Central overheads are allocated to research expenditure, shops' expenses, fundraising costs and charity administration on a variety of bases including floor area, head-count and time spent.

**Pension costs**
Pension costs are charged to the statement of financial activities so as to spread the cost of pensions over employees' working lives with Imperial Cancer Research Fund.

**Operating leases**
Operating lease rentals are charged in the statement of financial activities on a straight line basis over the length of the lease.

**Finance leases and hire purchase agreements**
Assets acquired under finance leases and hire purchase agreements are capitalised and the outstanding capital element of future instalments is included in creditors. The interest element is charged in the statement of financial activities so as to produce a constant periodic rate of charge on the outstanding obligation.

**Value Added Tax**
Expenditure subject to VAT which is not recoverable by Imperial Cancer Research Fund is shown inclusive of VAT. All other expenditure is shown exclusive of VAT.

**Foreign currencies**
Transactions in foreign currencies are recorded at the rate of exchange prevailing at the time of the transactions. Foreign currency balances are translated into sterling at the exchange rates prevailing at the balance sheet date. Any gains or losses arising from changes in exchange rates subsequent to the date of the transaction are included in the statement of financial activities.

**Designated funds**
Designated funds are amounts which have been put aside at the discretion of Council for specific projects. A designated fund has been created relating to the value of fixed assets owned by Imperial Cancer Research Fund. The funds used in the purchase of assets are not readily available to sustain ongoing expenditure and the creation of this designated fund reflects this. Due to the size of this fund and movements during the year, it is disclosed separately on the balance sheets.

[*Continued on following page*]

*Imperial Cancer Research Fund, continued*

A designated fund has been created relating to an amount set aside to finance expansion plans involving the building of new research facilities. Due to the size of this fund it is also disclosed separately on the balance sheet.

**Restricted funds**
Restricted funds are subject to specific conditions imposed by the donors or grant making organisations.

**Permanent endowment funds**
The capital of such funds must be held until the objectives of Imperial Cancer Research Fund, or those of the Trust deeds establishing each fund, are satisfied.

**Depreciation**
Depreciation is provided to write off the cost of fixed assets over their estimated useful lives on a straight line basis at the following annual rates:

| | |
|---|---|
| Freehold buildings | 4% |
| Leasehold buildings and research facilities | 4% or length of lease if shorter |
| Plant, fixtures and equipment | 5% to 25% |
| Shops leases, fixtures and fittings | 10% or length of lease if shorter |

**Investments**
Investments are stated at market value at the balance sheet date. It is Imperial Cancer Research Fund's policy to revalue immediately prior to selling so that no gain or loss arises on disposal. The statement of financial activities includes unrealised gains and losses arising from the revaluation of the investment portfolio in the year.

Cash deposits intended to be held for the long term are shown under investments in the balance sheet. All other cash deposits are included as bank balances in the balance sheet.

**Stock**
The value of donated goods held for resale in Imperial Cancer Research Fund shops is not reflected in the financial statements. Stocks of research consumables and goods bought in for resale are included at the lower of cost and net realisable value.

[*Continued on following page*]

*Imperial Cancer Research Fund, continued*

**Basis of consolidation**
The consolidated financial statements include the accounts of the two wholly owned subsidiary companies (Imperial Cancer Research Fund Trading Limited and Imperial Cancer Research Technology Limited) and our interest in associates.

## 3 FUNDS' STRUCTURE AND MOVEMENTS

**13.10** The accounting for separate funds within a charity is dealt with in paragraphs 36 to 38 of SORP and is covered in Chapter 5 **(5.11ff)**. This chapter concentrates on the notes to the accounts which help to amplify and explain the separate funds and their movements.

Paragraph 37 of SORP explains that whereas the accounts will *'provide a summary of the main funds, differentiating in particular between the unrestricted income funds, restricted income funds and endowment funds'*, the notes should give the details of material restricted funds, grouping them under suitable headings.

**13.11** Paragraph 49 of SORP goes on to say that *'the notes to the accounts should provide information on the structure of the charity's funds so as to disclose the individual fund balances and the reasons for them . . .'.*

**13.12** Such notes will include the following.

A summary showing:

- The assets and liabilities representing each fund, analysed between investments, fixed assets and net current assets.
- An explanation of how each fund has arisen and its purpose, with details of restrictions imposed. An indication should be given as to whether or not suitable resources are held in each fund to meet any restrictions eg if the funds have been given to be spent immediately, are they in liquid assets?
- Details of any funds in deficit. The Trustees Report should contain an explanation of any such fund and what action they propose to remedy the position.
- Explanations of material movements of funds.

**13.13** The requirement for an explanation of material movements of funds is contained in para 49(d) of SORP and essentially has three ingredients:

- details of material transfers between different funds;
- details of allocations to designated funds, and
- an explanation of the transfers or allocations and reasons for them.

In each case transfers or allocations should be shown gross, ie without any netting off.

**Comment**

**13.14** As the reconciliation of funds will have to include the transfers between funds, it is likely that most charities having more than one fund, will need only one note or possibly two to explain their funds structure and their movements.

> *Age Concern (National Council on Ageing): 31 March 2000*
>
> **Fund accounting**
> The Charity maintains various types of funds as follows:
>
> *Restricted funds*
> Restricted funds represent grants, donations and legacies received which are allocated by the donor for specific purposes.
>
> *Unrestricted funds*
> *Designated funds* are amounts which have been put aside at the discretion of the Trustees.
> *General unrestricted funds* represent funds which are expendable at the discretion of the Trustees in the furtherance of the objects of the Charity. Such funds may be held in order to finance both working capital and capital investment.

**13.15** The area which tends to cause the most confusion is that of transfers between funds. Take for example a capital restricted fund, the income of which can be applied for the general purposes of the charity. The income arising is unrestricted as will be the expenditure out of it, so no transfer is needed. Contrast this with a similar capital restricted fund, the income of which can be applied to make charitable grants within the general purposes of the charity. The application of the income is now restricted, if only slightly as it cannot be used for fundraising or general administration and the income will therefore be included in restricted income. As the charity's general purposes include making grants it is quite likely that in practice the trustees will periodically transfer cash from the restricted fund to the general fund to meet the cost of some of the grants. In the accounts these payments should in our view be shown in the Statement of Financial Activities in the restricted funds column as direct charitable expenditure, but they could equally be shown in the unrestricted funds column as being part of the general expenditure of the charity, the transfer from the restricted fund being shown below the line and explained in the notes.

**13.16** The very task of having to give an explanation of such a transfer should alert the charity accountant to the clumsiness of the treatment of the grant as unrestricted general expenditure in the first place. Far simpler to include it as expenditure of restricted funds.

*Alzheimer's: 31 March 1999*

Notes to the financial statements

**17. Restricted funds**

| | At 1 April 1998 Group AS RESTATED £ | Incoming resources £ | Resources expended £ | At 31 March 1999 Group AS RESTATED £ |
|---|---|---|---|---|
| Research | 86,956 | 373,713 | 736,885 | **(276,216)** |
| Regional development grants | 10,641 | 240,270 | 246,170 | **4,741** |
| Department of Health grants | (14,053) | 198,450 | 147,525 | **36,872** |
| Care service grants | 101,656 | 172,343 | 127,467 | **146,532** |
| Regions and branches | 263,559 | 332,959 | 211,082 | **385,436** |
| Other restricted | 25,272 | 74,918 | 76,382 | **23,808** |
| **National organisation** | 474,031 | 1,392,653 | 1,545,511 | **321,173** |
| Branches and support groups | 6,778,423 | 6,592,513 | 5,683,215 | **7,687,721** |
| National Lottery Charities Board | 42,935 | 338,029 | 364,618 | **16,346** |
| **Society** | 7,295,389 | 8,323,195 | 7,593,344 | **8,025,240** |

Restricted research funds are held for use in research involved with the cause and treatment of Alzheimer's disease and other dementias. Restricted regional development funds are held for use in the Central and Welsh regions. Restricted care service grants are held for use in a project developing and implementing quality care service standards and in a project relating to younger persons with dementia. Restricted other grants are held for use in a project relating to dementia in younger persons. Restricted regional, branch and support group funds are held for use within specific localities. Department of Health grant funds and other restricted funds are held for use in various projects. Restricted National Lottery Charities Board funds are held within branches and support groups to be used in projects in the specific localities.

## 4 CONNECTED CHARITIES

**13.17** Paragraph 31(c) of SORP says that the trustees' annual report should provide information on charities which are connected with it and with which it cooperates in the pursuit of its charitable objectives.

**13.18** The Glossary defines connected charities as those which have:

*'(a) common, parallel or related objects and activities; and either*

*(b) common control; or*
*(c) unity of administration.*

*Within this category may be charities which come together under one umbrella organisation.'*

Paragraph 158 of SORP says that a charity can be a related party of another charity, for example, if one is the trustee of the other, or if one has the power to appoint or secure a significant proportion of the charity trustees of the other, or if the two charities are subject to common control (for instance a majority of trustees in common).

**13.19** Paragraph 157 of SORP requires related party transactions to be disclosed in the notes to the accounts. Such transactions may include purchases, sales, leases, donations, the supply of services and making payments (see para 161 of SORP).

*'Only material transactions need to be disclosed . . .'* *(para 162)*

Paragraph 163 of SORP sets out details of the required disclosure for all related party transactions. For connected charities these can be summarised as follows:

(a) name of connected charity;
(b) description of the relationship;
(c) description of the transactions;
(d) the amounts involved;
(e) outstanding balances at the balance sheet date;
(f) any amounts written off; and
(g) any other elements of the transactions which are necessary for the understanding of the financial statements.

**13.20** To avoid unnecessary disclosure of information relating to connected charities, paragraph 165 of SORP lists examples of transactions which *'are unlikely to influence the pursuance of the separate independent interests of the charity . . . and which need not be disclosed unless there is evidence to the contrary'*. These include:

(a) unrestricted donations, other than material grants;
(b) minor or routine unremunerated services provided to the charity;
(c) the purchase from a charity of minor articles which are available to the public on the same terms; and
(d) services provided by one charity to another, eg the use of a village hall.

**13.21** Sometimes the connection between one charity and another is that of parent and subsidiary undertaking in which case consolidated accounts will be prepared. This is considered in the next section (**13.24ff**).

*Age Concern: 31 March 2000*

# Report of the Trustees

## Objects and activities

The National Council on Ageing's constitutional objective is "to promote the welfare of the aged in any manner which now is or hereafter deemed by law to be charitable".

The mission of the **National Council on Ageing (Age Concern England)** is *"to promote the well-being of all older people and help make later life a fulfilling and enjoyable experience."*

Its principal aims are:

- to promote positive attitudes towards older people and ageing;
- to influence and develop public policies that affect older people;
- to promote effective care for older people; and
- to encourage choice and opportunity for older people.

Age Concern England (ACE) is a central resource to over 800 autonomous Age Concern bodies which offer direct services to older people. ACE supports this work through the provision of information and policy, publications, grants, the training of professional and voluntary carers, campaigning, fundraising, research and the development of services for older people. This Report and Annual Accounts do not reflect the affairs of those autonomous organisations.

ACE also works closely with partner organisations in the UK concerned with the needs of older people; across Europe through *Eurolink Age*; and internationally through the *International Federation On Ageing*.

## Organisation

The **National Council** has 232 members who are nominated by Age Concern organisations and national and retirement organisations, and elected representatives of associate members. The council meets twice a year to discuss major policy issues and campaigns and receives a report from the **Board of Trustees**.

The constituent parts of the National Council also meet as **Fora** to discuss various issues of current concern and report to the Board of Trustees and to the National Council.

At its September 1999 meeting the National Council accepted proposals for the formation of Age Concern, a federation. Age Concern England will be a member of this federation which has a separate governance structure. A constitutional amendment will be placed before the National Council at its meeting in July 2000 to complete the proposals for the establishment of the federation.

The Board of Trustees meets four times a year and is responsible for the governance of the organisation. It receives reports from the **Finance Committee**, the **Membership Committee**, the **Training Advisory Committee** and the **Director General**.

*Age Concern: 31 March 2000*

## National organisations in membership

*as of 31 March 2000*

Abbeyfield Society
Action on Elder Abuse
Age Concern Cymru
Age Concern Northern Ireland
Age Concern Retired Staff Association
Age Concern Scotland
Age Endeavour
Almshouses Association
Alzheimer's Disease Society
Anchor Housing Trust
ARP050
Arthritis Care
Association of Charity Officers
Association of Directors of Social Services
Association of District Councils
Association of Metropolitan Authorities
Baptist Union of Great Britain
British Association Service to the Elderly (BASE)
British Association of Domiciliary Care Officers (BADCO)
British Association of Settlements
British Association of Social Workers
British Diabetic Association
British Geriatrics Society
British Medical Association
British Psychological Society
British Red Cross Society
British Society of Gerontology
Burtons Retirement Association
Carers National Association
Catholic Women's League
Centre for Policy on Ageing
Chartered Soceity of Physiotherapy
The Church Army
Church of England Board for Social Responsibility
Civil Service Pensioners' Alliance
Civil Service Retirement Fellowship
College of Occupational Therapists
Community Development Foundation
Community Matters
Confederation of British Industry
Counsel and Care
Disabled Living Foundation
Equal Opportunities Commission
Family Welfare Association
Hanover Housing Association
Health Visitors Association
Hearing Concern
Help the Aged
Institute of Health Services Management
The Institute of Human Ageing
International Association of Lions Clubs
Jewish Care
Library Association Retired Members' Guild
Limbless Association
Local Government Association
Methodist Homes for the Aged
NASUWT – Federation of Retired Members' Associations
National Association of Leagues of Hospital Friends
National Association of Local Councils
National Association of Mental Health (MIND)
National Association of Women's Clubs
National Association of Retired Police Officers (NARPO)
National Association of Retired Fire-fighters (NARF)
National Centre for Volunteering
National Council for Voluntary Organisations (NCVO)
National Council of Women of Great Britain
National Federation of Post Office and British Telecom Pensioners
National Federation of Women's Institutes
National Free Chuches Council
National Health Service Retirement Fellowship
National Housing Federation
National Institute of Adult Continuing Education
National Union of Teachers (Retired Teachers' Advisory Committee)
Occupational Benevolent Funds Alliance (OBFA)
Officers' Pensions Society
Patients Association
Pensioners' Voice
Physically Handicapped Able-Bodied (Phab)
The Pre-Retirement Association of Great Britain and Northern Ireland
Queen's Nursing Institute
Refugee Council
Research Institute for the Care of the Elderly (RICE)
Research into Ageing
Retired Executives Action Clearing House (REACH)
Rotary International in Great Britan and Ireland
Royal Association for Disability and Rehabilitation (RADAR)
Royal College of General Practitioners
Royal College of Nursing
Royal College of Psychiatrists
Royal Institute of Public Health & Hygiene & Society of Public Health
Royal National Institute for the Blind (RNIB)
Royal National Institute for the Deaf (RNID)
Royal Pharmaceutical Society of Great Britain
Royal Society for Mentally Handicapped Children and Adults (MENCAP)
Royal UK Beneficient Association (RUKBA)
St John Ambulance Brigade
Salvation Army
Sense
Social Care Association
Soldiers', Sailors' and Airmens' Families' Association – Forces Help (SSAFA Forces Help)
Soroptomist International UK Programme Action Committee
Stroke Association
Tinnitus Action
ToCH
Trades Union Congress
Transport and General Workers' Union (Retired Members Association)
UNISON
UNISON (Retired Members Section)
United Kingdom Federation of Business and Professional Women
University of the Third Age
Women's Royal Voluntary Service (WRVS)

### Comment

**13.22** The first point to note regarding the disclosure of information on connected charities is that SORP asks for this to be given in the annual report – not in the notes. This is reinforced by para 31(b) and (c) of SORP which in connection with the annual report says that the narrative information should include:

'(b) *a description of the organisational structure of the charity and how decisions are made. Where the charity is part of a wider network then the relationship involved should also be explained.*

(c) *a statement regarding the relationships between the charity and related parties and with any other charities and organisations with which it co-operates in pursuit of its charitable objectives.'* *(para 31)*

**13.23** Clearly, therefore, reference must be made to connected charities in the trustees' annual report, but the detail concerning the names and addresses and material transactions can be given in the notes to the accounts, to which reference should be made in the annual report (see also **13.71ff** regarding related party transactions generally).

## 5 SUBSIDIARY UNDERTAKINGS AND ASSOCIATED UNDERTAKINGS

**13.24** Paragraph 300 of SORP requires a parent charity to prepare consolidated accounts including all its subsidiary undertakings. The only exceptions are where the gross income of the group is below the audit threshold, currently £250,000, or the subsidiary undertakings' results are not material to the group, or the accounts have to be aggregated under charity legislation.

**13.25** Paragraph 302 of SORP says that consolidated accounts should be prepared for the reporting charity and its charitable subsidiaries *'whether or not the subsidiaries are also companies. However, where the subsidiary undertaking is a non-company charity it will normally be accounted for in the consolidated accounts in the same manner as a branch . . .'* — (see **5.28**).

**13.26** Disclosure notes relating to consolidation are contained in paragraphs 312 to 319 of SORP. In summary these are as follows:

- A separate comment in the Trustees' Annual Report concerning the performance of the subsidiaries.
- An accounting policy note of the method of consolidation and which subsidiaries are included and which excluded.
- Figures given in the notes should generally show the position for the group as well as for the parent undertaking.
- The total investment by the charity in its subsidiaries.
- The names of the subsidiaries, particulars of the charity's shareholding or other means of control, how their activities relate to the charity, the aggregate amount, if material, of the assets, liabilities and funds of each subsidiary and, if material a summary of the turnover, expenditure and profit or loss of each.
- If any subsidiaries are excluded or if consolidated accounts are not prepared *'the trustees should explain the reasons in a note to the chairty's accounts with reference to each excluded subsidiary undertaking'.* *(para 317)*

**Comment**

**13.27** Whilst the rules relating to consolidation are clear, there is a danger that the amalgamation of figures from both charitable and non charitable subsidiary companies and other undertakings may obscure some of the main messages contained in the accounts of a charity. This point is recognised in paragraphs 311 and 318 of SORP which recommend that trustees should choose appropriate line headings to reflect the underlying activities of the group and, if that is insufficient, segmented information should be given in the notes so that the results of the parent charity and each subsidiary undertaking are transparent.

*'Examples of items that should be separately disclosed include the cost of generating funds, management and administration and the costs of charitable activities.'* *(para 318)*

*National Trust: 28 February 1999*

**Note 9—National Trust Enterprises' Net Contribution**

The Trust is the owner of the National Trust (Enterprises) Limited, which is responsible for those activities of a commercial nature, such as trading and catering at properties and the mail order operation, which do not enjoy exemption from income tax as does most of the Trust's income. A deed of covenant has been entered into between the Trust and the Company, whereby the Company donates the whole of its surplus income to the Trust each year. The turnover and net contribution of The National Trust (Enterprises) Limited to Trust funds were:

| | **Turnover** | | **Contribution** | |
|---|---|---|---|---|
| | **1999** | 1998 | **1999** | 1998 |
| | **£'000** | £'000 | **£'000** | £'000 |
| Regional retailing | **18,103** | 17,939 | **2,291** | 2,232 |
| Regional catering | **14,617** | 14,793 | **2,158** | 2,763 |
| Holiday cottages | **3,097** | 2,812 | **1,262** | 1,112 |
| Head Office activities | **5,662** | 5,288 | **1,187** | 636 |
| Other regional activities | **2,844** | 2,847 | **905** | 975 |
| | **44,323** | 43,679 | **7,803** | 7,718 |
| Advertising, sponsorship and other income | **5,469** | 5,456 | **3,563** | 3,903 |
| | **49,792** | 49,135 | **11,366** | 11,621 |
| Amount payable to the National Trust | | | **(11,366)** | (11,621) |
| Retained in subsidy | | | – | – |

[*Continued on following page*]

The contribution represents the operating profit of The National Trust (Enterprises) Limited before any charge is made for the use of the Trust's property assets. The balance sheet of The National Trust (Enterprises) Limited is as follows:

| | 1999 | 1998 |
|---|---|---|
| | **£'000** | £'000 |
| Stock | **5,941** | 5,167 |
| Debtors | **391** | 588 |
| Cash | **42** | 45 |
| Creditors | **(5,633)** | (5,734) |
| Current account with the National Trust | **(741)** | (66) |
| Net Assets | – | – |

The current account with the National Trust is secured on the assets of the company, is repayable on demand and interest is charged at 2% over Barclays base rate on the monthly balance.

## 6 NETTING OFF

**13.28** Paragraphs 76 and 77 of SORP state:

*'All incoming resources should be reported gross whether raised by the charity or its agents. Netting off expenditure against income is only allowable for small fundraising events where it will not materially understate the gross incoming resources and gross resources expended for the event. However, in no case should the charity's own staff costs be netted off against the proceeds of any such events when reported in the accounts.'* *(para 76)*

*'Some receipts can be regarded as reimbursements and can be offset against the related expenditure charged in the statement of financial activities (though a separate asset must be shown in the balance sheet see paragraph 254). FRS 12 explains when this is possible, for instance, the receipt of an insurance payment will meet this criteria. However, the receipt of a grant to meet resources expended already paid or accrued as a liability will not be regarded as a reimbursement and cannot be netted off against the accrued liability.'* *(para 77)*

**13.29** The general rule should be that all income is shown gross. SORP sets out one exception to the above rule. Paragraph 76 of SORP refers to the profits obtained from some forms of occasional trading which are relieved from tax by Extra Statutory Concession of the Inland Revenue and permits netting off where both income and expenditure arising out of such on event are small and immaterial.

**13.30** However, para 76 of SORP clearly states that even in these situations the charity's own staff costs should not be netted off against the proceeds of any such events.

**13.31** Paragraph 77 of SORP distinguishes between netting off and the treatment of reimbursements. Insurance policy receipts following a claim are the obvious example.

**13.32** In the past charities have occasionally been tempted to net 'capital' grants off the cost of any asset purchased from the grant and capitalise and depreciate the net amount. Paragraph 193 of SORP makes it clear that this is not permissible:

*'If a fixed asset is acquired in full or in part from the proceeds of a grant it should be included at its full acquisition cost (or in the case of a joint arrangement at the gross value of the charity's share in the asset) without netting off the grant proceeds [see paragraph 328].'* *(para 193)*

**Comment**

**13.33** The rule against netting off is welcome as it not only ensures that the cost/benefit ratio of fundraising activities is disclosed, but also ensures that the scale of trading activities carried on by subsidiary companies is prominently disclosed. The rule forbidding the netting off of a grant against the cost of an asset purchased with the grant ensures that the asset is capitalised at its true costs or worth and that the depreciation charge is based on that cost, thereby ensuring that the full cost of the asset is charged to expenditure over its useful life.

## 7 INCOME FROM CHARITY SHOPS

**13.34** One of the main areas where 'netting off' is a particularly contentious and common area is the treatment of income from charity shops. However, paragraph 76 of SORP (see above) is categoric that all incoming resources, including proceeds from the sale of donated and bought goods, should be accounted for gross.

**13.35** Paragraph 106 of SORP requires that the income from charity shops should be included within the the Statement of Financial Activities heading 'Activities for generating funds'. Although requiring this categorization, the SORP acknowledges that income from the sale of donated goods might also be regarded as the realisation of a gift-in-kind. In the past many charities have taken this view and included the sale proceeds within donations and voluntary income. However, the SORP states that such income is essentially no different from trading income and hence should be classified as income from activities for generating funds.

*'Activities for generating funds can include selling donated goods and bought in goods, providing services to other than the charity's beneficiaries, licensing*

*arrangements, the letting of non investment property and many others. Whilst selling donated goods is legally considered to be the realisation of a donation in kind (see paragraph 95(c)), in economic terms it is similar to a trading activity and should be included in this section. Ancillary trades where the principal aim (whilst still providing a service to the beneficiaries) is to generate incoming resources to support or contribute to the other charitable activities, should also be included in this section. Sometimes all these activities are carried on separately and other times mixed together in a single enterprise.'*
*(para 106)*

**Comment**

**13.36** This is reasonable and easy to comply with if the charity shops only sell donated and bought in goods. If this is the case, in most instances, the shops will be operated directly by the charity.

**13.37** The situation becomes more complex where the shops sell a mixture of donated and bought in goods for resale and also sell a small amount of goods made by beneficiaries and incidentally provide information about the charity. SORP implies, at first glance, that the different types of activity should be treated differently in the accounts of the charity.

- The sale of goods made by the beneficiaries is not a trading activity. Income from the sale of such items, therefore, is deemed income from activities in furtherance of the charity's objects in accordance with para 103.
- The sale of donated and bought in goods is regarded as trading income and should be accounted for as explained above.

Paragraph 107 of SORP addresses this issue and permits all incoming resources from the shop to be classified as 'shop income' under 'activities for generating funds'. This is a common sense approach and is welcomed.

*'It may be possible to segregate the incoming resources and resources expended for each different type of activity (this may have to be done for tax purposes) but an enterprise carrying on a mix of activities will often be viewed as a single economic unit. Charity trustees should consider the balance of the activities being undertaken to determine the most appropriate place to include the incoming resources from such enterprises but having done this the mix of incoming resources need not be segregated further. For example a shop may mainly sell donated and bought in goods, but it may also sell a small amount of goods made by its beneficiaries and incidentally provide information about the charity. It would be acceptable to class all the incoming resources from the shop as "shop income" under "activities for generating funds".'*
*(para 107)*

The issue is further complicated where shops are operated through a trading subsidiary and sell a mixture of donated goods and bought in goods for resale. The sale of donated goods is not a trading activity and, in theory, could be carried out by the charity itself. It might be argued, therefore, that income from the sale of donated goods should be accounted for gross within activities for generating funds. The sale of bought in goods is a trading activity and will be carried out by the trading subsidiary and should be accounted for in that entity's accounts in accordance with normal accounting rules. All operating costs (excluding those incurred in the sale of donated goods) should be deducted from the proceeds to arrive at an accounting and a taxable profit, the latter of which will be paid over to the charity as a Gift Aid payment and shown as a receipt from the trading subsidiary in the accounts of the charity.

**13.38** There are a number of implications arising from this.

- Income from the sale of donated goods is credited gross directly to the charity's accounts even though the goods have been sold through a charity shop operated by a trading subsidiary of the charity. None of the overheads incurred by the trading subsidiary should be deducted from the sale proceeds. Instead, they should be shown as costs of generating funds.
- All other overhead costs (including apportioned salaries of shop staff) are deducted from the proceeds of the sale of bought in goods prior to calculating the Gift Aid payment to be made to the charity by the trading subsidiary.
- The shops need to maintain detailed records showing the proceeds from the sale of donated goods and the proceeds from the sale of bought in goods. In addition, to ensure that such records are accurate the two types of goods will have to be clearly identifiable within the shop.

**13.39** Clearly the practical problems caused by this differentiation of the sale of donated and bought in goods demands the application of a common sense solution. Two such solutions would appear to present themselves.

1 One solution is to split out the income from the sale of donated goods from that from the sale of bought in goods but to allocate overheads to each of the two categories. The gross sale proceeds of donated goods would then be shown as income from activities for generating funds in the charity's Statement of Financial Activities with the costs charged separately as costs of generating funds but both would be cross-referenced to a note showing gross proceeds and the expenses deducted to arrive at the net benefit to the charity. The sale of bought in goods less the remaining overhead costs would be accounted for within the subsidiary's

accounts and then shown on the charity's Statement of Financial Activities as part of 'Income from trading subsidiaries'. Oxfam's 2000 accounts provide an example of this approach to the problem as do those of the Imperial Cancer Research Fund for 1999.

2 An alternative solution is to account for all the sales, regardless of whether they arise from donated goods or from bought in goods, through the trading subsidiary and to show the total net income on the face of the charity's Statement of Financial Activities as 'Income from retailing activities'. The figure would be cross-referenced to a note to the accounts giving details of the two types of sale with no attempt to allocate expenditure between them.

**13.40** Of the two possible solutions, the first is more in keeping with the spirit of SORP and should, in most instances, provide a fair representation of the charity's activities while the second solution may be better at minimising the practical problems.

*OXFAM: 30 April 2000*

**2 Income**

**a. Donations**

| | 2000 £'000 Unrestricted | 2000 £'000 Restricted | 2000 £'000 Endowment | 2000 £'000 Total | 1999 £'000 Total |
|---|---|---|---|---|---|
| Committed Giving | 33,193 | 0 | 0 | 33,193 | 28,960 |
| Legacies | 8,163 | 0 | 66 | 8,229 | 7,307 |
| Donations, Appeals and Fundraising events | 8,369 | 5,537 | 0 | 13,906 | 16,260 |
| | 49,725 | 5,537 | 66 | 55,328 | 52,527 |

As explained in Accounting Policies Note 1, income is accounted for as soon as it is prudent and practicable to do so, that is once there is reasonable certainty as to the amount and entitlement.

At 30 April 2000, in addition to legacy income that has been included in the accounts on the above basis, Oxfam expected to benefit from a number of legacies from estates for which the administration had yet to be finalised. Oxfam's future income from these legacies is estimated at £1.3 million (1999: £1.2 million).

**b. Oxfam Shops**

This represents the net income from the sale of donated goods through Oxfam shops, after deduction of local and management expenses. Oxfam believes this most fairly represents the value to the charity of donated goods.

[*Continued on following page*]

*OXFAM, continued*

| | 2000 £'000 | 2000 £'000 | 1999 £'000 | 1999 £'000 |
|---|---|---|---|---|
| Turnover from donated goods* | | 42,972 | | 44,307 |
| Shop Operating Expenses | | (30,754) | | (27,768) |
| Management Expenses | | (3,415) | | (2,834) |
| **Oxfam Shops (net of Expenses)** | | **8,803** | | **13,705** |
| Donations—Unrestricted | 602 | | 638 | |
| —Restricted | 2,068 | | 957 | |
| | | 2,670 | | 1,595 |
| Net Income from Trading | | 11,473 | | 15,300 |

| | 2000 £'000 | 1999 £'000 |
|---|---|---|
| In addition to the sale of donated goods, the Oxfam shops also sold Oxfam Trading goods amounting to (inclusive VAT) | 11,015 | 11,121 |

*This includes rental income from sublet units of Oxfam shops of £0.6 million (1999 £0.6 million).

## c. Contribution from UK Government, the European Union and UN Agencies (restricted)

| | Net | | Gross | | Deferred | |
|---|---|---|---|---|---|---|
| | 2000 £'000 | 1999 £'000 | 2000 £'000 | 1999 £'000 | 2000 £'000 | 1999 £'000 |
| UK Government Department for International Development | 11,772 | 13,193 | 11,772 | 13,405 | 0 | (212) |
| European Union | 14,345 | 13,491 | 14,345 | 13,535 | 0 | (44) |
| UNHCR | 3,264 | 1,542 | 3,264 | 1,542 | 0 | 0 |
| Other UN Agencies | 200 | 342 | 200 | 342 | 0 | 0 |
| | 29,581 | 28,568 | 29,581 | 28,824 | 0 | (256) |

## d. Contribution from Other Agencies (restricted)

| | Net | | Gross | | Deferred | |
|---|---|---|---|---|---|---|
| | 2000 £'000 | 1999 £'000 | 2000 £'000 | 1999 £'000 | 2000 £'000 | 1999 £'000 |
| Members of Oxfam International | 9,089 | 6,689 | 9,089 | 6,689 | 0 | 0 |
| Non-UK Governments | 241 | 450 | 241 | 450 | 0 | 0 |
| Other International Agencies | 936 | 917 | 936 | 919 | 0 | (2) |
| Disaster Emergencies Committee | 14,731 | 9,393 | 14,731 | 9,393 | 0 | 0 |
| National Lottery Charities Board | 392 | 72 | 392 | 142 | 0 | (70) |
| Other UK Agencies | 23 | 98 | 23 | 106 | 0 | (8) |
| | 25,412 | 17,619 | 25,412 | 17,699 | 0 | (80) |

## e. Gifts in Kind

| | 2000 £'000 | 1999 £'000 |
|---|---|---|
| Blankets and Clothing | 342 | 1,672 |
| Food Aid received from World Food Programme | 1,092 | 4,070 |
| Food Aid received from European Union | 1,001 | 3,576 |
| | 2,435 | 9,318 |

[*Continued on following page*]

*OXFAM, continued*

### f. Miscellaneous Income

| | 2000 £'000 | 1999 £'000 |
|---|---|---|
| Deposit Interest—unrestricted | 1,493 | 1,573 |
| Deposit Interest—restricted | 152 | 0 |
| Sale of printed material | 151 | 0 |
| Surplus/(Loss) on Disposal of Fixed Assets | 68 | (89) |
| Investment Income | | |
| Quoted Investments | 6 | 43 |
| Cash held for investment (endowment income) | 102 | 13 |
| Rental income from investment properties | 7 | 0 |
| Nursery fees | 146 | 131 |
| Others | 11 | 3 |
| | 2,136 | 1,674 |

### g. Net Income from Trading Subsidiary

The total contribution of Oxfam Activities Limited to Oxfam was as follows:

| | 2000 £,000 | 1999 £'000 |
|---|---|---|
| Turnover | 14,962 | 15,707 |
| Less Expenses (excluding interest charged by Oxfam) | (11,483) | (11,691) |
| Net Profit for the Financial Year | 3,479 | 4,016 |
| Management Charge | (3,064) | (3,168) |
| | 415 | 848 |
| Donations Received for Oxfam by Oxfam Activities Limited | 15 | 61 |
| | 430 | 909 |

No charge is made to the trading subsidiary for rags provided from Oxfam shops. The profit of Oxfam Activities Limited is covenanted to Oxfam, so that there is no liability to Corporation Tax.

Interest on working capital was charged to the trading subsidiary of £335,000 (1999: £304,000), resulting in an overall profit for Oxfam Activities Limited of £0.1 million (1999: £0.6 million).

*Imperial Cancer Research Fund: 30 September 1999*

### Consolidated statement of financial activities for the year ended 30 September 1999

| | Note | Unrestricted funds £000 | Designated funds £000 | Restricted funds £000 | **Total 1999 £000** | Total 1998 £000 |
|---|---|---|---|---|---|---|
| **Incoming resources** | | | | | | |
| Fundraising: | | | | | | |
| Legacies | | **47,558** | – | – | **47,558** | 46,038 |
| Donations | | **15,296** | – | **1,335** | **16,631** | 12,890 |
| Regional activities | | **6,511** | – | **4,022** | **10,533** | 10,546 |
| Corporate fundraising | | **1,862** | – | **1,013** | **2,875** | 1,680 |
| Miscellaneous | | **128** | – | – | **128** | 662 |
| | | **71,355** | – | **6,370** | **77,725** | 71,816 |

[*Continued on following page*]

*Imperial Cancer Research Fund, continued*

| | Note | Unrestricted funds £000 | Designated funds £000 | Restricted funds £000 | **Total 1999 £000** | Total 1998 £000 |
|---|---|---|---|---|---|---|
| Other sources: | | | | | | |
| Grants | | – | – | **4,052** | **4,052** | 4,900 |
| Investment income | | **5,091** | – | **28** | **5,119** | 4,841 |
| | | **5,091** | – | **4,080** | **9,171** | 9,171 |
| Retail and trading operations: | | | | | | |
| Sales of donated goods in shops, including donations | | **25,795** | – | – | **25,795** | 24,602 |
| Trading subsidiaries' income | 2 | **10,226** | – | **23** | **10,249** | 11,616 |
| **Total incoming resources** | | **112,467** | – | **10,473** | **122,940** | 117,775 |
| Less: shops' expenses | 7 | **(20,796)** | – | – | **(20,796)** | (22,248) |
| trading subsidiaries' expenses | 2 | **(8,533)** | – | – | **(8,533)** | (9,274) |
| **Incoming resources available** | | **83,138** | – | **10,473** | **93,611** | 86,253 |
| **Resources expended** | 7 | | | | | |
| Direct charitable expenditure | | | | | | |
| Research expenditure | | **53,478** | – | **10,715** | **64,193** | 55,331 |
| Other expenditure: | | | | | | |
| Fundraising costs | | **19,842** | – | – | **19,842** | 14,482 |
| Management and administration costs | | **737** | – | – | **737** | 841 |
| **Total expenditure** | | **74,057** | – | **10,715** | **84,772** | 70,654 |
| **Surplus/(deficit) for the year** | | **9,081** | – | **(242)** | **8,839** | 15,599 |
| **Associates** | | | | | | |
| Net profit/(loss) on associates | 10 | **21** | – | – | **21** | (21) |
| **Other** | | | | | | |
| Net investment gains/(losses) | 9 | **5,372** | – | **87** | **5,459** | (245) |
| Transfer between funds | 14 | **(21,929)** | **21,929** | – | – | – |
| **Change in net assets** | | **(7,455)** | **21,929** | **(155)** | **14,319** | 15,333 |
| **Funds at 30 September 1998** | | **71,651** | **46,409** | **6,399** | **124,459** | 109,126 |
| **Funds at 30 September 1999** | | **64,196** | **68,338** | **6,244** | **138,778** | 124,459 |

The notes to these accounts form an integral part of the consolidated financial statements.

## 2 Net profit of trading subsidiaries

The principal activities of Imperial Cancer Research Fund Trading Limited ("TRADING") are the sale of bought in goods and the undertaking of other fundraising activities.

The principal activities of Imperial Cancer Research Technology Limited ("ICRT") are the generation of income from Imperial Cancer Research Fund inventions and fees for negotiating collaboration research and consultancy agreements. The results of the trading activities undertaken by the wholly owned subsidiary companies are detailed below:

[*Continued on following page*]

*Imperial Cancer Research Fund, continued*

| | TRADING 1999 £000 | ICRT 1999 £000 | **Total 1999 £000** | Total 1998 £000 |
|---|---|---|---|---|
| Turnover | **7,264** | **2,894** | **10,158** | 11,489 |
| Cost of sales | **(4,502)** | **(1,045)** | **(5,547)** | (6,169) |
| Total expenses | **(1,620)** | **(1,365)** | **(2,985)** | (3,104) |
| Interest receivable | **61** | **30** | **91** | 127 |
| Taxation | **–** | **(1)** | **(1)** | (1) |
| Profit after tax | **1,203** | **513** | **1,716** | 2,342 |
| Covenant and gift aid payments to Imperial Cancer Research Fund | **(1,203)** | **(513)** | **(1,716)** | (2,342) |
| Retained profits for the year | **–** | **–** | **–** | – |
| Reserves at 30 September 1998 | **3** | **–** | **3** | 3 |
| Reserves at 30 September 1999 | **3** | **–** | **3** | 3 |

## 8 DETAIL OF INCOME AND EXPENDITURE

**13.41** As discussed in Chapter 8 expenditure should be analysed according to its functional classification on the face of the Statement of Financial Activities. In other words, the analysis of expenditure contained within the Statement of Financial Activities should be sufficient to enable the reader to identify the defined charitable purpose for which the money was expended (eg hospice and healthcare services).

**13.42** In addition, the notes to the accounts should show the *'natural'* classification of expenditure (eg salaries, rent, premises costs etc).

*National Institute for Social Work: 30 June 2000*

### 3 Direct charitable expenditure

| | Unrestricted funds £ | Restricted funds £ | **Total 2000 £** | Total 1999 £ |
|---|---|---|---|---|
| **Research** | | | | |
| Salary, other staff and related costs | 1,102 | 324,518 | **325,620** | 322,996 |
| Dissemination and miscellaneous costs | 9,236 | 55,277 | **64,513** | 86,541 |
| | 10,338 | 379,795 | **390,133** | 409,537 |
| **Development** | | | | |
| Salary, other staff and related costs | 477,406 | 84,208 | **561,614** | 502,349 |
| Dissemination and miscellaneous costs | 12,897 | 3,262 | **16,159** | 79,986 |
| | 490,303 | 87,470 | **577,773** | 582,335 |
| **Information** | | | | |
| Salary, other staff and related costs | 233,078 | 69,125 | **302,203** | 234,485 |
| Books and publication costs | 48,426 | – | **48,426** | 60,235 |
| Dissemination and miscellaneous costs | 9,613 | 52,229 | **61,842** | 66,757 |
| | 291,117 | 121,354 | **412,471** | 361,477 |

[*Continued on following page*]

*National Institute for Social Work, continued*

| | Unrestricted funds £ | Restricted funds £ | **Total 2000 £** | Total 1999 £ |
|---|---|---|---|---|
| **Policy** | | | | |
| Salary, other staff and related costs | 20,789 | 56,322 | **77,111** | 129,115 |
| Dissemination and miscellaneous costs | 1,510 | 25,687 | **27,197** | 35,695 |
| | 22,299 | 82,009 | **104,308** | 164,810 |
| **Support costs** | | | | |
| Salary, other staff and related costs | 261,201 | – | **261,201** | 252,779 |
| Premises and office costs | 131,698 | 85,348 | **217,046** | 141,668 |
| Finance costs | 3,353 | – | **3,353** | 3,681 |
| Staff training | 8,122 | – | **8,122** | 2,356 |
| Dissemination and miscellaneous costs | 42,853 | – | **42,853** | 45,021 |
| | 447,227 | 85,348 | **532,575** | 445,505 |
| **Total direct charitable expenditure** | 1,261,284 | 755,976 | **2,017,260** | 1,963,664 |

## 5 Management and administration of the charity

| | Unrestricted funds £ | Restricted funds £ | **Total 2000 £** | Total 1999 £ |
|---|---|---|---|---|
| Premises and office costs | 87,091 | 24,494 | **111,585** | 101,823 |
| Legal and professional fees | 17,645 | – | **17,645** | 9,765 |
| Auditors' remuneration | 6,500 | – | **6,500** | 6,000 |
| Company secretarial costs | 50,805 | – | **50,805** | 45,004 |
| | 162,041 | 24,494 | **186,535** | 162,592 |

### Comment

**13.43** The above example illustrates the breakdown of the two categories of direct charitable expenditure and management and administration expenses incurred by the National Institute for Social Work into their natural classification.

**13.44** This classification is required to give the reader of the charity's accounts further insight into the charity's objects and to explain the expenditure it must incur in order to fulfil those objectives. A well-designed note will, for example, emphasise the fact that the charity may be heavily dependent on its staff, ie it is people oriented or that a large proportion of its expenditure is focused on maintaining properties, ie it is a heritage charity. Care needs to be taken to ensure that the natural classification of expenditure is meaningful and summarised into appropriate categories. For example, expenditure headings such as light, heat, rent, repairs to property, rates, rent etc, may be immaterial individually and may be better grouped together and disclosed as 'expenditure on premises' etc. The temptation to list every conceivable type of expense should be avoided as such detail will be excessive and will detract from the intended message of the overall accounts.

**13.45** If carefully designed the note providing details of the natural classification of expenditure can be combined with the need to provide and disclose other information such as employees' remuneration details (see **13.91**) and auditor's remuneration (see **13.103**). The 2000 accounts of the Church of England Children's Society illustrates how such a note can be designed in practice.

*Church of England Children's Society: 31 March 2000*

**5 Resources expended**

Analysis of resources expended (excluding shops operating costs)

| | Staff Costs £000 | Other £000 | Depreciation £000 | Total £000 |
|---|---|---|---|---|
| **Direct charitable expenditure** | | | | |
| Child care | 17,185 | 5,008 | 703 | 22,896 |
| Support costs | 1,905 | 1,157 | 156 | 3,218 |
| Campaigning and public education | 934 | 856 | 19 | 1,809 |
| | 20,024 | 7,021 | 878 | 27,923 |
| **Other expenditure** | | | | |
| Management and admininstration | 821 | 419 | 36 | 1,276 |
| Fundraising | 3,651 | 5,427 | 123 | 9,201 |
| 2000 | 24,496 | 12,867 | 1,037 | 38,400 |
| 1999 | 19,940 | 11,696 | 1,065 | 32,701 |
| Shops operating costs | 890 | 1,777 | 262 | 2,929 |

| | 2000 £000 | 1999 £000 |
|---|---|---|
| **Resources expended include:** | | |
| Operating lease rentals (land and buildings) | 1,405 | 1,810 |
| Depreciation charge | 1,298 | 1,183 |
| Auditors' remuneration (excluding VAT) [Society £37,000 (1999: £26,000)] | 39 | 28 |
| Audit fee for Prior Year Audits (excluding VAT) | 19 | 0 |
| Previous auditors' remuneration in respect of Tax Services (excluding VAT) | 17 | 16 |
| Previous auditors' remuneration of IT consultancy (excluding VAT) | 20 | 0 |
| | 37 | 16 |

All the net expenditure for the year of £2,691,000 (1999: £4,193,000) has been dealt with in the financial statements of the Society.

## 9 GRANTS PAYABLE

**13.46** Since the late 1980s there has been criticism of grant making charities over their secrecy and apparent unwillingness to disclose to whom they made grants and for what purpose. As a consequence the requirements for grants payable disclosure contained within the SORP are detailed and extensive.

### Definition

**13.47** SORP defines a grant as *'any payment which, in order to further its objects, a charity makes voluntarily to another institution or individual'*. The

SORP makes it clear that the definition does not include any payment made in consideration of the supply to the grant maker of assets or services, ie the grant must be given for nil consideration. If the payment is made in pursuance of a contract, it is not a grant.

### The requirements for disclosure

**13.48** Schedule 1 Part IV to the Charities (Accounts and Reports) Regulations 1995 states that the notes to the accounts of a charity should give particulars of any grant made by the charity to another institution, of which any relevant recommended practice requires disclosure. This clearly means that any disclosure required by the SORP must be included in the charity's accounts. SORP does recognise, however, that in many cases grant making represents only a very small part of a charity's activities. Paragraph 139 of SORP states that the detailed grant disclosure need only be given where grant making activities constitute 5% or more of the charity's resources expended:

*'If grant-making is material to a charity, the charity should provide an appropriate analysis and explanation of the grants which it makes. Whether grant-making is material will to some extent depend on the size of the charity and the importance of grant-making to its overall operation. If in any accounting year a charity makes grants totalling at least 5% of its total resources expended in that year the charity should regard its grant-making as material. However, there may be circumstances where the value of grants to an institution in an accounting year is material compared to the total institutional grants in that year and information regarding such grants could be useful to the users of the accounts and should be disclosed.'* *(para 139)*

### Comment

**13.49** This distinction is extremely sensible and ensures that for those charities where grant making is only a small part of their total activities, grant disclosure does not detract from the charity's other work.

### Specific disclosure requirements

**13.50** SORP itself splits grants payable into two categories: those payable to institutions and those payable to individuals and para 141 of SORP defines these two types of grant:

*'The analysis should clearly indicate whether grants are individual or institutional. An individual grant is one which is made for the direct benefit of the individual who receives it, for example to relieve financial hardship. All other grants should be regarded as institutional. For example, a grant which is made to an individual to carry out some research project should be regarded as*

*a grant to the institution with which the individual is connected rather than as a grant to the individual.'* *(para 141)*

The general aim of the grant disclosure is to enable the reader of the charity's accounts to gain a full appreciation of the scale and scope of the charity's grant making activities, as explained by para 142 of SORP:

*'For both individual and institutional grants, an analysis should be given which discloses the total number and the total value of the grants given for different charitable purposes. The charity should decide upon classifications which are appropriate for an understanding of its policy. For example, institutional grants may be grouped into categories covering social welfare, medical research, the performing arts, etc. Similarly, grants to individuals may be grouped in categories covering, for example, the welfare of people in financial need or help to people seeking to further their education. Some charities may decide that it is appropriate to provide further levels of analysis, for example, showing a geographical analysis of the number and value of grants made.'* *(para 142)*

### Grants payable to institutions

**13.51** Paragraphs 143 and 144 of SORP state:

*'In addition,* ***in the case of institutional grants****, and subject to paragraph 146, the trustees should disclose details, as specified in paragraph 144, of a sufficient number of institutional grants to convey a proper understanding of the charity's grant-making activities. The number of grants which is sufficient will vary with circumstances. Where a charity has made fewer than 50 material institutional grants in a year all the grants should be disclosed. Otherwise, the disclosure should cover at least the 50 largest institutional grants or any larger number which is necessary for the proper understanding of the charity's grant-making activity. There is no requirement to disclose any grants which are below £1,000 in total.'* *(para 143)*

*'The disclosure for institutional grants should include the name of the recipient institution and the number and total value of grants made to that institution in the accounting year. Where grants have been made to a particular institution for different charitable purposes, the number and total value of the grants made for each purpose should be disclosed. For example, a charity may have made grants to different officers of a particular university for different projects. As has already been explained (paragraph 141), the grants should all be treated as having been made to the institution but an analysis should be given of the number and total of grants made for each purpose.'* *(para 144)*

The analyses required, as set out above, need to be reconciled clearly to the amount for grants payable in the Statement of Financial Activities. In order to facilitate this reconciliation, it may be necessary to include within the list of grants a 'balancing category', ie the total of grants for which full details have not been disclosed.

**13.52** SORP does allow charities to withhold these details in cases where the trustees believe disclosure would prejudice either the furtherance of the purposes of the charity or those of the recipient. In such cases only the total number, value and general purpose of such grants should be disclosed in the accounts. However, details of any such grants, together with an explanation of the reason for non-disclosure, must be sent, in writing, to the Charity Commission prior to the trustees signing the accounts. In addition, para 146(c) of SORP requires that *'the trustees must confirm whether or not such details have been submitted to the Charity Commission in their trustees report'*.

**13.53** In its simplest form, therefore, the grants disclosure will be in the format set out in the example below, taken from the accounts of The Lord Ashdown Charitable Settlement.

*Lord Ashdown Charitable Settlement: 5 April 2000*

**1 Grants payable**

During the year ended 5 April 2000 the Trust made grants, and at 5 April 2000 had commitments in respect of grants, in the following categories:

| | **Payable** | For future years | | Payable |
|---|---|---|---|---|
| | **2000** | 2002 | 2001 | 1999 |
| | **£** | £ | £ | £ |
| Arts | **160,350** | – | 40,000 | 132,200 |
| Children/youth | **85,700** | – | 7,200 | 46,700 |
| Community | **1,443,922** | 450,000 | 612,862 | 1,771,902 |
| Disability | – | – | 15,500 | – |
| Education | **764,130** | 775,000 | 940,000 | 1,281,801 |
| Hospice and aged | **13,000** | – | – | 15,000 |
| Interfaith/race | **413,650** | 40,000 | 126,800 | 168,850 |
| Medical | **5,000** | – | 5,500 | 53,300 |
| Mental health | **4,500** | – | – | – |
| Preventative medicine | **38,000** | – | 4,000 | 52,500 |
| Students | **50,463** | – | 2,450 | 66,906 |
| Grants of £250 or under | **23,109** | – | – | 22,252 |
| | **3,001,824** | 1,265,000 | 1,754,312 | 3,611,411 |

In addition to the commitments existing at 5 April 2000, the charity has entered into a guarantee agreement whereby it guarantees the salary and pension contributions of the director of the London College of Jewish Studies (formerly Jews' College) for a period of three years commencing 1 May 2000.

[*Continued on following page*]

*Lord Ashdown Charitable Settlement, continued*

| Recipient | Charity registration number | Purpose of Grant | £ |
|---|---|---|---|
| **Arts** | | | |
| Ebony Steel Band Trust | 308026 | African Caribbean Youth | **72,000** |
| Lyndons Arts Trust | 1060068 | Community arts | **15,000** |
| Stephen Spender Memorial Trust | 1069077 | Artistic development | **20,000** |
| Yaa Asantewaa Arts Centre | 271449 | Black community Arts | **55,000** |
| **Children/Youth** | | | |
| Jewish Child's Day | 209266 | Children of Chernobyl | **15,000** |
| **Community** | | | |
| American Jewish Committee | 13.556.3393 | Community/Holocaust/projects | **47,965** |
| Bayswater Project | 294622 | Support for homeless families | **74,000** |
| Black Training Enterprise Group | 225922 | Black business development | **25,000** |
| Civil Liberties Trust | 228465 | Civil Liberties | **34,500** |
| Community Links | 1018517 | Community development work | **24,000** |
| Community Security Trust | 1042391 | Community | **26,000** |
| Conference of European Rabbis | U17422 | Community | **15,000** |
| Foundation for International Security | 327771 | Working towards international co-operation | **40,000** |
| Friends of the Hebrew University of Jersusalem | 209691 | Education | **40,000** |
| Institute for Jewish Policy Research | 252626 | Jewish education | **60,000** |
| Institute for Public Policy Research | 800065 | Educational development | **19,000** |
| Jewish Marriage Council | 214377 | Community | **14,000** |
| Jewish Memorial Council | 206565 | Community support | **50,000** |
| Joint Jewish Charitable Trust | 1060078 | Educational training | **175,000** |
| Kente | 1053663 | Black voluntary sector | **24,000** |
| London Print Studio | 1006900 | Community media | **26,500** |
| Lubavitch Foundation (London) | 227638 | Community development work | **25,000** |
| Maimonides Foundation | 1044028 | Interfaith work | **44,757** |
| The Noah Trust | 326523 | Healthcare development | **33,000** |
| Parent Network | 327136 | Parenting support | **20,000** |
| Reform Synagogues of Great Britain | 250060 | Chaplaincies | **135,000** |
| Runnymede Trust | 313767 | Racial awareness | **23,500** |
| Shelter | 263710 | Community development work | **23,000** |
| Voluntary Action Westminster | 243954 | Community development | **19,500** |
| Yakar Educational Foundation | 277818 | Cultural community centre | **134,875** |
| **Education** | | | |
| Centre for Advanced Professional Educators | 1060078 | Educational training | **150,000** |
| Clore Tikva Primary School | 1073942 | Education | **50,000** |
| Friends of Israel Education Trust | 271983 | Education | **33,925** |
| Holocaust Educational Trust | 327640 | Education | **25,000** |
| Jewish Preparatory School | 289066 | Education | **25,000** |
| Limmud | 327111 | Education | **27,000** |
| London School of Jewish Studies | U1742Z | Jewish education | **240,750** |
| Spiro Institute (London Jewish Cultural Centre) | 1013594 | History and culture | **187,375** |
| Carried forward | | | **2,069,647** |

[*Continued on following page*]

*Lord Ashdown Charitable Settlement, continued*

| Recipient | Charity registration number | Purpose of Grant | £ |
|---|---|---|---|
| Brought forward | | | **2,069,647** |
| **Interfaith/race** | | | |
| The 1990 Trust | 1012898 | Community development | **72,500** |
| Centre for Jewish Christian Relations | U17422 | Interfaith work | **13,000** |
| Council of Christians and Jews | 238005 | Interfaith work | **22,500** |
| Coventry Cathedral | n/a | Interfaith work | **20,000** |
| Detainee Support and Help Unit | 1073911 | Immigrant support | **25,000** |
| Foundation for the Care of Victims of Apartheid | 328686 | Welfare | **13,200** |
| Foreign Policy Centre | 1042046 | Multicultural development | **15,000** |
| International Council of Christians & Jews | 238005 | Interfaith work | **14,600** |
| Jews Council for Racial Equality | 281236 | Racial equality | **25,000** |
| Racial Equality in Europe Trust | 1021451 | Racial awareness | **20,000** |
| Stephen Lawrence Educational Trust | 1070860 | Black educational development | **20,000** |
| Yigal Allon Educational Trust | 327009 | Interfaith education | **18,000** |
| | | | **2,348,447** |
| Other grants | | | **653,377** |
| **Total of Annual Grants** | | | **3,001,824** |

**13.54** However, the requirement of para 140 of SORP for grants to be appropriately *analysed and explained* implies that the larger grant makers will have to give statistical information such as the number and value of grants given for specific activities, specific geographical locations and specific groups. Such information, which would normally be contained in a separate publication, will often be presented in the form of charts and diagrams.

## Grants to individuals

**13.55** Charities which give grants to individuals need only disclose the aggregate value of such grants and the total number given.

## Comment

**13.56** The disclosure of grants payable is a contentious area and a number of concerns have been voiced about the requirements of SORP.

*The Baring Foundation: 31 December 1999*

# International project grants

**In 1999 the Foundation made 18 grants to support work by UK organisations to develop the effectiveness of community and voluntary organisations working in Sub-Saharan Africa and Latin America.**

Awards were made for a number of activities, but chiefly for training work and the dissemination of good practice. Training activities included leadership courses for non-government organisations (NGOs) in Africa; training for community-based organisations (CBOs) and NGOs working with farmers, foresters and elderly people; and training in information and communication technology for refugee groups. Grants for dissemination included work to bring NGOs, CBOs and government officials together to discuss housing issues in Nairobi, Kenya; a collaboration between mental health experts from Africa and Latin America on a training manual for a global network; and a series of meetings to share ideas on how women's rights as employees can be monitored in Central America.

The types of activities and organisations funded in 1999 were similar to those funded in 1998. The average grant size was 27% higher which in turn meant fewer grants were awarded.

Photographer: Darren Saywell Photo courtesy of Wateraid

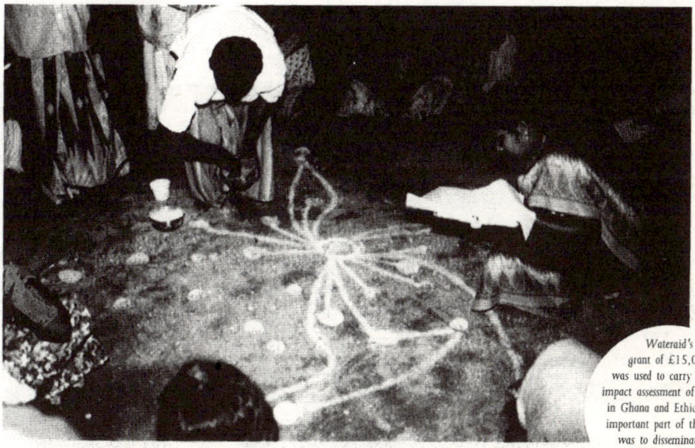

*Wateraid's grant of £15,000 was used to carry out an impact assessment of its work in Ghana and Ethiopia. An important part of this work was to disseminate the findings to local organisations.*

*The Baring Foundation, continued*

## International Grants: Key facts

**Summary of applications and grants**

| | 1999 | 1998 | 1997 |
|---|---|---|---|
| Number of applications | 67 | 68 | 50 |
| Number of eligible applications | 63 | 66 | 49 |
| Number of grants | 18 | 25 | 13 |
| Success rate of eligible applications | 29% | 39% | 29% |
| Total value of grants | £232,780 | £254,048 | £88,416 |
| Largest grant | £15,450 | £16,065 | £14,000 |
| Smallest grant | £6,200 | £2,500 | £1,700 |
| Average grant | £12,932 | £10,162 | £6,801 |

**What kinds of activities have been funded?**

| Activity | 1999 | | 1998 | | 1997 | |
|---|---|---|---|---|---|---|
| | Number | Value | Number | Value | Number | Value |
| Dissemination of good practice | 6 | £76,005 | 9 | £75,687 | 2 | £5,950 |
| Training | 9 | £117,145 | 12 | £133,498 | 3 | £31,282 |
| Feasibility or investigative study | 1 | £14,730 | 1 | £5,000 | 3 | £27,704 |
| Start-up funding or pilot project | 2 | £24,900 | 2 | £29,863 | 2 | £4,200 |
| Consultancy work | 0 | – | 0 | – | 3 | £19,280 |
| Participatory arts project | 0 | – | 1 | £10,000 | 0 | – |
| Total | 18 | £232,780 | 25 | £254,048 | 13 | £88,416 |

**What kinds of organisations have been funded?**

| Organisation | 1999 | | 1998 | | 1997 | |
|---|---|---|---|---|---|---|
| Arts | 0 | – | 1 | £10,000 | 0 | – |
| Environmental | 1 | £12,125 | 1 | £15,000 | 2 | £14,700 |
| Health | 1 | £12,981 | 3 | £25,200 | 2 | £19,000 |
| Overseas development (general) | 14 | £177,944 | 15 | £162,814 | 6 | £39,184 |
| Training | 1 | £14,730 | 2 | £18,784 | 0 | – |
| Community networks | 1 | £15,000 | 3 | £22,250 | 1 | £1,250 |
| Community care | 0 | – | 0 | – | 2 | £14,282 |
| Total | 18 | £232,780 | 25 | £254,048 | 13 | £88,416 |

**How have the grants been distributed geographically?**

| Country or region | 1999 | | 1998 | | 1997 | |
|---|---|---|---|---|---|---|
| Latin America | 3 | £37,125 | 7 | £76,220 | 3 | £21,700 |
| Sub-Saharan Africa | 12 | £153,075 | 17 | £165,328 | 6 | £41,766 |
| Both Africa and Latin America | 3 | £42,580 | 1 | £12,500 | 4 | £24,950 |
| Total | 18 | £232,780 | 25 | £254,048 | 13 | £88,416 |

*The Baring Foundation, continued*

# Small Projects

**In 1999, 56 new Small Projects grants were made to support small scale arts activities (projects costing less than £20,000 in all) in educational or community settings.**

The majority of grants were awarded to projects in which participants worked together, but without producing a final performance or public event. As in 1998, grants were made to a wide range of artforms, but the majority went to activities which combined artforms. No grants were given for activities on literature and storytelling or opera, but these are the categories which attract fewest applications. Grants were distributed widely throughout the UK, with the London region receiving the greatest number of grants. The south west was particularly successful, which is gratifying because this region had no grants in 1998. The number of grants and success rates of applications has remained largely unchanged since 1998.

Photographer: Richard Jennings Photo courtesy of Common Players

Common Players' grant of £4,000 gave young people in South West England a taste of life in a touring theatre company.

*The Baring Foundation, continued*

## Small Projects: Key facts

**Summary of applications and grants**

| | 1999 | 1998 | 1997 |
|---|---|---|---|
| Number of applications | 438 | 449 | 832 |
| Number of eligible applications | 362 | 359 | 592 |
| Number of grants | 56 | 56 | 64 |
| Success rate of eligible applications | 15% | 16% | 11% |
| Total value of grants | £178,356 | £161,774 | £178,146 |
| Largest grant | £5,000 | £5,000 | £5,000 |
| Smallest grant | £700 | £500 | £600 |
| Average grant | £3,185 | £2,911 | £2,784 |

**What kinds of activities have been funded?**

| Activity | 1999 | | 1998 | | 1997 | |
|---|---|---|---|---|---|---|
| | Number | Value | Number | Value | Number | Value |
| Feasibility or investigative study | 0 | – | 1 | £5,000 | 2 | £5,000 |
| Participatory project leading to a performance | 20 | £65,725 | 34 | £103,628 | 42 | £112,304 |
| Participatory arts project without a final product | 28 | £87,679 | 15 | £33,146 | 15 | £46,647 |
| Performance or exhibition | 7 | £21,952 | 5 | £17,000 | 4 | £11,195 |
| Training | 1 | £3,000 | 1 | £3,000 | 1 | £3,000 |
| Total | 56 | £178,356 | 56 | £161,774 | 64 | £178,146 |

**What artforms have been funded?**

| Artform | 1999 | | 1998 | | 1997 | |
|---|---|---|---|---|---|---|
| Combined artforms | 19 | £64,980 | 19 | £44,925 | 13 | £41,397 |
| Dance | 8 | £24,150 | 2 | £7,837 | 5 | £10,300 |
| Literature, poetry and storytelling | 0 | – | 2 | £5,000 | 5 | £11,260 |
| Media and film | 2 | £7,000 | 3 | £11,000 | 4 | £13,790 |
| Music | 6 | £17,700 | 7 | £17,271 | 11 | £29,490 |
| Opera and music theatre | 0 | – | 1 | £3,000 | 2 | £7,000 |
| Theatre, mime and puppetry | 16 | £53,042 | 13 | £44,400 | 10 | £25,022 |
| Visual arts and crafts | 5 | £11,484 | 9 | £28,341 | 14 | £ 39,887 |
| Total | 56 | £178,356 | 56 | £161,774 | 64 | £178,146 |

**How have the grants been distributed geographically?**

| Country or region | 1999 | | 1998 | | 1997 | |
|---|---|---|---|---|---|---|
| East Anglia | 6 | £20,500 | 3 | £7,186 | 2 | £9,400 |
| East Midlands | 0 | – | 1 | £3,000 | 1 | £3,000 |
| London | 12 | £44,816 | 18 | £53,028 | 22 | £61,464 |
| North | 2 | £6,500 | 3 | £6,040 | 2 | £3,650 |
| North West | 7 | £18,835 | 4 | £11,000 | 6 | £13,700 |
| South | 4 | £7,570 | 2 | £4,000 | 1 | £3,700 |
| South East | 2 | £6,250 | 0 | – | 4 | £8,590 |
| South West | 10 | £32,245 | 0 | – | 4 | £12,250 |
| West Midlands | 4 | £13,645 | 4 | £7,950 | 4 | £12,850 |
| Yorkshire & Humberside | 1 | £4,210 | 6 | £15,000 | 4 | £10,000 |
| Northern Ireland | 1 | £905 | 2 | £10,000 | 1 | £1,710 |
| Scotland | 4 | £12,500 | 8 | £27,000 | 8 | £23,947 |
| Wales | 3 | £10,380 | 5 | £17,570 | 5 | £13,885 |
| Total | 56 | £178,356 | 56 | £161,774 | 64 | £178,146 |

These concerns include:

(a) Why do the largest 50 grants have to be disclosed and not, for example, 50 of the largest projects or any other area of the charity's expenditure? The Charity Commission find grants more difficult to monitor than other charitable expenditure.
(b) Why distinguish between grants to individuals and grants to institutions?
(c) Will not such detailed disclosure detract from the overall message of the charity's accounts, particularly when the charity is not only involved in grant making? It should not if the detail is contained in the notes.
(d) What is the responsibility of auditors with regard to verifying grant disclosure details, particularly when the details are given in a separate publication? They must ensure that the accounts are not misleading in any material respect and if the accounts rely upon information contained in a separate document then, if material, the auditors will have to satisfy themselves that the content of that other document justifies the accounts' reliance upon it.

**13.57** The question of the recognition of liabilities is also very relevant with regard to grants payable. The recognition of liabilities is dealt with in Chapter 11 and so we only refer to it briefly here. Where a charity's trustees are under an unconditional obligation to make a grant (even if that obligation is only a moral one), and also if that grant is to be paid in a number of instalments over a number of years, it will be necessary to recognise, as expenditure, the full grant in the year in which the commitment is made and treat the amounts payable in future years as liabilities. However, where a grant commitment is made in principle, but it is conditional upon funds becoming available in the future to meet it, then it may not be appropriate to account for the grant as a liability but simply to disclose the commitment in the notes to the accounts.

## 10 CONCESSIONARY LOANS

**13.58** Many charities, particularly benevolent associations, make interest free loans (or loans with interest at non-commercial rates) to their beneficiaries, in furtherance of their charitable objectives. Although not explicitly required by SORP it is generally deemed good practice for the notes to the accounts of such charities to give information regarding such loans and that the charity should regularly consider whether such loans are recoverable or not.

### Comment

**13.59** Most charities should have little difficulty in meeting these requirements.

## 11 OVERHEAD COSTS

**13.60** SORP defines, in general terms, the main categories of expenditure to be shown on the Statement of Financial Activities, ie costs of generating funds (para 132), grants payable (para 138), costs of activities in furtherance of the charity's objects (para 147), support costs (para 148) and costs of management and administration (para 151).

**13.61** Paragraph 153 of SORP sets out the basic principles that should be applied in allocating overhead costs:

*'It is not practicable to define precisely what should be included under each expenditure heading as each charity's circumstances will be different. Furthermore, charities will often group expenditure under different headings for internal reporting purposes from those which should be disclosed in the annual accounts. In attributing costs the following principles should be applied:*

*(a) No part of expenditure incurred on activities falling directly within one cost category should be attributed to any other cost category.*
*(b) Items of expenditure which involve more than one cost category, for example the cost of running an office which houses both fundraising and charitable project support functions, should be apportioned on a reasonable, justifiable and consistent basis to the cost categories involved.*
*(c) Where costs should not be allocated to the categories in paragraph 60(i) (costs of generating funds) and 60(u)(a–c) (grants payable, costs of operating activities, and support costs) they should be included within the costs of management and administration of the charity.' (para 153)*

### Allocation of costs

**13.62** While it may be obvious to which category of expenditure many overheads relate, for example the salary of the fundraiser will be attributed to costs of generating funds, para 153(b) of SORP emphasises the possible need to apportion certain overheads between various expenditure heads. The basis of such apportionment may vary according to the type of overhead and the sophistication of the charity's accounting system but it should be reasonable, practicable to apply and be such that the same basis can be used from one year to another unless there is a fundamental change in circumstances.

**13.63** The importance of determining the bases for allocation should not be underestimated, nor should the time and thought charities will need to put into deciding on appropriate bases, particularly in the first year in which the revised SORP is applied.

**13.64** Typical examples of the ways in which costs can be apportioned are as follows.

FLOOR SPACE

**13.65** This may be used as a basis for allocating costs such as light, heat, rent, rates, maintenance of properties, property depreciation etc between the various headings of costs of generating funds, costs of activities in furtherance of the charity's objectives, support, and management and administration of the charity.

TIME SPENT

**13.66** The chief executive of the charity may spend his or her time involved in all aspects of the charity's activities. In order to allocate his or her salary across the appropriate headings it may be necessary to take a typical week in his or her working life and record the amount of time spent involved in each of the main expense categories. This information can then be used to determine percentages to be used when allocating the chief executive's annual salary for statutory accounts purposes. A similar exercise may be necessary for other staff members who are involved in several areas of the charity's work.

ACTUAL USAGE OF COMMON SERVICES

**13.67** By careful logging and recording, it may be possible to allocate certain overhead costs such as printing, postage, stationery, telephone, photocopying etc on an actual usage basis. This will probably only be applicable for charities with significant expenditure under any of these headings.

## Disclosure of basis used

**13.68** Whichever basis is used to allocate overhead costs across the headings shown on the face of the Statement of Financial Activities, Paragraph 154 of SORP requires: *'The basis and principles used for the allocation of all costs should be disclosed clearly in the accounting policies.'*

**13.69** In addition to disclosing the basis and principles adopted in allocating overhead costs para 152 of SORP requires:

*'There should be a clear analysis of all the major items of expenditure on management and administration in the notes to the accounts.'*

## Comment

**13.70** Common sense should be the guiding principle. The accounting policy note need not be too detailed. The following illustrations are taken from the examples accompanying SORP 2000.

*CC66—SORP 2000: Example Report and Accounts (Dorsetshire Drugs Advice Centre)*

(f) Resources expended are allocated to the particular activity where the cost relates directly to that activity. However, the cost of overall direction and administration on each activity, comprising the salary and overhead costs of the central function, is apportioned on the following bases which are an estimate, based on staff time, of the amount attributable to each activity:

| | |
|---|---|
| Charity Shop | 0% |
| Fund-raising and publicity | 15% |
| Advice and information | 20% |
| Outreach work | 20% |
| Training project | 30% |
| Management and administration of the charity | 15% |

*CC66—SORP 2000: Example Reports and Accounts (Aid overseas)*

(d) **Resources expended and basis of allocation of costs**
Expenditure is included when incurred.

Grants payable to partner organisations for relief and development projects are included in the SOFA when approved by the trustees and agreed with the other organisation. The value of such grants unpaid at the year end is accrued. Grants where the beneficiary has not been informed or has to meet certain conditions before the grant is released are not accrued but are noted as financial commitments.

Expenditure on operational programmes is recognised in the period in which it is incurred. A designated fund is established for expenditure which has been committed to projects, but remains unspent at the year end.

The majority of costs are directly attributable to specific activities. Certain shared costs are apportioned to activities in furtherance of the objects of the charity. Office costs and property related costs are apportioned on the proportion of floor area occupied by the activity. Staff costs and office costs are allocated in the same proportion as directly attributed staff costs.

(e) **Fund-raising costs**
These include the salaries, direct expenditure and overhead costs of the staff in offices in the UK who promote fund-raising, including events.

[*Continued on following page*]

*CC66—SORP 2000: Example Reports and Accounts (Aid overseas), continued*

(f) **Support costs**
Support costs represent the cost of core field offices and the costs incurred by UK based staff, directly providing support for the international programme, including management, policy and advocacy work and supervision and technical support for emergency programmes.

*CC66—SORP 2000: Example Reports and Accounts (The Higher College Charity)*

(d) **Resources expended**
Resources expended are accounted for on an accruals basis. Certain expenditure is apportioned to cost categories based on the estimated amount attributable to that activity in the year. These estimates are based on staff time or the floor area as appropriate. The irrecoverable element of VAT is included with the item of expense to which it relates.

Fuel supplied to the schools by a subsidiary company is treated as a cost of the schools, and the sale proceeds and associated costs are excluded from trading income and trading expenditure. Likewise, construction and repair costs, supplied to the Charity by its subsidiary, are capitalised or expensed and excluded from trading income and expenditure.

## 12 TRANSACTIONS WITH TRUSTEES AND RELATED PERSONS

**13.71** The Charities (Accounts and Reports) Regulations 2000 require disclosure of any transaction undertaken in the name of the charity (or on its behalf) in which any trustee, or person connected to a trustee, has a material interest. These requirements are linked closely with the need under FRS8 'Related party Transactions' (issued in October 1995) to disclose material transactions with those deemed to be a related party to the charity. The SORP ensures that charity accounting requirements are consistent with those of FRS8 by requiring disclosure, in a note to the accounts, of situations where the reporting charity or any institution connected with it (see below) enters into a 'related party transaction'. A related party transaction is one where the charity has a relationship with another party or parties (the related party) which might inhibit it from pursing its own separate interests. Paragraph 157 of SORP states that related parties include:

*'(a) a charity trustee or someone else who is related to the charity; and*
*(b) someone who is either connected with a charity trustee or to a person who is related to the charity'.* *(para 157)*

## Definitions

**13.72** In assessing whether a transaction needs to be disclosed or not the following definitions are important.

MATERIAL

**13.73** An item is defined as being material if its inclusion (or exclusion) would be likely to influence a reader of the report and accounts either in relation to the report and accounts as a whole or in relation to the context of which the item forms part. It is for the trustees to decide whether an item is material or not. The requirements are complex because they require consideration of whether the transaction is material to the related party, in addition to the charity. Hence, it is possible for a transaction to require disclosure even though it may be immaterial to the charity.

RELATED PARTIES

**13.74** Related parties include all of the following:

- 'Institution Connected with a Charity'

An institution is connected with a charity if it is controlled by (in Scotland managed or controlled by), or if a participating interest in it is beneficially owned by, the charity.

- 'Related to the Charity'

The following should be treated as related to the charity:

(a) any charity trustee and custodian trustee of the charity;
(b) any person or body with the power to appoint or remove a significant proportion of the charity trustees of the charity, or whose consent is required to the exercise of any of the discretions of those trustees, or who is entitled to give directions to those trustees as to the exercise of any of those discretions. All or a majority of the trustees should always be treated as a 'significant proportion'. Fewer than 50% of the trustees may be a 'significant proportion' if they collectively have a dominant influence on the operation of the charity, as, for example, is likely to be the case if

one body has the power to appoint/remove 7 of a body of 15 trustees, and 8 other different bodies had the right to appoint/remove 1 each.

(c) any institution connected with the charity, and any director of such an institution;
(d) any other charity with which it is commonly controlled;
(e) any pension fund for the benefit of the employees of the charity, and/or of any other person who is a related party of the charity;
(f) any officer, agent or employee of the charity having authority or responsibility for directing or controlling the major activities or resources of the charity; and
(g) any person connected to a person who is related to the charity.

● 'Connected with a charity trustee or to a person related to the charity'

The following should be treated as 'connected with a charity trustee' or 'connected to a person who is related to the charity':

(a) members of the same family or household of the charity trustee or related person who may be expected to influence, or be influenced by, that person in their dealings with the charity;
(b) the trustees of any trust, not being a charity, the beneficiaries or potential beneficiaries of which include a charity trustee or related person or a person referred to in (a) as being connected with a charity trustee or to a related person, as the case may be;
(c) any business partner of a charity trustee or related person, or of any person referred to in (a) or (b) as being connected with a charity trustee or to a related person, as the case may be;
(d) any body corporate, not being a company which is controlled entirely by one or more charitable institutions, in which:
    (i) the charity trustee has, or the charity trustee and any other charity trustee or trustees or person or persons referred to in (a), (b) or (c) above as being connected with a charity trustee, taken together, have a participating interest; or
    (ii) the related person has, or the related person and any other related parties of the charity, taken together, have a participating interest.
(e) Any person or body who makes available to the charity the services of any person or body as a charity trustee is connected with a charity trustee.

**13.75** Common control exists if:

(i) the same person, or persons have the right to appoint a majority of the charity trustees of both or all the charities; or
(ii) the same person, or persons, hold a majority of the voting rights in the administration of both or all of the charities.

Persons who are related with each other through family or business relationships should be treated as the same person for the present purposes.

**13.76** 'Controlled' means that the charity is able to secure that the affairs of the institution are conducted in accordance with its wishes.

**13.77** 'Participating interest' means that the charity:

'(a) *is interested in shares comprised in the equity share capital of the body of a nominal value of more than one fifth of that share capital; or*
(b) *is entitled to exercise or control the excerise of more than one-fifth of the voting power at any general meeting of the body.'*

**13.78** Thus a charity can be a related party of another charity, for example, if one is the trustee of the other, or if it has the power to appoint or remove a significant proportion of the charity trustees of the other, or if the two charities are subject to common control (ie a majority of the trustees in common). This should not, however, be interpreted as meaning that two charities are related simply because a particular person happens to be a trustee of both.

**13.79** The reasoning behind related party disclosure is one of transparency and demonstrating good stewardship. Any decision to enter into a transaction ought to be influenced only by the consideration of the charity's own interests. This requirement is re-inforced by legal rules which, in certain circumstances, can invalidate transactions where the charity's trustees have a conflict of interest.

**13.80** Transparency is particularly important where the relationship between the charity and the other party or parties might suggest that the transaction could possibly have been influenced by interests other than the charity's.

### Related party transactions

**13.81** Paragraph 161 of SORP states that related party transactions potentially include:

'(a) *purchases, sales, leases and donations (including donations which are made in furtherance of the charity's objects) of goods, property, money and other assets such as intellectual property rights to or from the related party;*
(b) *the supply of services by the related party to the charity, and the supply of services by the charity to the related party. Supplying services includes providing the use of goods, property and other assets and finance arrangements such as making loans and giving guarantees and indemnities;*

(c) *any other payments and other benefits which are made to trustees under express provisions of the governing document of a charity or in fulfilment of its charitable objectives.'* *(para 161)*

Transactions should be disclosed whether or not they are at arm's length.

**Disclosure**

**13.82** The disclosure requirements are summarised in para 163 of SORP:

*'The required disclosure is as follows (also see paragraph 238(c) re investments);*

(a) *the names(s) of the transacting related party or parties;*
(b) *a description of the relationship between the parties (including the interest of the related party or parties in the transaction);*
(c) *a description of the transaction;*
(d) *the amounts involved;*
(e) *outstanding balances with related parties at the balance sheet date and any provisions for doubtful debts from such persons;*
(f) *any amounts written off from such balances during the accounting year; and*
(g) *any other elements of the transactions which are necessary for the understanding of the financial statements.'* *(para 163)*

Clearly some transactions are such that they are unlikely to influence the pursuance of the separate independent interests of the charity. Such transactions need not be disclosed unless there is evidence to the contrary. Paragraph 165 of SORP gives the following examples of transactions where no disclosure is usually necessary:

'(a) *donations received by the reporting charity from a related party, so long as the donor has not attached conditions which would, or might, require the charity to alter materially the nature of its existing activities if it were to accept the donation (but any material grant by the reporting charity to a charity which is a related party should be disclosed);*
(b) *minor or routine unremunerated services provided to a charity by people related to it;*
(c) *contracts of employment between a charity and its employees (except where the employees are the charity trustees or people connected with them):*
(d) *contributions by a charity to a pension fund for the benefit of employees; (also see paragraph 172);*
(e) *the purchase from a charity by a related party of minor articles which are offered for sale to the general public on the same terms as are offered to the general public;*

(f) *the provision of services to a related party (including a charity trustee or person connected with a charity trustee), where the related party receives the services as part of a wider beneficiary class of which he is a member, and on the same terms as other members of the class (for example, the use of a village hall by members of its committee of management, as inhabitants of the area of benefit); and*

(g) *the payment or reimbursement of out of pocket expenses to a related party (including a charity trustee or person connected with a charity trustee – but see paragraphs 167 to 169).'* *(para 165)*

## Transactions with trustees

**13.83** All transactions, whether directly or indirectly, with a trustee (including persons connected with them), are deemed to be material and therefore require disclosure unless one of the exemptions in para 165 of SORP applies. The fact that remuneration has been paid to a trustee directly or indirectly by the charity or a company which the trustee controls must be disclosed, together with details of the source and the amount, the legal authority under which the payment was made (eg provision in the governing document of the charity, order of the Charity Commission, etc), and the reason for such remuneration. Similar disclosure is required when a person with a family or business connection has received such remuneration (ie when a connected person has received the remuneration). If no such remuneration has been received by trustees this fact must be stated. A company is deemed to be controlled by the trustees if they are able to exercise or direct the exercise of voting power at general meetings of the company.

**13.84** Similarly, where any expenses have been reimbursed to a trustee, the aggregate amount of the reimbursed expenses should be disclosed, together with the number of trustees who have been reimbursed during the year. If no expenses have been reimbursed this fact should be stated. Where expenses have been reimbursed, the nature of the expenses (eg travel, subsistence etc) should be disclosed.

Occasionally trustees act as agents for a charity and make pruchases on its behalf and are reimbursed for this expenditure, eg payment for office stationery or equipment. Such expenditure is not related to the services provided by the trustee and need not be disclosed. Similarly there is no need to disclose routine expenditure which is attributable collectively to the services provided by the trustees eg providing refreshments at a trustees meeting or hiring a room for the meeting.

## Comment

**13.85** SORP provides very prescriptive guidance to the preparers of accounts to determine whether a transaction requires disclosure as being one 'with trustees and related parties'. The decision as to whether a transaction should be disclosed depends on how the criteria set out above apply to the circumstances of the individual case. The ultimate decision on the disclosure or otherwise of a transaction with a trustee or a connected person of the charity rests with the trustees and, in cases of doubt, items should be treated as material and should be disclosed.

**13.86** When considering transactions, one should not forget the requirement to disclose details of transactions involving not only those connected to the charity but also those connected to the trustees. Further consideration should be given to not only the materiality of the transaction to the charity but also to the related party. For both trustees and auditors, the identification of these transactions will be difficult. Auditors and trustees may find that the use of an annual certificate completed by each trustee and by senior management in which such persons give details of disclosable transactions may be a useful starting point.

## 13 INDEMNITY INSURANCE

**13.87** If funds of the charity have been used to purchase indemnity insurance this fact, together with the cost of such insurance, should be disclosed in the notes to the accounts.

**13.88** The types of insurance to be disclosed would either protect the charity from loss arising from the neglect or default of its trustees, employees or agents, or indemnify the trustees against the consequences of any neglect or default on their part.

**Comment**

**13.89** Under s 310(3) of Companies Act 1985, a company may purchase for any officer or auditor insurance against any liability which by virtue of any rule of law would otherwise attach to him in relation to the company. Where any such insurance has been purchased or maintained in the year, that fact must be stated in the directors' report.

**13.90** If the charity indemnified trustees directly for the cost of any neglect or default on their part, this fact would need to be disclosed in the notes to the accounts as a transaction with a trustee (see **13.83**). Care is needed here as there are limitations on the extent to which a charity can indemnify trustees against the effects of their own actions – see Charity Commission Leaflet CC3 and **2.20 ff**.

## 14 EMOLUMENTS OF EMPLOYEES

**13.91** SORP requires the disclosure in the notes to the accounts of the costs of employing staff who work for the charity whether or not the charity itself has incurred the cost. This includes seconded and agency staff and staff employed by connected or independent companies. For instance, staff working for a charity may have contracts with and be paid by a connected company. Payments may also be made to third parties for the provision of staff (eg agencies), where such arrangements are in place and the costs involved are material in relation to the charity's expenditure, SORP requires that the notes to the accounts should include an outline of the arrangements in place, the reasons for them and the amounts involved.

### Comment

**13.92** This amount of disclosure is significantly greater than has been required in the past. Part of the reasoning behind it is to clearly demonstrate the true cost of providing the charity's services. However, it will also enable the reader of the charity's accounts to gain a better understanding of the charity's efficiency and of the scale of its activities.

### Specific disclosure

**13.93** Paragraph 172 of SORP sets out the specific disclosures required:

*'The total staff costs should be shown in the notes to the accounts giving the split between gross wages and salaries, employer's national insurance costs and pension contributions for the year. An estimate of the average number of full time equivalent employees for the year should be disclosed in the notes to the accounts providing sub-categories according to the manner in which the charity's activities are organised.'* *(para 172)*

**13.94** The notes should also show the number of employees whose emoluments for the year (including benefits in kind but excluding pension contributions) fell within each band of £10,000 from £50,000 upwards (ie from £50,001 to £60,000, from £60,001 to £70,000 etc). There is no requirement to provide this disclosure for bands into which no employee's emoluments fell in the current or preceding accounting period.

**13.95** In addition, for the first time SORP requires details to be given regarding pension details for staff whose emoluments exceed £50,000 per annum. Paragraph 174 of SORP states:

*'In addition pension details must be disclosed in total for higher paid staff in paragraph 173 as follows:*

*(a)* *contributions in the year for the provision of money purchase benefits (normally money purchase schemes); and*

(b) *the number of staff to whom retirement benefits are accruing under money purchase and defined-benefit schemes respectively.'* (para 174)

**Comment**

DEFINITION OF 'TOTAL EMOLUMENTS'

**13.96** SORP defines 'total emoluments' as remuneration and benefits-in-kind, in the same way as defined for taxation purposes. For tax purposes 'emoluments' includes 'all salaries, fees, wages, perquisites and profits whatsoever'. It would normally exclude contributions made by the employer to approved pension schemes which do not form part of the employee's taxable income.

**13.97** Redundancy costs would not normally be included in 'total emoluments', although, if material, their separate disclosure should be considered.

VOLUNTEERS AND PART-TIME EMPLOYEES

**13.98** SORP provides no guidance on the treatment of part-time employees and volunteers in determining the average number of employees of the charity. As volunteers are, by definition, excluded from those persons whose remuneration is included in 'total emoluments', they should similarly be excluded from the average number of employees of the charity. SORP recommends that the extent to which the charity is dependent on the services of unpaid volunteers should be appreciated from the narrative contained in the trustees' annual report or should be reported in the notes to the accounts.

**13.99** Similarly, SORP provides no guidance on the treatment of part-time employees in determining the average number of employees. The comparison of the 'average number of employees' with the total emoluments of the charity may not provide useful information to the reader if part-time employees were included as 'whole' employees. However, useful guidance is contained in Sch 4 of the Companies Act 1985. The Companies Act requires the disclosure of the average number of persons employed under contracts of service by the company and gives the method by which this average is to be calculated. This would require the inclusion by charities of all persons with a contract of employment, whether full or part-time, in the calculation of the average number of employees.

**13.100** If charities have a large number of part-time employees under contracts of employment, this may produce a misleading average number of employees. Charities which are not companies could overcome this problem by treating part-time employees as part-employees when calculating the average number of employees. The proportion of the working week for which the part-time employee works can be used to determine the proportion of an employee which should be included in the calculation of the average number of employees (ie if an employee works mornings only, they might be treated as half an employee when calculating the average number of employees). If this approach is used, it is suggested that the accounts should make clear that the disclosure is of full-time equivalents rather than full-time employees. However, it must be remembered that for incorporated charities the use of full-time equivalents disclosure is not permitted by the Companies Act.

BANDING OF EMOLUMENTS

**13.101** Surprisingly, SORP's requirement in respect of the banding of employees' emoluments goes further than the company law requirements which, for years ending on or after 31 March 1997, require the specific disclosure of the emoluments of the highest paid director only. For these Companies Act purposes, 'emoluments' excludes pension contributions made on behalf of the director, but includes benefits-in-kind. Incorporated charities may therefore need to make additional disclosure to meet these requirements.

SPLIT OF EMPLOYEE COSTS BY ACTIVITY AND THEIR NUMBER

**13.102** Paragraph 147 of SORP requires an analysis of expenditure on activities in furtherance of the charity's objects by functional classification. SORP suggests that this would include an analysis of 'salaries' and charities may consider that this analysis may provide more useful information if supplied with details of the average number of employees analysed in the same manner.

*Save the Children: 31 March 2000*

**5 Staff costs**

| | 2000 £'000 | 1999 £'000 |
|---|---|---|
| **Costs of staff on UK contracts:** | | |
| Wages and salaries | **17,656** | 17,224 |
| Employer's National Insurance | **1,134** | 1,175 |
| Employer's pension contribution | **1,551** | 1,124 |
| | **20,341** | 19,523 |

The average number or persons, including part-time staff, employed on UK contracts was 835 (1999 – 872). Approximately 2,364 (1999 – 2,120) staff were employed locally on overseas projects at a cost of £5,220,000 (1999 – £5,093,000).

[*Continued on following page*]

*Save the Children, continued*

| | **2000** NUMBER | 1999 NUMBER |
|---|---|---|
| The following number of employees (including those on short-term contracts) received emoluments within the bands shown: | | |
| Between £0 – £10,000 | **331** | 657 |
| Between £10,001 – £20,000 | **269** | 362 |
| Between £20,001 – £30,000 | **248** | 300 |
| Between £30,001 – £40,000 | **32** | 35 |
| Between £40,001 – £50,000 | **8** | 6 |
| Between £50,001 – £60,000 | **4** | 3 |
| Between £60,001 – £70,000 | **1** | 1 |
| Between £70,001 – £80,000 | **1** | 1 |

The highest paid employee received emoluments amounting to £79,497 in the year ended 31 March 2000.

Emoluments consist of normal remuneration salary and established cash value of benefits-in-kind.

Members of the Board of Trustees (who are all directors within the meaning of the Companies Act 1985) receive no remuneration for their services. Expenses reimbursed to Board members for travelling undertaken on behalf of Save the Children during the year amounted to £12,035 (1999 – £4,870).

Save the Children contributes to two defined benefit schemes administered by the Pensions Trust. At intervals of not more than three years, the schemes' assets are valued by the projected unit method by consulting actuaries who consider Save the Children's contribution rates and the value of the schemes.

The pension cost charged to the Consolidated Statement of Financial Activities is designed to spread the cost of providing pensions to the employees who are members of the schemes over their working lifetimes with Save the Children.

The latest actuarial valuation of the schemes' assets was at September 30, 1999. This reported a market value of £49,046,000, being sufficient to cover 100% of the benefits accrued to members. The most significant assumptions made in that valuation were:

| | |
|---|---|
| Rate of return on investments | 6.85% p.a. |
| Rate of increase in salaries | 4.5% p.a. |
| Rate of increase in equity dividends | 3.25% p.a. |

[*Continued on following page*]

*Save the Children, continued*

**The movement on the Staff Pensions Scheme account was:**

| | 2000 £'000 | 2000 £'000 | 1999 £'000 | 1999 £'000 |
|---|---|---|---|---|
| Balance at 1 April 1999 | | **4,959** | | 5,297 |
| Regular pension costs | **1,551** | | 1,462 | |
| Addition to provision/ (Amortisation of surplus) | **114** | | (388) | |
| Charge to Statement of Financial Activities | | **1,665** | | 1,124 |
| Contributions paid | | **(1,551)** | | (1,462) |
| **Balance at 31 March 2000** | | **5,073** | | 4,959 |

The balance represents the timing difference, calculated in accordance with SSAP24, between the charge to Consolidated Statement of Financial Activities and the contributions actually made.

*Alzheimer's Society: 31 March 2000*

**6 Staff Costs**
**Staff costs consist of:**

| | 1999 Group £ | 1998 Group £ |
|---|---|---|
| Wages and salaries | **6,949,186** | 6,358,237 |
| Social security costs | **565,151** | 474,511 |
| Pension costs | **208,978** | 147,661 |
| | **7,723,315** | 6,980,409 |

The average weekly number of employees for the year was as follows:

| | 1999 Group Full-time No. | 1999 Group Part-time No. | 1998 Group Full-time No. | 1998 Group Part-time No. |
|---|---|---|---|---|
| Care services | 117 | **583** | 114 | 579 |
| Information and education | 16 | **2** | 14 | 2 |
| Regional development and branch activities | 94 | **125** | 87 | 99 |
| Fundraising | 13 | **1** | 13 | 1 |
| Support services | 10 | **–** | 8 | – |
| | 250 | **711** | 236 | 681 |

[*Continued on following page*]

*Alzheimer's Society, continued*

The number of employees in salary bands (including pension contributions) in excess of £40,000 were as follows:

| | 1999<br>No. | 1998<br>No. |
|---|---|---|
| £40,000 – £50,000 | 5 | 1 |
| £50,001 – £60,000 | 0 | 1 |
| £60,001 – £70,000 | 1 | 0 |

Salary increases for members of the senior management team are approved biannually by the remuneration committee.

**Members of Council**
No trustee received any remuneration during the year (1998: NIL). Expenses reimbursed to all trustees during the year totalled £17,892 (1998: £14,854).

## 15 AUDITORS' AND INDEPENDENT EXAMINERS' REMUNERATION

**13.103** SORP requires the separate disclosure in the notes to the accounts of the total amounts payable to the charity's auditor or independent examiner in respect of:

(a) audit or independent examination services, ie the costs of their respective external scrutiny; and
(b) other services, such as taxation advice, consultancy, financial advice and accountancy.

**13.104** The total fees for each of the 'other services' must be analysed by the nature of the service provided (eg taxation advice, consultancy, financial advice and accountancy). Where the accounts are consolidated, the amounts to be disclosed should be the total for the whole group.

**13.105** In addition, where a charity has incurred other non-statutory costs of external scrutiny, eg the audit of a branch, the total of these costs should be identified and disclosed separately.

*The National Council on Ageing: 31 March 2000*

**Notes to the accounts**
*Year ended 31 March 2000*

**12 Net (outgoing)/incoming resources**

| | Group | | Charity | |
|---|---|---|---|---|
| | **2000** | **1999** | **2000** | **1999** |
| | **£'000** | **£'000** | **£'000** | **£'000** |
| Net (outgoing)/incoming resources for the year are stated after charging: | | | | |
| Auditors' remuneration: | | | | |
| For audit services | 68 | 48 | 26 | 11 |
| For audit services – previous year | 14 | (4) | 14 | (4) |
| For taxation services | 28 | 34 | 28 | 34 |
| For consultancy services | 20 | 18 | – | 10 |
| For internal audit services | 37 | 47 | 37 | 47 |
| For staff services | – | 48 | – | 48 |
| Interest payable | 151 | 167 | – | – |
| Depreciation of tangible fixed assets: | | | | |
| Owned assets | 2,080 | 1,764 | 1,336 | 1,168 |
| Operating lease rentals – motor vehicles | 243 | 234 | 243 | 234 |
| – land and vehicles | 1,896 | 1,739 | 1,896 | 1,714 |
| – other | 85 | 93 | – | – |
| Operating lease rentals receivable | (705) | (609) | – | – |
| Research and development expenditure | 4 | 33 | – | – |

## 16 EX GRATIA PAYMENTS

**13.106** Where ex gratia payments are made not as an application of funds or property for charitable purposes, but in fulfilment of a compelling moral obligation, the total amount should be disclosed in the notes to the accounts. 'Payments' for this purpose include the transfer of non-monetary benefits or other expenditure of any kind or waiver of rights to property to which a charity is entitled.

**13.107** The types of payment which may be included under this head would include the surrendering of part of a bequest where disinherited relatives of the deceased press a 'moral' claim to the estate.

**13.108** Payments which the trustees reasonably consider to be in the interests of the charity, ie more than a moral obligation, should not be treated as ex gratia even though there is no legal obligation to make them. For example, a redundancy payment over and above the statutory level may be made in order to motivate retained staff and hence benefit the charity.

**13.109** The nature and date of the authority for each ex gratia payment should be disclosed in the notes to the accounts where the trustees require the authority of the court, the attorney general or the Charity Commissioners to make such payment.

## 17 FIXED ASSETS

**13.110** Most of the disclosure requirements concerning fixed assets have been covered in Chapter 10. It may be helpful however to recap the main items here. Reference should be made to the examples given in that chapter which illustrate these requirements.

**13.111** Paragraphs 203–207 of SORP give a detailed explanation as to how the fixed assets held for use by the charity should be analysed:

- Freehold property, leasehold property, plant and machinery including motor vehicles, fixtures and equipment and assets in course of construction are all examples of likely headings.
- Changes in values of each from the beginning of the year to the end distinguishing between the cost or valuation of assets and their depreciation and giving figures of additions, disposals, revaluations, impairments and transfers.
- Separate totals for each class of asset, together with a combined total should be shown and the depreciation charge for the year for each should also be identifiable.

**13.112** Information on inalienable or historic assets which have not been capitalised should be given.

*'This should specify why the assets are considered to be inalienable or historic and be sufficient to enable the reader to appreciate the age and scale of these assets and what use is made of them. . .'.* *(para 215)*

Any amounts spent on acquiring inalienable and historic assets should also be disclosed.

**13.113** If any functional fixed assets have been revalued the notes should record:

- the name and qualification of the valuer;
- the basis of valuation;
- the historical cost (if available) and depreciation;
- date of the previous valuation; and
- if the value has not been updated, a statement by the trustees that they are not aware of any material changes.

**13.114** In the case of impairment in the value of a functional fixed asset, the notes should show *the methods used in the impairment review to determine the net realisable value and value in use. . .'. (para 230)*. Details of the valuer should also be given as set out in **13.113** above.

*Leeds Castle Foundation and Subsidiary: 28 March 1999*

**Notes to the Accounts**

**1 Accounting Policies**

**Fixed assets and depreciation**

**(a) Castle grounds, freehold land, buildings and castle contents**
No depreciation is provided on the value attributable to the assets acquired through the original gift, on other land and buildings held by the holding company, or on assets subsequently added by development expenditure. It is the policy of the company to carry out annually a full repairs and maintenance programme such that, the residual values of these assets based on prices prevailing at the date of acquisition or 1974 valuation, as applicable, are at least equal to their carrying value. Accordingly any depreciation would not be material. Carrying values are reviewed annually and provision is made, if necessary, for any impairment in value.

*Leeds Castle Foundation and Subsidiary: 28 March 1999*

**Notes to the Accounts**

**Tangible Fixed Assets—Group**

| | Castle ground and buildings | Castle contents | Freehold land and buildings | Equipment and motor vehicles | Total |
|---|---|---|---|---|---|
| | £ | £ | £ | £ | £ |
| COST OR VALUATION | | | | | |
| At Estate Duty Valuation 1974 | 500,000 | 867,586 | – | – | 1,367,586 |
| At cost | 5,785,867 | 506,908 | 1,912,049 | 1,679,471 | 9,884,295 |
| **At 30 March 1998** | **6,285,867** | **1,374,494** | **1,912,049** | **1,679,471** | **11,251,881** |
| Additions | 303,757 | 13,439 | 238,915 | 285,866 | 841,977 |
| Disposals | – | – | – | (152,724) | (152,724) |
| **At 28 March 1999** | **6,589,624** | **1,387,933** | **2,150,964** | **1,812,613** | **11,941,134** |
| DEPRECIATION | | | | | |
| At 30 March 1998 | – | – | – | 1,350,082 | 1,350,082 |
| Charge for year | – | – | – | 166,790 | 166,790 |
| Eliminated in respect of disposals | – | – | – | (112,127) | (112,127) |
| **At 28 March 1999** | – | – | – | **1,404,745** | **1,404,745** |
| **NET BOOK VALUE** | | | | | |
| **At 28 March 1999** | **6,589,624** | **1,387,933** | **2,150,964** | **407,868** | **10,536,389** |
| At 30 March 1998 | 6,285,867 | 1,374,494 | 1,912,049 | 329,389 | 9,901,799 |

**13.115** In the case of fixed asset investments, there will normally be a quoted market price to which reference may be made in the notes. If not the notes should indicate who is responsible for the valuation giving their qualification and position (eg trustee, employee or external valuer). An indication should also be given as to how the valuation was carried out.

**13.116** Paragraph 236 of SORP deals with the situation where the charity holds such a significant proportion of a company's shares that the quoted price may give an exaggerated view of the total value, bearing in mind the effect that a sale of such a large holding might have on the market. The trustees may in such circumstances make adjustments to the valuation but should give an explanation.

**13.117** An analysis of investment assets is required by para 238 of SORP, distinguishing between:

- investment properties;
- quoted investments, including unit trusts;
- shares in subsidiary companies;
- unlisted securities;
- cash held as part of the investment portfolio; and
- other investments.

There should be a further analysis between investment assets within the UK and those outside the UK.

Any holdings representing more than 5% of the total portfolio should be separately disclosed and any restrictions which might apply to the realisation of such assets (para 240).

## 18 COMMITMENTS

**13.118** *'Particulars of all material provisions for commitments accrued in the balance sheet as liabilities should be disclosed in the notes. Similar particulars of all material commitments in respect of specific charitable projects should be disclosed if they have not been charged in the accounts'.* *(para 256)*

**13.119** Where a provision has been made previously the note should show any movement during the year, ie payments made and further provisions required.

*The Leathersellers' Company Charitable Fund: 31 July 1999*

**Notes to the financial statements for the year ended 31 July 1999**

**15 Financial Commitments**

The Trustees of The Leathersellers' Company Charitable Fund have agreed, subject to continuing resources, to award grants of at least £1 million per annum. Of this sum, guaranteed and other recurrent grants already awarded subject to annual review are:

| Year ended 31 July | **1999** | 1998 | Movement in Commitments |
|---|---|---|---|
| | **£** | £ | £ |
| 1999 | 0 | 716,853 | (716,853) |
| 2000 | 822,892 | 625,573 | 197,319 |
| 2001 | 611,025 | 435,321 | 175,704 |
| 2002 | 481,931 | 273,002 | 208,929 |
| 2003 | 374,424 | 0 | 374,424 |
| | 2,290,272 | 2,050,749 | 239,523 |

These grants are payable from future income.

**Comment**

**13.120** Paragraph 258 of SORP says that *'the notes should distinguish between those commitments included on the balance sheet as liabilities and those that are intentions to spend and are not included . . .'* and then goes on to list the details of each that should be disclosed. Whilst it seems sensible to give details of commitments which are included as liabilities, it seems to us that it would be more appropriate in the case of material intentions for future expenditure to set up a designated fund and key any explanatory note to that. This is provided for in para 49 of SORP and following.

## 19 GUARANTEES

**13.121** Paragraph 260 of SORP requires the disclosure of *'all material guarantees given by the charity and the conditions under which liabilities might arise'* for the charity as a result of the guarantees.

**Comment**

**13.122** Examples would include the guarantee of a bank overdraft of a trading subsidiary or of a loan obtained by an employee or beneficiary of the charity. In this case it is suggested that the disclosure should include the amount of the guaranteed overdraft or loan at the balance sheet date and the maximum amount of the guarantee.

**13.123** Where consolidated accounts are prepared, it is suggested that any guarantees given by the parent charity to its subsidiary charities should be disclosed, even if the results and assets and liabilities of the subsidiary charities concerned are included in the consolidated accounts. This is because, technically, consolidated accounts are additional to the entity accounts of the charity and if the charity is seeking to avoid filing more than the consolidated accounts it must ensure that all disclosures relevant to the entity are made. See Chapter 5 on Consolidation.

## 20 CONTINGENT ASSETS AND LIABILITIES

### Definition

**13.124** A contingent asset is *'a possible asset that arises from past events and where existence will be confirmed only by the occurrence of one or more uncertain future events not wholly within the entity's control.' (Appendix 1)*

A contingent liability is:

*'(a) A possible obligation that arises from past events and whose existence will be confirmed only by the occurrence of one or more uncertain future events not wholly within the entity's control; or*

*(b) A present obligation that arises from past events but is not recognised in the primary statements because:-*

*(i) it is not probable that a transfer of economic benefits will be required to settle the obligation;*
*or*

*(ii) the amount of the obligation, cannot be measured with sufficient reliability.'*

### Treatment as accrual or not

**13.125** The degree of certainty, timing and measurement of the prospective asset or liability will dictate whether or not it should be brought into the accounts. It is this decision which marks the distinction between an actual asset or liability which should be accrued in the accounts and a contingent asset or liability which should not. If the decision is that the asset or liability is contingent then the only concern is its materiality and how it should be disclosed, if at all.

### Disclosure of contingency

**13.126** In respect of each contingency which is required to be disclosed, the accounts should show:

(a) the nature of the contingency;

(b) the uncertainties which are expected to affect the ultimate outcome; and

(c) a prudent estimate of the financial effect, where an amount has not been accrued, at the date the accounts are approved. Where it is not practicable to make such an estimate, a statement to this effect should be included — see para 267 of SORP.

**13.127** Where a contingent loss may be capable of being reduced by a related counter-claim (eg an insurance claim), the amount accrued or disclosed should take into account the probable result of any such counter-claim. Full details of such counter-claim should be disclosed in the accounts.

*RSPCA: 31 December 1999*

**Notes to the accounts**

**10 Contingent liabilities**
The Society is the legal tenant for 13 properties where the beneficial tenant is an RSPCA branch. In the event of the financial failure of the beneficial tenant the Society would be obliged to continue the tenancy.

## 21 LOAN LIABILITIES

**13.128** A note to the accounts is required if any asset of the charity is subject to a mortgage or charge given as security for a loan or other liability.

**13.129** Such a note should disclose:

'*(a) particulars of the assets which are subject to the mortgage or charge;*
*(b) the amount of the loan or liability and its proportion to the value of the assets mortgaged or charged.*' *(para 270)*

**13.130** SORP also requires the disclosure in the notes to the accounts of all inter-fund loans existing at the balance sheet date, including details of amounts, interest and repayment terms. This disclosure can be in a summarised form if necessary.

**13.131** Separate disclosure is required of amounts loaned to trading subsidiaries, including details of any security provided by the subsidiary.

### Comment

SECURITY GIVEN ON BEHALF OF OTHERS

**13.132** Although not specifically stated in SORP, disclosure requirements for secured loans will cover not only secured loans of the charity, but also security given in respect of another person's liabilities.

PRESENT VALUE OF ASSETS

**13.133** It is interesting that SORP requires disclosure of the proportion of the secured loan to the value of the assets on which it is secured. As this is an attempt to disclose how much of a charity's liabilities are covered by the assets on which they are secured, it is assumed that for the purposes of this disclosure, 'value' should be taken to be the market value or realisable value of the charity's secured assets.

CHAPTER 14

# Summarised accounts

## 1 INTRODUCTION

**14.1** In addition to producing an annual trustees' report and full accounts prepared in accordance with applicable legislation such as the Charities Act 1993 or companies legislation many charities also produce, and publish, an annual review.

**14.2** An annual review typically contains only summarised accounts or summary financial information rather than the full audited accounts and is normally produced for public consumption. Summarised accounts will comprise an extract (possibly in abbreviated form) from the full accounts of the Statement of Financial Activities, the balance sheet and some of the notes to the accounts. Summary financial information, on the other hand, comprises financial data expressed purely by way of statistics, charts, diagrams, narrative, etc. The inclusion of summarised accounts or summary financial information in an annual review enables the charity to communicate key financial information to readers who may not be familiar with accounts, so providing them with an overview of the charity's financial activities. It also provides the charity with an opportunity to concentrate on a particular target audience and to emphasise more clearly, often with the aid of charts and diagrams, the salient points within the accounts. For example, a charity may wish to highlight a particular area of its work and use the annual review in order to appeal for more funds for those activities.

**14.3** It is essential, however, that the annual review, including the summarised accounts or summary financial information, is consistent with the full audited accounts and does not give a false picture. It is also important to remember that a full annual report and accounts should always be prepared, regardless of the intended circulation of any summarised accounts.

**14.4** If summarised accounts are produced, or if summary financial information is provided, they should follow certain general principles which are set out in the SORP. Charitable companies must follow the provisions of s 240 of the Companies Act 1985 concerning non-statutory financial statements but there are no legal provisions for other charities.

## 2 SORP AND LEGISLATIVE REQUIREMENTS

**14.5** Paragraphs 295 to 297 of SORP set out the general principles to be applied when preparing summarised accounts.

*'Summarised financial statements are to be accompanied by a statement, signed on behalf of the trustees, indicating:*

*(a) that they are not the statutory accounts but a summary of information relating to both the Statement of Financial Activities and the balance sheet;*
*(b) whether or not the full financial statements from which the summary is derived have as yet been externally examined (whether audit, independent examination, or reporting accountants report); and*
*(c) where they have been externally examined whether there was an unqualified report;*
*(d) where the report is qualified, contains an explanatory paragraph or emphasis of matter, sufficient details should be provided in the summary financial information to enable the reader to appreciate the significance of the report;*
*(e) where branch accounts are produced it must be clearly stated that the summary is for the branch only and has been extracted from the full accounts of the main charity (giving its name);*
*(f) details of how the full annual accounts, the external examiners report (as applicable) and the trustees report can be obtained;*
*(g) the date on which the annual accounts were approved; and*
*(h) for charities registered in England and Wales, say whether or not the annual report and accounts have been submitted to the Charity Commission.' (para 295)*

*'If the full accounts have been externally examined (either audited, independently examined or subject to a reporting accountants report) the external examiner should attach a statement giving an opinion as to whether or not the summary financial information is consistent with the full annual accounts.' (para 296)*

*'Any other summary financial information in whatever form which does not include information on the Statement of Financial Activities and the balance sheet must be accompanied by a statement signed on behalf of the trustees as to:*

*(a) the purpose of the information;*
*(b) whether or not it is from the full annual accounts;*
*(c) whether or not these accounts have been audited, independently examined or subject to a reporting accountants report;*
*(d) details of how the full annual accounts, trustees report and external examiners report (as appropriate) can be obtained' (para 297)*

## 3 HOW THE INFORMATION IS SHOWN

**14.6** The wide diversity of charities and the different emphasis each places on its objectives and needs means that, in particular, there is a wide variety as to the manner in which charities design and produce summarised accounts or summary financial information. In the pages that follow it is only possible to give a few examples. However, prizes are awarded annually to charities producing the most imaginative and effective reports. The prizes and awards are sponsored by *Accountancy* and the Charities Aid Foundation, and readers wishing to see how other charities present their summarised accounts and summary financial information may obtain details from either of these organisations.

### The basic minimum

**14.7** The 1999 Review of the RAF Benevolent Fund provides an example of the basic minimum that needs to be produced if a charity wishes to produce summarised accounts. The example illustrates the inclusion of a statement by the auditors stating that the information is consistent with the full audited accounts and a statement by the trustees that the auditor's report on the full accounts was unqualified. In most cases it would be unsuitable to quote the auditor's report and in the case of incorporated charities the Companies Act 1985 strictly forbids this.

**14.8** In addition to producing the summarised accounts some charities also give summary financial information either in the form of a short narrative financial review or in the form of charts and diagrams.

### A financial review

**14.9** A short financial review, often presented in the form of a treasurer's report, is an extremely useful tool for highlighting a particular aspect of the accounts or for giving further explanation on the charity's finances. Many readers of the charity's annual review will find narrative easier to understand than figures.

**14.10** The report, which can be in the form of a short financial commentary, can be used to enable the reader to appreciate how the charity's funds have been applied, the purposes for which assets are held and the charity's reserve policy. More importantly, in terms of fundraising and marketing, the report can set out the charity's financial position in terms of its future plans and commitments, and emphasise worries concerning future funding.

**14.11** An example of such a financial review published to accompany accounts is that of ChildLine. In its 1999 Annual Review the charity's

*Royal Airforce Benevolent Fund: 31 December 1999*

## Summarised Accounts

Year ended 31 December 1999

| | Charity 1999 | Charity 1998 | *Group 1999 | *Group 1998 |
|---|---|---|---|---|
| STATEMENT OF FINANCIAL ACTIVITIES | £000 | £000 | £000 | £000 |
| **Incoming Resources** | | | | |
| Royal Air Force Voluntary Income | 1,859 | 1,803 | 1,859 | 1,803 |
| Other Voluntary Income | 7,368 | 5,997 | 7,393 | 6,063 |
| Investment Income | 5,219 | 5,156 | 5,242 | 5,196 |
| Other Income | 1,439 | 1,459 | 2,254 | 2,084 |
| Trading Income | – | – | 182 | 336 |
| **TOTAL INCOMING RESOURCES** | **15,885** | **14,415** | **16,930** | **15,482** |
| **Resources Expended** | | | | |
| Direct Charitable Expenditure** | 13,175 | 11,122 | 13,510 | 11,441 |
| Fund Raising and Publicity | 1,115 | 949 | 1,115 | 949 |
| Management and Administration | 954 | 1,069 | 971 | 1,140 |
| **TOTAL RESOURCES EXPENDED** | **15,244** | **13,140** | **15,596** | **13,530** |
| **Net Incoming Resources** | 641 | 1,275 | 1,334 | 1,952 |
| **Gains on Investments** | 22,062 | 17,706 | 22,062 | 17,706 |
| **Net Movement in Funds** | 22,703 | 18,981 | 23,396 | 19,658 |
| Fund Balances Brought Forward on 1 January 1999 | 164,336 | 145,355 | 168,698 | 149,040 |
| **FUND BALANCES CARRIED FORWARD AT 31 DECEMBER 1999** | **187,039** | **164,336** | **192,094** | **168,698** |
| BALANCE SHEET | | | | |
| **Fixed Assets** | 4,448 | 3,560 | 17,906 | 16,165 |
| **Loans to Beneficiaries** | 10,925 | 10,776 | 10,925 | 10,776 |
| **Investments** | 161,236 | 136,292 | 161,236 | 136,292 |
| **Net Current Assets** | 10,430 | 13,708 | 2,027 | 5,465 |
| **TOTAL NET ASSETS** | **187,039** | **164,336** | **192,094** | **168,698** |
| **Capital and Income Funds** | | | | |
| Endowed | 4,034 | 3,333 | 4,034 | 3,333 |
| Restricted | 2,423 | 2,321 | 2,423 | 2,321 |
| Unrestricted | 180,582 | 158,682 | 185,637 | 163,044 |
| | **187,039** | **164,336** | **192,094** | **168,698** |

* Group – Consists of Charity and Connected Organisations, as detailed in Full Annual Report and Accounts

** In addition to the amount of Direct Charitable Expenditure shown, capital expenditure on behalf of beneficiaries amounted to £1.938m compared to £2.283m in 1998.

*Royal Airforce Benevolent Fund, continued*

## Report of the Auditors to the Council of The RAF Benevolent Fund

We have examined the summarised accounts set out on page 16.

**Respective Responsibilities of the Trustees and the Auditors**

You are responsible as Trustees for the preparation of the summarised accounts. We have agreed to report to you our opinion on the summarised accounts' consistency with the full accounts, on which we reported to you on 30 May 2000.

**Basis of Opinion**

We have carried out the procedures we consider necessary to ascertain whether the summarised accounts are consistent with the full accounts from which they have been prepared.

**Opinion**

In our opinion the summarised accounts are consistent with the full accounts for the year ended 31 December 1999.

Ernst & Young
Registered Auditor
London 30 May 2000

## Trustees' Report and Accounts

The summarised accounts on the opposite page have been extracted from the audited annual accounts of the Charity which were approved by Trustees on 30 May 2000. These summarised accounts may not contain sufficient information to allow a full understanding of the financial affairs of the Charity. A copy of the full Annual Report and Accounts has not yet been but will be submitted to the Charity Commission. For further information the full Annual Report and Accounts, including the unqualified report of the Auditors, should be consulted. A copy can be obtained from the Fund's offices at 67 Portland Place, London, W1N 4AR.

Signed on behalf of the Trustees
by Sir Adrian Swire on 30 May 2000.

treasurer uses such a report to highlight the importance of voluntary income to the charity and the need for further money to meet the increasing demands placed on the charity's resources.

*ChildLine: 31 March 1999*

**ChildLine** Annual Review 1999

# THE FINANCIAL YEAR

### Income

Following two excellent fundraising years, ChildLine has struggled to maintain such a strong performance this year, in the face of ever-increasing competition for people's money. The total raised was £6 million. Even so, we were able to help 13% more children than last year, thanks to the continuing support of business and the general public. Approximately 10% of our annual income comes from statutory grants and we rely on voluntary income for the remaining 90% – a huge proportion compared to many other charities. We cannot overestimate the value of the work done by our volunteer counsellors and indeed their generous service makes a significant financial contribution to ChildLine.

### Expenditure

Our total expenditure was almost £7 million, which matched our target but left us with an income shortfall. We spent £5 million on our counselling service, a 10 per cent increase over last year. As ever, we have been extremely conscious to keep administration costs to an absolute minimum. Administration represents only 1% of our total expenditure, and we managed to reduce these costs this year by more than £7,000.

### Reserves

ChildLine does not have the significant reserves and endowments that many older charities have built up over a long period. Our financial loss of £1 million this year has reduced our reserves from £2.6 million to £1.57 million. This represents less than two and a half months' operating costs. We are taking steps to remedy this situation in order to build up reserves to an acceptable level in forthcoming years.

### The future

We are working hard to build up our level of income, and have in place for next year a vigorous and imaginative fundraising strategy. Income from new sources, and good communication with our existing supporters – both individuals and companies – will be crucial.

If we are to answer more of the thousands of calls children try to make to ChildLine every day, it is essential that we are able to maintain the growth we have achieved in the service we provide to children.

Paddy Linaker
(Honorary Treasurer until October 1999)

Bryan Graham
(Honorary Treasurer from October 1999)

**INCOME** 1998/99

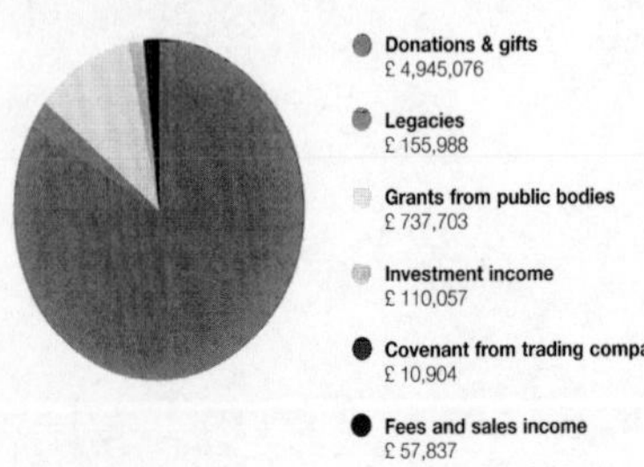


**EXPENDITURE** 1998/99

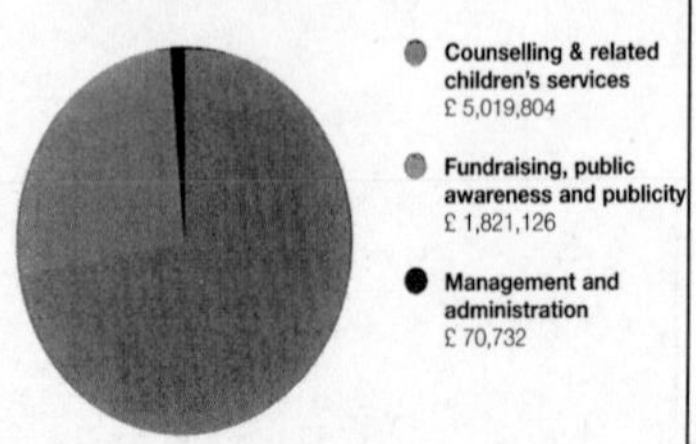

## Charts and diagrams

**14.12** Charts and diagrams are also often used by charities to provide readers of the annual review with a clear picture of the charity's finances. If charts and diagrams are to succeed in illustrating the facts they should be clear, striking and original in design.

**14.13** Charts and diagrams may be used to show a variety of information including where the charity obtains its resources from, how those resources are spent either in total or in specific areas and to provide trend analyses over a past number of years.

**14.14** Sense, for example, provide pie charts showing a breakdown of both income and expenditure, and a chart detailing the growth in income over a three year period. The chart illustrates clearly the sources of income and the proportion of expenditure devoted to direct charitable work, administration, fundraising etc.

**14.15** A similar approach was adopted by The Bible Society in its 1999 Annual Review. Diagrams were used to indicate how income was expended. This highlighted the proportion of income devoted to direct charitable activities.

## The target audience

**14.16** The essential ingredient to producing useful and meaningful summary financial information, be it summarised accounts or charts, diagrams, etc, is to remember your target audience.

**14.17** The summarised accounts published by Shelter in their 1999/2000 Annual Report are an excellent example of a charity tailoring the information to the people it is trying to get its message across to. As many of those supporting Shelter will have little experience of reading detailed financial statements, the summarised accounts contain a detailed commentary on each category of income and each type of expenditure head.

## Faults to be avoided

**14.18** Despite the general principles for summarised accounts and summary financial information being set out clearly within SORP, charities continue to make a number of mistakes when producing this information. The most common faults found by the judges of the Charity Annual Report and Accounts Award can be summarised as follows.

*Sense: 31 March 2000*

# Sense finances

## Growth in turnover

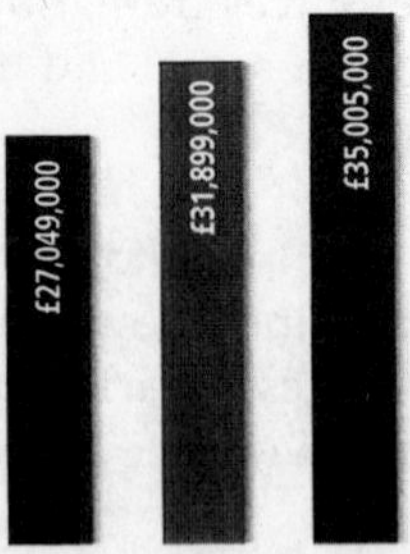


Thanks to the dedication of staff, volunteers and supporters, this year we have increased our annual turnover by a further 10% to £35 million.

However this increase has been achieved against the backdrop of a financially challenging year. Sales in our shops, in line with the charity shop sector, fell below the budgeted level and expenditure on residential services was higher than budgeted. As a result, unrestricted cash reserves at the end of year were less than the equivalent of four weeks turnover, which is three weeks less than our target level.

A more detailed explanation of Sense's financial affairs is given in the full Annual Report and Accounts – copies of which can be obtained from Sense on 020 7272 7774.

**Ian Miller**, Treasurer

## Income

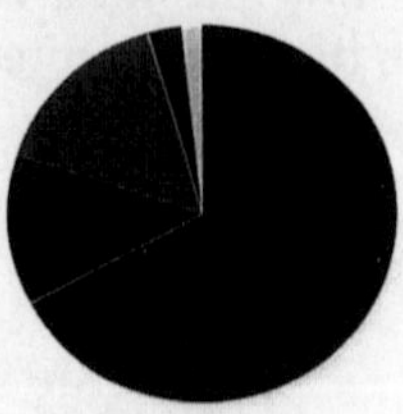

| **Where our funds come from** | **£000** |
|---|---|
| ● Fees for Sense services | 23,538 |
| ● Fundraising | 4,499 |
| ● Shops | 5,367 |
| ● Grants | 1,011 |
| ● Other | 590 |
| Total | **35,005** |

## Expenditure

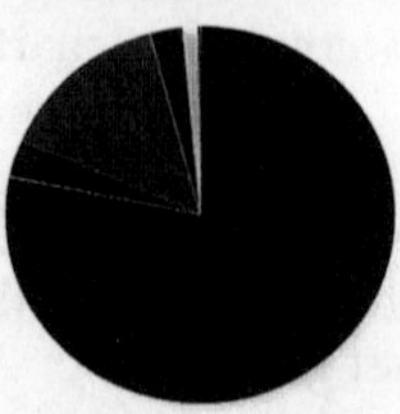

| **How the money is used** | **£000** |
|---|---|
| ● Sense services | 27,403 |
| ● Fundraising | 1,140 |
| ● Shops | 4,946 |
| ● Information and awareness | 973 |
| ● Administration | 442 |
| ● Funds for future projects | 101 |
| Total | **35,005** |

## Auditor's statement

**Our report of the Association's full report and accounts for the year ended 31 March 2000 was unqualified. In our opinion the summarised accounts set out on this page are consistent with the full report and accounts of Sense, The National Deafblind and Rubella Association, for the year ended 31 March 2000.**

**Pricewaterhouse Coopers, Chartered Accountants and Registered Auditors, 28 June 2000**

12 TOUCHING PEOPLE'S LIVES

*The Bible Society: 1999*

**Bible Society carries out a variety of projects each year in order to fulfil its mission goals. The annual report commentary highlights many of this year's projects. Here are the financial details.**

| | £'000 |
|---|---|
| ***Major events*** | |
| Greenbelt | 45 |
| The Time of Our Lives Anglican Millennium youth event | 16 |
| The Bible and Racial Attacks Conference with black majority churches | 5 |
| Churches Advisory Council for Local Broadcasting (CACLB) Conference | 6 |
| Denominational and other events | 8 |
| ***Church resources and activities*** | |
| Storytelling -- in partnership with the Northumbria Community | 73 |
| Other church resources and activities | 16 |
| ***Public theology activities – taking the Bible beyond the Church*** | |
| Imagining Tomorrow conference | 25 |
| Education track | 32 |
| *Heartland* – *Vogue* magazine campaign | 79 |
| Other public theology projects | 2 |
| ***Investments in future activities*** | |
| Public campaigning for the Bible | 85 |
| *The Cry* – continued development | 92 |
| *The Miracle Maker* – film launch in 2000 | 29 |
| ***Other Bible advocacy*** | |
| *The Bible in Transmission* – campaigning publication | 33 |
| The Gospel and Our Culture activities | 12 |
| ***Research projects*** | |
| Research into Use of the Bible | 8 |
| Total project activities | 566 |

14 Report and Summarised Accounts

## *The Bible Society: 1999*

*Many factors have conspired to make the Bible a largely closed book in Western culture today, not least developments in the academic world. Partnership with Bible Society has made possible the exciting development of the Scripture and Hermeneutics Seminar which meets yearly to address key issues that could help facilitate the re-opening of the Book for our culture.*

Revd Dr Craig Bartholomew, Research Fellow, School of Theology and Religious Studies, Cheltenham and Gloucester College of Higher Education

# Summary of numbers

### Income

| | |
|---|---|
| Individuals | 1,870 |
| Other | 202 |
| Legacies | 2,412 |
| Investments | 1,159 |
| Sales revenue | 2,087 |
| Faith Comes by Hearing | 255 |
| Action Groups | 350 |
| Churches | 630 |
| Bible a Month Club | 1,014 |
| | **9,979** |

### Expenditure

| | |
|---|---|
| Fundraising | 1,421 |
| Administration | 382 |
| National programme | 3,769 |
| International programme | 4,718 |
| | **10,290** |

### International programme

| | |
|---|---|
| Africa | 1,180 |
| Americas | 1,085 |
| Asia Pacific | 520 |
| Middle East | 473 |
| Central & Eastern Europe | 1,460 |
| | **4,718** |

### National programme

| | |
|---|---|
| Project costs | 566 |
| Grants | 250 |
| Trading costs | 1,876 |
| Staff & other costs | 1,077 |
| | **3,769** |

Geographical analysis of international programme

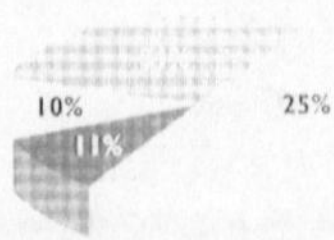


25% Africa
23% Americas
11% Asia Pacific
10% Middle East
31% Central & Eastern Europe

National programme

15% Project costs
7% Grants
49% Trading costs
29% Staff & other costs

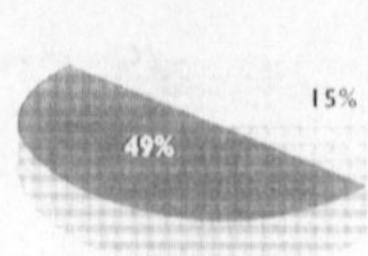


Where the money came from

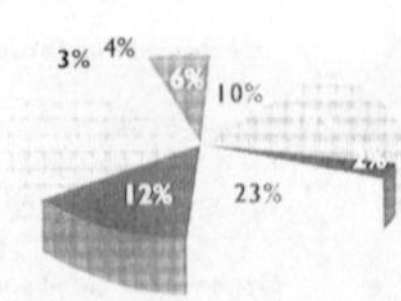


19% Individuals
2% Other
23% Legacies
12% Investments
21% Sales revenue
3% Faith Comes by Hearing
4% Action Groups
6% Churches
10% Bible a Month Club

How we used it

14% Fundraising
4% Administration
37% National programme
45% International programme

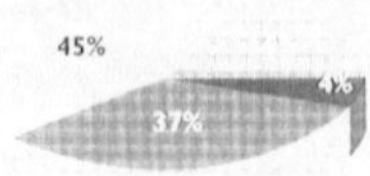


Report and Summarised Accounts

*Shelter: 31 March 2000*

## Where does Shelter's income come from?

- DONATIONS AND LEGACIES 56.5% £14.7 million
- GRANTS 15.4% £4.0 million
- SHELTER SHOPS 21.5% £5.6 million
- OTHER MERCHANDISING 1.2% £0.3 million
- PUBLICATION SALES 1.5% £0.4 million
- TRAINING INCOME 0.8% £0.2 million
- INVESTMENT INCOME 0.4% £0.1 million
- OTHER INCOME 2.7% £0.7 million

**TOTAL £26 MILLION**

## How each pound is spent

- HOUSING SERVICES 47.6% £12.1 million
- CAMPAIGNING & EDUCATION 9.5% £2.4 million
- NATIONAL/REGIONAL FUNDRAISING 17.3% £4.4 million
- SHELTER SHOPS 21.7% £5.5 million
- OTHER MERCHANDISING 1.2% £0.3 million
- MANAGEMENT & ADMINISTRATION 2.7% £0.7 million

**TOTAL £25.4 MILLION**

**Donations and legacies**
Donation and legacy income received from individual donors, trusts, school children, religious groups and businesses totalled £14.7 million this year. This represents an increase of £3.1 million on the previous year and we are indebted to our donors for their generous and continuing support. We are especially grateful to one individual, whose bequest contributed to 50 per cent of this year's legacies.

**Grants**
Shelter received £4.0 million in grant income from local and district authorities, central government, the London Boroughs Grants Unit and other organisations during the year.

**Shelter Shops**
Shelter Shops completed a successful but difficult year of growth contributing £5.6 million income, an increase of 23.5 per cent against last year.

**Other merchandising**
Sales of new merchandise including Christmas cards and other gifts in the Christmas catalogue totalled £0.3 million.

**Publication sales**
Sales of Shelter's publications on legal, financial and research matters relating to housing totalled £0.4 million in the year.

**Training income**
Training programmes for housing professionals and related organisations totalled £0.2 million.

**Investment income**
Income generated on Shelter's investment portfolio in the year totalled £0.1 million.

**Other income**
Other income of £0.7 million relates to legal services, rent and service charges, legal aid franchising income and community legal service income.

**Housing services**
Expenditure on Shelter's housing aid services totalled £12.1 million, an increase in spend of £0.5 million on the previous year. Due to restructuring Shelter has been able to provide both an increase and improvement in services for less money.

**Campaigning and education**
Shelter spent £2.4 million on its continuing campaign for long-term solutions to the problem of homelessness and bad housing as well as raising public awareness of these issues through its publications etc.

**National/regional fundraising**
Total fundraising costs for the year, including salaries and overheads, totalled £4.4 million and generated an income of £14.7 million. Even in difficult times Shelter trebled its investment through careful fundraising.

**Shelter Shops**
Shelter Shops expenditure totalled £5.5 million, and with its continued programme of expansion was able to contribute £0.1 million to Shelter.

**Other merchandising**
Other merchandising costs totalled £0.3 million.

**Management and administration**
Central costs reflect the central and administrative costs of Shelter, such as the costs of managing the charity's assets, complying with constitutional and statutory requirements, and the costs of organisational management. Central costs have increased to £0.7 million representing investment in IT and other key infrastructure elements essential to maintaining Shelter's charitable activities.

30 **Shelter** Annual Report 1999/2000

OMISSIONS

**14.19** Several charities produce an extract of their statement of financial activities only, failing to provide a summary of their balance sheet. Others omit to refer to the full audited accounts or fail to provide a warning statement.

ADAPTATION OF ACCOUNTS

**14.20** Some charities adapt the information contained within their full accounts or exclude certain information from the summarised statements altogether, such as the results of trading subsidiaries. If summary financial information such as charts and diagrams are produced, it is essential that these are consistent with the information in the full accounts and that creative license is not taken too far.

PROOF-READING

**14.21** Often typographical errors are not spotted at the proof-reading stage.

**14.22** Sadly, all of these faults can detract from the overall message portrayed by the summarised accounts.

CHAPTER 15

# Scottish, Irish and exempt charities

## 1 INTRODUCTION

**15.1** Many people, particularly those living in England, think that there is one law governing all charities in the United Kingdom and that they are subject to the supervision of the Charity Commissioners. This is not so. Some may think that it would be better if it were so but that is unlikely to happen for some time, if at all, given the political climate of 2001 with the pressures for and against European federation on the one hand and devolution on the other.

**15.2** The Charity Commissioners in England and Wales were established in the 19th century in response to the specific needs of England and Wales at that time. In particular, because of the cost and delay experienced by petitioners in the Court of Chancery, it was thought fit to establish a speedier and cheaper way of helping trustees of charitable foundations to obtain the court's permission to do things in connection with their trust to facilitate its development for the benefit of its beneficiaries.

**15.3** It was also recognised that some so-called charitable foundations were run more for the benefit of the kith and kin of the founder than for the beneficiaries.

**15.4** The Charity Commissioners therefore were established to represent the interests of all those objects of charity in England and Wales, the poor, the sick, the young and the old, as well as foundations to promote the arts, sciences and other charitable objects.

**15.5** Certain charitable activities were regarded by Parliament as having adequate protection and control already and were therefore left outside the control of the Charity Commissioners. These included:

(a) Scottish charities;
(b) Irish charities (non Northern Irish charities); and

(c) those exempted by the Charities Act, mainly bodies which were already well regulated by other statutes such as:

   (i) registered places of public worship;
   (ii) ancient schools and universities; and
   (iii) museums, galleries, the British Library.

The list of exempt charities has been brought up to date and is included in Sch 2 to the Charities Act 1993.

**15.6** The purpose of this chapter is to identify those charities which are not subject to the Charity Commission in whole or in part and to see to what extent they need not comply with the precepts put forward in the rest of this book.

## 2 EXEMPT CHARITIES

**15.7** All charities which fall within Schedule 2 of Charities Act 1993 are exempt from the jurisdiction of the Charity Commissioners. They are, however, required by the Charities Act to keep proper accounting records and to produce accounts and to make these available to the public on request.

**15.8** The way in which exempt charities keep their accounting records and prepare accounts is dependent upon the regulations that each has to obey. Thus universities will follow their particular SORP and account in accordance with the requirements of the Higher Education Funding Council. Friendly, Industrial and Provident Societies have their own reporting procedures. Churches, museums, and exempt scholastic institutions will report under their own specific statutes.

**15.9** The charities' SORP will, however, apply to the form and content of all exempt charities' reports and accounts, unless superseded by another SORP as in the cases of universities, common investment funds and registered social landlords.

**15.10** As time goes on it is possible that more SORPs, specific to certain charitable activities will be developed and, if these relate to exempt charities, they will supersede the charities' SORP. At present, however, the Accounting Standards Board is reluctant to recognise any more sub-sectors with a need for a specific SORP.

## 3 SCOTTISH CHARITIES

**15.11** In Scotland the regulation of charities is in the hands of the Scottish Executive and the Revenue. The Secretary of State for Scotland has exercised his powers under sections 4(4)(a) and 5(3), (5) of the Law Reform (Miscellaneous Provisions) (Scotland) Act 1990 to make the Charities Accounts (Scotland) Regulations 1992.

**15.12** In brief these require that:

(a) 'a recognised body' (ie a charity) shall produce annual accounts giving an income and expenditure account and balance sheet; and
(b) an auditor shall be appointed by the trustees and his report will be annexed to the balance sheet and income and expenditure accounts.

**15.13** Section 3 of the regulations allows a recognised body to produce a receipts and payments account and 'statement of balances' if its gross receipts are less than £25,000 pa.

**15.14** Section 4 requires the accounts to be signed by one of the trustees, authorised by the other trustees, to signify their approval. It also sets out in detail by reference to Schedule 1 of the regulations the form and content of the balance sheet and the income and expenditure account.

**15.15** Inexplicably, these regulations were issued while the original Charities SORP Review Committee was deliberating its recommendations and before the discussion document was issued. As a result, some of the main recommendations of the SORP are not reflected in the Regulations. There is no requirement to produce a Statement of Financial Activities as a primary accounting statement; investments may be classified in the balance sheet separately from fixed assets and current assets; and they may be shown at historical cost rather than market value.

**15.16** To overcome this lack of harmonisation the original 1995 SORP contained a number of paragraphs specific to Scottish charities. In the revised SORP this has been reduced to one paragraph which is as follows:

> *'Whilst the remit of the Charity Commission does not extend to Scotland the content of this SORP is intended to apply except where it would be inappropriate to do so. The legislation in Scotland relating to the form and content of non-company charities' report and accounts is the Law Reform (Miscellaneous Provisions) (Scotland) Act 1990 and regulations made thereunder. In particular, this legislation requires Scottish non-company charities to prepare, as a primary statement, an Income and Expenditure*

*Account; this statement should be provided in addition to those statements required under this SORP. In a small number of cases the disclosure requirements may be more onerous than those set out in the SORP and in such cases the legislative requirement must be followed.'* *(para 19).*

**15.17** In many cases the Statement of Financial Activities (SOFA) can be adapted to include the Income and Expenditure account. As for charitable companies, however, (see paras 331–343 of SORP) Scottish charities, both incorporated and unincorporated, which have permanent endowments will have to produce their Income and Expenditure Account as the primary statement and include the SOFA as a prominent note. The word 'prominent' was included in the 1995 SORP to emphasise the importance of the SOFA as a primary statement.

**15.18** It is recommended that the income and expenditure account be shown in columnar form in order to keep separate the restricted funds from the unrestricted funds.

**15.19** There should be the same level of disclosure in the notes to the accounts to support the income and expenditure account as is required in the rest of the SORP for the Statement of Financial Activities.

**The exceptions**

**15.20** Paragraph 139 of SORP concerns the disclosure of grants payable to institutions. Whilst all other charities need only disclose grants if they exceed 5% of total expenditure Scottish charities are required by regulations to disclose grants exceeding the greater of 2% of the gross income from all sources and £1,000.

**15.21** The threshold for small charities in Scotland is £25,000. Those with incomes below this figure need only prepare a receipts and payments account and a statement of balances. Above this figure they must produce full accounts on the accruals basis. In England and Wales the similar threshold is £100,000.

**15.22** The audit and independent examination requirements also differ:

(a) in England and Wales an unincorporated charity needs no external scrutiny if its income is below £10,000 pa. No such exemption applies in Scotland;
(b) the same charity with income of between £10,000 and £250,000 may, in England and Wales, opt for an independent examination. In Scotland this option is available to such a charity with an income between £0 and £100,000; and
(c) a full audit is required for the charity if its income exceeds these figures, ie over £250,000 in England and Wales and £100,000 in Scotland.

**Comment**

**15.23** The differences between the accounting and auditing requirements of Scottish and English or Welsh charities apply only to unincorporated charities. If they are companies or friendly societies they will be subject to their relevant statutes which apply throughout the UK. It must be regarded as a pity that such important measures as resulted from the Deregulation Task Force should not have been extended to Scotland at least as regards the regulations governing the form and content of accounts and the audit requirements.

**15.24** In March 2000 an independent commission was set up to review and reform charity law in Scotland. The commission is due to report back in the spring 2001. It is to be hoped therefore that in the near future the regulations governing the accounts of Scottish charities will be brought more closely in line with those of English and Welsh charities. In the meantime, unincorporated Scottish charities should comply with the Charities Accounts (Scotland) Regulations 1992 and, insofar as it does not conflict with these regulations, the SORP.

**15.25** When preparing accounts for a national charity with operations in England and Scotland, it is important to establish at the outset whether it is an English charity with Scottish branches or vice versa. All reporting and accounting requirements will follow from the answer. If these are separate charities in both countries it is likely that each will have to prepare separate reports and accounts even if an overall national report is also produced. This will be to satisfy the different regulatory authorities, the Inland Revenue in Scotland and the Charity Commission and Inland Revenue in England.

## 4 IRISH CHARITIES

**15.26** Charities in the Republic of Ireland are governed by the Irish Charities Acts 1961 and 1973, neither of which require charities to register or to prepare and submit accounts. In practice they are required to prepare accounts by the tax authorities from whom they claim repayments of tax — para 21 of SORP.

**15.27** The accounting bodies in the Republic of Ireland have given their backing to the charities SORP, hence the reference in para 12 of SORP to its application to all charities in the Republic of Ireland regardless of their size, constitution or complexity.

**15.28** It can be expected therefore that those charities in the Republic of Ireland which present audited accounts showing a true and fair view will follow the recommendations of the SORP. This may be reinforced by legislation similar to the Charities Acts for England and Wales.

**15.29** Charities in Northern Ireland are governed by the Charities Act (Northern Ireland) 1964 and the Charities (Northern Ireland) Order 1987. There is no charity commission for Northern Ireland. Responsibility for charities in Northern Ireland rests with the Department for Social Development. They do not maintain a register but can require accounts to be filed in certain circumstances. Trustees are required to keep proper accounts but these are not defined in the Act — para 20 of SORP.

**Comment**

**15.30** With all the other legal complications affecting the constitutions of the Republic of Ireland and Northern Ireland, it is unlikely that conformity of charity legislation will be high on any agenda. So it will largely depend upon the general acceptance and application of the recommendations of the SORP, to achieve consistency of approach and compatibility.

**15.31** There are many examples of English charities with branches in Ireland, and Irish charities with branches in England. It is important that these should report their full responsibilities and activities and not limit themselves to their own country. The SORP shows how to do this.

## 5 COMMON INVESTMENT FUNDS

**15.32** A disproportionate amount of the text of the Charities (Accounts and Reports) Regulations 1995 is given to the special position of common investment funds, so much so that in the Core Guide issued by the Home Office Voluntary Services Unit in November 1995 it was edited out entirely. This is because there are only about 20 common investment funds in existence. Similarly they are not mentioned in the Charity Accounts 2001 framework.

**15.33** Suffice it to say here that common investment funds are charities established by schemes made by the Charity Commission. They are administered by trustees who appoint investment managers to manage the funds and a corporate trustee to hold them and oversee the investment manager in a similar manner to a unit trust. Trustees of other charities are then invited to invest in the units issued by the common investment fund. The essential distinction between these funds and 'pooled' funds is that the trustees of a common investment fund are entrusted with funds belonging to charities of which they are not necessarily trustees, whereas trustees of 'pooled' funds have to have control of the trusts which pool their funds together.

**15.34** Essentially the accounts of a common investment fund are drawn up to comply with the requirements of authorised unit trusts. These are designed to show their total returns on investments with comparisons to relevant indices as well as an income and expenditure account and balance sheet.

## Comment

**15.35** Following discussions between the Charity Commission and the managers of Common Investment Funds during 1998 and 1999 amendments have been made to the constitution of Common Investment Funds to bring them within the jurisdiction of the Financial Services Authority. With the appointment of a Corporate Trustee, each Common Investment Fund is now in a similar regulatory framework to that of an authorised unit trust. Indeed the only significant difference is that CIFs have a supervisory board of trustees who have responsibility for appointing the corporate trustee, the investment managers and auditors and for establishing the investment guidelines.

CHAPTER 16

# The auditor and the independent examiner

## 1 INTRODUCTION

**16.1** The purpose of this chapter is to explain the statutory requirement for audit or other external scrutiny of accounts within the charity sector, and to explain the role and responsibilities of the auditor or other scrutineer of the accounts. The chapter is written from the perspective of the client, in order to understand the role of the audit; it does not purport to be an auditing treatise.

**16.2** The Charities Act 1993 also introduced the concept of 'independent examination' for smaller, unincorporated charities and this is also dealt with in this chapter.

### What is an audit?

**16.3** Within the context of auditing standards, an audit of a set of financial statements (or 'accounts' as they are frequently referred to) is:

*'An exercise whose objective is to enable auditors to express an opinion whether the financial statements give a true and fair view of the entity's affairs at the period end or of its profit or loss (or income or expenditure) of the period then ended and have been properly prepared in accordance with the applicable reporting framework (for example, relevant legislation and applicable accounting standards) or, where statutory or other specific requirement prescribe the term, whether the financial statements "present fairly".'*

**16.4** For an unincorporated charity, the auditor is required to express an opinion that the accounts give a true and fair view of the charity's state of affairs at the year end, and of its incoming resources and application of resources (as shown within its SOFA (Statement of Financial Activities) for its financial year ended at that date, and have been properly prepared in accordance with the Charities Act 1993 (the relevant legislation)). In carrying out an audit, the auditor has to consider applicable financial reporting or accounting standards, together with professional auditing standards. The audit of an incorporated charity is conducted in accordance with the requirements of the Companies Act 1985.

**16.5** The form and content of auditors' reports on the accounts of charities follow the basic principles and procedures established by Auditing Standard SAS 600 *Auditors' Reports on Financial Statements.* These principles and procedures are now well established.

**16.6** The form of auditors' report under SAS 600 clearly distinguishes the respective responsibilities of trustees and auditors – it is the charity's trustees who are responsible for the preparation of accounts, while the auditors are responsible for reporting an independent opinion on those accounts. Trustees frequently do not fully appreciate their responsibilities in this respect. Charity law requires the trustees to prepare accounts for each financial year, which give a true and fair view of the charity's financial activities during the year and of its financial position at the end of the year (assuming the charity is not entitled to prepare accounts on the alternative 'receipts and payments' basis). In preparing accounts giving a true and fair view, the trustees will need to follow best practice and accord with the recommendations of the Statement of Recommended Practice *Accounting by Charities.* Preparation of accounts involves:

- selecting suitable accounting policies and applying them consistently;
- making judgements and estimates that are reasonable and prudent;
- stating within the accounts whether applicable accounting standards and (for unincorporated charities exceeding £100,000 pa gross income – See Appendix 3) statements of recommended practice have been followed (subject to any material departures being disclosed and explained within the accounts);
- preparing the accounts on the 'going concern' basis unless it is inappropriate to presume that the charity will continue in operation.

**16.7** The trustees are responsible for keeping accounting records which disclose, with reasonable accuracy at any time, the financial position of the charity and which enable them to ensure that the accounts comply with appropriate legislation or regulations or governing document (for example, trust deed). The trustees are also responsible for safeguarding the assets of the charity, and for taking reasonable steps for the prevention and detection of fraud and other irregularities.

**16.8** The benefit of an audit is primarily the assurance that the trustees receive from an external scrutiny, in accordance with statutory requirements and professional standards, of the charity's activities over the financial period and the state of affairs at a given point in time – the balance sheet date.

**What is an independent examination?**

**16.9** Following the Charities Act 1993, all but the smallest charities are required to have some form of independent examination of their accounts. Where neither gross income nor total expenditure of the charity (see definition in Appendix 3) for the year in question exceed £10,000 no such scrutiny is required. An unincorporated charity, whose income and/or expenditure is not more than £250,000 in the current financial year and in both of the preceding two years, may elect to have an independent examination – this is a form of independent scrutiny that falls short of the full requirement of an audit. Independent examination is only appropriate for unincorporated charities. A charity which is a company must comply with the audit requirements of the Companies Act 1985, unless it is able to take advantage, for example, of the exemptions from audit.

**16.10** Independent examination was a new concept introduced by the Charities Act 1993. As mentioned above, it is a less onerous form of scrutiny than an audit and provides less assurance. An independent examination involves:

- a review of the accounting records kept by the charity — this is something that is not required of a charitable company audit exemption report;
- a comparison of the accounts presented with the accounting records;
- a review of the accounts and the consideration of any unusual items or disclosures identified.

**16.11** The depth of work carried out during an independent examination is less than an audit: for example, verification procedures are only necessary when material concerns or doubts arise during the examination and where satisfactory explanations cannot be obtained from the trustees.

**16.12** A procedural basis or framework defining how the reporting duties of the independent examiner must be met are contained within the General Directions, issued by the Charity Commissioners. These Directions, together with guidance of operational procedures and methods to help the examiner, are contained within the Charity Commissioners' publication, *'The Carrying out of an Independent Examination – Directions and Guidance Notes'*.

**16.13** The report of an independent examiner is required to state whether or not any matter has come to his attention in connection with the examination which gives reasonable cause to believe that in any material respect:

- proper accounting records have not been kept;
- the accounts do not accord with such accounting records;
- the accounts fail to comply with relevant regulations.

**16.14** The independent examiner is also required to state in his report whether or not any matter has been identifed, in connection with the examination, to which attention should be drawn to enable a proper understanding of the accounts to be reached.

**16.15** Where they have become apparent, additional details that need to be included within the report are:

- any material expenditure or action contrary to the trusts of the charity;
- any failure to provide information or explanations to which the examiner is entitled;
- evidence that accounts prepared on an accruals basis (under s 42(1) of the Charities Act 1993) are materially inconsistent with the trustees' annual report. (An example of an unqualified report of an independent examiner is contained within the Charity Commissioners' publication *The Carrying out of an Independent Examination*, see Appendix 2.)

**16.16** As can be seen from the form of independent examiner's report, a positive opinion on the accounts does not need to be supported by a body of detailed evidence, nor is an opinion required as to whether the accounts show a 'true and fair view'. As can be seen, however, the benefits of an independent examination are a level of scrutiny commensurate with the relative size and materiality of the charity and the clearly defined items required by the regulations.

## 2 REQUIREMENT FOR EXTERNAL SCRUTINY

**16.17** Whether a charity requires an audit, independent examination or audit exemption report depends upon whether it is:

(a) a charitable company subject to the Companies Act 1985 (CA 1985);
(b) an unincorporated charity, subject to the Charities Act 1993; or
(c) an exempt charity, subject to its own charter, Act of Parliament, or other legislation.

### Unincorporated Charities

**16.18** Where a (b) type of charity's gross income or total expenditure in the financial year (or its immediately preceding financial year or the financial year before that) exceeds £250,000 the charity's accounts must be audited. The audit must be carried out by a registered auditor being a company auditor eligible for appointment in accordance with CA 1989 s 25 or by regulations made under Charities Act 1993 s 44.

**16.19** Where such a charity's gross income or total expenditure for the financial year exceeds £10,000 but does not exceed £250,000 and the charity is not otherwise obliged to have an audit, the trustees may elect to have the accounts either:

- examined by an independent examiner; or
- audited by a registered auditor.

**16.20** An independent examiner (as explained below) is an independent person who is reasonably believed by the trustees to have the requisite ability and practical experience to carry out a competent examination of the accounts. The Charity Commissioners' view is that the appointment of an independent examiner relates to an individual rather than to a partnership or company.

**16.21** If, within 10 months of the end of the charity's financial year, no audit or independent examination has been carried out, the Charity Commissioners may by order require the accounts to be audited by a registered auditor.

**16.22** Where a charity's gross income and total expenditure on the above basis do not exceed £10,000, the accounts of the charity need not be independently examined, under the so-called 'light touch' regime for small charities, brought about by the Deregulation and Contracting Out Act 1994. This is subject, always, to the Charity Commissioners' right by order to require an audit (Charities Act 1993 s 43(4)).

**16.23** Where an auditor is appointed by the Charity Commissioners in these circumstances, the auditor's remuneration and any expenses of such an audit is recoverable from the charity trustees who are personally liable, jointly and severally, for the expenses, or where such recovery is not practicable, from the funds of the charity.

### Incorporated Charities — audit exemption

**16.24** A charitable company which meets the 'total exemption conditions' in respect of a financial year is exempt from the requirement to have its accounts audited in respect of that year.

Furthermore, charitable companies which meet 'report conditions' are exempt from the requirement to have their accounts for that year audited provided the directors make a report to the charity's members, in accordance with the CA 1995 s 249C.

**16.25** the 'total exemption conditions' are met by a charitable company in respect of a financial year if:

(a) it qualifies as a 'small company' in relation to that year;
(b) its 'gross income' in that year is not more than £90,000; and
(c) its balance sheet total for that year is not more than £1.4 million.

**16.26** The 'report conditions' are met by a charitable company in respect of a financial year if:

(a) it qualifies as a 'small company' in relation to that year;
(b) its 'gross income' in that year is more than £90,000 but not more than £250,000; and
(c) its balance sheet total for that year is not more than £1.4 million.

**16.27** 'Gross income' means the charity's income from all sources, as shown in its income and expenditure account. The maximum gross income figures are to be proportionately adjusted where the charitable company's financial 'year' is not, in fact, 12 months.

**16.28** Companies taking advantage of the audit exemptions must include in their balance sheet a statement by the directors to the effect that:

(a) for the year in question the company was entitled to exemption from audit under s 249A(1) [*total exemption*] or 249A(2) [*exemption with accountant's report*] [*as the case may be*];
(b) no notice by a member or members requesting an audit pursuant to s 249B(2), in respect of that year, has been deposited;
(c) the directors acknowledge their responsibilities for:
    (i) ensuring that the company keeps accounting records which comply with s 221, and
    (ii) preparing accounts which give a true and fair view of the state of affairs of the company as at the end of the financial year and of its results for the financial year in accordance with the requirements of s 226, and which otherwise comply with the requirements of the Act relating to accounts.

**16.29** The accountants report required, for the purposes of CA 1985 s 249A(2), is to be prepared by a 'reporting accountant'. It has to state whether in the opinion of the reporting accountant:

(a) the accounts of the company of the financial year in question are in agreement with the accounting records kept by the charitable company under s 221; and
(b) having regard only to, and on the basis of, the information contained in those accounting records, those accounts have been drawn up in a manner consistent with the provisions specified in s 249C(6), so far as applicable to the company, concerning: the form and content of company accounts; related/subsidiary undertakings; and directors' emoluments and other benefits.

The report also has to state that in the opinion of the reporting accountant the company satisfied the statutory requirements for exemption from audit of the accounts for the year and did not, at any time within that year, fall within any of the categories of companies not entitled to exemption.

**16.30** Generally, a reporting accountant for the purposes of audit exemption has to be a member of one of the recognised accounting bodies and be either engaged in public practice or eligible as a company auditor or independent reporting accountant.

## 3 SELECTION CRITERIA FOR INDEPENDENT EXAMINER

**16.31** An independent examiner does not have to hold a professional accountancy qualification, but must be a person suitable for the circumstances of the charity. The Charity Commissioners strongly recommend that trustees of charities with gross assets in excess of £1 million, or gross income of £100,000 or more, should select a qualified accountant to carry out the independent examination. Such accountant need not necessarily be a registered auditor. A commensurate understanding of accountancy principles and accounting standards is nevertheless required in other cases where the accounts are prepared on an accruals basis. The Charity Commission guidance under the Charities Act 1993 s 43(7)(a) clearly points out, an independent examiner must:

- be an independent person;
- have, in the opinion of the trustees, the requisite ability and practical experience; and
- be able to carry out a competent examination of the charity's accounts.

**16.32** 'Independence' means that the examiner should have no connection with the charity trustees, which might inhibit an impartial conduct of the examination. Such individuals as the charity's trustees themselves, anyone closely involved in the administration of the charity, major donors or beneficiaries of the charity or any close relative, business partner or employee of any of the preceding would be deemed inappropriate.

**16.33** As to 'requisite ability', as mentioned above, it is difficult to envisage anyone other than an accountant familiar with accountancy principles and accounting standards being competent to examine accounts prepared on an accruals basis. (For other accounts and small uncomplicated charities, a bank manager or local authority treasurer, for example, may be competent.)

**16.34** 'Practical experience' involves experience of the financial administration of a charity or other institution of similar nature, structure and size, or prior experience as an independent examiner or investigator. An independent examiner should be conversant with the Charity Commission Directions, and the requirements of an independent examiner's report prescribed in accordance with the regulations. Where accruals accounts are concerned, the examiner should also be conversant with the regulations as to form and content of the accounts and the charities SORP.

**16.35** It is the charity trustees' responsibility to ensure that the prospective independent examiner is appropriate for the assignment. The terms of engagement should be recognised in a letter of engagement between the trustees and the independent examiner.

## 4 WHO CAN BE AN AUDITOR?

**16.36** Eligibility for the appointment as auditor of a charity is determined by whether a person (or firm) is:

- a registered auditor, eligible to act as company auditor under Companies Act 1989 s 25; or
- a person eligible for appointment as auditor of the charity under regulations made under Charities Act 1993 s 43.

## 5 WHAT IS THE AUDITOR OR INDEPENDENT EXAMINER REQUIRED TO DO?

### Reporting

**16.37** Under s 43, it is the duty of the auditor or independent examiner, as the case may be, to make a report on the accounts of the charity (prepared under Charities Act 1993 s 43(1) (Accruals Accounts), or s 42(3) (Receipts and Payments Accounts)). The report should be addressed to the charity's trustees (unless the auditor has been appointed by the Charity Commissioners). In the case of a membership association where the charity's governing instrument requires a report to the members, it should be addressed to both. In preparing his report, the auditor is required to carry out such investigations as will enable him to form an opinion as to the matters specified (in sub-paras (e) and (f) of regs 6(2) or (3) as the case may be (see below)). The elements/contents required to be contained in the respective reports may be compared as follows (regs 6 to 7):

<table>
<tr><th colspan="3">AUDITORS' REPORTS AND<br>REPORTS OF AN INDEPENDENT EXAMINER COMPARED<br>(Unincorporated Charities)</th></tr>
<tr><th>Regulation 6(2)<br>Audit of Accruals accounts prepared under<br>s 42(1)</th><th>Regulation 6(3)<br>Audit of Receipts and Payments accounts prepared under<br>s 42(3)</th><th>Regulation 7<br>Independent Examination under<br>s 43(3)</th></tr>
<tr><td colspan="3">Name of charity concerned</td></tr>
<tr><td colspan="3">Name and address of auditor(s) or independent examiner</td></tr>
<tr><td colspan="3">Signed by auditor or independent examiner</td></tr>
<tr><td colspan="2">States auditor eligible within s 43(2)(a) (or (b)) of Charities Act 1993 (eg is a 'Registered auditor')</td><td>Specifies any relevant professional qualifications or professional body of which the independent examiner is a member</td></tr>
<tr><td colspan="3">Report dated and financial year to which accounts relate specified</td></tr>
<tr><td colspan="2">Specifies that report is in respect of an audit carried out under Charities Act 1993 s 43 and in accordance with regulations under s 44</td><td>Specifies that report is in respect of an examination carried out under Charities Act 1993 s 43 and in accordance with directions given by Commissioners under s 43(7)(b)</td></tr>
</table>

| | | |
|---|---|---|
| Auditors opinion:<br>• Accounts comply with requirements of Regulation 3 (or 4)<br>• Give a true and fair view of state of affairs and incoming resources and application of resources. | Auditors opinion:<br>• Account and statement properly present receipts and payments for the year and assets and liabilities at year end<br>• Account and statement adequately distinguish any material special trust or other restricted fund | Statement whether or not any matter has come to the examiner's attention, giving reasonable cause to believe that in any material respect:<br>• where examination of accruals accounts under s 42(1) Ch A 1993, accounts do not comply with any requirements of Regulations 3 or 4 (except requirements to show 'true and fair view' Sch 1 Pt III para 1 of Regulations)<br>• accounting records not kept in accordance with s 41 Ch A 1993<br>• the accounts do not accord with the accounting records |
| Statement of opinion (if applicable) and grounds for forming it where:<br>• accounting records not kept in accordance with s 41 Ch A 1993<br>• accounts do not accord with accounting records | Statement of opinion (if applicable) and grounds for forming it where:<br>• accounting records not kept in accordance with s 41 Ch A 1993<br>• account and statement do not accord with accounting records | Statement whether or not any matter has come to examiner's attention to which attention should be drawn in report to enable a proper understanding of accounts |

[*continued on following page*]

| | | |
|---|---|---|
| | | Statement, where apparent to the examiner, where:<br>• any material expenditure or action appears not to be in accordance with the trusts of the charity |
| • any information or explanation where entitled under Regulation 8 not afforded | • any information or explanation where entitled under Regulation 8 not afforded | • any information or explanation where entitled under Regulation 8 not afforded |
| • information in accounts inconsistent in any material respect with annual report under s 45 Ch A 1993 | | • any information (in s 42(1) accruals accounts) inconsistent in any material respect with annual report prepared under s 45 Ch A 1993 |

## 6 DUTIES OF AUDITORS – CORPORATE CHARITIES

**16.38** For a corporate charity, in accordance with Companies Act 1985, s 237, the auditors are required to carry out such investigations as will enable them to form an opinion as to whether:

- proper accounting records have been kept by the charitable company, and whether proper returns adequate for their audit have been received from branches not visited by them; and
- the charitable company's individual accounts are in agreement with the accounting records and returns.

**16.39** The auditors are required to state in their report if they are of the opinion that proper accounting records have not been kept, or proper returns, adequate for their audit, have not been received from branches not visited by them, or if the company's individual accounts are not in agreement with the accounting records and returns.

**16.40** The auditors are also required to state in their report if they fail to obtain all the information and explanations which, to the best of their knowledge and belief, are necessary for the purposes of their audit. Where the disclosure requirements of information relating to the emoluments and other benefits of trustees/directors are not complied with in the annual accounts, the auditors are required to provide the necessary particulars within their report, so far as they are reasonably able to do so.

**16.41** Contrasting the duties of an auditor of a corporate charity with those of the auditor of an unincorporated charity, as set out in the table above, reveals some significant differences:

- the requirement to form an opinion as to the adequacy of branch returns, under the Companies Act 1985 is not included under the Charities Act 1993 for the auditor of an unincorporated charity with branches;
- the Companies Act 1985 does not require auditors to give the grounds for forming their opinion, as is required by the Charities Act 1993 (see table above).

## 7 AUDITING STANDARDS

**16.42** The auditor of a charity is required to carry out his work having regard to Auditing Standards issued by the Auditing Practices Board (APB). Statements of Auditing Standards (SASs) govern the work of the auditor. These SASs contain the basic principles and essential procedures with which auditors are required to comply in the conduct of any audit of financial statements. The APB also issues Practice Notes which assist auditors in the application of Auditing Standards to particular sectors. In October 1996 the APB issued a Practice Note on 'Charities'.

**16.43** The regulatory framework in which the charity auditor conducts his work is, therefore, determined by the Charities Act 1993, together with supplementary regulations in the case of an unincorporated charity, or the Companies Act 1985 (as amended) in the case of a charitable company, and also the professional requirements of Auditing Standards. The table set out below details the current statements of auditing standards which govern the work of auditors.

**APB Statements of Auditing Standards**

| | |
|---|---|
| | *Responsibility* |
| SAS 100 | Objective and general principles governing an audit of financial statements |
| SAS 110 | Fraud and error |
| SAS 120 | Consideration of law and regulations |

| | |
|---|---|
| SAS 130 | The going concern basis in financial statements |
| SAS 140 | Engagement letters |
| SAS 150 | Subsequent events |
| SAS 160 | Other information in documents containing audited financial statements |
| | *Planning, controlling and recording* |
| SAS 200 | Planning |
| SAS 210 | Knowledge of the business |
| SAS 220 | Materiality and the audit |
| SAS 230 | Working papers |
| SAS 240 | Quality control for audit work |
| | *Accounting systems and internal control* |
| SAS 300 | Accounting and internal control systems and audit risk assessments |
| | *Evidence* |
| SAS 400 | Audit evidence |
| SAS 410 | Analytical procedures |
| SAS 420 | Audit of accounting estimates |
| SAS 430 | Audit sampling |
| SAS 440 | Management representations |
| SAS 450 | Opening balances and comparatives |
| SAS 460 | Related parties |
| SAS 470 | Overall review of financial statements |
| SAS 480 | Service organisations |
| | *Using the work of others* |
| SAS 500 | Considering the work of internal audit |
| SAS 510 | The relationship between principal auditors and other auditors |
| SAS 520 | Using the work of an expert |
| | *Reporting* |
| SAS 600 | Auditors' reports on financial statements |
| SAS 601 | Imposed limitation of audit scope |
| SAS 610 | Reports to directors or management |
| SAS 620 | The auditors' right and duty to report to regulators in the financial sector |

## 8 'WHISTLE BLOWING'

**16.44** Under reg 6(5) of the Regulations, an auditor of an unincorporated charity is required to communicate in writing to the Charity Commissioners any matters which come to his attention (in his capacity as auditor) relating to the activities or affairs of the charity (or any institution or body corporate connected with the charity) which the auditor reasonably believes is (or is likely to be) of material significance for the exercise of the Charity Commissioners' functions under Charities Act 1993 s 8 (general power to institute enquiries) or s 18 (power to act for the protection of charities).

**16.45** The Regulations do not require auditors to perform any additional audit work for the purposes of the statutory duty of 'whistle blowing' and nor are they required specifically to seek out any breaches of the requirements applicable to a particular charity. However, auditors should anticipate any requirements and include procedures within their planning to ensure that members of the audit team are able to recognise reportable matters that may be encountered during the audit.

**16.46** The types of matter which give rise to a duty to report to the regulator are those which, in the auditors' opinion, are of material significance in determining whether action may be appropriate in order to protect the property of the charity, or ensure that its property is used for proper purposes. This would, of course, exclude minor breaches of trustees' obligations. The statutory duty on the auditors to report to the Charity Commissioners arises primarily from the identification of any significant loss, or misapplication, of the charity's property or funds, or from the identification of a significant risk to the charity's property or maladministration or misuse of assets (Practice Note p 61 para 24).

**16.47** The following matters may give rise to a statutory duty to report to the Commissioners.

- **Maladministration and inadequacy of direction and control.** Incompetence, poor judgement, indifference, recklessness may all be evidence of a failure to exercise proper control over the administration and management of a charity's affairs. Uncertainty of charity trustees' responsibilities, poor consideration of policy or strategy matters by the trustee body, or weak control by the trustees (for example rubber stamping decisions made by a dominant chief executive or senior staff) may be other examples of a serious weakness in management.
- **Significant breaches of the charity's trusts or of legislative requirement.** Material failures to operate within the charity's constitution may give rise to a duty to report. This could include reckless investment, disregard of professional advice or the

application of funds for purposes outside the charity's objects or contrary to any special trust. A breach of legal duties or obligations may similarly give rise to a duty to report; these could include contraventions of fundraising regulations, breaches of tax exemptions, failure to keep proper accounting records, obstruction of auditors in the course of their work or, for example, a trustee receiving remuneration without proper power or consent.

- **Deliberate misuse of charity property.** Misuse or misappropriation of the property of the charity may result from false accounting, theft or misappropriation by any trustee, employee, volunteer, agent or third party, where no report has been made to the police or the Charity Commissioners. Generally, where there is reasonable cause to doubt the honesty or integrity of a trustee or trustee body, a duty to report arises.

**16.48** It should be noted that the 'whistle blowing' duty at present applies only to charities established in England and Wales which are unincorporated. Charitable companies incorporated or registered under the Companies Act 1985 are not covered by the 1995 Regulations, although the Department of Trade and Industry has indicated its intention to introduce legislation at the earliest opportunity to bring such companies on to an equal footing with other charities. Auditors of charitable companies identifying matters that would otherwise be reportable do have the right to report to an appropriate authority in the public interest, on the lines of SAS 120 *Consideration of Law and Regulations*, but whether this gives sufficient coverage to counterbalance the weight of client confidentiality considerations remains to be seen. The law needs to be the same for both classes of charity.

## 9 CONTRACTUAL REQUIREMENTS OF THE AUDITOR

**16.49** In addition to carrying out the statutory audit, in accordance with Charities Act 1993 or Companies Act 1985, as the case may be, the auditor may carry out specific contractual assignments at the request of the trustees. For example, the trustees may request the auditor to comment on the nature and adequacy of the internal controls of the organisation, or matters such as management reporting, budgeting or forecasting with a view to enabling the trustees to fulfil their obligations. Matters of particular concern, for example, irregularities, suspicion of fraud, weaknesses in the accounting system, could also be the subject of a special investigation by the auditor. All these special assignments are quite separate from the statutory responsibilities of the auditor to express an opinion on the annual accounts of the charity.

## 10 WHAT IS THE INDEPENDENT EXAMINER REQUIRED TO DO?

### The relative merits of audit and independent examination

**16.50** Where charities' gross income or expenditure per year exceeds £10,000, but not £250,000 (in the current or either of the two preceding financial years), the trustees must choose to subject the accounts of the charity to independent examination or audit, provided there is no stipulation within the governing document of the charity specifically for an audit. The decision whether to have an audit or independent examination will depend upon several factors, including cost and the level of reassurance required.

**16.51** If the trustees require specific advice that is outside the scope of an independent examiner, who may be a private individual for example, they are always entitled to seek that advice from the most appropriate source, including independent professional accountants. The trustees will always need to weigh up the costs and benefits of the type of external scrutiny that they require and ensure that they receive value for money – a particularly pertinent factor where charitable funds are concerned. Certainly, for a small charity, if the audit in itself adds no value, it may well be best to opt for an independent examination. This will be particularly appropriate, for example, where the charity is closely controlled and subject to direct supervision by the trustees personally.

**16.52** In essence, an audit provides a high positive level of assurance; an independent examination on the other hand, provides only a moderate and negative assurance in the sense of reporting only by exception. The independent examination makes no attempt to provide an opinion on whether the accounts show a true and fair view.

**16.53** In considering the accounting records, the review work carried out within an independent examination is made with a view to identifying *major* failures to maintain accounting records in accordance with s 41 Charities Act 1993, whereas under the principles of audit, procedures are carried out with a view to forming an opinion of whether accounting records have been maintained in accordance with the statutory requirements. An independent examination does not necessarily involve substantive testing, that is examining source documentation, obtaining independent third party confirmations or physical inspection of assets, for example. Unless the analytical review work of an independent examination shows unusual items, for which the trustees cannot give satisfactory explanations, no substantive testing is required under independent examination.

**16.54** Whenever accruals based accounts are prepared, it will be seen that the major differences between audit and independent examination are:

- the level of overall independent assurance;
- whether or not an opinion on a true and fair view is required;
- whether accounting records are maintained to a satisfactory level required by statute;
- whether the comfort of detailed substantive testing is required.

**16.55** From the above, it will seem that in many instances an independent examination will provide a perfectly adequate level of assurance.

**16.56** For accounts prepared on the basis of receipts and payments, where the gross income or total expenditure exceeds £10,000 but does not exceed £100,000, an independent examination would normally be more appropriate, in the absence of special requirements of funding bodies, or of the membership in the case of an unincorporated association.

**16.57** The auditors of an unincorporated charity, which prepares accounts on a receipts and payments basis, are not required to issue an opinion in 'true and fair view' terms, but to report that in their opinion the receipts and payments account, and statement of assets and liabilities 'properly present' the receipts and payments of the charity for the year under review, together with its statement of assets and liabilities as at the year end.

## 11 COMMENTS AND CONCLUSIONS

**16.58** Wherever a charity has a choice between an audit and independent examination, an audit is invariably preferable for those organisations with a high profile, as this represents a high risk for the trustees' reputations. As mentioned above, for a small, closely controlled, low risk organisation, perhaps with few volunteers and no 'members', an independent examination may be preferable.

**16.59** As the Charity Commissioners relate in their Direction and Guidance Note: *The Carrying out of an Independent Examination,* the independent examiner must obviously be competent for the task and be familiar with accountancy methods – but does not need to be a practising accountant.

CHAPTER 17

# Tax exemptions and charities

## 1 GENERAL

**17.1** There is no overall tax exemption for charities. The lack of a general exemption means that awareness of the tax issues and careful organisation are sometimes necessary if charities are to keep their tax liabilities to the minimum, and preserve their funds for charitable works.

Important exemptions exist for income tax, corporation tax and capital gains tax, as do significant reliefs for stamp duty and value added tax.

**17.2** Many of these exemptions have been added or amended over the years, and a major criticism of the way charity tax exemptions operated was that there were a number of glaring inconsistencies in the way exemption for direct and indirect taxes often worked. The overall government review of charity taxation expected in the last edition of this book has resulted in a number of changes to charity tax enacted in the Finance Act 2000 to address this issue. VAT exemptions and reliefs are dealt with in Chapter 20.

## 2 INCOME TAX AND CORPORATION TAX

**17.3** Reliefs from income tax, extended to corporation tax by s 9(4) of TA 1988, are contained in s 505 of TA 1988. This is not a general exemption from taxation, but provides a range of specific exemptions for which claims must be submitted. These claims must be made within six years of the end of the tax year or corporation tax accounting period to which the claim relates.

Claims for repayment of income tax suffered on investment income or of transitional relief (see **17.10**) are made on form R68 obtainable from the Inland Revenue on request.

**17.4** The last few years have seen a fundamental change in UK taxation — the switch to self-assessment. This now affects charities which in the past were often not required, in practice, to file a full tax return and accounts with the Inland Revenue. Now any charity, whether constituted as a trust or company, must self-assess its income and gains if required by notice to file a tax return. This regime operates for charities constituted as companies in respect of all accounting periods ended on or after 1 July 1999, and for charitable trusts from the 1999/2000 tax year.

**17.5** There are special supplementary pages to the standard tax returns which charities must complete if called upon to do so (copy of forms in Appendices). These pages form part of the tax return of the charity, and require the disclosure of figures, exempt income and gains, related expenses and details of a charity's general administration expenses and assets. It is important to note that these pages legally constitute the charity's claim to tax exemption. The charity must also declare:

- that all its income and gains are exempt; and
- that all income and gains have been applied for charitable purposes only; or
- that some income or gains may not be exempt, or may not have been applied for charitable purposes.

At present, the Inland Revenue have said that not all charities will be required to make these returns every year, but that returns will be issued to charities on a random basis.

**17.6** Whilst most of the information required to file these forms will be readily available from the charity's accounting records, some of the questions demand such a degree of detail that further sub-analysis of the records may be needed. For example, one question asks for the total amount of grants made by the charity, splitting these between those made within the UK and those outside.

More importantly, however, the person responsible for the form should carefully consider the implications of the answers to the question. Some of these are carefully chosen to reveal the extent to which the charity may not be applying its income and gains for charitable purposes only, eg making grants outside the UK without taking reasonable care to ensure that they are applied for charitable purposes, or making loans to a subsidiary company at less than a commercial rate of interest (see **18.13**).

## The exemptions

**17.7** Section 505 of TA 1988 exempts:

(a) profits or gains taxable under Schedule A or D, arising in respect of rents or other receipts from any estate, interest in or right over any land, whether situated in the United Kingdom or elsewhere, to the extent that the profits or gains:
  - (i) arise in respect of rents or receipts from an estate, interest or right vested in any person for charitable purposes; and
  - (ii) are applied to charitable purposes only;

(b) (i) income chargeable under Schedule D Case III, for example, interest, annuities and other annual payments, including covenants, and some royalties;
  - (ii) income that would be taxable under Schedule D Case III if UK-sourced, but which is not so sourced, and is therefore taxable under Schedule D Case IV or V;
  - (iii) dividends and other distributions taxable under Schedule F;
  - (iv) dividends and other distributions taxable under Schedule D Case V because they have an overseas source, but which would be taxable under Schedule F if they had a UK source;

(c) public revenue dividends on securities in the name of trustees, taxable under Schedule D, to the extent that the dividends are applicable and applied only for the repair of any cathedral, college, church or chapel, or other building used only for the purposes of divine worship;

(d) profits of trade carried on by a charity, whether in the UK or elsewhere, if the profits are applied solely to the purposes of the charity and either;
  - (i) the primary purpose of the charity, or
  - (ii) work in connection with the trade is mainly carried on by beneficiaries of the charity;

(e) profits accruing in respect of a lottery under ss 3 or 5 of the Lotteries and Amusements Act 1976 (or its Northern Ireland equivalent) where the proceeds are applied solely to the charity's purpose.

The exemption for public revenue dividends applied for the repair of cathedral, college, church or chapel, or other building used only for divine worship was introduced by the Finance Act 1996, and means that local appeals such as 'Friends of the Church Steeple' are now exempted.

## Small trades

**17.8** A major change introduced by the Finance Act 2000 s 46 is the addition of a general exemption for small trades carried on by charities.

The profits of any trade will be exempt either where gross trading or other income chargeable under Schedule D Case I or Case VI does not exceed certain limits, or the charity could reasonably have expected at the beginning of any year that the limits would not be exceeded.

The limit is the greater of two sums:

(a) £5,000; and
(b) the lesser of £50,000 and 25% of a charity's total income.

**17.9** Exemption applies on the condition that the income or profits received by the charity are applied solely for charitable purposes. Where not all income or gains are so applied, restrictions of a charity's tax exemptions may occur (see **17.29**). There is a subtle difference between the wording of the condition attaching to exemption for most types of income, which must be applied for charitable purposes only, and that for trading income (both in TA 1988 s 505 and FA 2000 s 46, where the income has to be applied solely to the purposes of the charity, ie ploughed back into the charitable activity.)

A number of types of income or profits are not exempted by TA 1988 s 505. Schedule E income is not exempt, but this is not relevant since individuals cannot themselves be charities.

**17.10** The exemption in respect of Schedule F income ceased to have effect from 6 April 1999, when Advance Corporation Tax (ACT) was abolished, since, as a consequence, the tax credit on UK dividends became notional and not repayable. This change alone was calculated by some observers to cost the charity sector as a whole about £400 million. To soften the blow, transitional relief was introduced to enable charities to obtain payment of a sum additional to the dividend on a sliding scale until 2003/2004, as follows:

| | |
|---|---|
| 1999/2000 | 21% of the dividend |
| 2000/2001 | 17% |
| 2001/2002 | 13% |
| 2002/2003 | 8% |
| 2003/2004 | 4% |

## Trading activities

**17.11** Trading profits are not exempted unless as described above, namely carried out by the beneficiaries of the charity or in the course of the carrying out of a primary purpose of the charity, or within the limits introduced by the Finance Act 2000 s 46.

The tax issues relating to trading activities carried on by charities, and the ways in which the profits of trading activities carried on for the benefit of charities can flow through in a form which is exempt under TA 1988 s 505, are discussed in detail in Chapter 18.

**Interest and annual payments**

**17.12** Exemption from income and corporation tax applies to all forms of interest, whether annual or short and with a UK or overseas source. It also includes interest payable gross by building societies.

**17.13** The question as to what constitutes an 'annual payment' for tax purposes is dealt with in more detail at **19.3** below in connection with deeds of covenant. Suffice to say that it must be pure profit in the charity's hands, so that a charity receiving an annual payment does not have to do anything to earn it, nor be obliged to offer anything in return.

**17.14** Copyright or other royalties may constitute annual payments, especially if given or bequeathed to the charity, but care needs to be taken where a charity takes action to exploit such rights, as such activities can often constitute trading.

**Land transactions**

**17.15** Annual profits or gains not otherwise assessable for tax are included under Schedule D Case VI. These are not exempted unless derived from land (see TA 1988 s 505(1)(a)).

**17.16** Thus, for example, copyright income enjoyed by a charity may be taxable. Prior to 1995/96, income from furnished lettings also fell to be taxable in this way. From 1995/96 onwards, however, furnished lettings carried on by a charity constituted as a trust have been technically chargeable under Schedule A, and exempt, whereas the same income to a charitable company would still be within Schedule D Case VI and taxable, but for a Revenue concession.

**17.17** ICTA 1988 s 776 imposes a charge to tax under Schedule D Case VI where land is obtained, held or developed with the sole intention of realising a gain on its disposal. It is believed that the Inland Revenue do not accept that TA 1988 s 505(1)(a) exempts a charge under s 776. Thus, where disposal of property is contemplated that could lead to a gain, particularly where charitable trustees, in carrying out their duties diligently, seek to share in a developer's profit, advice should be sought before proceeding (see *Page v Lowther* [1983] STC 199, where the trustees did exactly that and were caught by s 776). Alternatively, the Revenue could seek to remove exemption from such a disposal by assessing the transaction as an adventure in the nature of trade. Either way, professional advice should be obtained before entering into any significant land transaction.

## Fundraising events

**17.18** Fundraising events that might technically be defined as trading are exempted from income and corporation tax provided they fulfil the requirements for VAT exemption laid out in Chapter 20. This is a substantial improvement on the reliance on the extra-statutory concession ESC C4 which applied before the Finance Act 2000, as this put regular or substantial events outside the exemption.

**17.19** Following the new alignment of the direct and indirect tax exemptions concerning the raising of money through holding events, the criteria for exemption are laid out in full in Chapter 20. By keeping within those criteria, a charity will be exempt from both income or corporation tax and VAT.

## Miscellaneous exemptions

**17.20** A number of other minor exemptions from tax can be found elsewhere in the legislation. Charities are exempted from special charges in connection with certificates of deposit by the TA 1988 s 56(3)(c). They are also exempted from the accrued income scheme (TA 1988 s 715(1)(d)) and from the 40% tax charge on the repayment of pension fund surpluses (TA 1988 s 601(4)).

## Contemplative orders

**17.21** ESC B10 grants specific relief to contemplative religious communities and their members, as some communities are not entitled to the exemptions from tax contained in s 505. This is because purely contemplative orders are not seen as carrying on the charitable purpose of the advancement of religion because their activity is inward looking rather than evangelistic. The question of to whom the income of such a community actually belongs is another difficult point to determine.

**17.22** ESC B10 assists with these difficulties. It allows an amount being equal to an individual's personal allowance to be regarded as the income of a member of the community, and the aggregate of the members' personal allowances to be offset against the income of the community. Where this aggregate exceeds actual income, the excess can be used against capital gains in that tax year. Carry forward of the excess used to be allowed, but this is no longer possible, with the exception of allowances unused as at 5 April 1995, which can be carried forward until exhausted.

## Anti-avoidance

**17.23** In addition to the anti-avoidance legislation contained in TA 1988 s 776 relating to capital gains on land (see **17.15**), the Revenue has significant other powers to counteract the abuse of charitable status. Although there is no general exemption from tax for charities, favourable exemptions make charitable status an attractive prospect for the avoidance of tax. The general lowering of income tax rates and their combination with CGT rates has reduced the number of artificial schemes somewhat, but traps remain to catch the greedy, which may unfortunately catch the unwary as well.

**17.24** Developments in this field include recent agreement to closer co-operation between the Revenue and Customs and Excise. VAT anti-avoidance legislation is well developed, and recent increases to Customs' powers to restrict the formation of VAT groups may well impact on many charities. This is discussed in Chapter 20.

**17.25** For direct tax, the TA 1988 s 703 deals with the cancellation of tax advantages accruing from certain transactions in securities. Exempt bodies are not outside this legislation, which was made clear in *Commissioners of the Inland Revenue v Universities Superannuation Scheme Ltd* [1997] STC 1. In this case a company purchased its own shares from the appellant, a pension scheme otherwise exempt from tax, giving rise to a distribution. The monies received by the appellant consisted of repayment of capital and a dividend. They then claimed a tax credit of over £850,000. The Revenue challenged this as the credit had arisen from a dividend which was of an 'abnormal amount', and they succeeded in raising an assessment under Case VI for the amount of the tax credit. Advance clearance should be sought from the Revenue's Technical Division if this section could apply to a transaction.

**17.26** Sections 235 and 236 of TA 1988 used to deny exemption from Schedule F dividends where a charity received pre-acquisition dividends from a company where it controlled more than ten percent of the shares. These sections were repealed with effect from 6 April 1999 on the abolition of ACT.

### Claiming relief

**17.27** Charities should remember that claims for relief from tax under the TA 1988 s 505 can be made as soon and as often as they wish, providing they hold the necessary tax vouchers. It is not necessary to wait until the end of the tax year, or to accumulate vouchers to a specific threshold.

**17.28** In addition, it is possible to receive interest gross on certain holdings. The Bank of England will pay interest on government securities gross on receipt of an application accompanied by the charity registration slip issued by the Charity Commissioners. Banks and building societies will also pay interest gross as long as they are provided with proof of charitable status. It is important to provide this proof when the relevant account or deposit is opened, to avoid tax being deducted automatically.

## 3 CAPITAL GAINS TAX

**17.29** Charities are exempt from CGT provided that the gains are applied for charitable purposes, except in one circumstance. To prevent temporary charities being used to avoid liability to CGT, s 256(2) of TCGA 1992 revokes the exemption where assets held on charitable trusts cease to be subject to such trusts. If this occurs, the trustees are treated as if they had disposed of and immediately reacquired the assets at open market value. The gain on the deemed disposal is chargeable to CGT. Assessments must be raised by the Inland Revenue within three years of the end of the year of assessment in which the asset ceases to be held on charitable trusts.

**17.30** Unfortunately, as with several anti-avoidance provisions, this withholding of exemption can affect genuine transactions by charities, as well as transactions with the aim of avoiding tax. One example would be where property has been given to a charity for a fixed term, after which it passes to a member of the donor's family. The Charity's trustees would then be liable for CGT on the unrealised gains attaching to the property when passed on. This treatment can carry back to any earlier disposals that were reinvested in other assets which continued to be held at the end of the fixed term. This carry back is not restricted by the six year limit. The carry back to previous disposals may also be made on those who were trustees at the time of those disposals, rendering them potentially personally liable to CGT. Therefore, trustees in such a situation must ensure that they retain sufficient assets to meet this liability before they transfer the property to the ultimate beneficiary, and obtain an indemnity from them.

**17.31** Another situation in which this can be an issue is where a charity has run its course, and no longer has charitable objects to which income and gains can be applied. Trustees in this position should apply to the Charity Commissioners for a scheme under s 16 of the Charities Act 1993, to widen the charitable objects of the charity in order that property can continue to be held with the income and gains being applied for charitable purposes.

## 4 APPLICATION FOR CHARITABLE PURPOSES ONLY

**17.32** For CGT purposes, a gain is not a chargeable gain if it accrues to a charity and is applied for charitable purposes (TCGA 1992 s 256).

For income and corporation tax, TA 1988 s 505 requires income or profits to be applied to charitable purposes only. Examples of such income are explored in the next chapter. Although a charity's administrators may think that this is a simple condition to meet, being a charity and application for charitable purposes are not one and the same thing. Three questions are raised by these conditions:

- What constitutes application for charitable purposes?
- To what extent can income or gains be accumulated?
- What happens to income or gains applied for non-charitable purposes?

### Application

**17.33** Charitable purposes have been defined in Chapter 1. To recap, Lord McNaghten's judgment in *Income Tax Special Purposes Comrs v Pemsel* [1891], summarised charitable purposes as the relief of poverty, the advancement of education, the advancement of religion, and other purposes beneficial to the community. Provided the charity applies its income and gains within the bounds permitted by its articles or trust deed, and within these charitable purposes, there should be no problem. However, there are sometimes grey areas or differences of emphasis as to what does or does not come within charitable purposes. Often there can also be significant delays between the receipt of income or gains and their application, specifically where funds are being built up for a specific but long-term project or charitable purpose. If there appears to be no application of funds, the Inland Revenue may seek to withdraw or deny the tax exemptions available to a charity.

### Accumulating income

**17.34** The question of application was the subject of the Court of Appeal case, *IRC v Helen Slater Charitable Trust Ltd* [1981] STC 471. This case was concerned with the payment of income by the trustees of the appellant to the trustees of the Slater Foundation Ltd, another charitable company, with the same trustees as the first. The Inland Revenue claimed that as the money paid over had been accumulated to no specific purpose, had not been spent, and, they believed, there had not been any change in the beneficial ownership of the funds, the payment did not constitute application for charitable purposes.

**17.35** The court held that, despite the trustees of both charities being the same people, they were separate trusts, with no power in law to direct the affairs of the other. The appellant trustees had, therefore, applied the funds for charitable purposes, by passing them to another charity. The recipient charity had received a capital sum, and was therefore only liable to account for the application of any income arising therefrom.

**17.36** Although the case was not decided on the precise point, the remarks of Lord Justice Oliver in the *Helen Slater* case are of prime importance. In commenting on two conflicting dicta of the judges in the earlier case of *General Nursing Council for Scotland v IRC* [1929] 14 TC 645, he said:

'Charitable trustees who simply leave surplus income uninvested cannot, I think, be said to have applied it all, and, indeed, would be in breach of trust. But if the income is reinvested by them and held, as invested, as part of the funds of the charity, I would be disposed to say that it is no less being applied for charitable purposes than if it is paid out in wages to the secretary'.

**17.37** As the Revenue in the *Helen Slater* case had conceded that, subject to the trustees not acting ultra vires, accumulation for a specific purpose does represent application for charitable purposes, the only problem appears to lie with accumulation for general purposes. The remarks of Lord Justice Oliver seem to indicate that even general accumulations can constitute application for charitable purposes. This is as long as the very minimum that has been done by the charity in question is consciously to reinvest any surplus income so that it can be said to have been applied. However, the point is still not totally free from doubt, and it may be legislated in the future or tested again by the Inland Revenue through the courts in an extreme case. However, the Inland Revenue did mount an attack in the case of *Nightingale Ltd v Price* [1996] STC (SCD) 116 before the Special Commissioners. They had sought to deny charitable exemption under the precursor of TA 1988 s 505 on the grounds that the income received by way of covenant from the property development and trading subsidiaries of the charitable company Nightingale Ltd was not applied for charitable purposes. The income was re-lent at interest to a property holding company controlled by the director of the charity and the charity's subsidiary companies. The Inland Revenue was not successful before the Special Commissioners, who found that the income was applied for charitable purposes only, since the charity's policy was to increase its own resources by lending money to subsidiaries and associated companies at high rates of interest. The Inland Revenue did not pursue this case through the courts, and it remains to be seen whether they will attempt to pursue a similar case in the future.

**17.38** To counter avoidance by using the *Helen Slater* principle, an amendment to TA 1988 s 505(2) was made in FA 1996. This provides that any payments by one charity to another, being not for full consideration, not otherwise chargeable to tax, or otherwise eligible for relief under s 505(1), are taxable under Schedule D Case III as an annual payment. This follows the *Slater* case in that the charity making the payment has applied those funds for charitable purposes, but requires the recipient also to show that they have applied the funds for charitable purposes. The recipient can still claim exemption for tax on these grounds, and the donor does not, despite some earlier interpretations to the contrary, have to deduct tax before making the payment.

**17.39** Where, however, the recipient charity is not resident in the UK, it may not be subject to the requirement to demonstrate to the Inland Revenue that it has applied the money it receives for charitable purposes. In such cases, the onus of proving that the money has been applied for charitable purposes falls on the UK-resident donor charity. In these circumstances, the TA 1988 s 506(3) requires the donor charity to take reasonable steps to ensure that the money is used by the foreign charity for charitable purposes. Any failure to do this, or carelessness by a UK charity in these circumstances, would leave the donor charity in the UK within the rules on non-qualifying expenditure, and faced with a consequent restriction of its tax exemptions. This legislation is primarily designed to counter artificial tax avoidance schemes. If care is taken bona fide charities with operations overseas and their supporters in the UK should have no problems in satisfying the statutory requirements.

## Application for non-charitable purposes

**17.40** Positive misuse of a charity's income in applying it for non-charitable purposes is rare, but inadvertently using income for such purposes can endanger the tax exemptions of any charity, however well-intentioned. There are two ways in which the application of income can slip into dangerous territory; administration costs and non-charitable activity. While the Revenue allows that reasonable administrative costs are necessary for the achievement of a charity's objects, and are therefore indirectly applied for charitable purposes, they or the Charity Commission can investigate excessive administration costs. Although this is a subjective question, expenditure by the officers of a charity that is seen as 'extravagant', such as unnecessary foreign trips, is an example of what could be investigated (see Chapter 8 for the accounting requirements concerning administrative expenses).

**17.41** A strict legal definition of charitable purposes would exclude activities that are political. An occasional foray into this field, subject to the rules governing non-qualifying expenditure, will generally be tolerated by the Revenue, but sustained and significant political or other non-charitable activity will not be. Activity at such a level should be contained within a separate body with separate sources of income if at all possible. The worst case scenario if this is not done is that a charity's tax exemptions may be totally withdrawn, and their very charitable status may be in danger.

## 5 NON-QUALIFYING — RESTRICTION OF TAX EXEMPTION

**17.42** Reference has been made earlier in this chapter to 'non-qualifying' expenditure and restriction of tax exemptions. New rules were laid down in the Finance Act 1986 to deal with the problem of non-qualifying expenditure. These are now contained in the TA 1988 ss 505 and 506. The TA 1988 Sch 20 specifies the types of investments which are regarded as qualifying investments and loans for the purposes of s 506.

**17.43** The basic rules for calculating the amount of any restriction of tax exemption for non-qualifying expenditure are contained in the TA 1988 s 505(3). This lays down that if in any chargeable period a charity has:

(a) relevant income and gains not less than £10,000; and
(b) relevant income and gains exceeding qualifying expenditure; and
(c) the charity incurs or is deemed to have incurred non-qualifying expenditure, tax relief will be restricted.

**17.44** The amount of income and gains to which the restriction applies is found by comparing the excess of relevant income and gains over qualifying expenditure with the amount of non-qualifying expenditure. Tax exemption is withdrawn for so much of the excess of relevant income and gains over qualifying expenditure as does not exceed the amount of non-qualifying expenditure.

**17.45** For the purposes of this test, relevant income and gains do not necessarily include all the income and gains a charity receives. Relevant income and gains are only those income and gains which would be taxable if they were not exempted by TA 1988 s 505(1) or TCGA 1992 s 256(1).

**17.46** Qualifying expenditure includes all expenditure in the period laid out solely for charitable purposes, and any commitments made for such expenditure to be entered into in the period. It will obviously include any investments, loans or expenditure connected with them and permitted by Sch 20. It also includes reasonable fundraising and administration expenditure. Where, however, the charity makes payments to bodies outside the UK, it will only be regarded as making qualifying expenditure provided the charity concerned has taken reasonable steps to ensure that their payment will be applied for charitable purposes. Non-qualifying expenditure, in addition to investments or loans outside Sch 20, will include all non-chargeable expenses, for example, trading expenses, political activities, excessive administration costs etc.

**17.47** Thus, the purpose of the legislation is to penalise any charity which misapplies its income and gains, by denying tax relief on the appropriate proportion of its income and gains up to the limit of the expenditure misapplied. The de minimis limit should not be forgotten in that, for the rules on non-qualifying expenditure to apply, the charity must have relevant income and gains of £10,000 or more in any one year. In addition, relevant income and gains do not include any income or gains which are exempt under separate provisions from TA 1988 s 505(1) or TCGA 1992 s 256. Contrast the following examples.

**17.48** In Example 1, Charity X has the following income:

| | £ |
|---|---|
| Grants from other UK charities | 250,000 |
| UK dividend income | 50,000 |
| Gift Aided donations | 40,000 |

Its expenditure comprises:

| | |
|---|---|
| Grants to UK charities | 30,000 |
| Administration costs (of which 60% is deemed excessive by the Inland Revenue) | 100,000 |
| Grants to overseas bodies (£80,000 of which was handed over without prior research on the part of Charity X to a little known tax haven charity which promptly misappropriated it) | 180,000 |

Charity X will have its tax exemptions and reliefs restricted as follows:

| | **Income** | **Relevant Income** |
|---|---|---|
| | £ | £ |
| Grants from other UK charities | 250,000 | 250,000 |
| UK dividend income | 50,000 | 50,000 |
| Gift Aided donations | 40,000 | 40,000 |
| | 340,000 | 340,000 |

| | **Total expenditure** | **Qualifying expenditure** |
|---|---|---|
| | £ | £ |
| Grants to UK charities | 30,000 | 30,000 |
| Administrative expenses | 100,000 | 40,000 |
| Grants to overseas bodies | 180,000 | 100,000 |
| | 310,000 | 170,000 |

**17.49** Thus, non-qualifying expenditure is £140,000. The excess of relevant income and gains over qualifying expenditure is £170,000. Charity X will therefore have its tax reliefs and exemptions restricted by the lesser of these two amounts, and will therefore pay tax on £140,000 of relevant income and gains.

**17.50** In Example 2, in the same year, Charity Y, with exactly the same qualifying and non-qualifying expenditure as Charity X, has the following income:

| | £ |
|---|---|
| Grants from UK charities | 150,000 |
| UK dividend income | 50,000 |
| Donations from the public (including £40,000 donations under Gift Aid) | 140,000 |

The computation for Charity Y is:

| | **Income** | **Relevant Income** |
|---|---|---|
| | **£** | **£** |
| Grants from UK charities | 150,000 | 150,000 |
| UK dividend income | 50,000 | 50,000 |
| Donations | 140,000 | 40,000 |
| | 340,000 | 240,000 |

Whereas non-qualifying expenditure, as for Charity X, is £140,000, the excess relevant income and gains over qualifying expenditure is only £70,000 (£240,000 less £170,000). Charity Y will therefore suffer restriction of its tax reliefs and exemptions only on £70,000 of relevant income, the lesser of the two amounts. In other words, part of the non-qualifying expenditure is effectively deemed to have been met from income which is not relevant income.

**17.51** Example 3, that of Charity Z, illustrates another point. Its income is:

| | £ |
|---|---|
| UK dividends | 100,000 |
| Capital gains | 115,000 |
| Donations from the public (including £10,000 under Gift Aid) | 45,000 |

Expenditure is as follows:

| | £ |
|---|---|
| Qualifying expenditure being payments to beneficiaries | 225,000 |
| Necessary administrative costs | 25,000 |
| Political donation | 10,000 |

The computation is:

| | **Income** | **Relevant Income** |
|---|---|---|
| | £ | £ |
| UK dividends | 100,000 | 100,000 |
| Capital gains | 115,000 | 115,000 |
| Donations | 45,000 | 10,000 |
| | 260,000 | 225,000 |

| | **Total expenditure** | **Qualifying expenditure** |
|---|---|---|
| | £ | £ |
| Payments to beneficiaries | 225,000 | 225,000 |
| Administrative costs | 25,000 | 25,000 |
| Political donation | 10,000 | - |
| | 260,000 | 250,000 |

**17.52** Here, for Charity Z, the excess of relevant income over qualifying expenditure is £NIL. Thus, despite the £10,000 political donation ranking as non-qualifying expenditure, Charity Z suffers no restrictions of its tax reliefs or exemptions because it is the lesser of the two amounts, in this case £NIL, which quantifies the amount of the restriction.

**17.53** It is perhaps ironic that legislation which was introduced to combat tax avoidance or malpractice by charities does not always result in a restriction of tax relief, whereas previously it was recognised that a charity had to apply income and gains for charitable purposes only.

**17.54** Nevertheless, any charity which does fall foul of the non-qualifying expenditure rules can be faced with difficulties. This is because, where the aggregate of all expenditure exceeds relevant income and gains in the period, as for Charity Z in Example 3, the proportion of the excess which represents non-qualifying expenditure in the period is actually carried back and treated as non-qualifying expenditure of previous periods.

**17.55** In Example 4, Charity XYZ has the following income and expenditure:

| | | £ |
|---|---|---|
| 1997/98 | Relevant income | 200,000 |
| | Qualifying expenditure | 150,000 |
| | Non-qualifying expenditure | NIL |
| 1998/99 | Relevant income | 200,000 |
| | Qualifying expenditure | 150,000 |
| | Non-qualifying expenditure | NIL |

| | | £ |
|---|---|---|
| 1999/2000 | Relevant income | 200,000 |
| | Qualifying expenditure | 150,000 |
| | Non-qualifying expenditure | 140,000 |

**17.56** Thus, not only will Charity XYZ suffer restriction of tax relief in 1999/2000 on £50,000 of income (being the excess of relevant income over qualifying expenditure of £50,000 which is less than non-qualifying expenditure), expenditure for the year exceeded relevant income by £90,000. This is all attributed to non-qualifying expenditure. The carry-back rules, which are contained in TA 1988 s 506(3) and TA 1988 Sch 20 Part III are brought into operation. Prior to 1999/00, Charity XYZ suffered no tax restriction, because even though its relevant income and gains exceeded qualifying expenditure by £50,000 per annum, it had no non-qualifying expenditure. Now Charity XYZ is deemed to have incurred £90,000 of non-qualifying expenditure for 1998/99, giving rise to a restriction of tax exemption of £50,000 of income and gains for that year. The tax relief lost is ascertained using the normal formula. A further £40,000 non-qualifying expenditure is deemed to have been incurred in 1997/98.

**17.57** TA 1988 s 506(4) defines as non-qualifying expenditure any investments or loans made in the period which are not qualifying investments or loans as defined in TA 1988 Sch 20. The list of qualifying investments contained in Sch 20 paras 1–10 is not surprising, but may give problems from a strictly technical standpoint. Permitted investments include:

(a) any investments falling within Parts I, II, and III of Sch 1 of the Trustee Investments Act 1961, except those in Part II para 13 (mortgages etc);
(b) any investment in a common fund established under the Charities Acts;
(c) any land other than an interest in land held as security for a debt;
(d) any quoted shares or securities, including those quoted on the Unlisted Securities Market;
(e) any units in a unit trust authorised under the Financial Services Act 1986;
(f) any interest-bearing deposits with authorised banks or deposit takes, so long as the deposits are not part of any back-to-back arrangement providing finance for a third party;
(g) any loan or investment outside these categories provided that the Inland Revenue is satisfied that it is made for the benefit of the charity and not for tax avoidance purposes.

An interesting point is that the Unlisted Securities Market is no longer in existence, rendering this section of Sch 20 without impact. The effective 'replacements' for the USM, the Alternative Investment Market and OFEX, are not included within the specifically qualifying investments listed in Sch 20. However, the Inland Revenue regard stocks quoted on AIM as being listed on a recognised stock exchange for the purposes of the relief for gifts of quoted shares to charity in FA 2000 s 43 – see **19.43** below. It appears that AIM stocks would be regarded as qualifying but OFEX investments should be considered on a case by case basis as to whether they are qualifying investments.

**17.58** The definition of a qualifying loan is further extended to include non-interest-bearing bank current accounts, loans to other charities, and loans to beneficiaries of the charity made in the course of carrying out the purposes of the charity. One notable omission from qualifying expenditure is investment in unquoted companies, whether by share capital or loan. However, such investment is permissible provided there is no tax avoidance motive and it can be shown to the satisfaction of the Inland Revenue that it is for the charity's benefit. The potential problem this might pose in relation to trading activities is discussed in Chapter 18.

## 6 VALUE ADDED TAX

**17.59** There is no general relief from VAT available to charities. Once the registration threshold of taxable supplies has been exceeded, a charity must register and account for VAT as any other trader. This is a complex area, discussed in Chapter 20.

## 7 INHERITANCE TAX

**17.60** The aspects of inheritance tax relating to giving to charity are considered in Chapter 19. Charities themselves benefit from the relief in the Inheritance Tax Act 1984 s 58(1)(a), which applies to charities constituted in the form of a trust. Charities constituted as trusts are almost invariably drawn up as discretionary trusts.

**17.61** The relief applies to the charges made under the system by which a periodic ten-year charge is imposed on discretionary trusts. This system involves tax being due, albeit at a reduced rate, on the value of the assets held by a discretionary trust on every tenth anniversary of its foundation. Property held for charitable purposes only by permanently charitable trusts is exempted from this periodic charge.

**17.62** If the property ceases to be held for charitable purposes, however, the charge can be triggered unless it is given to another charity or applied for such purposes. It will also arise if the trustees make a disposition reducing the value of the settled property otherwise than for charitable purposes.

## 8 BUSINESS RATES AND COUNCIL TAX

### Business Rates

**17.63** Local taxation is divided into business rates, which apply to businesses, and council tax, which applies to individuals.

Charities receive a mandatory reduction of 80% on uniform business rates. Further relief, up to the total amount otherwise due, can be given to charities at the discretion of local authorities. Following the case *Oxfam v City of Birmingham District Council* [1976] AC 126, the Rating (Charity Shops) Act 1976 was introduced, which entitles charity shops to qualify for the relief, provided that they wholly or mainly sell donated goods, and the profits are applied for charitable purposes.

### Council Tax

**17.64** Council tax is chargeable on private dwellings, and is determined by the value of the property, graded in eight valuation bands, A to H. Certain properties can be exempt from the tax, and occupants may qualify for reductions or discounts. Charities also receive both specific and partial exemptions. Subject to these properties where charities will be liable to council tax are:

- residential care homes, hostels, nursing or mental homes;
- staff flats or accommodation in residential property;
- houses in multiple accommodation;
- convents, monasteries, and church houses.

**17.65** Properties exempt from council tax include those occupied only by students, or as armed forces' barracks and married quarters. Also included are properties that are vacant for certain reasons, including those waiting to be occupied by a minister of religion, or vacated by someone who has gone into care, or gone to care for another person. Residential properties owned by charities that are vacant for up to six months are partly exempt.

**17.66** Claims must be made for other reductions. The disabled reduction scheme applies where at least one resident is substantially and permanently disabled, and the property contains either space for a wheelchair to be used inside, or a room other than a kitchen, bathroom or toilet, mainly used by that person and essential to their needs. Under the scheme, valuation can be on the band below the one that would otherwise apply, apart from Band A.

**17.67** Where all adult residents of a property fall into the following categories, council tax is reduced by 50%. If one resident is outside the categories, the reduction is 25%, but if two or more are outside, there is no reduction. The categories are:

- patients in homes receiving treatment or care in a residential care home, nursing home, mental home or hostel;
- some care workers, where the person being cared for receives specified benefits and the carer is resident and works at least 35 hours per week (the spouse or child of the recipient is excluded);
- care workers employed by the Crown, a charity or a local authority, or introduced by such to a third party, where they reside in premises provided by their employer, work at least 24 hours per week, and do not earn more than £30 per week.

**17.68** If a claim for relief under the above schemes is rejected, an appeal can be made to a Valuation Tribunal.

## 9 BENEFITS IN KIND, STAMP DUTY, BETTING DUTY

**17.69** Where charities act as employers, they are subject to the normal PAYE (pay as you earn) and NIC (National Insurance Contributions) regimes. Where a director of a charity has total emoluments of less than £8,500, expenses reimbursed to that director are not subject to the benefits in kind legislation. Volunteer drivers who are paid a mileage allowance may be seen as receiving a taxable profit element if the allowance paid exceeds amounts necessary to merely reimburse the cost of fuel and running costs. The Revenue can tax this profit element, and so it would be more sensible to limit mileage allowances to agreed rates published by the Revenue.

**17.70** The introduction of the national minimum wage may affect charities that make nominal payments to volunteers. Where such payments are being considered, a charity should carefully structure the method by which they are made.

**17.71** Charities are not liable for stamp duty on conveyances, transfers or sales or leases (FA 1982 s 129), but where stamp duty does apply, it will apply to the full amount of the consideration for sale, including VAT, where that tax is applicable. VAT does not apply to the amount paid to the Inland Revenue as stamp duty, as this does not form part of the consideration for the supply for VAT purposes (SP 11/91).

**17.72** Small lotteries or raffles incidental to exempt entertainments, or private lotteries or societies lotteries defined by ss 4 and 5 of the Lotteries and Amusements Act 1976, may be organised by a charity and exempt from pool betting duty. Additional regulations govern lotteries run by charities, which were introduced in 1994. Information about them can be obtained from the Gaming Board.

## 10 LANDFILL TAX

**17.73** Landfill tax is a tax per tonne of waste disposed of at licensed landfill sites. It is accounted for by landfill site operators. Bodies registered for landfill tax that make 'qualifying contributions' to approved bodies can get credit for landfill tax paid or payable in respect of 90% of the amount of each qualifying contribution in any accounting period. This credit can only be claimed, however, up to 20% of the annual landfill tax liability of the contributing body.

**17.74** An approved body for the purposes of landfill tax is one that is concerned with the environment, including the fields of waste management, reclamation, pollution control, and that is precluded from distributing any profit it may make. Any charities active in areas as described above may wish to seek advice in order to attract as many qualifying contributions as possible by maximising the extent of the credit available for contributors.

CHAPTER 18

# Tax and trading activities of charities

## 1 GENERAL PRINCIPLES

**18.1** The requirement to find continual sources of income with which to pursue the objects of a charity results in competition both between charities, and between charitable and commercial concerns. Where this competition involves adventures in the nature of trade, direct and indirect taxation must be taken into account. Continual trading activities such as the operation of charity shops are one example of charities entering the world of business, while occasional activities, such as the sale of Christmas cards, are another.

**18.2** 'Trade' for direct tax purposes is not the same as 'business' for VAT purposes. The latter is discussed in Chapter 20. However, it should always be kept in mind that if a charity is doing anything that could be construed as making supplies in return for a consideration, VAT will be an issue. If a charity is trading for the purposes of TA 1988, the making of supplies for VAT purposes is a near certainty.

**18.3** Unless a specific exemption is available, trading profits are taxable, no matter what the motive for the activity or the use made of the profits. This is because if the charity was in competition with commercial traders, a blanket exemption would unfairly disadvantage non-charitable traders, and would distort competition. This rationale applies to both direct tax, and, under the EC Sixth VAT Directive, to VAT. One specific exemption available is that the sale of donated goods is not treated as trading for the purposes of TA 1988, being seen as the conversion of a donation into cash, and is zero-rated for VAT, which avoids a VAT charge to charities or to their customers. This is one area in which both taxes treat the same subject in the same way.

## 2 SECTION 505 EXEMPTION

**18.4** The exemption for trading income is far stricter than that for other income under TA 1988 s 505. The conditions to be met in this case are that:

- the trade is exercised in the course of the actual carrying out of a primary purpose of the charity; or
- the work in connection with the trade is mainly carried out by the beneficiaries of the charity.

Thus, where a museum, zoo, or art gallery charges for admission, they are achieving their charitable goals, carrying out their primary purpose of advancing education and art. The same applies for orchestras etc charging for tickets to a performance.

**18.5** A typical example of beneficiaries of a charity carrying out work in connection with trade is where a charity established to help disabled people sets up a workshop to employ them, and sells the items manufactured.

**18.6** Where a charity is trading, whether all year round or on an occasional basis, its profits will only escape tax if the trade is within these specific exemptions. If a charity carries on trading activities on a regular basis which are not within either of the two exemptions, problems will result. At best, the profits of the trade will be liable to tax, but the rest of the charity's tax exemptions will be unaffected. At worst, where the trading activity becomes so significant that it has effectively become the *raison d'être* of the organisation, the charity may be held not to be pursuing exclusively charitable objects, and its charitable status may be vitiated so that all tax exemptions are lost.

**18.7** A further point needs to be made on the working of the exemption. Instead of stipulating that the profits must be applied for charitable purposes only, the exemption makes it a condition that the profits must be applied *solely to the purposes of the charity*. Thus, in an extreme case, if a charity established for strictly educational purposes only and trading as such were to make a large donation for famine relief out of profits, it would be liable to tax on those profits. Even though the trade was exercised in the course of carrying out the primary purpose of the charity, and even though the payment was applied for charitable purposes in a general sense, the exemption would not apply because profits were not applied solely for the purposes of the charity itself. Thus, the wording of the legislation encourages a charity with an exempt trade to plough back all profits into the same activity.

## 3 SMALL TRADERS

**18.8** A new measure, introduced by the Finance Act 2000 s 46, allows charities to carry on small trading operations, such as the sale of

Christmas cards or commemorative items, without the complications of setting up a trading subsidiary or the danger of becoming subject to tax.

**18.9** Providing that the governing instrument of a charity allows it, non-qualifying trading is now, within certain limits, exempt from tax. The maximum trading income allowed (and charities should note that this is *income*, not profit) is £5,000 per annum, or, if over this amount, up to the lesser of 25% of total incoming resources or £50,000. Profits must be applied solely for the use of the charity. There is also room in the Finance Act 2000 for these amounts to be accidentally exceeded, as exemption applies where the charity had *reasonable expectation* that they would be within the relevant limit. This applies for both the expectation of the level of income from trading, and the expectation of the level of total incoming resources.

## 4 TRADING SUBSIDIARY

**18.10** Where more substantial trading activities are carried on, standard procedure is to set up a trading subsidiary company to carry on the trade while the parent charity concentrates on qualifying charitable activities. A deed of covenant was previously the most popular means of changing profit liable to corporation tax in the hands of the subsidiary into an annual payment exempt from tax in the hands of the charity itself. The Finance Act 2000 s 41 effectively abolished the tax effect of deeds of covenant, and treated all payments to be made under existing deeds as Gift Aid payments. Transfer of profit is now achieved using the Gift Aid provisions, whereby the gross amount is paid over to the charity, who need make no claim for the tax, and the company is able to get tax relief on the amount paid over. Deeds of covenant already in existence with payments due after 1 April 2000 will now be within the Gift Aid scheme, and the existing deed qualifies as the declaration necessary. For full details of the new Gift Aid rules, see Chapter 19.

**18.11** Providing the necessary capital to set up a subsidiary is a contentious area. As subscription for the share capital of an unquoted company is not a qualifying investment within Sch 20 of TA 1988, it can only be qualifying expenditure if the Revenue can be satisfied that it is for the benefit of the charity, and not for the avoidance of tax. As a trading subsidiary is commonly set up to avoid taxing a charity on its trading profits, it can be argued that funding the subsidiary is non-qualifying expenditure.

**18.12** The continuing funding of a subsidiary suffers from many of the same problems. The financial situation of most charities means that they would be loath to tie up large sums of money in share capital which would not be easily accessible, and that the working capital of the company is therefore likely to be substantially funded by borrowing. To borrow from a bank or other outside source may be difficult, given the payment of profits up to the parent charity. The subsidiary may find it difficult to achieve sufficient liquidity to repay the borrowing.

**18.13** Therefore, funding is often achieved by a loan from the parent charity. Given that the trustees have to apply funds for charitable purposes, this must be at a commercial rate of interest, and the Charity Commission also requires that the loan be secured, wherever possible. This is also not specifically covered by the TA 1988 Sch 20 Part II, so can also only be regarded as qualifying expenditure where the Inland Revenue is satisfied that the loan is made for the benefit of the charity, and not for the avoidance of tax.

**18.14** However, accepted practice is that the use and loan funding of trading subsidiaries by parent charities, unless being blatantly used to misappropriate funds or otherwise misuse charitable status, has the tacit approval of the Revenue. In support of the practice is also that most charities will have strong reasons for trading through a subsidiary that are unconnected with tax avoidance, for example, preservation of charitable status, and compliance with their governing instrument. Statement of Practice SP3/87 implies very strongly that no attempt will be made to attack such a structure, providing the charity's affairs are in order.

**18.15** Trading involves risk, and this may not sit well with the responsibility of managing a charity. A charity's governing document may also prevent the carrying on of trade, either at all, or at 'significant' levels. Prior to the Finance Act 2000, the Charity Commission advised and required charities to use a subsidiary company for trading, with the benefits of limited liability. This may be expected to continue as there are a number of areas where charity responsibility should be separated from trading risk.

**18.16** A Charity Fundraising Pack is available, combining information from the Inland Revenue, Customs and Excise, and the Charity Commissioners. The packs are available from all three bodies, whose addresses are included in the Appendix. The information provided includes advice concerning the establishment and maintenance of a trading subsidiary, with reminders about the requirements to stay within the powers laid out in a charity's governing document and within the terms of charity law with regard to avoiding undue risk or speculation. In order to be seen as being for the benefit of the charity, the trading company should be run on efficient lines, and aim to make a profit. All decisions concerning such a company, in the course of setting it up and in the course of its operation, should be recorded. The Inland Revenue have published detailed guidance notes on this topic and others for charities. These notes can be accessed on the Inland Revenue website at www.inlandrevenue.gov.uk/charities.

## 5 PROFIT SHEDDING COVENANTS

**18.17** One method of passing trading income up to the parent charity was for the subsidiary to covenant all or part of its profits to the charity in each successive accounting period. Such covenants have now been replaced by the extension of the Gift Aid scheme to cover payments by companies to their parent charities. Nevertheless, many charities will prefer to maintain a profit-shedding covenant from their subsidiary for greater security. Although the Deed of Covenant per se has no tax effect, the payments made under it are still tax-effective under the Gift Aid scheme. More importantly, the covenant is still a legally binding document requiring the company to pay its profits to the charity.

**18.18** A covenant converted trading income, which would have been taxable if the trade was carried on by the charity, to an annual payment specifically exempt from tax. Tax-efficiency was realised by having the payment qualify as a charge on income for the covenanting body.

**18.19** All charitable covenants must be capable of exceeding three years. Prior to 1 April 1997, the payment had to be made within the period to which it related in order to qualify as a charge on income for the purposes of corporation tax. After that date, new rules were specifically introduced governing subsidiary companies wholly owned by charities, allowing the payment to qualify as a charge if paid within nine months of the end of the relevant period. This allowed time for proper determination of the amount to be paid and avoiding the possibility of a tax liability for the company if their actual profits exceeded those forecast when the payment was made. This retrospective element has been extended to Gift Aid.

## 6 DIVIDENDS BY A SUBSIDIARY TO A CHARITY

**18.20** An alternative method of passing trading income up to a charity was by means of a dividend. However, the above concession for covenants did not apply, and the dividend had to be paid within the accounting period to which it relates. It would therefore be an estimate of income for the year.

**18.21** Also, charities are not entitled to repayment of tax credits after 5 April 1999, when ACT was abolished (see **17.10**). Given the timeframe of the sliding scale of transitional relief, this method of passing up profits will be totally ineffective by 2004. Under F(No 2)A 1997 s 35, transitional relief gives a repayment of a part of the gross distribution, the dividend plus tax credit, equal to:

| Tax year | percentage repayment |
|---|---|
| 1999/2000 | 21% |
| 2000/01 | 17% |
| 2001/02 | 13% |
| 2002/03 | 8% |
| 2003/04 | 4% |

**18.22** In the past, and before the abolition of ACT, this was an acceptable way of transferring a subsidiary's profit to a charity, particularly where the rate of ACT and the small companies' rate of corporation tax were the same.

## 7 PAYMENTS BY A COMPANY TO A CHARITY UNDER GIFT AID

**18.23** The Gift Aid scheme can be used by individuals or companies to make donations to a charity in a tax efficient manner. Prior to the Finance Act 2000, where the donation was made by a company, the recipient charity reclaimed the tax withheld on the payment in the same way as for a deed of covenant payment, the company treating the donation as a charge on income. As the payment had to be made within the year to which it related, if the actual and estimated profit was at variance, problems could ensue. Where profits exceeded the amount paid over, the company would be liable to tax on the excess. Where the profits did not reach the level of the payment, the company would be left with a loss, which could lead to the company becoming insolvent.

**18.24** From 1 April 2000, the company simply pays over the gross amount and claims tax relief on that, with no claim required or allowed by the charity.

**18.25** The Gift Aid scheme has also been extended by the Finance Act 2000 ss 40 and 41 to cover payments that would previously have been made under a deed of covenant. Existing covenants simply move within the new scheme, with the covenant documentation serving as that necessary for the Gift Aid rules to apply. The Finance Act 2000 s 40(7) allows trading subsidiaries of charities to make the Gift Aid payment up to nine months after the end of the accounting period. The scheme is described in more detail in Chapter 19, as it can also be used by individuals to make payments to charities.

## 8 CHOOSING THE MOST SUITABLE METHOD

**18.26** The most recognised and reliable method of passing trading profits up to a charity was, prior to changes in the Finance Act 2000, a deed of covenant. As this has now been brought within the scope of the Gift Aid scheme, Gift Aid will become the most widely used method going forward.

**18.27** The deed of covenant was preferred previously because it was the only method that could be paid on a provisional basis. However, the amended system brought in by the Finance Act 2000 removes the requirement for companies to deduct tax from their donations or to give a declaration to the charity. Also, as payments can now be made after the accounting period to which they refer, the problems of over- or underestimation should no longer be an issue.

## 9 VAT IMPLICATIONS

**18.28** Chapter 20 deals with the VAT aspects of charities trading, but it should be mentioned now that a profit motive is not necessary to make trading an activity subject to VAT. Any supply of goods or services for a consideration is a supply for the purposes of VAT. Although the VAT legislation does not define 'business' exactly, it does state that it includes every trade, profession or vocation.

**18.29** If a charity chooses to establish a trading subsidiary, this can mean that the company, rather than the parent charity, is liable to register for VAT. Although this can be a desirable outcome from the point of view of the parent, a close eye must be kept on its relationship with its subsidiary; supplies between the two may result in a VAT cost to the parent, or in a need for it to register.

**18.30** As VAT applies to turnover rather than to profits, if a charity is making trading profits that embroil them in direct tax consideration, VAT will almost certainly be an issue. However, it is possible for both direct and indirect taxes to generate problems quite independently of each other, and it should not be assumed that safety from one point of view will prevent unfortunate repercussions from the other.

## 10 SPONSORSHIP

**18.31** Sponsorship has such a wide meaning in charities and charity fundraising activities that it is imperative that clear thought is given to the direct and indirect tax implications of the transactions or activities to be carried out. At its most innocent, for example, a sponsored bicycle ride by an individual in support of his favourite charity, this form of sponsorship will be totally outside the scope of tax. At its most commercial, for example, a charity's endorsement in commercial advertising of a commercial product, significant direct and indirect tax liabilities may be at stake. At their most complex, sponsorship deals, such as affinity credit card schemes and the like, may be a mixture of these two extremes.

**18.32** The penalties for ignoring the underlying commerciality of sponsorship deals can be very serious for charities, and significant tax liabilities to income or corporation tax and VAT can be incurred if correct structures are not set up.

**18.33** When considering the structure of a sponsorship deal from a tax point of view, it is essential to analyse the component parts of the arrangements thoroughly. In this type of activity both Customs and Excise and the Inland Revenue will look closely at the substance of the transactions. Customs will regard the commercial element of any sponsorship deal as a taxable supply, but it may be possible to persuade them that only part should be regarded as subject to VAT, with part being regarded as a philanthropic donation. The Inland Revenue is likely to take a far stricter approach and tax the whole payment as relating to the sale of advertising services.

**18.34** This is particularly true where a charity, in some sort of joint venture, allows its name or logo to be used by a commercial organisation. The marketing by a charity of its name or logo directly to a commercial organisation which then advertises its support for the charity can be regarded either as promotional trading, or as the sale of copyright or trademark by the charity. Either activity would be subject to VAT and direct tax.

**18.35** The Inland Revenue's booklet CS2, *Trading by Charities*, is very helpful, and devotes a short chapter to business sponsorship. It highlights the fact that there are two sides to the issue of sponsorship:

- where the charity acknowledges a business sponsor's support;
- where the business sponsor makes use of the charity's good name or image.

**18.36** Where a charity merely acknowledges the support of a corporate benefactor, trading will not be in point. Where something beyond mere acknowledgement is involved, for example, widespread use of the sponsor's logo or mention of its products, the Inland Revenue will seek to tax sponsorship money as trading income.

**18.37** Where a charity lends its good name alongside that of a corporate sponsor, some sort of income liable under Sch D will arise. Where the charity takes no positive steps to assist the sponsor to exploit its name, the receipts will be treated as annual payments exempt under Sch D Case III. Where the charity goes further and sells its mailing list, or allows its logo to endorse a sponsor's products, the receipts will be treated as trading income. The technical appendix on Trading by Charities in the 'Guidance Notes for Charities' on the Inland Revenue website gives some useful pointers to the attitude of the Inland Revenue in various instances.

**18.38** This whole area has been complicated even more by the requirements in the Charities Act 1992 ss 58 and 59 that '*commercial participators have written agreements with charities setting out the terms under which money is paid to charity and the way in which it reaches the charity*'. It has been thought that the very existence of such a contract created a liability under Sch D Case VI (not exempted from tax) where none previously existed. Our understanding is that this is not the case, although the Inland Revenue's *Technical Bulletin Issue 20* at p 265 does indicate other types of income under Sch D Case VI which the Inland Revenue will seek to tax, for example, underwriting commission. There is no doubt, however, that the requirement for these formal commercial participators' agreements has made life more complex since, as in a typical affinity card deal, where there are transactions between the charity and the sponsor, such agreements will have to be in place with all parties. Any attempt to short-circuit this procedure could lead to an attack on grounds of trading if only the charity is party to the transactions. In another way, however, it is quite helpful in analysing the nature of the transactions to decide whether trading or some other taxable activity is in point.

**18.39** The solution to the problem of sponsorship being considered as trading for income tax or corporation tax purposes and making taxable supplies for VAT purposes may, therefore, be to use a trading subsidiary company. Wherever possible, pure trading deals should be routed through the trading subsidiary. A mixed transaction should be split into its commercial and philanthropic component parts, the commercial element being routed through the trading subsidiary, and the philanthropic element being paid direct to the charity, making use of available tax reliefs including the Gift Aid provisions. Obviously, purely philanthropic gifts should go straight to the charity, again using Gift Aid where necessary.

**18.40** Where there are complex sophisticated sponsorship and promotional deals, it may be that the only safe way to proceed is to agree the

VAT and income and corporation tax treatment in advance, in principle with both Customs and Excise and the Inland Revenue. This can cause charity fundraisers and commercial sponsors some frustration at the time it takes to reach agreement, but the risk of making expensive mistakes should not be underestimated. Even a simple decision, correct in principle, to route a sponsorship deal through a trading subsidiary can give rise to problems if the subsidiary does not have the necessary legal rights to exploit the name or logo of its charitable parent.

**18.41** Care also needs to be taken where joint ventures or activities are concerned. Ideally, joint ventures constituted as such are to be avoided, as they may require separate VAT registration, and it is often more beneficial from a tax point of view if a commercial organisation takes all responsibility for VAT related matters. Detailed planning advice needs to be taken in advance on both the VAT and direct tax implications of each sponsorship promotion.

CHAPTER 19

# Tax incentives to donors

## 1 GENERAL PROPOSITION

**19.1** There is no general relief from tax granted to a taxpayer who makes a gift to charity. However, a number of major and specific reliefs have been used and developed over the years, culminating in the changes to broaden the scope of Gift Aid.

## 2 DEEDS OF COVENANT

**19.2** Prior to the Finance Act 2000, a deed of covenant could be used to make tax-efficient donations to charities. Covenants can be made by individuals or by companies, as explained in Chapter 18. Although still possible to make, and binding in law, their tax effect has now been subsumed within the Gift Aid scheme, discussed later (see **19.11 ff**). It is likely that charities will still be happy for people to enter into deeds of covenant, as they result in a long-term obligation for the donor to give. Deeds of covenant can, and should, for the purposes of tax efficiency, be drawn up to be 'Gift Aid compliant'.

**19.3** Under TA 1988 s 347A(7), a covenanted payment to a charity had to be capable of exceeding three years, and was a charge on income for the donor. Covenants were annual payments for tax purposes, and are therefore exempt under TA 1988 s 505 in the hands of the recipient charity. To qualify, the payments had to:

- be made under a legally binding obligation;
- have a quality of recurrence (although the amounts might differ);
- be pure income profit in the hands of the recipient charity.

'Pure income profit' means that the donor gave the amount on the same basis that a pure donation is made; they did not receive, or expect to receive, any service or other supply in return for their gift. Although the amounts payable over the term of the covenant might differ, they had to be calculated on a consistent basis.

**19.4** The 'pure income profit' rule was breached in only two ways in the case of covenanted subscriptions to membership charities:

(a) by Inland Revenue concession where certain minimal benefits were allowed;
(b) by FA 1989 s 59, which allowed a charity to reclaim tax on a covenant whilst providing benefits to the covenantor if the sole or main purpose of the charity was the preservation of property or the conservation of wildlife, and the only benefit provided was that of free or reduced admission to view that property or wildlife.

FA 1989 s 59 has been abolished by s 40(7) of the Finance Act 2000, but similar provisions have been included in the extended Gift Aid legislation (FA 2000 s 39(5), (5E)).

**19.5** Deeds needed to be signed and 'delivered', and the document had to state clearly that it was, in fact, a deed of covenant. The required documentation has been simplified under the Gift Aid scheme as amended by the Finance Act 2000. Deeds of covenant stated whether the annual amount payable was net or gross of basic rate income tax, with individual donors usually using net covenants. Gross covenants were usually used by companies.

**19.6** Whether expressed net or gross of basic rate income tax, an individual donor was deemed to have deducted this from the annual payment, and only paid the net amount to the charity. The charity then reclaimed the tax deemed to have been paid. Provided the donor had a personal tax liability at least equal to the basic rate tax on the gross amount received by the charity, they did not have to pay any tax to the Inland Revenue. Companies always had to withhold income tax from the covenanted donations and pay over the tax to the Inland Revenue. The charity then claimed repayment from the Inland Revenue.

**19.7** If an individual donor's personal liability was insufficient to meet the tax due on the gross amount, they would be assessed to tax on the shortfall. In practice, the Revenue did not insist on such assessments where the recipient charity undertook not to reclaim the tax.

**19.8** Deeds of covenant were one of the most popular and tax efficient ways of giving to charity. However, they had their complexities, such as the need to ensure that the deed was valid in law. The personal incentive for individuals to donate using a deed of covenant was that, as well as the charity benefiting from the gross amount of a covenanted payment although the donor only pays the net, the donor was also able to set the gross amount against their income for relief from higher rate tax. Charities favoured deeds of covenant because they had a legally binding agreement to receive a particular sum of money for a period of years.

## 3 DEPOSITED COVENANTS

**19.9** A variation on a regular deed of covenant was a deposited, or loan, covenant. This system entailed the donor paying over the whole net amount of the donation under the covenant by way of an interest-free loan, usually repayable on demand. The charity was empowered to resort to the loan for satisfaction of the annual payment due under the covenant. This meant that the charity had the use of the whole amount covenanted from its inception, but derived the tax advantages over the life of the covenant. Higher rate relief was available to the donor every time the charity resorted to the loan for the annual amount. The letter of loan usually also contained a waiver clause, under which any remainder of the loan would not be repayable were the donor to die before the expiry of the covenant period.

## 4 COVENANTED DONATIONS BY COMPANIES

**19.10** The ability to make payments to charity under a deed of covenant was not restricted to individuals, or the subsidiary company of a charity as mentioned in Chapter 18. Unconnected companies could also make covenanted donations, although, unlike those from individuals, those donations required the company to withhold and pay to the Revenue the tax due on the payment covenanted. They remained a charge on income, but as this type of charge is not wholly and exclusively for the purposes of the company's trade, there was no carry forward or back for corporation tax loss purposes.

## 5 DONATIONS TO CHARITY: GIFT AID

**19.11** The Gift Aid scheme was introduced in 1990. Prior to the Finance Act 2000, the minimum donation to qualify for the scheme was £250. The Millennium Gift Aid scheme, time-limited to 31 December 2000, set a minimum donation of £100, able to be paid in instalments. Millennium Gift Aid was abolished by the Finance Act 2000.

**19.12** The Gift Aid scheme can be used by individuals as well as companies, and now replaces the deed of covenant system, for donations by individuals made or due after 6 April 2000, and by companies after 1 April 2000. There is no minimum limit for giving under the system, and the certification requirements have been simplified from those in force before the Finance Act 2000.

**19.13** It is now possible to make Gift Aid donations over the telephone or the Internet, as it is not necessary for the donor to sign a paper declaration. However, it is still incumbent upon charities to provide written notification to the donor of the circumstances of their donation (see **19.19** regarding Gift Aid declarations).

**Lower rate and higher rate taxpayers**

**19.14** Tax relief is now available on Gift Aid payments by donors who pay income tax at a rate below the basic rate. Other extensions brought in by the Finance Act 2000 allow relief to payments by donors paying capital gains tax, and allow higher rate tax relief to both income tax and CGT. Gift Aid donations are deemed to be net of basic rate tax. The basic rate band of the donor for the year of donation is increased by the grossed-up amount. This means that a higher rate taxpayer gets higher rate tax relief on the grossed-up amount of the donation, whether against income tax or against capital gains tax. Entitlement to personal reliefs is restricted, where necessary, to ensure that income tax or capital gains tax equal to the tax 'deducted' from the donation is actually paid.

**19.15** For example, in 2000/2001, Mr X earned income of £80,000. Tax of £24,952 was deducted under PAYE.

| | |
|---|---|
| Income | 80,000 |
| Personal allowance | 4,385 |
| Taxable income | 75,615 |

Mr X made a Gift Aid donation of £15,600 (net) to a local animal sanctuary, which received a tax refund of £4,400. Mr X's tax position is therefore:

| | |
|---|---|
| Taxable income | 75,615 |
| Starting rate | 152 |
| Basic rate band | 5,914 |
| Basic rate withheld on donation | 4,400 |
| Higher rate liability | 10,886 |
| Total tax payable | 21,352 |
| Difference from tax under PAYE | 3,600 |

The charity therefore receives £15,600 + £4,400 tax refund, equalling £20,000.

Mr X pays £3,600 less tax than he would do if he did not make the donation. The effect on his income is therefore £15,600 – £3,600, making an equivalent net payment of £12,000.

If Mr X is prepared for his net payment to be the £15,600 originally donated, his net donation should be £20,280. This grosses up to £26,000 added to his basic rate tax band, and results in a higher rate tax saving of £4,680. The effect on his income is therefore £20,280 - £4,680, which equals an equivalent net payment of £15,600.

This means that the charity receives the net donation of £20,280 plus a tax refund of £5,720, equalling the grossed-up total of £26,000. Thus the charity receives £6,000 more than under the original calculation with Mr X still only reducing his income by £15,600 when all the tax reliefs unwind.

**Benefits to donors**

**19.16** Although in principle, donations should be pure gifts, a limited amount of benefits are allowed to be provided to donors. An acknowledgement of a donation is permissible provided it does not amount to commercial advertising (this is also a concern from a VAT point of view, and is discussed in Chapter 20). The free or reduced-price viewing of a property or wildlife, where the support of which is the primary aim of the charity in question, is also allowed to the donor and their family, provided that any member of the public could make such a donation.

**19.17** Aside from these two specific allowances, there is a sliding scale of the monetary value of benefits, for example, free or reduced entry fees, or publications, which a donor can receive.

| **Donation** | **Maximum benefit allowed** |
|---|---|
| £0 – 100 | 25% value of donation |
| £101 – 1,000 | £25 |
| £1,000 + | 2.5% value of donation up to a maximum of £250 |

Where the benefits received are regular, but cover a period of less than 12 months, they should be grossed up to 'annualise' the amount of benefit received, and the limits applied as above. This would apply, for example, where a donation resulted in six 'free' copies of a monthly publication. The relevant limit would be that which applied to the 'annualised' donation (in this case, the donation would be doubled to find the limit). The annualised amount of benefit received would be the value of the benefit if received continuously over the year (again in this case, double the value of the benefit actually received).

**19.18** An interesting variation to the rules on donor benefits is the possibility of making 'split payments', as set out in *Getting Britain Giving*, the Revenue's Guidance Note for charities after the Finance Act 2000. This states:

*'Where the value of benefits would exceed the limits in the donor benefit rules, the donor may specify that part of his or her payment is to be treated as payment for the benefits and part is to be treated as a donation. Provided the donor specifies this before, or at the time of making the donation, the part of the payment that is specified as a donation may qualify as a Gift Aid donation, provided it satisfies all the conditions for the tax relief.'*

Although this may mitigate the restrictions that the donor benefit rules apply, specifying that part of what is otherwise a 'donation' is payment for benefits might be regarded as trading, and therefore be subject to the restrictions on charity trading set out in **17.11** and Chapter 18. Customs and Excise' attitude towards split payments may also be problematic, given their approach in previous cases explored (see **20.72**).

### Gift Aid declarations

**19.19** Charity covenant records were subject to random audit by the Inland Revenue. Charities therefore had to be very organised in the way they dealt with covenants and reclaimed tax from the Inland Revenue. At one time, original deeds of covenant had to be produced to the Inland Revenue, and at all times there needed to be a clear audit trail from the covenant to the amount of any tax repayment claim. Gift Aid record-keeping requirements are equally stringent. Whether a one-off donation or a covenant is involved, Gift Aid declarations will be required from individuals. The old Gift Aid certificates whereby a donor had to certify his or her donation have been replaced by a more flexible Gift Aid declaration. A charity will need a declaration before it can reclaim tax on gifts from individuals. No declaration is required in respect of company donations because a company's Gift Aid payments are made gross and there is no tax to reclaim.

**19.20** Declarations may be given at any time, whether before, at the time of, or after the gift concerned. They may be phrased to cover just one or a series of donations, and can be made in writing or orally. A written declaration by an individual must contain the following details:

- the donor's name and address;
- the name of the recipient charity;
- a description of the donation;
- a declaration that the donations are to be treated as Gift Aid donations;
- a note explaining that the donor must pay tax equal to the tax recoverable by the charity.

Curiously enough, there is no requirement for the declaration to be signed. Charities can design their own declaration, provided the above details are all present.

**19.21** Where a declaration is made orally, for example, in a telephone response to a television appeal, the charity has to send the donor a written record of the oral declaration, showing:

- all the details provided by the donor (name, address, etc);
- a note explaining that the donor must pay sufficient tax to match the charity's reclaim;
- a note of the donor's right to cancel the donation within thirty days;
- the date of the declaration and the date of the written record.

**19.22** Gift Aid records will be subject to Inland Revenue audit, and a clear audit trail needs to be maintained in the charity's records. These records may be computerised, but as a bare minimum they should comprise:

- Gift Aid declaration;
- copies of written records of oral declarations;
- correspondence with donors;
- bank statements and paying-in records;
- accounting records showing receipts.

The records should be retained for six years minimum.

## 6 PAYROLL GIVING

**19.23** The payroll giving scheme allows employees to give to charities through their payroll, before the deduction of income tax (but after the deduction of National Insurance). From 6 April 1996 there was a £1,200 annual limit on payroll giving, but this was disapplied with effect from 6 April 2000.

**19.24** The conditions for operating such a scheme are as follows:

- deductions are to be made in accordance with a scheme approved by the Inland Revenue (or a standard scheme of the kind so approved);
- payments must be made through an approved agent, which must pay over the amounts deducted to the charity or charities of each individual employee's choice;
- sums deducted can only be so withheld by the employer at the request of the employee (this is a voluntary employee-driven scheme, not a compulsory employer-driven scheme).

**19.25** Regulations for the approval of any scheme or agency under the payroll giving scheme are contained in the Charitable Deductions (Approved Schemes) Regulations 1986, SI 1986/2211.

**19.26** Although a useful tax incentive for an employee, it can be administratively demanding for the employer. Such a scheme can only come into operation if both employer and employees agree to operate a machinery by which:

- the employer contracts with an approved agency;
- the employer makes the deductions requested by each individual employee and gives tax relief under a 'net pay' arrangement of applying PAYE;
- entry into the scheme is entirely voluntary on the part of each individual employee;
- the amounts deducted are paid to an agency which distributes the money exactly in accordance with the wishes of each employee.

**19.27** Approved agencies also have a significant administrative workload, in that they must:

- be charities themselves;
- act in accordance with the wishes of each individual employee;
- take care gifts only go to bona fide charities;
- ensure the proper records are kept and returns made to the Inland Revenue;
- distribute the gifts promptly, and ensure that no refunds can be made.

**19.28** A further change made by the FA 2000 s 38 was to introduce a scheme whereby the government will pay a ten percent supplement on the amounts paid over, which will apply up to and including 5 April 2003. Where payroll agencies issue donors with vouchers to pass on to the charities of their choice, the supplement may be added to the value of the voucher. It is hoped that this will encourage more people to give through their payroll.

## 7 BUSINESS GIFTS

**19.29** Donations to charity by businesses are not, (unless made under the Gift Aid scheme, or of qualifying shares and securities), normally deductible for tax purposes unless they are wholly and exclusively for trade purposes. For example, a butcher's gift of meat to the old people's home he supplies throughout the year could be said to be protecting and improving his customer relationships. The gift must be reasonable in amount and either boost the goodwill of the business or encourage staff morale.

**19.30** Normally TA 1988 s 577 disallows business gifts and entertaining, except where any gift is less than £10 in value and carries a conspicuous advert for the donor. However, s 577(9) specifically permits a deduction for gifts to charity provided that they fall within the general Schedule D 'wholly and exclusively' rule. ESC B7 effectively extends the relief in s 577(9) in relation to gifts to bodies without charitable status. This is provided that the gift is allowable under normal Schedule D rules and made to a body or association established for educational, cultural, religious, recreational or benevolent purposes which is local in relation to the donor's business activities. The gifts must not be connected with, or restricted to persons connected with, the donor.

**19.31** The Inland Revenue's June 1996 *Tax Bulletin* sets out the tax treatment of trading stock donated to charities. Provided that the stock was originally manufactured or purchased for sale, later donation to charity in the course of trade will not cause the cost to be disallowed for tax purposes, nor lead the Inland Revenue to attribute any deemed market value sale proceeds. Market value would normally be imputed where stock is disposed of otherwise than in the course of a trade. The Inland Revenue give the example of surplus sandwiches and other perishable goods being given to charities for the homeless as being made in the course of a trade, since the donation is the most commercially effective way of disposing of stock which would otherwise become unsaleable. It should be noted that there is also a specific relief in the TA 1988 s 84 in respect of trading stock or assets used in business which are donated to designated educational establishments. The relief applies where the stock or assets would qualify as machinery or plant in the hands of the educational establishment, eg computers, or laboratory equipment.

## 8 EMPLOYEE SECONDMENTS AND DONATED SALARIES

**19.32** One way in which a growing number of employers have been helping charities is by seconding staff or management to charities to help them with the organisation or the establishment of a project. The employer continues to pay the seconded employee's salary and associated costs, eg pension, and National Insurance. Under normal rules, this expenditure, while the employee is working for the charity, is not deductible. The TA 1988 s 86 contains legislation first introduced in 1983 to permit the employer to continue obtaining a tax deduction in such circumstances, providing that the employee secondment is of a temporary nature. Temporary is not defined in the legislation, and so takes its normal meaning. It follows that the charity and the employer must intend, at the very least, that the arrangement in relation to that particular employee will be for a limited period of time.

**19.33** Some individuals, usually in religious orders, donate their services to their charitable trust or order. This may include services for which they are paid a salary, for example, teaching or nursing. As individuals, they would, after deducting personal allowances, obtain no tax relief for the gift of their services to charity. The solution is for the individual concerned to gift their income, including any salary, to the charity under the Gift Aid scheme. In theory, they should always withhold income tax from their payment, but in practice the PAYE district issues a no-tax coding so that the charity receives the gross salary direct.

## 9 INTEREST FREE LOANS

**19.34** Interest free loans can be a very simple and straightforward way of providing a charity with income. The cost to the lender is usually only the net after-tax income he would have derived, while the charity, being exempt on the income generated by the deposit, receives the gross amount.

**19.35** Technically, the provision of such an interest free loan can be caught by the revocable settlement provisions in the TA 1988 Part XV Ch III which, if imposed, would tax the lender on the income received by the charity. The Inland Revenue does not seek to invoke this legislation in respect of tax free loans to charities, provided that:

- the loan is in cash;
- there are no arrangements as to how the loan should be invested or the income therefrom repaid;
- the loan will be repaid in cash and not by transfer of any assets; and
- the loan is not part of any wider arrangement.

## 10 GIFTS OF CAPITAL ASSETS

**19.36** The normal CGT treatment for the gift of a chargeable asset is that the giver is deemed to have disposed of the asset for market value at the time of the gifting. However, TCGA 1992 s 257 amends these rules where gifts of chargeable assets are made to charities. It treats them as being for such consideration that neither gain nor loss arises on the disposal. This relief only applies to gifts of chargeable assets. It does not extend to the sale by the donor of assets where the proceeds are then given to charity.

**19.37** If a donor has an asset or assets which they wish to use to benefit a charity, they should consider whether it is more beneficial to give the assets direct to the charity, or for the donor to realise the asset and then donate the proceeds. In order to determine this, the donor should estimate his total income tax and capital gains tax for the year.

If the asset is realised by the donor, and a gain arises, there will be a liability to CGT (subject to annual exemptions etc). The amount available for the charity will then be the sale proceeds less the amount of CGT. If this amount is paid to the charity under Gift Aid, it will be deemed to be net of basic rate tax, which the charity can then recover.

**19.38** For example, ignoring the annual exemption:

If Mr C, a higher rate taxpayer, sells a bureau for which he originally paid £16,000, and realises £18,000 from the sale, his chargeable gain is £2,000. CGT of £800 is then due. The amount available to the charity is £18,000 - £800 = £17,200.

If this amount is grossed up, the charity should also receive a tax refund of £4,851, giving a total to them of £22,051. Provided Mr C has paid sufficient tax (whether income tax or CGT, and at whatever rate) he will receive higher rate tax relief on this amount. As the tax relief exceeds the CGT due on the disposal, Mr C gets a reduction in his cumulative tax bill of £4,051.

**19.39** However, if the gain on the realised asset is large enough, this treatment will not be appropriate. For example, if the antiques market developed a sudden surge in the value of bureaux, and Mr C discovered he could sell his bureau for £40,000, his chargeable gain would be £24,000. The CGT on this would be £9,600, giving a net to be paid to the charity of £30,400. When grossed up, however, even if Mr C had sufficient tax liability to cover the relief available, the tax refunded to the charity and relieved for Mr C would only be £8.574. As the CGT on the disposal exceeds this, Mr C would suffer an increase in his tax bill of £1,026, whereas the charity would receive in total only £38,974. In this case, it would be more efficient for Mr C to gift the asset direct to the charity, leaving him with no extra tax to pay, and the charity with the full value of the disposal of the asset (£40,000).

**19.40** If the donor does not have sufficient tax liability to cover any relief due under the Gift Aid provisions, they should also gift the asset directly to the charity, thereby avoiding any complications of their tax position.

| | | |
|---|---|---|
| Sale proceeds | 18,000 | 40,000 |
| Cost of Asset | 16,000 | 16,000 |
| Chargeable Gain | 2,000 | 24,000 |
| CGT @ 40% | 800 | 9,600 |
| Net amount for charity | 17,200 | 30,400 |

| | | |
|---|---|---|
| If net paid via Gift Aid | | |
| Gross up | 22,051 | 38,974 |
| Basic rate tax | 4,851 | 8,574 |
| Amount received by charity | 22,051 | 38,974 |
| Donor's tax relief net of CGT liability | 4,051 | (1,026) |

## 11 INHERITANCE TAX

**19.41** All transfers of value to charity, whether lifetime gifts or legacies on death, are exempt from IHT provided the gift is absolute. The exemption will be lost if the gift is dependent upon a condition which is not satisfied within 12 months of transfer. It will also be lost if the gift is defeasible (capable of being annulled or made void) or takes effect only after the termination of another interest. The exemption is also disallowed by IHTA 1984 s 23(4) if the donor, their spouse or other connected person retains any interest in the property given.

**19.42** Where an individual wishes to leave money to charity in their will, great care is needed in the drafting. This is especially important where other bequests bring about a liability to tax, and a residue is left to charity. Unless the will is drafted so that the other specific bequests bear their own tax, the tax thereon will be payable out of, and thus reduce, the residue available to the charity.

## 12 CHARITABLE TRUSTS AND FOUNDATIONS

**19.43** The broadening of the scope of the Gift Aid scheme in the Finance Act 2000 may have removed one incentive for setting up a personal trust or foundation to enable charitable giving. The administration required under the deed of covenant scheme could be considerable, and setting up a trust to which the appropriate donations could be made or a capital sum transferred simplified this.

**19.44** Despite this recent change, there are still very sound reasons for setting up a charitable foundation. Providing such a trust is drawn up properly, and achieves charitable status, it may make donations as the trustees wish, as long as they are within the charitable purposes laid out in the trust deed. Normally the whole of the income in a small charitable trust such as this would be disposed of in each year. Income tax can be reclaimed, and donations made gross. The recipient does not necessarily need to be a charity.

**19.45** Personal charitable trusts or foundations can also have commercial and long-term tax planning implications. If what is transferred to such a vehicle by the settlor is a number of shares in a private company, or significant income-producing assets, a company's independence may thus be preserved, or IHT liabilities mitigated. Such charitable trusts can also be augmented by further donations.

## 13 SECURITIES AND SHARES

**19.46** Finance Act 2000 s 43 introduced a new relief for gifts of certain shares or securities. Where such securities or shares are gifted to a charity, or sold to a charity for less than their value, the donor receives a deduction from income or profit on the difference between the value of the shares and the consideration received. This treatment applies from 6 April 2000 for individuals, and 1 April 2000 for companies.

**19.47** Eligible shares and securities are those registered on a recognised stock exchange, units in unit trusts, shares in open-ended investment companies, and some holdings in foreign collective investment schemes. Interestingly, they also specifically include shares traded on the Alternative Investment Market, although the holding of such shares by a charity is not automatically a qualifying investment (see **17.57**). The ability for donors of shares to claim relief on the full market value of the shares at the date of gift will be a significant incentive to charitable giving both by successful entrepeneurs floating their companies and those people with large investment portfolios on which significant capital gains have been accrued.

CHAPTER 20

# Charities and VAT

## 1 GENERAL FRAMEWORK

**20.1** Charities have no general relief from Value Added Tax (VAT), and the supremacy of EU law over domestic legislation limits the ability of the Treasury to alter the VAT regime in any significant way.

**20.2** VAT law is shaped by the EC Sixth Directive, whereas charity law throughout the EU is different from state to state. Although the Directive allows for certain supplies to be exempt from VAT, and limits some of these exemptions to charities, public bodies, or other non-profit making bodies, it does not mandate any specific VAT treatment for charities. This area remains the responsibility of domestic legislation, albeit within the parameters laid down by the Directive. There is provision in Annex H of the Directive for the supply of goods and services by organisations recognised as charities and engaged in welfare or social security work to be subject to reduced rates of VAT (as long as they are not otherwise exempt) but this is not a requirement on member states.

**20.3** In essence, VAT is charged on the supply by a registered person of goods or services in the course of a business. The main stumbling block for charities is that this includes 'all forms of supply, but not anything done otherwise than for a consideration'. Hence a large part of charitable activity, being for no consideration, is outside the scope of VAT.

**20.4** In the interests of equity, the regime aims to avoid any unfair advantage resulting to one supplier over another. For this reason, where charities undertake activities that bring them into direct competition with commercial entities, they are subject to the same rules for VAT purposes. A general relief for charities would be anti-competitive.

**20.5** Benefits are extended to charities in the form of specifically exempted or zero rated supplies. These are contained in the Value Added Tax Act 1994 as follows:

| | | |
|---|---|---|
| **Exempt:** | Schedule 9 | Group 6 (Education) |
| | | Group 7 (Health and Welfare) |
| | | Group 12 (Fundraising) |
| **Zero Rate:** | Schedule 8 | Group 4 (Aids for Blind People) |
| | | Group 12 (Aids for the Handicapped) |
| | | Group 15 (Sales of donated goods and advertising) |

Exemptions from VAT, or reduced rates such as the zero rate in the UK, are allowed under the provisions of the EC Second Directive, whereby such treatment may apply for 'clearly defined social reasons and for the benefit of the final consumer'. In the case *EC v UK* (C-416/85), it was held that zero rating could extend to supplies made higher up in the production 'chain' provided they were 'sufficiently close' to the final consumer to be of benefit to them.

## 2 THE ZERO RATE

**20.6** When a supply is zero rated, it is supplied with VAT chargeable at zero per cent; the supply is taxable, and so allows for input tax recovery, but there is, in effect, no VAT charged to the recipient. The specific zero rating provisions available to charities include being able to zero rate the sale of donated goods, and also to receive medical goods and advertising services free from VAT. Supplies in the course of constructing certain buildings, or altering protected buildings, can be zero rated by the supplier if the recipient charity issues a certificate stating that zero rating is applicable. These supplies will be discussed at greater length in the sections on property and zero rating (see **20.29**).

**20.7** The zero rate is not available in every member state of the EU, and is only available in the UK during such time as the transitional arrangements allowed by the EC Sixth Directive are in place. Although it seems unlikely that full harmonisation, with its attendant uniformity of VAT rates and other VAT issues, will happen any time in the near future, it must be remembered that the zero rate is a transitional provision, and will not be around forever.

## 3 EXEMPTION FROM VAT

**20.8** Supplies that are exempt from VAT must not be confused with supplies at the zero rate, or those which are outside the scope of VAT. Exempt supplies are within the VAT regime. Most of the supplies made by welfare charities are exempt. Whilst this means that they do not have to charge VAT on the value of the supplies, it also severely restricts the charity's ability to recover VAT on its inputs (see **20.16**).

**20.9** Some exempt supplies, such as financial services, are exempt no matter who provides them, but others are only exempt under special circumstances, usually being contingent on the provider being an eligible body for the purposes of that supply. The requirements charities need to meet for the exemption for supplies of health or education are contained in Sch 9 Groups 6 and 7 of the VAT Act 1994. Some fundraising events are exempt, as is the supply of welfare services, which will be discussed in relation to health (see **20.59**).

## 4 REGISTRATION

**20.10** When considering VAT, the first issue a charity must confront is whether it should be registered. Registration is mandatory once the threshold of taxable supplies is exceeded. For 2000/2001, the limit is £52,000, among the highest in the EU, which allows charities making smaller supplies to function outside the VAT regime. There is talk, of a lowering of the threshold, or introduction of a 'two-tier' registration system which could draw many presently unregistered charities within the value added net. Only taxable supplies, at the standard or zero rates, count towards turnover for the purposes of the registration threshold. Whether or not a profit is made on these supplies is irrelevant; it is on the level of turnover, not profit, that the threshold is established. The value of non-business activities such as income from donations and grants do not count towards turnover.

**20.11** If supplies are made below the registration threshold, registration can be voluntary, but only if Customs and Excise are satisfied that the registrant intends to make taxable supplies. A charity making no business supplies is not eligible to register. If eligible, a charity may be able to register branches or sections separately, or register in a group with other entities under common control. Regional branches of a charity can register individually, providing each branch is eligible.

**20.12** In order for separate registrations to be allowed, Customs and Excise must be satisfied that the bodies applying for them are genuinely separate. Separation may be held to be artificial where the persons carrying on the different activities are closely bound to one another by financial, economic or organisational links. Customs can direct persons to be treated as a single taxable person where they deem it necessary for the protection of the Revenue.

## 5 GROUP REGISTRATION

**20.13** If several branches are registered, or the charity and any subsidiary companies, they can, at present, register as a group. This means that only one VAT number is held by all the members, and one member, the 'representative member', is responsible for rendering returns for the whole group. Supplies made by any member are deemed to be made by the representative member. Thresholds, output tax and input tax apply to the group as a whole, not to individual entities. Supplies between group members are not supplies for VAT purposes, and so can be made free from VAT.

**20.14** However, Customs and Excise have the power to refuse any applications relating to group treatment, mandate that a group dissolves, that specific members leave or join, or that a group be formed, as they deem necessary for the protection of the Revenue. The situation may arise in the future where only fully taxable entities are able to form a VAT group, but, at the present time, the option is still technically available to charities and other bodies with restrictions in input tax recovery.

**20.15** The nature of the liability of a VAT group may cause special problems for charities, in that every group member is jointly and severably liable for the tax due and the obligations of the group. It may be beyond the authority of a trustee to bring the liabilities of a trading subsidiary onto a charitable trust.

## 6 INPUT TAX RECOVERY

**20.16** Charities are in a different position from commercial concerns for VAT purposes because not all of their activities are in the sphere of business, and it is only on business activities that VAT applies. Certain activities like making or receiving grants, or providing services free of charge, are not business activities and so are outside the scope of VAT. Where supplies are made for a consideration, they are business supplies, and, as far as VAT is concerned, business is business, and charities do not receive special treatment. Unless their activities are covered by either the general provisions for exemption or zero rating or those specifically aimed at charities, VAT will be chargeable as normal.

**20.17** 'Business' includes every trade, profession or vocation, and is thus a far wider term than 'trading' is for income or corporation tax purposes. Furthermore, while the concept of trading implies a fundamental profit motive, it is not necessary to have an overriding profit motive to be within the scope of VAT. It is making a supply for a consideration, rather than any profit margin, that can lay an activity open to VAT.

**20.18** A charity can undertake activities under three 'headings': non-business, exempt, or taxable supplies. Input tax recovery is restricted to VAT incurred in the course of making taxable supplies, and so a two-stage calculation process is required to establish recovery where a charity is active in all three areas:

(a) **business/non-business apportionment** — split the activities between business (ie exempt or taxable supplies) and non-business (ie outside the scope);
(b) **partial exemption calculation** — calculate the proportion of input tax which is recoverable (partial exemption).

**Business/non-business apportionment**

**20.19** The first stage in the calculation process is to determine what proportion of VAT incurred can be attributed to the carrying on of business activities.

**20.20** Tax on inputs relating wholly to business activities is input tax, and is carried forward to the partial exemption calculation. Tax on inputs relating wholly to non-business activities is not input tax within the strict meaning of the VAT Act 1994, and is not carried forward, and not recoverable. Where tax is incurred on inputs which relate to both business and non-business activities, an apportionment should take place to determine the proportion which can fairly and reasonably be attributed to business activities.

**20.21** There is no 'standard method' for performing this attribution, and any method used must be confirmed in writing with Customs and Excise. Possible bases for attribution include the proportion of business income to total income, floorspace used wholly for business purposes over total floorspace, or staff numbers used wholly for business purposes over total staff numbers. Given that charities will often be receiving significant amounts of income from donations, it may be desirable to look at methods other than the income-based approach. Any method proposed to Customs and Excise will need to produce a 'fair and reasonable' result before they will approve its use.

**Example 1**

**20.22** For example, Charity X has several areas of activity. It solicits donations to support its non-business activities, runs a school, and publishes books. VAT on inputs relating wholly to the publication of books or running the school is carried forward to the partial exemption calculation. VAT suffered on inputs relating wholly to the soliciting of donations and the carrying on of non-business activities is not carried through. VAT not wholly relating to either activity needs apportioning.

The income from donations is £100,000. School fees are £150,000 and income from selling books is £50,000. Therefore, if apportionment were to be done on an income-based method, the calculation would be:

$$\text{VAT to be apportioned} \times \frac{(150k + 50k)}{(150k + 50k + 100k)} = 67\% \text{ VAT through to partial exemption calculation}$$

All the activities are carried on at one site. The fundraising office is very small, taking up only $10m^2$. The school takes up $300m^2$, and the printing press takes up $190m^2$. If the apportionment were to be based on floorspace, therefore, the calculation would be:

$$\text{VAT to be apportioned} \times \frac{(300 + 190)}{(300 + 190 + 10)} = 98\% \text{ VAT through to partial exemption calculation}$$

Alternatively, staff numbers could be used. The fundraising team consists of six people working full time. There are 30 members of staff at the school, and 14 working the printing press. The calculation on this basis would therefore be:

$$\text{VAT to be apportioned} \times \frac{(30 + 14)}{(30 + 14 + 6)} = 88\% \text{ VAT through to partial exemption calculation}$$

One can see from these three calculations that the basis of apportionment can significantly affect the amount of VAT which is carried through to the partial exemption calculation.

**Partial exemption**

**20.23** The input tax wholly related to business activities and the proportion of input tax attributed to business activities by the business/non-business apportionment is carried forward to the next stage in the calculation process, the partial exemption calculation.

**20.24** It must now be determined what input VAT relates to taxable supplies and what to exempt supplies. That which is wholly related to the making of taxable supplies is recoverable in full through a charity's VAT registration. That which is wholly related to the making of exempt supplies is irrecoverable. This is called *direct attribution*. Where VAT cannot be so directly attributed, a partial exemption apportionment is required.

**20.25** There is a standard method for apportioning such overhead or 'pot' input tax. This applies the ratio of taxable supplies to total business supplies to the pot input tax. An 'on account' calculation is required each quarter followed by an annual calculation which adjusts the sum of the four quarters to actual over the year.

**20.26** If a charity wishes to use a non-standard method of apportioning their pot input tax, for example one based on floorspace, staff numbers or any other criteria not matching the standard method, they can propose their alternative method to Customs and Excise for approval as a *special method*. This method must produce a 'fair and reasonable' result if its use is to be approved.

**20.27** Incidental supplies of land such as the sale of properties or the granting of leases, are prohibited by the standard method from impacting on the calculated recovery rate, although if the supply is taxable, all wholly attributed input tax can of course be recovered. This measure aims to prevent distortion of recovery. If a special method is agreed, Customs and Excise may also wish to exclude some other activities from the calculation in an attempt to reach the most 'fair and reasonable' result.

**Example 2**

**20.28** Charity X, therefore, has brought forward the VAT wholly related to business activities and that attributed to business activities using whichever method was settled upon and approved by Customs and Excise. They now need to calculate their partial exemption method, which will let them know how much input tax incurred is actually recoverable.

The two business activities of Charity X are the running of the school (an exempt activity) and the printing and selling of books (a taxable activity). The input tax which can be directly attributed to the running of the school is not recoverable. That which is directly attributed to the running of the printing press is fully recoverable. The 'pot', as before, can be apportioned in several different ways.

The standard method takes the taxable income of Charity X and compares it with the total business income. This method does not require Customs and Excise approval, although they are allowed to direct the use of another method if they deem it necessary for 'the protection of the Revenue'. As before, income from school fees is £150,000, and from the printing press, £50,000. The standard method calculation would therefore be:

$$\text{Input tax} \times \frac{50\text{k}}{(150\text{k} + 50\text{k})} = 25\%\ \text{input tax recoverable.}$$

Alternatively, Charity X could propose a special method. As before, the floorspace of the school is $300\text{m}^2$, and that of the printing press is $190\text{m}^2$. The calculation based on floorspace would therefore be:

$$\text{Input tax} \times \frac{190}{(300 + 190)} = 61\%\ \text{input tax recoverable.}$$

Another special method to propose could be based on staff numbers. As before, 30 members of staff work in the school and 14 in the printing press. The calculation would therefore be:

$$\text{Input tax} \times \frac{14}{(30 + 14)} = 32\% \text{ input tax recoverable.}$$

As with the business/non-business method of apportionment, the basis of the partial exemption calculation can make a significant difference to the actual amounts recoverable by a charity. While Charity X might prefer to base their calculations on floorspace, Customs and Excise would need to be convinced that such a recovery rate would produce a fair and reasonable result.

## 7 PROPERTY

**20.29** Some of the reliefs from VAT available to charities are in the sphere of property. Zero rating is allowed on supplies in the course of construction of a building, or the first sale of a new construction or conversion, provided the property in question is used for a relevant residential purpose or a relevant charitable purpose. An approved alteration to a listed building can also benefit from this relief if for one of these purposes. A relevant charitable purpose is use by a charity otherwise than in the course or furtherance of a business, or use as 'a village hall or similarly in providing social or recreational facilities for a local community' (VATA 1994 Sch 8 Group 5 note 6(b)). A relevant residential purpose encompasses a wide range of residential accommodation as well as dwellings (see **20.36**).

**20.30** In order to benefit from the zero rating allowed to such property, including the zero rating of supplies in the course of its construction, the charity must issue a zero rating certificate. In the case of construction services, the contractor must hold the certificate before zero rating the work; certificates cannot be issued on a retrospective basis. If a zero rated disposal of a property, such as the sale of the freehold of a new building or the grant of a new lease of a major interest in a new building, is to be made, the tax treatment must also be supported by a certificate. It is recommended that a charity confirms the eligibility for zero rating of the project in question before issuing a certificate, as penalties equal to the difference between tax paid and tax due can result if a certificate is incorrectly issued. The eligibility of a project for zero rating, either as being for a relevant residential purpose or a relevant charitable purpose, is not always a straightforward decision, and has been the subject of several court cases.

### A relevant charitable purpose

**20.31** The difficulty of establishing use 'otherwise than in the course or furtherance of a business' was mentioned earlier; profit is not the benchmark of being in business. If a charity uses a building in connection with trading, fundraising, or other activities where supplies are made for a consideration, the building cannot qualify as being for a relevant charitable purpose unless the non-business use of the building exceeds 90%, or is used as a village hall 'or similarly'. The Customs Extra-Statutory Concession which came into effect on 1 June 2000 allows for the 90% use to be calculated based on time used, or floorspace or user numbers, although the latter two require Customs and Excise approval, as does the application of the 'time used' method for a part, rather than the whole, of a building. Customs guidance on what constitutes a 'village hall or similarly' is regarded by many as being too narrow for practical application.

**20.32** Customs and Excise consider that each 'village hall' has a committee that is an independent charity whose objects are to provide community meeting places for the whole community. The ownership and management of the village hall is usually vested in local trustees drawn from representatives of local groups who use the facilities of the hall. While the concession 'or similarly' may avoid this condition having to be met in every case, Customs' view on the use of such a building is equally restrictive:

> *'The buildings are usually small scale, the primary feature being a meeting room or hall. They are hired out for use by a range of local clubs and groups, also for wedding receptions, birthday parties, playgroups and other leisure interests. They are essentially multipurpose, being let out for a multitude of public and private uses'.*

**20.33** Where use as a village hall is concerned, the key case is that of Jubilee Hall (*Jubilee Hall Recreation Centre Ltd v Customs and Excise Comrs* [1999] STC 381), which is a listed building used by a charity to provide recreational facilities in Covent Garden. It was determined not to be a village hall 'or similarly' in the Court of Appeal case in December 1998, on the grounds that it was a commercial concern of a scale which could not reasonably be termed 'a village hall'. It was also held to be of an overly specialised nature, not being used for 'a multitude of public and private uses'.

**20.34** However, another case, *Bennachie Leisure Centre Association v Customs and Excise Comrs* (1996) VAT Decision 14276, allowed zero rating of a property on the grounds that, although a similar kind of establishment to *Jubilee Hall*, membership of the leisure centre was automatic within a certain geographical area, and that area, in the Scottish highlands, was easier to define as a 'local community' than the neighbourhood of Covent Garden. The point about the need for a multitude of uses was not upheld.

**20.35** When considering this point, it should be remembered that the Court of Appeal decision in *Jubilee Hall* is binding on all lower courts, whereas the tribunal decision in *Bennachie* is not. The decision in *Jubilee*

*Hall* can only not be followed where there is significant difference of facts from that case. Therefore, where business activities are carried on, to qualify as being for a relevant charitable purpose would seem to be effectively restricted to the multipurpose, small-scale properties envisaged by Customs. A high degree of specialisation and commercial intent will reduce the probability of qualifying for the relief.

### A relevant residential purpose

**20.36** Uses of property which qualify for zero rating as for a relevant residential purpose include children's homes, homes for the elderly, disabled, or those addicted to drugs or alcohol, hospices, residential accommodation for students and school pupils, and residential religious establishments. Hotels and hospitals are specifically excluded from being for a relevant residential purpose, as 'residents' of such buildings can reasonably be expected to leave them and return home. Following two tribunal cases, *Urdd Gobaith Cymru v Customs and Excise Comrs* (1997) VAT Decision 14881, and *Denman College v Customs and Excise Comrs* (1998) VAT Decision 15513, however, Customs extended their interpretation of residential accommodation for students or school pupils to accommodation for short-term courses.

**20.37** The basic rule for determining whether a building qualifies as being for a relevant residential purpose is that it should be the sole or main residence of at least 90% of its residents. In short, a home, an institution or similar establishment used as a main or sole place of abode for children, elderly persons, terminally ill people, students, disabled people, members of armed forces or members of religious orders qualifies for relief for the same reasons as any private housing scheme does.

### Alterations

**20.38** Unless it is listed, zero rating of construction services does not extend, even if the purpose of the property is a qualifying one, to conversion, reconstruction or alteration of an existing building. Enlargements or extensions are also prohibited from the relief, and the construction of an annexe can only be included if it is used for a relevant charitable purpose, and is capable of functioning as a separate building with independent means of access.

**20.39** In the recent tribunal case of *Grace Baptist Church v Customs and Excise Comrs* (1999) VAT Decision 16093, however, the tribunal consulted the Shorter Oxford English Dictionary to aid in establishing the definition of an annexe, and, finding it to be 'a supplementary building or wing', pointed out that this meant that an annexe could be either a separate or a connected building, so long as it is a (lesser) building supplemental to another (greater) one. It remains to be seen whether the view of this one tribunal will have any effect on Customs and Excise guidance, as tribunal decisions are only binding on the parties to a specific case. The ruling could be overturned by a Customs appeal to a higher court, or be held only to apply in this one particular case. Charities are advised in this, as with all cases, not to pin all their hopes on a tribunal ruling in a similar case, but to use such rulings to support, rather than to comprise, their argument.

**Change of use**

**20.40** Where a building, allowed zero rating for being for a qualifying purpose, is used within ten years of completion for a non-qualifying purpose, provisions exist within Schedule 10 of the VAT Act 1994 to charge the VAT at standard rate. This applies both to grants of an interest in a building, and to change in use by the occupier.

**20.41** Where a grant is made of the building, and it is not used for a qualifying purpose after the grant, the grant is deemed to be taxable. There is no loss to the revenue, as output tax being due on the grant validates recovery of input tax on the acquisition, which would have been charged had zero rating not applied. However, it does mean that the person being granted the interest will be charged VAT, and may also be liable to include the asset within the Capital Goods scheme. Also, if the parties are connected, the provisions of Schedule 6 of the VAT Act 1994 operate to prevent the grant being for less than market value. This section allows Customs to require the grantor to account for output VAT on the open market value of the supply to the connected party.

**20.42** Where use is changed without an interest being granted, this will be more prejudicial to the person owning the building in question. If use ceases to be qualifying, they must account for VAT on the amount they paid to acquire it (previously zero rated). Unless the new use is taxable, the input tax will be a total cost. This could affect, for example, a hospice whose activities merge with those of a hospital, or use by a charity that develops from non-business to exempt business use. The occupant may also need to include the asset within the Capital Goods Scheme.

**20.43** Where goods or services are acquired that are not capital items, there is still the possibility of adjustment of recovery to reflect use under the clawback provisions set out in VAT Regulations 1995, SI 1995/2518, Regulation 108. This provides for repayment of recovered input VAT where the use or intended use of goods or services changes within six years of the initial deduction. Thus, where input tax is recovered in full because the item to which it refers is intended to be used in making a taxable supply, an exempt supply is made instead, the taxpayer must repay all the input tax on that item to Customs and

Excise. These provisions also work for 'payback' in Regulation 109, where items purchased with a view to making exempt supplies are later used in the course of taxable activities.

## Capital Goods Scheme

**20.44** The acquisition and disposal of property can impact on recovery over a longer period of time if any supplies are received or made that fall within the Capital Goods Scheme. The scheme applies to capital items, which are interests in property worth over £250,000, and computers worth over £50,000. In the case of computers, and interests in land which have less than ten years to run, the scheme applies for five years. If the interest in land is for longer than ten years, the scheme applies for ten years.

**20.45** The Capital Goods Scheme applies where a partly exempt entity acquires capital items, and ensures that input tax recovery fairly reflects the use made of the capital item over the relevant period of time. The disposal of a capital item is excluded from the partial exemption calculation so that dealings in this area do not distort input tax recovery. The initial recovery of input tax on acquisition of a capital item is adjusted over the period appropriate, either five or ten years, to reflect any change in recovery rates over that time. The charity recovers VAT at the recovery rate appropriate at the time of acquisition, and thereafter makes adjustments to reflect any change in recovery rates.

**20.46** The treatment of the disposal of a capital item if still within the time frame of the scheme will also affect recovery. If the disposal is taxable, the recovery rate for each year thereafter is 100%, but if it is exempt, the recovery rate is nil. The difference between the original recovery rate and the rate applicable on disposal is applied to the fraction for each year after disposal until the term of the scheme runs out. For example, where a person in the Capital Goods scheme disposes of a building within the scheme's time-frame, recovery will depend on the liability of the disposal. If the person opts to tax the property, and charges VAT on the disposal, which occurs after five years, with five years of the scheme still to run, the recovery rate for the final five years is 100%. If this person did not opt to tax, and made the disposal exempt from VAT, the recovery in the last five years would be 0%.

If we assume that the original recovery rate was 50%, and that the fraction for each of the ten years of the scheme is £10,000, the results for the two examples are:

**Where VAT is charged:** five years × (£10,000 × (100% – 50%) = £25,000 recovery

**Where VAT is not charged:** five years × (£10,000 × (0% – 50%) = £25,000 payment due to Customs & Excise

**Investment property**

**20.47** The holding of property for investment purposes is an issue for some charities. Whereas interest and dividend income is outside the scope of VAT (non-business), and dealing in shares is exempt, rental income can be taxable or exempt depending upon circumstance or choice. The renting of residential accommodation is always exempt from VAT, but if a charity holds investments in the form of commercial property, they have the option to elect to waive exemption from VAT. The sale of freehold commercial property less than three years old is standard rated, but otherwise the grant of an interest in land is exempt unless an option is taken.

**20.48** The option to tax, or election to waive exemption, enables supplies of the property to be taxable. The charity is then able to recover all VAT incurred directly attributable to the property, as it is used to make taxable supplies. Its value may not be included within the partial exemption calculation for recovering indirectly attributable input tax. Customs and Excise must be notified when an election has taken place, and where exempt supplies have previously been made in connection with the property, prior permission must be granted in writing before an election can be made.

**20.49** Schedule 10 also includes provisions to disapply an option where the person constructing or converting the property (the developer of the land) or the person responsible for financing such development expect or intend an exempt use to be made of the property. This will affect planning structures where, for example, a trading subsidiary opts to tax the renting of a property to its parent charity in order to recover the VAT on development costs, if the use of the property by the charity will be exempt.

## 8 SPECIFIC RELIEFS

**20.50** The taxable status of supplies to and from an entity, despite there being no blanket relief from VAT, and despite the stress placed by the EC Sixth Directive on the need to prevent distortion of the regime, does in certain circumstances change where that entity is a charity, as we have seen in the case of certain properties.

**Zero rating of advertising services**

**20.51** Prior to the introduction of VAT (Charities and Aids for the Handicapped) Order 2000, SI 2000/805, which enacts the changes announced in the 2000 Budget, zero rating relief for charity advertising was restricted to adverts used to either raise funds or make known the objects of the charity. Recruitment advertising was standard rated. The introduction of the statutory instrument, which came into effect on 1 April 2000, extends the scope of this relief in one direction while significantly restricting it in several others. As most if not all charities suffer some restriction on their input tax recovery, being charged VAT on advertising will be a substantial cost.

**20.52** The new relief applies to 'the right to promulgate an advertisement by means of a medium of communication with the public', and supplies of services (and closely related goods) of design or production of such an advertisement. The amended relief therefore does not rely on the content of the advertisement, and applies both to previously qualifying adverts, and those for recruitment or other purposes. Zero rating applies to pre-printed paperboard collecting boxes, pre-printed collecting envelopes, and lapel stickers.

**20.53** Prior to the changes announced in Budget 2000, the relief applied to pre-printed letters solely appealing for money. However, possibly the greatest blow to charities which results from the new rules is that the relief does not now apply where any persons who are reached by whatever particular medium used have been *selected*, by or on behalf of the charity. 'Selected' includes being selected by address, *or at random*. This means that 'mailshots' and door-to-door leafleting are now outside the relief. Charities who rely on annual appeals, or otherwise make use of mailshotting to gain much-needed income, will be sorely hurt by this new restriction.

**20.54** The relief includes online advertising, but not on a charity's own website. A website is deemed to belong to a charity even if it is hosted by somebody else. This means that the costs incurred in the setting up and maintaining of a website for a charity does not fall within the relief, and are therefore liable to VAT at the standard rate. This will be a significant cost for charities, and in stark contrast to the professed modernisation of the tax system which is receiving so much press.

**20.55** The relief also only applies to services and goods of producing an advertisement which are bought in; any inputs used 'in-house' at the charity to produce their own adverts do not qualify. This means that engaging an independent advertising company to prepare the necessary advertisements, in the course of which they will engage sub-contractors such as printers, designers, etc, will be zero rated. However, if a charity uses its own advertising department and uses the same sub-contractors for the work that the independent company uses, this will be standard rated.

**Zero rating of supplies of drugs, medicines and aids for the handicapped**

**20.56** Zero rating also applies to supplies for the use of blind or handicapped people, or medicinal products supplied to a charity providing care or treatment, or undertaking research. The adaptation of goods for use by handicapped people, or providing either access to buildings or facilities in residential homes or other charitable buildings, can also be zero rated. Charities can zero rate the supply of surgical appliances, stair lifts or other equipment for the benefit of handicapped persons when they are supplied for that person's domestic or personal use. SI 2000/805 extended the relief for providing, extending or adapting bathrooms, washrooms or lavatories to those within day-centres where at least 20% of the users are handicapped.

**20.57** 'Handicapped' in VAT law means chronically sick or disabled. An interpretation of 'chronically sick' was given in the case of *Tempur Pedic (UK) Ltd* (1996) VAT Decision 13744, when the tribunal chairman stated that this was where *'the conditions last a long time, and are not soon over, and those suffering are ill, or unhealthy, or suffering from an ailment'*. According to Customs and Excise, 'disabled' includes mental disability, and those who are blind, partially sighted or suffer from acute hearing loss can also qualify. Spectacles and hearing aids are specifically excluded from relief. The condition must have a significant detrimental effect on the ability of the individual to carry out day-to-day activities. Those who are frail simply because of old age are not considered to be 'handicapped'. However, where the physical condition of the person in question is so impaired on account of old age or as the result of a chronic condition that he or she cannot get about without a wheelchair or a walking aid, he or she can in the ordinary and accepted sense of the term be said to be 'disabled'.

## 9 EXEMPTION

**20.58** The basis for allowing certain activities to be exempt from VAT, thereby preventing a tax cost to the recipient but also causing hardship to the supplier in the form of irrecoverable VAT, is in the EC Sixth Directive. This is one area where the nature of the supplier as much as the nature of the supply is crucial to the VAT liability of the supplies being made. Exemptions for certain activities in the public interest are mandatory, but some of them are allowed to be exempted when provided by 'bodies other than those governed by public law', provided they satisfy at least one of the following four conditions. Member states allowing this extension of exemption may require more or all of the conditions to be met by suppliers. The conditions are:

- that the body is not systematically aiming to make a profit;
- that it is managed and administered on a voluntary basis;

- that they charge prices approved by public authorities;
- that '*exemption of the services concerned shall not be likely to create distortions of competition such as to place at a disadvantage commercial enterprises liable to value added tax*'.

**Exemption of health and welfare services**

**20.59** As the provision of healthcare is exempt from VAT, the provision of zero rated supplies such as surgical appliances or medicinal products may be included as part of an exempt supply of healthcare, rather than zero rated as supplies in themselves. With effect from 1 January 1998, the Value Added Tax (Drugs, Medicines and Aids for the Handicapped) Order, SI 1997/2744 prevents such goods from being supplied to patients at the zero rate if they are provided in conjunction with exempt in-patient care at a nursing home or hospital.

**20.60** Exemption applies to welfare services supplied otherwise than for profit as well as the provision of healthcare. 'Welfare' includes '*the provision of care . . . designed to promote the physical or mental welfare of elderly, sick, distressed or disabled persons*' (VATA 1994 Sch 9 Group 7 note 6(a)). It also includes the '*protection of children and young persons, or the provision of spiritual welfare by a religious institution as part of a course of instruction or a retreat*'.

**20.61** Before the tribunal decision in *Watford Help in the Home Service v Customs and Excise Comrs* (1998) VAT Decision 15660, Customs took the view that this 'care' was restricted to services such as bathing, feeding or dressing a patient. Services such as cooking or cleaning were excluded from exemption because they did not qualify as 'care'. After the *Watford* case, Customs and Excise issued Business Brief 24/98, which explained their revised interpretation of the extent of the exemption.

**20.62** Routine domestic tasks provided by charities (or public bodies) on a not-for-profit basis are now also exempted from VAT where the recipient has been assessed as being unable to carry out the tasks safely, adequately, or without significant pain or discomfort. More information on the treatment of routine domestic tasks can be found in VAT Information Sheet 6/99. As this was a change in interpretation rather than in law, retrospective application of exemption to routine domestic tasks can be done, subject to the normal three year cap and unjust enrichment rules.

**Agency staff**

**20.63** Business Brief 3/00 contained the latest news at the time of writing regarding the discussion of staff agency fees. Where in the past, charities have used agency staff, they were only charged VAT on the agency's profit margin, not on the wages paid to the individual worker. However, planned changes following a DTI consultation, that VAT is due on the whole amount paid to the agency, mean that VAT costs could be increased for those buying care in their own homes. Customs and Excise believe that the agencies act as principals, and therefore their whole supply is subject to VAT.

**20.64** In response to the furore which welcomed this news, Customs and Excise have announced an Extra-Statutory Concession for home care services provided to individuals. Although not yet finalised at the time of writing, it will allow businesses providing home care services to exclude salaries and related costs from the value of their supply; in other words, VAT will still only be due on the agency's commission. However, as this concession only applies to individuals buying in home care services, charities using agency staff to provide care, whether in an individual's residence or a residential home or hospice, will still be charged VAT on the full amount charged by the agency. As the provision of welfare by charities is exempt, this VAT will be a total cost.

**20.65** Where an individual does receive home care services from an agency, they will need to provide evidence, such as a written declaration, that they are in need of the services. The concession will apply to the provision both of personal care and routine domestic tasks.

### Exemption of education

**20.66** In the UK, the condition for the extension of exemption of education is that the supplier must be an 'eligible body'. Apart from being a school or university, this is a body that '*is precluded from distributing and does not distribute any profit it makes; and applies any profits made ... to the continuance or improvement of such [educational] supplies*'. The onus of proving that one is not making a profit for VAT purposes is on the charity, and is not automatically accepted by Customs and Excise. The exemption for education also applies to supplies of research, but only where both supplier and recipient are eligible bodies.

**20.67** In the UK, schools and universities can provide educational services, as registered medical professionals can provide health services, exempt from VAT however much profit they may make. This is because they automatically fall within the exemption without reference to profit. The exemption used to apply only to education supplied 'otherwise than for profit', the same proviso that applies to welfare services. This was, arguably, in conflict with the Sixth Directive condition that a supplier 'shall not systematically aim to make a profit'.

**20.68** This conflict was explored in the Court of Appeal case of *Bell Concord Educational Trust Ltd v Customs and Excise Comrs* [1989] STC 264, which concerned itself with the difference between aiming to make a profit, and making a profit secondary or incidental to the main aim of the provider, that being in this case to provide education. Thereafter the exemption was changed to the current wording, which seems better to reflect the intention of the EC Sixth Directive. However, no such change has been made to the exemption for welfare services, which retains the 'not for profit' condition.

## 10 INVESTMENT MANAGEMENT

**20.69** Where charities hold investments, fund administration can be another headache from a VAT point of view, as income-bearing assets in a varied portfolio may differ markedly in their treatment. As already mentioned, interest and dividend income is outside the scope of VAT, and investment property can be either exempt or taxable, depending on the availability and desirability of the option to tax. Dealings in money, shares or other securities are, in the main, exempt from VAT.

## 11 CONFLICT WITH DIRECT TAX RULES

**20.70** The non-complementary nature of the UK tax system means that an approach that seems to maximise revenue from a direct tax point of view might leave a charity open to unfortunate VAT consequences. Similarly, the best approach to take for VAT might have disadvantageous consequences when direct tax implications are considered. Expert advice on all aspects of administering a charitable trust, fund, or investment portfolio should be taken before any method is set in stone. This advice extends to all fundraising activities.

**20.71** An example of the unhelpful nature of the interaction of direct and indirect taxes is where a person makes a donation to a charity. The Inland Revenue allows for a *de minimis* limit on reciprocal supplies made to the donor which can be disregarded. Customs and Excise make no such allowances. For a donation to be outside the scope of VAT, it has to be a 'true' donation, where the donor receives *nothing* in return. 'Challenge activities', such as sponsored walks or fun runs, are outside the scope, but where income can be categorised as consideration for a supply, VAT must be considered.

**20.72** The consideration received need not be commensurate with the value of the supply to be subject to VAT. In the case of *Tron Theatre Ltd v Customs and Excise Comrs* [1992] STC 177, the charity claimed that where it received £150 for refurbishing seating, most of the amount received was a donation, freely given, and only a small part was consideration for a supply. The 'supply' in this case was a brass plaque on a 'sponsored' seat, a right to priority bookings and a limited edition print. This argument was rejected by the Court of Session, as it was ruled that the charity would not have provided these supplies for less than the full amount received.

**20.73** Therefore, the full amount was the consideration subject to VAT, even though the open market value of the supplies might have been less than £150. This leads to the unfortunate situation where a charity, by making some small supply as an incentive to encourage charitable giving, may put itself into a worse position for the purposes of VAT than if they offered no such incentives or inducements.

## 12 SPONSORSHIP

**20.74** This approach to donations may have suggested to some that the treatment of sponsorship is also subject to VAT. VAT must be charged to the sponsor, and then recovered by him insofar as his recovery rate allows. A fortunate offshoot of this is that sponsorship income will increase the charity's taxable supplies, and be eligible to be included in the partial exemption calculation. Before one becomes too cheered by this, the downside of the VAT status of sponsorship is that it may be the factor that requires a charity to register for VAT, with the associated disadvantages of administrative complexity, the pressures of compliance, and the need to charge VAT on *all* taxable supplies.

**20.75** Affinity credit card schemes have already been mentioned in Chapter 18. An affinity group may provide the credit card company with a variety of services — introduction of clients; product development; marketing and promotion etc. None of these fall within the financial exemptions for VAT. Exemption is allowed for '*intermediary services by a person acting in an intermediary capacity*'. However, in setting up a card scheme between its members and a financial institution, an affinity group is unlikely to be involved in work preparatory to the conclusion of contracts, which is necessary for exemption to apply. Therefore, the affinity group's supply to the credit card company will be taxable. A charity considering such a step will need to charge VAT if registered, and, if not registered, remember that the value of their supplies will contribute towards taxable turnover.

## 13 ROYALTIES

**20.76** Charitable trusts or foundations set up with the aim of preserving the works or memory of individuals should be aware that royalty payments are consideration for taxable supplies of the right to make use of the intangible, be it the written word, a picture or piece of music etc. As it is common practice for persons paying royalties to self-bill, it is important to remember to inform them that VAT is due, especially if registration occurs after the relationship with them has begun. Self-billing requires Customs permission.

**20.77** Where royalties are paid by a taxable body in another country, the 'supply' is in the country where the other body belongs. This means that if the recipient is within the EU and using the supply for the purpose of their business, the charity can charge no tax but still recover input VAT courtesy of VAT Regulations 1995, SI 1995/251, Regulation 103, and the recipient has to account for VAT in their country. If the recipient is outside the EU, the same treatment applies. However, as the supplies are deemed to be supplied where received, they are not made in the UK, and as such cannot be included within the partial exemption calculation of the supplier, although all directly attributable input tax can be recovered. This is because the recovery of directly attributable input tax is specifically allowed, with the supply being treated *as* a taxable supply, but it is *not* a taxable supply, and cannot therefore be included in the calculation.

## 14 FUNDRAISING EVENTS

**20.78** The exemption for fundraising events was extended by the 2000 Budget. Fundraising events are exempt from VAT provided that they satisfy the requirements of VAT (Fund-raising Events by Charities and Other Qualifying Bodies) Order 2000, SI 2000/802. Customs and Excise have also issued a draft notice 701/59, giving their views on the application of the amended exemption. The exemption applies to the admission fees, sale of programmes and advertising therein, sponsorship specifically for the event, and goods sold there by the charity. However, the relief only applies to the *outputs* of the charity, not the inputs. VAT on any purchases will therefore be charged as normal, and irrecoverable.

**20.79** According to Customs, a fundraising event is an event organised and promoted exclusively to make money for a charity or qualifying body. Social events which make incidental profits do not qualify, nor do regular or continuous activities such as the running of a shop. Examples of events that could qualify include balls, dances, performances, fetes, exhibitions or auctions.

**20.80** Prior to the coming into force of SI 2000/802 on 1 April 2000, events had to be 'one-offs' to qualify for exemption for VAT, and within the provisions of Inland Revenue Extra- Statutory Concession ESC C4 to be exempt from direct tax. The statutory instrument enacting the changes announced in Budget 2000 means that the indirect and direct tax exemptions are now co-ordinated. A body meeting the requirements for VAT exemption automatically qualifies for exemption from income tax and corporation tax.

**20.81** The wording of SI 2000/802 requires the primary purpose of an event to be raising money, and it should be promoted as such, before exemption can apply. This is an alteration of the previous treatment, which allowed for an event to qualify for exemption as long as raising money was a significant purpose of holding the event. The stipulation that an event must be promoted as being for the primary purpose of raising funds should also be noted. This raises the question of how narrowly Customs will construe this requirement. It would appear that this will be used to prevent the promotion of events to be for the entertainment of the attendees, with incidental profits going to charity, rather than an event being organised specifically for the benefit of a particular charity or charities, with any entertainment value being incidental.

**20.82** A charity is now allowed to hold up to 15 events of the same kind at the same location in a financial year and exempt them from VAT. Where a financial year is for a period of less or more than a calendar year, the number of allowed events is adjusted by multiplying the number of days in the financial year by 15, and then dividing the result by 365. The exemption also applies to events held for the same reasons by a 'qualifying body', or by a wholly owned subsidiary of a charity, providing all the profits are payable to the charity. Where events are organised by more than one charity or qualifying body, the 15 event limit applies to the number of events carried on involving any of the participating bodies.

**20.83** A 'qualifying body' includes a non-profit-making body within the scope of Sch 9 Group 9 of the VAT Act 1994, in particular, trade unions and professional associations. It also includes non-profit-making membership organisations with aims of a political, religious, patriotic, philosophical or philanthropic nature.

**20.84** A qualifying body can also be a non-profit-making body which is an eligible body for the purposes of the Sports, Sports Competitions and Physical Education group. These are required to be not subject to commercial influence. SI 2000/802 also requires them to have as their principal purpose the provision of facilities for people to take part in sport or physical education. Finally, eligible bodies for the purposes of the Cultural Services exemption are also qualifying bodies. These are bodies managed and administered on a voluntary basis, which do not distribute profits, and carry on the activities of allowing admission to a museum, gallery, exhibition or zoo, or a theatrical, musical or choreographic performance of a cultural nature.

**20.85** There is included in SI 2000/802 an 'anti-competition' clause. This states that the exemption does not apply to any supply that would be likely to create distortions of competition where similar activities are carried on by commercial concerns unable to qualify for the exemption. Customs say that this clause will only be used where there is 'potential to distort the relief', which would appear to mean that it will only be invoked where the relief is being actively exploited and charitable status misused. However, the clause remains in the legislation, and charities planning events should take note of any similar events happening near them, in case this clause could be invoked.

**20.86** A significant point to be aware of is that if the 15 event limit is exceeded, *all* the events will be taxable at the standard rate, not just those which exceed the limit. This means that if a charity mistakenly exceeds the limit, they will have to retrospectively account for VAT on the income of the previous events, thus reducing their income. VAT would therefore be due not only on ticket sales and sales of goods at the event, but also advertising and sponsorship income received.

**20.87** Where an event is taxable, VAT is due on the amount *required* for admission, etc. Thus, it is possible for a charity to set a minimum charge liable to VAT, and then suggest a further amount to be made as a donation. However, this will only be outside the scope of VAT if a true donation; in other words, a person *must* be allowed admission if they only pay the minimum set charge. No additional benefits must be conferred by the payment of any amount above the minimum charge, or the whole amount will be deemed to be consideration, and therefore taxable. Again to prevent distortion of competition, where the event is a performance of some sort, the minimum set charge may not be less than the usual price of admission/seating at a similar commercial event. Where the event is a dinner, dance or similar function, the minimum total sum upon which the organisers will be liable for VAT will not be less than their total organisation costs.

**20.88** Although 'location' is not defined, a prudent reading would be that it applies to a catchment area or local population rather than to a specific building or site. Customs' view is that 'location' is the geographical area within which an activity takes place. Thus, for an event that uses 'general use premises' such as a field or community hall, the location would be the area in which the field or hall is sited, rather than being the particular field or hall.

**20.89** Also, following the extension of the zero rate to online advertising, another example of the gradual modernisation of VAT law is that exemption also applies to events accessed wholly or partly by means of electronic communications. This means that 'web-cast' events are able to qualify for exemption, provided that their primary purpose is to raise funds, and they are promoted as such.

**20.90** There is no time limit put on the duration of an event by SI 2000/802, but the provision of incidental accommodation may only fall within the exemption if it does not exceed two nights, whether or not consecutive. Where accommodation is not incidental to an event, this can result in the whole event failing to qualify for exemption. The exemption cannot apply to any supplies made which fall within the Tour Operators' Margin Scheme. This specifically applies to businesses which buy in and resell holiday and other travel services.

**20.91** Small scale events, such as coffee mornings and jumble sales, which are deemed not to pose the risk of distortion of trade, can be excluded from the 15 annual events, provided that the gross weekly takings do not exceed £1,000.

## 15 SALE OF GOODS

**20.92** The supply of donated goods by a charity or a 'profits-to-charity' person, whether they are sold or let on hire, is zero rated. This covers goods sold in a charity shop or at a charity auction, or if supplied having been made available to two or more 'specified persons'. Whether people go to a charity auction for a bargain, or to exceed open market value for a good cause, VAT does not impact as it does where inducements are offered to encourage people to donate.

**20.93** Prior to the changes announced in Budget 2000, donated goods had to be held out for sale to the general public to qualify for zero rating. VAT (Charities and Aids for the Handicapped) Order 2000, SI 2000/805, however, allows for goods to be let on hire rather than sold, and also allows supplies to be targeted at specified persons. These are persons who are handicapped, or entitled to a specified benefit, or both. The benefits specified are income support, housing benefit, council tax benefit, income-based job-seeker's allowance, working families' tax credit and disabled person's tax credit.

**20.94** If the sale is by a trading company rather than the parent charity, which may be a direct tax requirement, then zero rating will still apply if they are a 'profits-to-charity' person. A 'profits-to-charity' person is a person who has agreed in writing to transfer the profits from the supplies and lettings of the goods to a charity, or whose profits therefrom are otherwise payable to a charity. If a trading subsidiary is governed by the requirement to pass all profits up to the parent charity, they will, therefore, qualify as a profits-to-charity person.

**20.95** The sale of bought-in or manufactured goods is treated for VAT purposes as if a commercial enterprise. Only goods donated specifically for resupply are eligible for zero rating. Where goods are donated for use by the charity and subsequently resold, or donated for use as a raffle prize, zero rating does not apply. Bequeathed property only qualifies if bequeathed specifically for sale, or for export.

**20.96** The export of goods is zero rated, treated as being a supply made in the UK for business purposes. This means that if goods are exported in the course of a non-business activity, the charity exporting them can still recover the VAT on costs. This is a significant concession for charities distributing aid overseas.

**20.97** Other than where these reliefs apply, trading activities are subject to VAT as normal. As well as bought-in goods, this may apply to other supplies such as Christmas cards, stationery etc. Yet again proving the complexity of the VAT system, however, goods sold as part of a fundraising event follow the treatment of the event, and are therefore exempt from VAT.

## 16 ADMINISTRATION OF VAT

**20.98** Once registered, a charity is responsible for accounting for VAT the same as any other registered entity. Returns are typically required to be rendered every three months, but can be allowed or directed to be submitted monthly. Charities can take advantage of the annual accounting scheme or the cash accounting scheme if they meet the relevant criteria.

**20.99** The annual accounting scheme is available to businesses that regularly pay tax to Customs, have been trading for 12 months or longer, and expect their next year's turnover to be £300,000 or less. The scheme is optional, but if they wish to join the scheme, a trader need only submit one return each year. They still have to make payments on account, based on their estimated liability for the year. Customs makes the estimation on the basis of past performance of the business and any information provided about the business' future prospects.

**20.100** The cash accounting scheme permits businesses with a turnover of less than £350,000 to account for VAT by reference to payments made and received. The VAT account of a trader using the cash accounting scheme must also reference amounts to dates of payments, not dates of invoices. The main advantages of the scheme are automatic bad debt relief and the deferral of time for payment where extended credit is given.

The 2000 Pre-Budget Report includes a proposal to raise the limits on annual accounting *and* cash accounting to a consolidated turnover level of £600,000. There is also the possibility of a 'flat-rate scheme' being available for bodies with a turnover of £100,000 per annum or less, although the details of this are not yet available. These changes should be introduced in April 2001, and charities should keep their eyes peeled for details.

**20.101** It is important to remember that turnover for the purposes of VAT does not include income from non-business activities or exempt supplies.

## 17 PENALTIES

**20.102** If returns or payments are rendered late or not at all, or Customs and Excise believe that they are incorrect, assessments can be issued. Assessments can cover a maximum period of three years prior to the date of the assessment, unless fraud is a factor, in which case the limit is 20 years. Surcharge liability notices will be issued when returns are late or missing, requiring punctual compliance for the following 12 months, known as the surcharge period. If a second return is defaulted on within that period, the trader will be liable to a penalty of 2% of the tax due on that return, and the surcharge period will be extended for another 12 months. The penalties rise per defaulted return within the surcharge period, to 5%, 10%, and finally 15%. Customs may not always implement the 2% or 5% penalties where the amount due would be less than £200, but the surcharge period will still be extended.

**20.103** Penalties can also be imposed if an entity does not register when it is supposed to. The penalty for failure to register is an amount equal to 5% of the net VAT liability between the date registration was due and the date notification was made, where registration was no more than 9 months late. Where registration is between 9 and 18 months late, the penalty is 10% of net tax due, and if registration is more than 18 months late, the penalty is fixed at 15% of net tax due. Charities do not receive any dispensation from the penalty regime. The only mitigation available to them is that available to all traders. Penalties may be mitigated if a 'reasonable excuse' can be proved, but ignorance of VAT law is not usually accepted as such.

**20.104** If an error in past VAT dealings is detected, Customs and Excise should be notified as soon as it is discovered. If the net amount of errors discovered in one accounting period is less than £2,000, this can be corrected on the VAT return for the period of discovery without fear of penalty. If the errors exceed £2,000, separate notification, called a voluntary disclosure, is necessary, and interest may be charged. Making a voluntary disclosure of an error before Customs and Excise discover it will usually prevent a penalty from being levied. Therefore it is always best to voluntarily disclose any errors, even if interest is charged, as this will avoid a penalty. It is also possible to argue to mitigate interest charged. Customs and Excise may refuse to accept voluntary disclosures where they have been submitted after notification of a VAT visit has been received. This is because they may believe that the error was only disclosed to prevent it being discovered at the visit, which could result in a penalty.

**20.105** If any taxpayer refuses to disclose an error to Customs and Excise, and their VAT advisor is a member of the Institute of Chartered Accountants of England and Wales, the advisor is required by professional standards to consider ceasing to act for the taxpayer. The taxpayer's permission is needed before information is passed on to a new advisor, but a refusal would result in misgivings on the part of the new advisor, who may then ask to see correspondence held by the taxpayer. It is unlikely that they would continue to act if this request was also refused. It is therefore not possible to 'hide' refusals to disclose by changing advisors.

**20.106** Charities may be proportionately more likely to seek rulings from Customs and Excise than other traders, for example, regarding the zero rating of property or whether or not they qualify as an eligible body for the purposes of exempting the services they provide. If Customs and Excise issue an assessment or a ruling with which a charity disagrees, provided that all outstanding returns have been submitted and all payments deemed to be due have been paid, an appeal can be lodged with the VAT and Duties Tribunal. In special circumstances, Customs may be satisfied that the assessment would cause hardship if prior payment was insisted upon, and so this may not always be necessary. Such crucial cases as *Watford Help in the Home Service* and *Urdd Gobaith* resulted from charities appealing against Customs and Excise rulings and establishing a change in Customs' interpretation of benefit to all. The cost of making an appeal should be taken into account before any precipitate action is taken. Taxpayers are entitled to represent themselves before a tribunal, but the complex nature of many of the matters a charity may wish to appeal often require expert advice and counsel to be sought, and professional representation.

**20.107** Although the appeals process can be long drawn out, it must be remembered that Customs and Excise decisions may not be final. If a charity disagrees with the facts on which Customs have made a decision, or with the legal basis of their argument, there is the possibility of convincing a tribunal or higher court to rule against them. The highest court of appeal in the UK is the House of Lords, although cases can be referred to the European Court of Justice. However, this is not a court of appeal, and the Community legal order knows no system of 'common law' precedent. Therefore, its rulings are binding only on the parties involved, not on future proceedings where a similar question arises. Rulings can, however, result in changes in treatment, such as the movement of non-profit organisations with political, patriotic, religious, philosophical, philanthropic or civic aims within the exemption for trade unions and professional bodies which followed the ECJ's ruling against the Italian Republic.

## 18 CONCLUSION

**20.108** At 17.5%, VAT is a tax which can take a significant slice from income or capital otherwise meant for charitable purposes. Especially in relation to capital assets, positive regard to the impact of VAT and to its management and administration will not guarantee no VAT charge, but will ensure that the net cost is kept to a minimum, and that the probability of interest charges or penalties is minimal.

APPENDIX 1

# Useful addresses

| | |
|---|---|
| Buzzacott | 12 New Fetter Lane,<br>London EC4A 1AG<br>Telephone: (020) 7556 1200 |
| Charities Advisory Trust | Radius Works, Back Lane,<br>Hampstead, London NW3 1HL<br>Telephone: (020) 7794 9835 |
| Charities Aid Foundation | Kings Hill, West Malling, Kent<br>ME19 4TA<br>Telephone: (01732) 520000<br>Fax: (01732) 520001 |
| Charities Deposit Fund and Charities Official Investment Fund | St Alphage House, 2 Fore Street,<br>London EC2Y 5AQ<br>Telephone: (020) 7588 1815 |
| Charity Commission<br>—Northern Office | 2nd Floor, 20 Kings Parade, Queens<br>Dock, Liverpool, L3 4DQ<br>Telephone: 0870 333 0123 |
| —South Western and Western Countries | Woodfield House, Tangier, Taunton,<br>Somerset TA1 4BL<br>Telephone: 0870 333 0123 |
| —Central Register | Charity Commission, Harmsworth<br>House, 13–15 Bouverie Street, London,<br>EC4Y 8DP<br>Telephone: 0870 333 0123 |
| —Internet address | http://www.charity-commission.gov.uk |

All Charity Commission offices have access to the same central register of charities although accounts etc are filed regionally. The Commission have set up telephone helplines. See the end of this Appendix for details.

| | |
|---|---|
| Directory of Social Change | 29 Stephenson Way, London NW1 2DR<br>Telephone: (020) 7209 4949 |

| | |
|---|---|
| Friendly Societies | Registrar of Friendly Societies, Victory House, 30–34 Kingsway, London WC2B 6ES<br>Telephone: (020) 7663 5000 |
| Housing Associations/Social Landlords | The Housing Corporation, 149 Tottenham Court Road, London W1P 7BN<br>Telephone: (020) 7393 2000 |
| —England and Wales | National Federation of Housing Associations, 175 Gray's Inn Road, London WC1X 8UP<br>Telephone: (020) 7278 6571 |
| —Scotland | Scottish Federation of Housing Associations, 38 York Place, Edinburgh EH1 3HU<br>Telephone: (0131) 556 5777 |
| —Northern Ireland | Northern Ireland Federation of Housing Associations, Carlisle Memorial Centre, 88 Clifton Street, Belfast BT13 1AB<br>Telephone: (028) 9023 0446 |
| Inland Revenue Financial Intermediaries and Claims Office ('FICO') (Trusts & Charities)<br>—England, Wales and Northern Ireland | (formerly Claims Branch (Trusts & Charities))<br><br>St. John's House, Merton Road, Bootle, Merseyside L69 9BB<br>Telephone: (0151) 472 6000 |

The switchboard has direct lines which will allow you to get straight through to the person who will deal with your enquiry.

| | | |
|---|---|---|
| Direct Helpline numbers will be: | Covenants | (0151) 472–6037 |
| | Gift Aid | (0151) 472–6038 |
| Additional lines for Gift Aid enquiries are: | | (0151) 472–6055 |
| | | (0151) 472–6056 |
| If you have a general enquiry: | | (0151) 472–6036 |
| If you do have a reference number: | | |
| Last digit of reference 1, 3 or 5 | | (0151) 472–6039 |
| 2 or 4 | | (0151) 472–6034 |
| 6, 7 or 8 | | (0151) 472–6035 |
| 9 or 0 | | (0151) 472–6040 |

| | |
|---|---|
| —Scotland | Trinity Park House, South Trinity Road, Edinburgh EH5 3SA<br>Telephone: (0131) 552 6255 |
| InterChange | Valby Street, London NW5 3NQ<br>Telephone: (020) 7267 9421 |

| | |
|---|---|
| National Council for Voluntary Organisations | Regent's Wharf, 8 All Saints Street, London N1 9RL<br>Telephone: (020) 7713 6161 |
| National Institute for Social Work | Mary Ward House, 5/7 Tavistock Place, London WC1H 9SS<br>Telephone: (020) 7387 9681 |
| Northern Ireland Council for Voluntary Action | 127 Ormeau Road, Belfast BT7 1SH<br>Telephone: (028) 9032 1224 |
| Northern Ireland Charities Unit Department of Finance and Personnel | Rosepark House, Upper Newtownards Road, Belfast BT4 3NR<br>Telephone: (028) 9052 0400 |
| Official Custodian for Charities | Charity Commission, Official Custodian's Division, Harmsworth House, 13–15 Bouverie Street, London EC4Y 8DP<br>Telephone: 0870 333 0123 |
| Scottish Council for Community and Voluntary Organisations | 19 Claremont Crescent, Edinburgh EH7 4QD<br>Telephone: (0131) 556 3882 |
| Scottish Home and Health Department | Civil Law and General Division, Room 227(b), St. Andrew's House, Regent Road, Edinburgh EH1 3DG<br>Telephone: (0131) 556 8400 |
| Voluntary Services Unit (Home Office) | Horseferry House, Dean Ryle Street, London SW1P 2AW<br>Telephone: (020) 7273 4000 |
| Wales Council for Voluntary Action | Information Office, Council for Voluntary Action of Wales, Llys Ifor, Crescent Road, Caerphilly, Mid Glamorgan CF83 1XL<br>Telephone: (1222) 869224 |
| Customs and Excise | New Kings Beam House, 22 Upper Ground, London SE1 9PJ<br>Telephone: (020) 7620 1313 |
| VAT Education Team | Thomas Paine House, 2 Angel Square, Torrens Street, London EC1V 1TA<br>Telephone: (020) 7865 3000 |
| Association of Chief Executives of Voluntary Organisations | 31–33 College Road, Harrow, Middlesex HA1 1JE<br>Telephone: (020) 8424 2334 |
| Scottish Charities Office | Crown Office, 25 Chambers Street, Edinburgh EH1 1LA<br>Telephone: (0131) 226 2626 |

| | |
|---|---|
| Legislation Monitoring Service for Charities | 12 Little College Street, London SW1P 3SH<br>Telephone: (020) 7222 1265 |
| Institute of Charity Fund-raising Managers | Central Offices, Market Towers, 1 Nine Elms Lane, London SW8 5NQ<br>Telephone: (020) 7627 3436 |
| Gaming Board for Great Britain, Lotteries Section | Berkshire House, 168/173 High Holborn, London WC1V 7AA<br>Telephone: (020) 7306 6269 |
| Charity Finance Directors' Group | Camelford House, 89 Albert Embankment, London SE1 7TP<br>Telephone: (020) 7793 4000 |

## CHARITY COMMISSION HELPLINES

**The Charity Commission has set up telephone helplines to answer enquiries from members of the public and charities on specific areas:**

| Subject | Location | Telephone number |
|---|---|---|
| General enquiries | | 0870 333 0123 |
| Press office | London | (020) 7674 2333 |
| Annual returns by registered charities | Liverpool | (0151) 703 1515 |
| Control of fundraising | London | 0870 333 0123 |
| The number for hearing and speach impaired callers using a minicom is | | 0870 333 0125 |

APPENDIX 2

# Charity Commission publications

| | |
|---|---|
| *CC1* | Charity Commission Publications (7/2000) |
| *CC2* | Charities and the Charity Commission (7/2000) |
| *CC3* | Responsibilities of Charity Trustees (9/99) |
| *CC3a* | Responsibilities of Charity Trustees: A Summary (8/99) |
| *CC4* | Charities for the Relief of the Poor (1/2000) |
| *CC6* | Charities for the Relief of Sickness (3/2000) |
| *CC7* | Ex Gratia Payments by Charities (1/95) |
| *CC8* | Internal Financial Controls for Charities (7/99) |
| *CC9* | Political Activities and Campaigning by Charities (9/99) |
| *CC9a* | Political Activities and Campaigning by Local Community Charities (2/97) |
| *CC10* | Annual Report for 1998: A Summary (5/99) |
| *CC11* | Payment of Charity Trustees (9/2000) |
| *CC12* | Managing Financial Difficulties and Insolvency in Charities (1/2000) |
| *CC13* | The Official Custodian for Charities' Land Holding Service (3/95) |
| *CC14* | Investment of Charitable Funds: Basic Principles (8/2000) |
| *CC14a* | Depositing Charity Cash (8/99) |
| *CC18* | Use of Church Halls for Village Hall and Other Charitable Purposes (3/96) |
| *CC19* | Charities' Reserves (6/99) |
| *CC20* | Charities and Fund-Raising (4/2000) |
| *CC20a* | Charities and Fund-Raising: A Summary (9/99) |
| *CC21* | Registering as a Charity (4/2000) |
| *CC22* | Choosing and Preparing a Governing Document (8/2000) |
| *CC23* | Exempt Charities (7/99) |
| *CC24* | Users on Board: Beneficiaries Who Become Trustees (3/2000) |
| *CC25* | Resolving Charity Disputes: Our Role (3/2000) |
| *CC27* | Providing Alcohol on Charity Premises (7/96) |
| *CC28* | Disposing of Charity Land (6/96) |
| *CC29* | Charities and Local Authorities (4/96) |
| *CC32* | Trustee Investments Act 1961: A Guide (8/99) |
| *CC33* | Aquiring Land (3/95) |

*CC35* Charities and Trading (4/2000)
*CC36* Making a Scheme (9/99)
*CC37* Charities and Contracts (1/2000)
*CC38* Expenditure and Replacement of Permanent Endowment (4/94)
*CC40* Disaster Appeals (8/94)
*CC43* Incorporation of Charity Trustees (6/99)
*CC44* Small Charities: Alteration of Trusts, Transfer of Property, Expenditure of Capital (5/99)
*CC45* Central Register of Charities (11/95)
*CC47* Inquiries into Charities (2/2000)
*CC48* Charities and Meetings (10/2000)
*CC49* Charities and Insurance (6/96)
*CC50* Getting in Touch with the Charity Commission (6/96)
*CC51* Charity Accounts: The New Framework (6/99)
*CC52* Charity Accounts: Charities Under £10,000 Threshold (4/99)
*CC54* Accounting for the Smaller Charity (9/99)
*CC55* Accruals Accounting for the Smaller Charity (9/99)
*CC56* The Carrying Out of an Independent Examination Directions and Guidance Notes (3/96)
*CC57* Receipts and Payments Accounts Pack (7/98)
Introductory Notes
*CC57(a)* Accounting Statement
*CC57(b)* Independent Examiner's Report on the Accounts
*CC57(c)* Trustees' Annual Report (Accompanying Receipts and Payments Accounts)
*CC58* Accruals Accounts Pack (7/98)
Introductory Notes
*CC58(a)* Accounting Statement (Accruals Accounts)
*CC58(b)* Independent Examiner's Report on the Accounts
*CC58(c)* Trustees' Annual Report (Accompanying Accruals Accounts)
*CC60* The Hallmarks of a Well-Run Charity (7/2000)
*CC61* Charity Accounts 2001: The Framework (1/2001)
*CC62* Charities SORP 2000: What Has Changed? (10/2000)
*CC66* SORP 2000: Example Reports and Accounts (11/2000)
Accounting and Reporting by Charities: Statement of Recommended Practice (SORP 2000) (10/2000)
*RR1* The Review of the Register of Charities (3/99)
*RR2* Promotion of Urban and Rural Regeneration (3/99)
*RR3* Charities for the Relief of Unemployment (3/99)
*RR4* The Recreational Charities Act 1958 (8/2000)
*RR5* The Promotion of Community Capacity Building (11/2000)
*RR6* Maintenance of an Accurate Register (11/2000)
A Guide to the Charities Acts 1992 and 1993 (3/97)

## Also Available

### Charity Commission Video—Its a Question of Trust (9/98)

The Charity Commission describe the video as follows.

> 'Its a Question of Trust is our video and support publication. The video is 18 minutes long and is divided into modules covering areas such as the governing document and key trustee responsibilities, which are backed up by information in the accompanying publication.
>
> The video is available in English, Welsh and in subtitled version of both languages. It costs £12.00 which includes postage and two copies of the support publication. To obtain a copy please write to Public Relations, the Charity Commission, Harmsworth House, 13–15 Bouverie Street, London EC4Y 8DP enclosing a cheque for £12.00 made payable to the Charity Commission.'

### Statement of Recommended Practice: Accounting by Charities (known as the Charity SORP) (10/95)

The Charity Commission describe the publication as follows.

> 'This publication explains how charities should prepare their accounts in accordance with widely agreed best practice. By following the recommendations of SORP, charities will improve the quality of their accounts and annual reports. Copies are available from our Liverpool office. Every charity is entitled to one free copy but otherwise it costs £5. Ring 0870 333 0123.'

### Charity Accounts and Reports: Core Guide (produced by the Home Office)

The Charity Commission describe the Core Guide as follows.

> 'This includes a copy of the Regulations, relevant extracts from the legislation and a commentary. Copies are available from the Stationary Office (telephone 0870 600 5522 (message menu system)) priced £11.00. ISBN 011-341156-1.'

### Translated Summary Guidance

The Summary guidance is described as follows by the Charity Commision.

> 'We produce the following summary guidance in Arabic, Bengali, Cantonese, Gujerati, Kurdish, Somali, Urdu, Vietnamese, in addition to Welsh:

- SG1—Registering as a charity
- SG2—Administration for charity trustees
- SG3—Financial management for charity trustees
- SG4—Resolving charity disputes

These are not currently available on the website but you can order them free of charge using our on-line publications order form or by telephoning our publication Request Answer phone on 01823 345 427.

For more details on translated guidance you can contact Sush Amar by email on samar@charity-commission.gov.uk or by telephone on 0207 674 2462.'

For details on other publications,
email publication@charity-commission.gov.uk.

APPENDIX 3

# Charity Commission definition of gross income and total expenditure

THE NOTE FROM THE CHARITIES (ANNUAL RETURN) REGULATIONS 1997 TO DETERMINE THE SIZE OF INCOME OF AN ACCOUNTABLE CHARITY

**Gross Income**

This is the total recorded income of the charity in all unrestricted and restricted funds but **not** resources received as capital (endowment) funds.

You should calculate income before deduction of any costs or expenses.

Therefore you should include the following in income:

- donations (including covenanted donations), grants, gifts, legacies, covenants and subscriptions (see note);
- tax refunds;
- investment income (including interest receivable, dividends and rents);
- gross receipts from the sale of goods or services in furtherance of the charity's objectives;
- gross proceeds from fund-raising; and
- other income, when trustees decide to spend expendable capital they should include the amount spent as 'other income', this is because capital receipts are not included as income when they first come into the charity (see note).

And you should exclude the following from income:

- receipt of a loan by the charity;
- loan repayments to the charity;
- proceeds of sale of investments and fixed assets; and
- gains or profits on disposal of investments and fixed assets.

**Total Expenditure**

You should include gross expenditure shown in the accounts of the relevant funds.

You should include the following in expenditure:

- expenditure relating to the objects of the charity including grants, donations, cost of services provided and support costs;
- management and administration costs of the charity;
- fund-raising and publicity costs;
- interest payable; and
- **when accounts are prepared on an accruals basis:** depreciation or amortisation of assets held.

And you should exclude the following from expenditure:

- making of a loan;
- repayment of a loan;
- purchase of investments and fixed assets; and
- losses on disposal of investments and fixed assets.

**Note:** Donations, etc, which the giver expects will be, or may be, retained for investment by the charity are capital, and should be excluded. Other capital donations should be excluded, eg gifts of land and buildings to be retained and used for a particular charitable purpose.

Where accruals accounts are prepared, the figure for **gross income** is the total of–

- the incoming resources of the charity's restricted and unrestricted income funds (other than gains on disposal or on revaluation of fixed assets) these figures will be entered in the statement of financial activities under paragraph 3(a) of Part 1 of Schedule 1 to the Charities (Accounts and Reports) Regulations 1995 (but any amount included under paragraph 3(a)(iv) which represents gains on the disposal of functional fixed assets should be left out for the purposes of this return); and
- any figure entered under paragraph 3(c) of that Part relating to a transfer from expendable endowment capital funds to income funds.

The figure for total expenditure is the total of the figures entered under paragraph 3(b) of that Part (but leaving out any amount which represents losses on the disposal of functional fixed assets).

APPENDIX 4

# Stages of an audit

The work of an auditor can be broken down into four main stages, as follows:

(a) defining and agreeing terms of audit engagement;
(b) planning, controlling and recording audit work;
(c) obtaining appropriate audit evidence from audit work; and
(d) reporting and expressing audit opinion on accounts.

The stages of an audit, set out above, reflect the basic objectives and general principles of auditing standards. In undertaking an audit, auditors:

(a) carry out procedures designed to obtain *sufficient* and *appropriate* audit evidence in order to determine with *reasonable confidence* whether the accounts are free of *material mis-statement*;
(b) evaluate the overall presentation of the accounts in order to determine that they have been prepared in accordance with *relevant legislation* and *accounting standards*; and
(c) issue a report containing a clear expression of their opinion on the accounts (SAS 100).

In expressing an opinion on a set of accounts, auditors provide a level of assurance that is reasonable in the circumstances of the work being carried out but, being based on a combination of facts and professional judgement, cannot be an absolute level of assurance or 'correct'.

In carrying out an audit, auditors are required to comply with the ethical guidance of their relevant professional bodies. Ethical principles, which underlie an auditor's responsibilities, include those of integrity, objectivity, independence and confidentiality, in addition to the basic expectation of professional competence and due care.

## Agree engagement terms

It is important that the client charity and the auditors agree on the terms of engagement and that these terms are recorded in writing (SAS 140). An engagement letter documents and confirms:

(a) client's acceptance of the auditor's appointment;
(b) respective responsibilities of the trustees or directors and of the auditors, including any statutory responsibilities;
(c) scope of the audit engagement; and
(d) the form of any report required of the auditor.

Terms of engagement must be agreed, in writing, at the outset of any audit appointment. Thereafter, both parties should regularly review the terms of engagement to ensure that they remain relevant and appropriate, and any updating should be confirmed in writing.

It is important that all trustees of the charity should be aware of, and agree, the terms of engagement, giving a detailed description of the audit work to be undertaken. Where day-to-day running of a charity is delegated to executive staff, those executives, for example the chief executive, should be aware of the terms of the auditor's engagement.

Matters that need particular reference within the letter of engagement may include:

(a) auditor's responsibility (or otherwise) for the audit of special income, such as government or local authority grants;
(b) the requirement for special reports (arising out of (a) above);
(c) the respective responsibilities of trustees and auditors, with respect to fraud and other irregularities and to the consideration of laws or regulations that may materially affect the accounts, or conduct of the charity's business or operations; and
(d) the scope of the charity's accounts, including the identification and accounting treatment of branches, or connected entities (SORP).

APPENDIX 5

# Rights of auditors

## OBLIGATIONS OF TRUSTEES CONCERNING AUDITORS (UNINCORPORATED CHARITIES)

The auditor must carry out such investigations as will enable him to form the opinion required to be stated in his auditor's report (see example auditors' reports).

Under s 44(1)(d) Ch A 1993 an auditor or independent examiner has the right of access to any books, documents or other records (however kept – for example, computer records) which relate to the charity and which he considers it necessary to inspect for the purposes of carrying out the audit or independent examination (Reg 8(1)). An auditor or independent examiner is also entitled to require information and explanations from past or present charity trustees or trustees for the charity, or from past or present officers or employees of the charity. If any person fails to afford the auditor or independent examiner any facility to which he is entitled, as set out above, the Charity Commissioners may (by order) under s 44(2) give such directions (as they consider appropriate) to that person or the charity trustees, to ensure that the default is made good. Where, in any proceedings for negligence, default, breach of duty or breach of trust against an auditor or independent examiner, a Court determines that the auditor or independent examiner has acted honestly and reasonably a Court may relieve the auditor or independent examiner from liability on such terms as it thinks fit. [CA 1985 s 727/Ch A 1993 s 44(3).]

APPENDIX 6

# Auditors ceasing office

Where an auditor, for any reason, ceases to hold office, he is required to send to the charity trustees a statement of any circumstances in connection with his ceasing to hold office, which he considers should be brought to their attention. If he considers that there are no such circumstances, a statement is required that there are none. It is the auditor's responsibility to send a copy of the statement outlining circumstances of ceasing to hold office (but not a statement of no such circumstances) to the Charity Commissioners.

**Dispensations from audit or independent examination**

Regulation 9 empowers the Commissioners, in certain circumstances, to dispense with the requirement for audit or independent examination under the Charities Act 1993 s 43(2) or s 43(3). These circumstances include:

(a) where an equivalent audit is carried under another statutory provision, eg by the Audit Commission under local government or NHS legislation, or by the Comptroller and Auditor General;
(b) where a charity is 'dormant', eg where there have been no transactions to be shown in the accounting records in the financial year; and
(c) where, in exceptional circumstances, an independent examination rather than an audit, is justified.

All the above circumstances (required by Regulation 9) require the charity's trustees to supply the Charity Commissioners with any report with respect to the accounts that the Commissioners may request.

APPENDIX 7

# Example engagement letter: unincorporated charity audit (accruals basis)

Our ref

The Trustees

Dear Sirs

1 The purpose of this letter is to set out the basis on which we act as auditors of the charity and the respective areas of responsibility of the trustees and of ourselves. We have been appointed as auditors under section 43 of the Charities Act 1993.

**Responsibilities of trustees and auditors**

2 As trustees of the above charity, you are responsible for ensuring that the charity maintains proper accounting records and for preparing financial statements which give a true and fair view and have been prepared in accordance with the Charities Act 1993 and regulations thereunder. You are also responsible for making available to us, as and when required, all of the charity's accounting records and all other relevant records and related information, including minutes of trustees' meetings and of all appropriate management meetings.

3 As trustees of a charity, you are under a duty to prepare an annual report for each financial year complying in its form and content with regulations made under the Charities Act 1993. You are also required to have regard to the Statement of Recommended Practice ('SORP') 'Accounting by Charities', issued by the Charity Commissioners for England and Wales. Charities' accounts and accounting practices are expected to comply fully, as appropriate, with the SORP.

4 We have a statutory responsibility to report to you as trustees whether in our opinion the financial statements comply with the

requirements of The Charities (Accounts and Reports) Regulations 1995 and The Charities (Accounts and Reports) Regulations 2000 and give a true and fair view of the state of affairs of the charity at the end of the financial year and of the incoming resources and application of the resources of the charity in that year. In arriving at our opinion, we are required to consider the following matters, and report on any in respect of which we are not satisfied:

4.1 whether proper accounting records have been kept by the charity in accordance with section 41 Charities Act 1993;

4.2 whether the financial statements are in agreement with the accounting records;

4.3 whether we have obtained all the information and explanations to which we are entitled for the purpose of our audit;

4.4 whether the information in the trustees' statutory annual report is materially consistent with that in the financial statements.

5 In addition, there are certain other matters which, according to the circumstances, may need to be dealt with in our report; For example, non-compliance with a requirement of regulations to be made under Charities Act 1993.

6 We have a professional responsibility to report if the financial statements do not comply in any material respect with applicable accounting standards, unless in our opinion the non-compliance is justified in the circumstances. In determining whether or not the departure is justified we consider:

6.1 whether the departure is required in order for the financial statements to give a true and fair view; and

6.2 whether adequate disclosure has been made concerning the departure.

7 Our professional responsibilities also include:

7.1 including in our report a description of the trustees' responsibilities for the financial statements where the financial statements or accompanying information do not include such a description; and

7.2 considering whether other information in documents containing audited financial statements is consistent with those financial statements.

## Duty to report to Charity Commissioners

8 We have a statutory duty to report to the Charity Commissioners such matters (concerning the activities or affairs of the charity or any connected institution or body corporate) of which we become aware during the course of our audit which are (or are likely to be) of material significance to the Commissioners in the exercise of their powers of inquiry into, or acting for the protection of, charities. (Regulation 6(5) The Charities (Accounts and Reports) Regulations 1995.)

## Scope of audit

9 Our audit will be conducted in accordance with the Auditing Standards issued by the Auditing Practices Board and will include such tests of transactions and of the existence, ownership and valuation of assets and liabilities as we consider necessary. We shall obtain an understanding of the accounting systems and internal controls in order to assess their adequacy as a basis for the preparation of the financial statements, and to establish whether proper accounting records have been maintained by the charity. We shall expect to obtain such relevant and reliable evidence as we consider sufficient to enable us to draw reasonable conclusions therefrom.

## Reporting to the trustees

10 The nature and extent of our procedures will vary according to our assessment of the charity's accounting system and, where we wish to place reliance on it, the internal control system, and may cover any aspect of the charity's operations that we consider appropriate. Our audit is not designed to identify all significant weaknesses in the charity's systems but, if such weaknesses come to our notice during the course of our audit which we think should be brought to your attention, we shall report them to you. Any such report may not be provided to third parties without our prior written consent. Such consent will be granted only on the basis that such reports are not prepared with the interests of anyone other than the charity in mind and that we accept no duty or responsibility to any other party as concerns the reports.

## Representations by trustees

11 As part of our normal audit procedures, we may request that you provide written confirmation of oral representations which we have received from you during the course of the audit on matters having a material effect on the financial statements.

## Documents issued with the financial statements

12 In order to assist us with the examination of your financial statements, we shall request sight of all documents or statements, including the trustees' report, which are due to be issued with the financial statements. If it is proposed that any documents or statement which refer to our name, other than the audited financial statements, are to be circulated to third parties, please consult us before they are issued.

## Irregularities, including fraud

13 The responsibility for safeguarding the assets of the charity and for the prevention and detection of fraud, error and non-compliance with law or regulations rests with yourselves. However, we shall endeavour to plan our audit so that we have a reasonable expectation of detecting material misstatements in the financial statements or accounting records (including those resulting from fraud, error or non compliance with law or regulations), but our examination should not be relied upon to disclose all such material misstatements or frauds, errors or instances of non-compliance as may exist.

## Other matters

14 We shall not be treated as having notice, for the purposes of our audit responsibilities, of information provided to members of our firm other than those engaged on the audit (for example, information provided in connection with accounting, taxation and other services).

## Other services

15 If you request that we provide other services, the terms under which we provide these other services will be dealt with in a separate letter. We will also agree in a separate letter of engagement the provision of any services relating to investment business advice as defined by the Financial Services Act 1986.

## Data Protection Act

16 In accordance with the Data Protection Act 1998, we are required to obtain your consent to process data relating to your affairs. Data, for the purposes of the Act, includes not only information about you in our computerised database, but also manual records contained in our filing system. Your acknowledgement to the terms of this letter will constitute grant of such consent.

## Confidentiality

17 We confirm that where you give us confidential information we shall at all times keep it confidential, except as required by law or as provided for in regulatory, ethical or other professional pronouncements applicable to our engagement.

18 You agree that it will be sufficient compliance with our duty of confidence for us to take such steps as we in good faith think fit to preserve confidential information both during and after termination of this engagement.

## Quality of service

19 We aim to provide you with a service with which you will be completely satisfied. If at any time you would like to discuss with us how our services to you could be improved or if you are concerned with the service you are receiving, please let us know by contacting [ ] the engagement partner, or [ ], Chairman of the firm.

20 We undertake to consider any comments carefully and promptly and do all we can to explain the position to you. We undertake to do anything reasonable to resolve any problems and if you are still not satisfied you may, of course, take up matters with the Institute of Chartered Accountants in England and Wales by whom we are regulated for audit purposes.

## Fees

21 Our fees are computed on the basis of the time spent on your affairs by the partners and our staff, and on the levels of skill and responsibility involved. We will confirm all fee arrangements in writing.

22 Unless otherwise agreed, our fees will be billed at appropriate intervals during the course of the year and will be due on presentation. Any queries concerning an invoice must be raised within 30 days of the invoice date.

23 Expenses properly incurred whilst we are engaged to carry out professional services on your behalf, whether at your premises or elsewhere, are charged at cost, in addition to our fees. Such expenses may include travelling, subsistence, accommodation, report production and any special telecommunication or computing charges.

**Applicable law**

24 This engagement letter shall be governed by, and construed in accordance with, English law. The Courts of England shall have exclusive jurisdiction in relation to any claim, dispute or difference concerning the engagement letter and any matter arising from it. Each party irrevocably waives any right it may have to object to an action being brought in those Courts, to claim that the action has been brought in an inconvenient forum, or to claim that those Courts do not have jurisdiction.

**Agreement of terms**

25 Once it has been agreed, this letter will remain effective from one audit appointment to another until it is replaced. We shall be grateful if you would confirm in writing your agreement to these terms, by signing and returning the enclosed copy of this letter, or let us know if they are not in accordance with your understanding of our terms of engagement.

Yours faithfully,

We confirm that this letter reflects our understanding of the terms of your engagement and agree to its contents.

Signed for, and on behalf of, the trustees of

..............................................................

Trustee

..............................................................

Date

APPENDIX 8

# Model Gift Aid declaration

**Gift Aid declaration**

Name of Charity ..........................................................................................

Details of donor

Title .........................Forename(s) ..................................Surname ................

Address .........................................................................................................

.........................................................................................................

...................................................................Postcode ................

I want the charity to treat

*the enclosed donation of £............

*the donation(s) of £........................which I made on ...../ ...../ .....

*all donations I make from the date of this declaration until I notify you otherwise

*all donations I have made since 6 April 2000, and all donations I make from the date of this declaration until I notify you otherwise

as Gift Aid donations.

*NB. Charities do not have to include all these statements on their declarations, but con choose whichever is appropriate.*

**See overleaf for notes**

**Notes**

1. You must pay an amount of income tax and/or capital gains tax at least equal to the tax that the charity reclaims on your donations in the tax year (currently 28p for each £1 you give).

2. You can cancel this declaration at any time by notifying the charity.

3. If in the future your circumstances change and you no longer pay tax on your income and capital gains equal to the tax that the charity reclaims, you can cancel your declaration (see note 1).

4. If you pay tax at the higher rate you can claim further tax relief in your Self-Assessment tax return.

5. If you are unsure whether your donations qualify for Gift Aid tax relief, ask the charity. Or ask your local tax office for leaflet IR 65.

6. Please notify the charity if you change your name or address.

# Charity X: sponsorship and Gift Aid declaration form

**CHARITY X: SPONSORSHIP AND GIFT AID DECLARATION FORM**

We, who have given our names and addresses below, and who have ticked the box entitled '(✔)Gift Aid?', want the above charity to reclaim tax on the donation detailed below, given on the date shown. We understand that each of us must pay income tax or capital gains tax equal to the tax reclaimed by the charity on the donation.

| Full name | Address | Post code | Amount pledged | Amount given | Date given (dd/mm/yy) | Gift Aid? (✔) |
|---|---|---|---|---|---|---|
| | | | | | | |
| | | | | | | |
| | | | | | | |
| | | | | | | |
| | | | | | | |
| | | | | | | |
| | | | | | | |
| | | | | | | |
| | | | | | | |
| | | | | | | |
| | | | | | | |
| | | | | | | |
| | | | | | | |
| | | | | | | |
| | | | | | | |
| | | | | | | |
| | | | | | | |

| | |
|---|---|
| Total donations | £ |

*To be completed by the charity:*

Date sums collected passed to charity:

Total income tax to be reclaimed on above donations: £

# APPENDIX 10

# Trust and estate charities form

Inland Revenue

*Income for the year ended 5 April 2000*

**TRUST AND ESTATE CHARITIES**

*Fill in these boxes first*

Name of trust

Name of charity, if different

Tax reference

***If you want help, look up the box numbers in the Notes on Trust and Estate Charities.***

## *Claim to exemption*

- Charity repayment reference **7.1**
- Charity Commission Registration Number or Scottish Charity Number **7.2**

If the trust is a charity are you claiming exemption from all tax on all or part of your income and gains? **YES** **NO**

Have all income and gains that you are claiming to be exempt from tax been, or will they be, applied for charitable purposes? **YES** **NO**

## *Return period*

- Are you returning information for the year ended 5 April 2000? **YES** **NO**
- If 'No', what period does this Return cover?

Period begins **7.3** / / and ends **7.4** / /

- Are accounts to be enclosed with the Return? **YES** **NO**

If 'No', explain why **7.5**

## *Repayments*

| | Income Tax | Transitional relief |
|---|---|---|
| • Amount already claimed on form R68 or R68(MGA) | **7.6** £ | **7.7** £ |
| • Total repayment/payment due | **7.8** £ | **7.9** £ |
| and | | |
| • further repayment/payment due | **7.10** £ | **7.11** £ |
| or | | |
| • amounts overclaimed | **7.12** £ | **7.13** £ |

## *Income on which you are claiming exemption*

Non-exempt amounts should be entered in the appropriate parts of the Return.

| | |
|---|---|
| • Total turnover from exempt trading activities | **7.14** £ |
| • Investment income | **7.15** £ |
| • UK land and buildings income | **7.16** £ |
| • Deed of covenant | **7.17** £ |
| • Gift Aid or Millennium Gift Aid | **7.18** £ |
| • Other charities | **7.19** £ |
| • Legacies | **7.20** £ |
| • Other donations | **7.21** £ |
| • Other, for example, commissions, fees, small fund raising | **7.22** £ |

*continued over*

SA907

BMSD 12/99net

TRUST AND ESTATE TAX RETURN ■ CHARITY PAGES TCH1

## *Expenses as included in the charity accounts*

| | | |
|---|---|---|
| • Trading costs | 7.23 | £ |
| • UK land and buildings | 7.24 | £ |
| • All general administration costs | 7.25 | £ |
| • All grants and donations made in the UK | 7.26 | £ |
| • All grants and donations made outside the UK | 7.27 | £ |
| • Others (not entered elsewhere on the Return) | 7.28 | £ |

## *Assets*

| | Disposals in year | Held at 5 April 2000 |
|---|---|---|
| • Tangible fixed assets | 7.29 £ | 7.30 £ |
| • UK investments (excluding controlled companies) | 7.31 £ | 7.32 £ |
| • Shares in, and loans to, controlled companies | 7.33 £ | 7.34 £ |
| • Overseas investments | 7.35 £ | 7.36 £ |
| • Loans and non-trade debtors | | 7.37 £ |
| • Other current assets | | 7.38 £ |
| • Were all investments qualifying investments, and were loans made qualifying loans, within Part I or II of Schedule 20 ICTA 1988? | YES | NO |
| • Value of any non-qualifying investments and loans | | 7.39 £ |
| • Number of subsidiary or associated companies you control at 5 April 2000 | | 7.40 |

## *Claim*

**I claim exemption from tax**

7.41

Signature

Date

Print name in full here

Status or capacity in which you are signing

7.42

***Additional information***

BMSD 12/99net

APPENDIX 11

# Company tax return form: charity supplementary pages

Inland Revenue

**Company Tax Return Form**
*Charity Supplementary Pages*
*For accounting periods ending on or after 1 July 1999*

## Information

Charity name

Tax reference

/ /

Period covered by these *Supplementary Pages* *(cannot exceed 12 months)*

From *(dd/mm/yyyy)* / / To / /

**Important points**

- ***These Supplementary Pages** will form the Charity's claim to exemption that its income and gains have been applied for charitable purposes only.*
- ***Please enter '0'** where appropriate.*
- ***How often** you are asked to make a return will depend on the extent and nature of your activities.*
- ***These Pages,** when completed, form part of the company's return.*
- ***These Pages set out** the information we need and provide a standard format.*
- ***These Pages are covered by** the Declaration you sign on page 1 of the form CT600.*
- ***The warning shown on the form CT600 about prosecution, and the advice about late and incorrect returns, and late payment of tax also apply to these Pages.***

**You need to complete these *Supplementary Pages* if**

- ***the Charity claims exemption from tax on all or any part of its income and gains.***

## Claim to exemption

**This section should be completed in all cases**

Charity repayment reference

Charity Commission Registration number; or Scottish Charity number *(if applicable)*

During the period covered by these *Supplementary Pages*:
*Put an 'X' in the box if 'Yes'*

- The company was a Charity and is claiming exemption from all tax on all or part of its income and gains
- All income and gains are exempt from tax and have been, or will be, applied for charitable purposes only

or

- Some of the Charity's income and gains may not be exempt or have not been applied for charitable purposes only, and I have completed the form *CT600*
  *See Note 7 on page 2 of these Pages*

**I claim exemption from tax**

Signature

Date *(dd/mm/yyyy)* / /

Status

Name *(in capital letters)*

*Except where a liquidator has been appointed, any person who is authorised to do so may sign on behalf of the company. A photocopy of a signature is not acceptable.*

BS12/00

CT600E Charity Supplementary Pages

2 **CT600E Supplementary Pages (2000)**

## Notes to help you complete the Charity Supplementary Pages

**Repayments (Boxes E1/E1a and E2/E2b)**

1. In Boxes E1/E1a:
   - Enter the amount of income tax and transitional relief claimed on forms R68 for the period covered by these Pages.
   - This should relate only to income arising in the period.
   - Do not include amounts claimed for earlier periods.
2. In Box E2/E2b enter the total amount due for income received in the period on which the Charity can claim.

**Trading income (Box E5)**

3. Enter details of the turnover of trades, the profits of which will be exempted by S505(1)(e) ICTA 1988.

   If the charity has carried on a trade during the return period which falls outside the exemption, complete the *Short* or *Detailed calculation* on the form *CT600*. Do not include in the calculation sources of income which are otherwise exempt from tax. Also complete the *Summary* and *Declaration* on page 1 of the form *CT600*.

**Other sources (Box E13)**

4. Enter details in Box E13 of the total income received from sources other than those included in the boxes above. If the amount in Box E13 includes income which is assessable under Case VI of Schedule D (for example, the profit from a single transaction or isolated service of some kind, which do not amount to trading under Case I of Schedule D), then complete the *Short calculation* in the form *CT600*, entering the income assessable at box 13. Also complete the *Summary* and *Declaration* on page 1 of the form *CT600*.

**Investments and loans within Sch 20 ICTA 1988 (Box E26)**

5. Qualifying investments for the purposes of S506 ICTA 1988 are specified in Part I, Sch 20 ICTA 1988.

   Qualifying loans for the purposes of S506 ICTA 1988 are specified in Part II, Sch 20 ICTA 1988.

   Any loan or other investment not specified may be accepted as qualifying where the loan or other investment is made for the benefit of the charity and not for the avoidance of tax (whether by the charity or any other person). Any claim must first be approved by Inland Revenue (Charities).

**Investments and loans made outside Sch 20 ICTA 1988 (Box E27)**

6. If the charity has made any investments or loans which do not fall within Sch 20 ICTA 1988 and no claim is to be made, enter the total of such investments or loans in Box E27.

**Restriction of relief for non-qualifying expenditure.**

7. Relief under S505(1) ICTA 1988 and S256 TCGA 1992 may not be available.

   The Charity should attach a calculation of restriction of relief under S505(3) ICTA 1988 and send it with this return. If you need help with this calculation please contact the IR (Charities) technical helpline. For Charities in England, Wales and Northern Ireland the telephone number is 0151 472 6051/6062. For Charities in Scotland the telephone number is 0131 777 4107.

**Subcontractor payments**

8. If the Charity has made payments under the Construction Industry Scheme enclose forms CIS25.

## Repayments

**Enter details of repayments/payments for income arising during the period covered by these Supplementary Pages**

*See Notes 1 and 2 on page 2 of these Pages*

| | Income Tax | Transitional Relief |
|---|---|---|
| E1/E1a Amount already claimed in period using form R68 or R68(MGA) | E1 £ | E1a £ |
| E2/E2b Total repayment/payment due | E2 £ | E2b £ |
| and either | | |
| E3/E3c Further repayment/payment due *Where E2/E2b is more than E1/E1a* | E3 £ | E3c £ |
| or | | |
| E4/E4d Amounts overclaimed in period *Where E1/E1a is more than E2/E2b* | E4 £ | E4d £ |

## Information required

**Enter details of any *income* claimed as exempt which is received from the following sources. Enter the figure included in the Charity's accounts for the period covered by these Supplementary Pages**

*Non-exempt amounts should be entered on the form CT600 in the appropriate boxes*

| Source | Amount |
|---|---|
| E5 Enter total turnover from exempt trading activities *See Note 3 on page 2 of these Pages* | E5 £ |
| E6 Investment income *Exclude any amounts included on the form CT600* | E6 £ |
| E7 UK land and buildings *Exclude any amounts included on the form CT600* | E7 £ |
| E8 Deed of Covenant *Exclude any amounts included on the form CT600* | E8 £ |
| E9 Gift Aid or Millenium Gift Aid *Exclude any amounts included on the form CT600* | E9 £ |
| E10 Other Charities *Exclude any amounts included on the form CT600* | E10 £ |
| E11 Legacies | E11 £ |
| E12 Other donations | E12 £ |
| E13 Other sources (for example, commissions, fees, small fund-raising) *See Note 4 on page 2 of these Pages* | E13 £ |

**Enter figures of *expenditure* as shown in the Charity's accounts for the period covered by these Supplementary Pages**

| Source | Amount |
|---|---|
| E14 Trading costs *In relation to exempt activities in box E5* | E14 £ |
| E15 UK land and buildings *In relation to exempt activities in box E7* | E15 £ |
| E16 All general administration costs | E16 £ |
| E17 All grants and donations made within the UK | E17 £ |
| E18 All grants and donations made outside the UK | E18 £ |
| E19 Other expenditure not included above, or in calculating figures entered on the form CT600 | E19 £ |

*Continued on page 4*

4 CT600E Supplementary Pages (2000)

*Continued from page 3*

| **Charity Assets** | **Disposals in period (total consideration received)** | **Held at the end of the period** |
|---|---|---|
| E20/E20a Tangible fixed assets | E20 £ | E20a £ |
| E21/E21b UK investments (excluding controlled companies) | E21 £ | E21b £ |
| E22/E22c Shares in, and loans to, controlled companies | E22 £ | E22c £ |
| E23/E23d Overseas investments | E23 £ | E23d £ |
| E24e Loans and non-trade debtors | | E24e £ |
| E25f Other current assets | | E25f £ |
| E26 Put an 'X' in this box if all investments and loans made by the Charity in the accounting period were qualifying investments or loans within Part I or II of Sch 20 ICTA 1988. *See Note 5 on page 2 of these Pages* | | E26 |
| E27 Value of any non-qualifying investments and loans. *See Note 6 on page 2 of these Pages* | | E27 £ |
| E28 Number of subsidiary or associated companies the Charity controls at the end of the period | | E28 |

**What to do when you have completed these *Supplementary Pages***

*Follow the advice shown under 'What to do when you have completed the return' on page 2 of the form CT600.*

# Index